Living with Earthquakes
in California:
A Survivor's Guide

_by_

Robert S. Yeats

Oregon State University Press
Corvallis

Cover: Collapsed building and burned area at Beach and Divisadero in the Marina District, San Francisco, damaged during the Loma Prieta Earthquake of October 17, 1989. Damage was caused by liquefaction and lateral movement of artificial fill that had been emplaced after the 1906 San Francisco Earthquake. Lateral movement caused rupture of underground gas lines, which then caught fire. Photograph by C.E. Meyer, U.S. Geological Survey.

The paper in this book meets the guidelines for permanence and durability of the Committee on Production Guidelines for Book Longevity of the Council on Library Resources and the minimum requirements of the American National Standard for Permanence of Paper for Printed Library Materials Z39.48-1984.

Library of Congress Cataloging-in-Publication Data
Yeats, Robert S.
  California earthquakes : a survivor's guide / Robert S. Yeats.
—1st ed.
     p. cm.
Includes bibliographical references and index.
  ISBN 0-87071-493-7
  1. Earthquakes--California. 2. Earthquakes--California--Safety measures. I. Title.
  QE535.2.U6 Y42 2001
  551.22'09794--dc21
                                        00-011859

Oregon State University Press
101 Waldo Hall
Corvallis, OR 97331-6407
541-737-3166 • fax 541-737-3170
http://osu.orst.edu/dept/press

OREGON STATE
UNIVERSITY

Contents

〜

Preface

My professional life changed irrevocably on a February morning in 1971, on an oceanographic expedition off the Galápagos Islands. As I headed for work in the science lab, I heard reports on the shortwave radio about a massive earthquake in Los Angeles. People had been killed, freeways had collapsed, and a fault scarp had suddenly appeared in the shady neighborhoods of the northern San Fernando Valley. A few months earlier, I had interviewed for a job at California State University at Northridge, and if I had taken it, my family would have been in harm's way at the same time I was looking at deep-sea cores in the tropics.

A few months later, I was hired for the summer by F. Beach Leighton, a professor of geology at Whittier College who had started a consulting business in engineering geology in the Los Angeles area. One of my jobs was mapping the area around the Olive View County Medical Center, which had been destroyed by the earthquake only a few months after it had been completed. I saw first hand the power of Nature: a toppled stairwell, a crumpled basement, bent streetlight poles, shattered ground on the hills above the Medical Center. I wandered inside, where I noticed the clock had stopped at exactly 6 A.M., the time of the earthquake; the bulletin boards told of planned events that never took place.

I knew the geology well. I had been an exploration geologist for Shell Oil Company in southern California, and I had mapped the faults that turned out to be the source of the earthquake. During my Shell days, I had no idea these faults were earthquake hazards. No one else did, either.

So I wrote research proposals and received funding from government agencies as well as oil companies to evaluate the earthquake hazards of the faults I had previously studied for their oil possibilities. Geologists are natural historians, accustomed to figuring out the past, but the next earthquake was in the future and we needed to learn something about which faults were dangerous and which ones were not. It was exciting, and it also gave my students and me a sense of purpose: not simply learning about geology for its own sake but trying to make a difference in people's lives and their safety. We mapped the faults, and we published our papers.

But after a while, I began to wonder whether it was more important to discuss earthquakes with my scientific colleagues or, instead, with my wife, my next-door neighbor, or the State

Living with Earthquakes

in California:

A Survivor's Guide

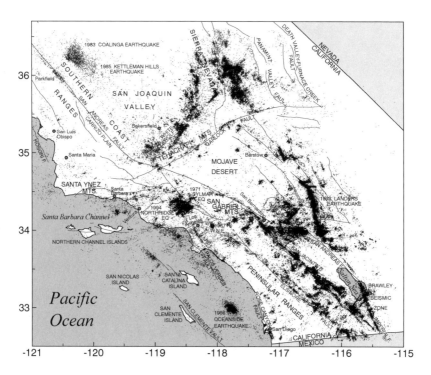

Earthquakes recorded by the Southern California Seismic Network between 1975 and 1998, located by a new technique taking into account varying speeds of earthquake waves through different kinds of rock. Nearly 300,000 earthquakes were located. From a paper in the Journal of Geophysical Research by K.B. Richards-Dinger and Peter Shearer of the University of California, San Diego. Thin curved lines are active faults. Note that some active faults are highlighted by earthquakes, but others are not, including much of the San Andreas Fault.

Legislature. This question answered itself when more earthquakes arrived.

I always learned about these earthquakes from nonscientists. My barber and friend, Bob Minnick, told me about the Whittier Narrows Earthquake of October 1, 1987. Before I could catch my breath, TV stations and newspapers began to call me, and armed with virtually no information, I suggested that it was probably on the Whittier Fault. (It wasn't.)

I was heading home from work on October 17, 1989 when I heard on the radio about the Loma Prieta Earthquake. The phone rang nonstop until almost midnight, and I pontificated to the media that the earthquake had ruptured the San Andreas Fault. (It hadn't.)

Finally, on January 17, 1994, my wife Angela called me out of bed to look at TV reports of another big Los Angeles earthquake.. As I watched TV images of collapsed freeways, burning houses, devastated shopping centers, and a burning gas line on Balboa Boulevard, I once again was awestruck by the power of the very faults I was trying to understand. After the Northridge Earthquake, the phone kept ringing for several days because my students and I had mapped the faults in the area of the earthquake. I became a media resource (read: "talking head"), so along with my colleagues I was asked which fault had caused the earthquake. We were all wrong. It turned out to be an eastern extension of a fault that I had mapped, but I had published a paper saying that the eastern extension was inactive.

However, the media's interest in what I was doing made me wonder whether it was enough to publish papers on the faults we were mapping, communing only with my scientific colleagues. Nobody paid much attention to us until an earthquake struck, and then we were big news. As I talked to reporters and to my nonscientific friends, I came to the conclusion that Californians, like Oregonians where I now live, were woefully uninformed about earthquakes, and also not very interested—unless the earthquake struck where they lived. Telling people California has an earthquake problem is like telling them about carpenter ants in the basement or about high blood pressure and high cholesterol—they don't really care until it happens to them.

But the sheer size of the earthquake problem dwarfs other concerns we face: the possibility of thousands of fatalities and tens of billions of dollars in damage. Suddenly, earthquake science stopped being fun for me; as a scientist, I began to feel like the watchman on the castle walls warning about barbarians at the gate, begging people to take me seriously.

How could I convince people they ought to be taking more steps to protect themselves against earthquakes, just as they would against fire?

The solution to my problem came at the university where I teach. Oregon State University had recently adopted a baccalaureate core curriculum that includes courses that synthesize and integrate student learning at the advanced undergraduate level. One of the components of the new curriculum is a course relating the discoveries of science to their impact on technology and on society.

In 1995, I offered to teach a course that told the story of the scientific recognition of the earthquake problem in the Pacific Northwest and of how society responded to it in terms of legislation, building codes, insurance premiums, elementary school curricula, and individual and community preparedness. The course was first taught in winter term, 1997, to a large class on campus and also was televised on three cable channels in Oregon. The class notes written for this course served as the nucleus of a book, *Living with Earthquakes in the Pacific Northwest*, published by Oregon State University Press in 1998.

The course drew students from across the University spectrum. I required a five-page term paper on a topic related to earthquakes. Although the prospect of reading nearly two hundred term papers was daunting, it turned out to be the most gratifying part of the course. Students wrote lesson plans for third graders, devised retrofit plans for their parents' houses, suggested new designs for earthquake-resistant bridges, outlined community response strategies and potential escape routes from an impending tsunami, and even pondered the feasibility of surfing a tsunami!

Surfing a tsunami can't be done, but surfing the Internet allowed students even in distant learning sites, far from a university library, to get up-to-the-minute information, so that in some cases the students learned about new developments before I did. I was reminded again of the awesome creative potential of motivated undergraduates—some only a few years out of high school, others returning to school in mid-life. Some of these term papers enriched my own experience and knowledge and thereby enriched this book.

Although *Living with Earthquakes* was written for the students in these classes, it served a larger community as well: families concerned about earthquake hazards in making decisions about where to live, legislators presented with bills to expand (or reduce) earthquake protection, insurance actuaries wondering how much to charge for earthquake insurance, high school principals and teachers trying to figure out why they must conduct earthquake drills in schools, local officials considering stricter ordinances for regulating growth while avoiding lawsuits, and the growing number of people involved professionally in emergency preparedness. With better knowledge about what is (and is not) possible, people might make more informed decisions.

Buoyed by the success of *Living with Earthquakes in the Pacific Northwest*, I embarked on a more ambitious project: telling the earthquake story of California. I concluded that the existing books about California earthquakes focus more on the spectacular features of damage and faulting and less on construction standards and earthquake preparedness. So much of the story was still untold. What about earthquake insurance in California? Why can't we forecast earthquakes as effectively as we forecast hurricanes?

In contrast to the book on the Northwest, the California story turned out to be an adventure: the tale of how Californians first refused to admit they had an earthquake problem, but eventually they enacted legislation that is now the most advanced in the world. In addition, my scientific colleagues and I have also been involved in an adventure, or perhaps it could be called a detective story. How little we knew in 1971, after the Sylmar Earthquake. At that time we were focused on prediction research, but that was premature. Our focus now is more on strengthening our communities against earthquakes. The technological advances have been awesome: satellite measurement of crustal deformation, state-of-the art seismographs, and advanced computer systems that permit us to churn through billions of bits of data. It has been an exciting time to be an earthquake scientist. I hope this book is able to transmit to you some of the thrill of scientific discovery, letting you know what we have learned but also where we are still up against the unknown.

Writing both books led me into subject areas in which I was woefully uninformed, and here I had a lot of help from others in seeking out information and in reviewing chapters. My thanks go to Clarence Allen and Kerry Sieh of Caltech; Jack Watts of State Farm Insurance Co.; Richard J. Roth, Jr. of the California Department of Insurance; Amy Bach of United Policyholders; Ian MacGregor of the National Science Foundation; Peter Shearer of the University of California San Diego; Brian Atwater, William Ellsworth, Thomas Hanks, David Hill, Patricia McCrory, Alan Nelson, Steve Obermeier, David Oppenheimer, Ross Stein, and Wayne Thatcher of the U.S. Geological Survey; Roy Hyndman of the Pacific Geoscience Centre; Kenji Satake of the Geological Survey of Japan; Chris Goldfinger, Steve Dickenson, Tom Miller, and George Moore of Oregon State University; Ray Weldon of the University of Oregon; Scott Burns of

Portland State University; Lori Dengler of Humboldt State University; Jill Andrews of the Southern California Earthquake Center; Bill Bryant, Jim Davis, and Earl Hart of the California Division of Mines and Geology; Diane Murbach of the City of San Diego; and Eldon Gath of Earth Consultants International. Also, I learned much from the delegates to the annual meeting of the Western Seismic Safety Policy Advisory Council in Victoria, B.C. in October, 1997; a conference in Seaside, Oregon, sponsored by the Geological Society of America, on Cascadia earthquakes; and from the annual meetings of the Southern California Earthquake Center (SCEC). SCEC was particularly helpful because it brings together geologists, seismologists, seismographers, geodesists, engineers, and emergency services professionals in an informal setting so that we can learn from one another.

Illustrations make a book, and I received original photographs and drawings—some never before published—from Brian Atwater, Lori Dengler, Chris Goldfinger, Ken Hudnut (of the Southern California Integrated GPS Network), Sarah Nathe (of the California Office of Emergency Services), Steve Obermeier, David Oppenheimer, Kenji Satake, Peter Shearer, Charles Rubin (of Central Washington University), and Chris Walls (of Earth Consultants International). The color slide collection of the National Oceanic and Atmospheric Administration, available from the National Geophysical Data Center, was the source of several photographs. The drawings were prepared by Kristi Whaley, Matt Gregory, Emily Oatney, and Mazhar Qayyum; the computer-generated topographic maps were prepared by Scott Lillebo with the help of Jon Kimerling. Dave Reinert digitized photographs and illustrations available only in hard copy. Thorough and constructive edits were provided by Lori Dengler of Humboldt State University, Eldon Gath of Earth Consultants International, and my wife Angela, who pointed out my scientific jargon. An earlier draft was edited by George Moore. Jo Alexander of OSU Press edited the final manuscript and carried the project through to completion.

The success of this book will depend on how successful I am in convincing individuals and communities to fortify themselves against a catastrophe that might not strike in our lifetimes. Ultimately, the book's value may be measured after the next large earthquake, when we ask ourselves, "Were we ready?"

Robert S. Yeats
Corvallis, Oregon

∽ Part I ∽
Boosters and Quakers:
Three Centuries of People
and Earthquakes in California

"And from there [Earthquake and Thunder] went south . . . They went south first and sank the ground . . . Every little while there would be an earthquake, then another earthquake, and another earthquake . . . And then the water would fill those depressed places."

Yurok story told to A. L. Kroeber in his book, *Yurok Myths*

"The plain facts are that earthquakes in California . . . kill far fewer people than the cyclones in the Middle West, the flood tornadoes in the South Coast states, and the lightning storms and heat waves along the Atlantic states kill every year. Californians don't wholly approve of earthquakes, but they prefer them to cyclones or tornadoes or floods or protracted heat or lightning storms. All of the earthquakes which have occurred in California since it was discovered nearly four hundred years ago have not killed so many people as one or two great cyclones of the Middle West."

William Randolph Hearst, editorial in the *New York American* after the San Francisco Earthquake of April 18, 1906.

Before the San Francisco Earthquake of 1906

Californians have always known they could be struck by earthquakes, including the Yuroks of the north coast, whose legend quoted above might refer to a great earthquake they endured in 1700 A.D. But except for oral traditions, the earthquake experience of Native Americans is lost to us.

The first record-keepers were the Spanish, who, under the leadership of Gaspar de Portolá, founded San Diego, Alta California's first town and presidio, in 1769. Two weeks later, Portolá left San Diego on an expedition to Monterey Bay. On July 28, Portolá's party was shaken by an earthquake along a river they called Río de los Temblores, River of Earthquakes—now known as the Santa Ana River. As described by Miguel Costansó, "At this place, we experienced a terrible earthquake, which was repeated four times during the day. The first vibration or shock occurred at one o'clock in the afternoon, and was the most violent." Portolá's party felt aftershocks as they crossed the Los Angeles Basin, the last one occurring on the Los Angeles River on August 3 as they departed the area, headed north.

The Spanish reported earthquakes rather matter-of-factly, as though familiar with them from Mexico or Spain. Indeed, the great Lisbon Earthquake of 1755, which was felt over the entire Iberian Peninsula, would have been experienced by many of the California explorers, which might explain why they were not surprised to find that the new lands they had discovered experienced earthquakes as well.

In the next few decades after the founding of San Diego, Franciscan priests, beginning with Father Junípero Serra, established missions from San Diego to San Francisco. These missions, in some cases surrounded by small settlements of Indians and Europeans, were a tenuous foothold on the California coast. They were lonely outposts of church and empire, and times were hard. Adding to their woes were frequent earthquakes, which damaged or destroyed the new churches and outbuildings and caused loss of life. The worst of these struck southern California on December 8 and 21, 1812, but earthquakes twelve years earlier had also resulted in considerable damage. The Spanish experienced earthquakes everywhere they had founded missions, from San Francisco to San Diego, and horrified as they must have been, they buried the dead, repaired the churches, and carried on.

Mexico, including its California outpost, achieved independence from Spain in 1822. Even before independence, the Americans, with little personal knowledge of earthquakes, had been arriving in large numbers, first as hunters of the sea otter and as traders and later as settlers, opening up the interior. Finally, in 1848 Mexico ceded California to the United States, and everything changed. That was the same year gold was discovered at Sutter's Mill in the foothills of the Sierra, and California—a forlorn, distant frontier under the Spanish and Mexicans—became the destination of tens of thousands of gold-seekers. This was the beginning of American expansion westward, and by 1869 the Central Pacific Railroad had connected the East Coast to California. Wealth created by gold mining, land speculation, and the development of an agricultural empire in the Great Valley became focused on the boom town of San Francisco. As in the rest of the United States in the last half of the nineteenth century, unbridled capitalism reigned supreme, with San Francisco, California's largest city, the seat of power. To flourish, railroad barons needed to attract Easterners to California. They circulated wondrous claims about fortunes to be made and the therapeutic values of living in the gentle climate of southern California—including a cure for tuberculosis. Boosterism was the name of the game.

Great earthquakes struck the Central Coast Ranges in 1857 and Owens Valley east of the Sierra Nevada in 1872. But so few people lived in the affected areas that these earthquakes had no dampening effect on the promotion and explosive growth of California.

However, the Bay Area had been experiencing large earthquakes even during the Mexican period, in 1836 and 1838. The first big one under American rule struck on October 8, 1865, centered near San Jose, but resulting in severe damage to the San Francisco City Hall. Mark Twain, then a journalist who had just been fired from his job at the San Francisco *Morning Call*, apparently believed he could boost his sagging fortunes when he found himself caught in what came to be called the Great San Francisco Earthquake: "As I turned the corner, around a frame house, there was a great rattle and jar . . . there came a really terrific shock; the ground seemed to roll under me in waves, interrupted by a violent jiggling up and down . . . at that moment, a third and still severer shock came, and as I reeled about on the pavement, trying to keep my footing, I saw a sight! The entire front of a tall four-story brick building in Third street sprung outward like a door and fell sprawling across the street, raising dust like a great column of smoke!"

The second "Great San Francisco Earthquake" struck three years later, on October 21, 1868, centered across the bay in Haywards (now Hayward) on the Hayward Fault. San Leandro was severely damaged, including its courthouse, as were Haywards and San Francisco, and at least thirty people were killed. Surely, with two earthquakes in such close succession damaging California's largest city, an organized effort would be mounted to protect the population—then numbering about 150,000—from future earthquakes.

It was not to be. The Chamber of Commerce appointed a committee of wealthy merchants to assure the financial markets of the East Coast that there was "no damage to well-constructed buildings. Total loss on property will not exceed $300,000." A committee of scientists appointed by the Chamber of Commerce documented damage closer to $1.5 million. One of the scientists, George Davidson, stated in a newspaper interview years later that "the result of our investigation was so startling that we never published our report. It was thought that to do so would frighten people who intended to come here and settle." Davidson later wrote that a businessman who headed the main committee "declared that it would ruin the commercial prospects of San Francisco to admit the large amount of damage and the cost thereof, and declared he would never publish [the report]."

However, Josiah D. Whitney, who headed the Geological Survey of California, wrote that "earthquakes are not to be bluffed off. They will come, and will do a great deal of damage." Funds for Whitney's survey were terminated six years later, in 1874. The Legislature was interested in gold, not earthquakes.

So the 1865 and 1868 earthquakes had no long-term effect. Earthquakes were part of the raw frontier that was California. People simply cleaned up after an earthquake and continued to make money and sell land. Author Bret Harte was ahead of his time when he wrote in 1866, after the first "Great San Francisco Earthquake": "In spite of the fears of alarmists, I do not think that the prosperity and future of California is disturbed by these shocks, and I believe that there is more danger . . . from the concealment of facts, or the tacit silence of the public press on this topic, than in free and open discussion of the subject . . ." This statement would apply only too well to the San Francisco Earthquake that was to follow forty years later.

From San Francisco to Long Beach (1906–1933)

On April 18, 1906, at 5:12 A.M., the great San Francisco Earthquake rocked California from Humboldt County on the north to San Benito County on the south. San Francisco, by that time the ninth-largest city in the United States, was devastated. Many buildings collapsed, and water mains, gas lines, and sewer lines ruptured. Escaping gas quickly caught fire, but because of the broken water mains, the Fire Department had no water to fight the fires. A great conflagration fanned by high winds raged for three days, destroying a large part of the city.

The official death toll was less than five hundred people, but even at the time, that figure was believed to be too low. As Jack London wrote in *Colliers*, "An enumeration of the dead will never be made. All vestiges of them were destroyed by the flames." A recent study showed that at least three thousand people died (Hansen and Condon, 1989). More than two hundred thousand were left homeless, and refugee camps were set up in Golden Gate Park and the Presidio of San Francisco. Property damage was estimated at $500 million—more than $10 billion in today's dollars. The 1906 earthquake and fire combined to create the greatest natural disaster in the history of the United States, until Hurricane Andrew struck Florida in 1992.

The earthquake threatened one of California's greatest assets—its reputation as a Mecca for the good life and for making money—particularly because it trashed California's largest and most dynamic city, one that was symbolic of California itself. To counter this insult to the state's image, newspapers, business interests, and chambers of commerce embarked on a massive cover-up: a rewriting of history to de-emphasize the earthquake and magnify the role of the fire. Why? Fires were a common experience in American cities, and Chicago, Boston, and Baltimore had been severely damaged by great fires in the recent past. San Francisco was not unique in experiencing a great fire, whereas an earthquake would expose a severe flaw in the California dream. Insurance companies were more likely to pay up if a building were destroyed by fire rather than by an earthquake. If it could not be denied that a building had collapsed rather than burned, then the cause could be laid to shoddy workmanship.

On the day after the earthquake, as fires raged in the city, Governor Pardee told the Governor of Massachusetts that "[d]estruction was wrought by fire far more than by earthquake." James Horsburgh of the Southern Pacific Railroad, the most dominant business in the State, advised chambers of commerce to say that "San Francisco did not suffer greatly from the earthquake." The *Los Angeles Times* claimed that "There are more deaths annually by lightning in almost any State of the Union, outside of the Pacific Coast, than all the deaths from earthquake in California." Picture postcards of the disaster were retouched to minimize earthquake damage.

Because of the cover-up, the San Francisco Earthquake, like the 1865 and 1868 earthquakes before it, would not lead to any improvements in building standards nor any moves toward earthquake preparedness. The same was true for the selection of building sites. Debris from the earthquake was pushed into the Bay to reclaim land for an exposition in 1915 advertising San Francisco's recovery from the disaster. This "made land" would fail in the Loma Prieta Earthquake in 1989, repeating on a small scale in the Marina District the fires and devastation of 1906 (see Chapter 9).

In contrast, the Japanese government, following a catastrophic earthquake in 1891, had embarked on a major earthquake research program, including the construction of seismographs that recorded seismic waves from the San Francisco Earthquake at the Imperial University of Tokyo, where seismograms were read and pondered by the world's leading seismologist at the time, Professor Fusakichi Omori.

The San Francisco Earthquake did lead to a scientific inquiry directed by Andrew C. Lawson, a geology professor at the University of California. Funds to investigate the earthquake were obtained not from the U.S. government or the State of California but from a private foundation, the Carnegie Institution of Washington. A State Earthquake Investigation Commission was established with Lawson as its chairman and some of the leading scientists of the day as members, among them John C. Branner (who would later become president of Stanford University), Harry Fielding Reid of Johns Hopkins University, and Grove Karl Gilbert of the United States Geological Survey, who happened to be in the Bay Area on another assignment. Professor Omori of Japan arrived in California a month after the earthquake and was made an associate member of the Investigation Commission.

Gilbert had already visited the village of Lone Pine east of the Sierra, destroyed by the 1872 Owens Valley Earthquake. He found a fault in Lone Pine that had ruptured and moved the ground sideways, and he concluded that this fault had caused the earthquake. He saw the same thing in Marin County, north of San Francisco: sideways motion on the San Andreas Fault, named by Lawson thirteen years before. Branner discovered roads near the Stanford campus that were offset by the same fault. Clearly, the San Andreas Fault was the culprit. Armed with this knowledge and with financial support from the Carnegie Institution, geologists followed the trace of the fault from Shelter Cove on the north to the southeastern California desert. Lawson took another look at the 1868 Haywards Earthquake and found that it, too, was the result of motion on a fault that he traced right across the University of California campus, close to his own office.

The Lawson report was largely an accounting of what had happened, describing the geology of the surface rupture and the damage caused by the earthquake. It was a research report; it failed to issue a call for action to upgrade California's building codes or to locate other earthquake faults in the state.

Instead, Professor Omori was quoted in newspapers as stating that San Francisco would not in the near future suffer another earthquake like that of April 18. The *San Francisco Chronicle* quoted him as saying that "the city of San Francisco and the surrounding country will be free from these great earthquakes for fifty years or more" and "[i]n all probability . . . there will never be an earthquake in the State as severe as the one in April." Omori might have been reassuring San Franciscans that the aftershocks that continued to rattle the Bay Area were to be expected after an earthquake, and these aftershocks were not signs that another great earthquake was imminent. But his remarks were seized upon by the business and booster community as support for their claim that the main concern for the future was fire, not earthquake.

Commission member Gilbert had a different reason for suggesting that San Francisco might not be struck by a great earthquake in the near future. Gilbert had described the fault scarp (a steep slope or cliff) formed during the 1872 Owens Valley Earthquake, and he had observed similar scarps along the Wasatch Fault, which runs through Salt Lake City, Utah. In a letter to the *Salt Lake City Tribune* in 1883, he wrote: "The old maxim, 'Lightning never strikes the same spot twice' is unsound in theory and false in fact; but something similar might truly be said about earthquakes. The spot which is the focus of an earthquake . . . is thereby exempted for a long time. And conversely, any locality on the fault line . . . which has been exempt from earthquake for a long time, is by so much nearer to the date of recurrence . . ."

Applying this reasoning to the San Andreas Fault, Gilbert would conclude that the section that ruptured in 1906 would not rupture again for a long time. As he wrote in 1906, he was interested in testing this idea—as was Harry Reid, who wanted to search for evidence that strain might again be building up on the fault.

Gilbert's view of the 1906 rupture is still held today, as discussed further in Chapter 8. But this does not mean that other faults that didn't rupture in 1906 or 1868 would not be the source of an earthquake. Omori's discussion of aftershocks and Gilbert's views on earthquake recurrence were taken out of context to reinforce what California boosters wanted the world to hear.

It seems strange that members of the Earthquake Commission—especially Gilbert and Omori—were not more concerned about the impact of their statements on the general public. The Commission did not take a stand on upgrading the quality of building construction, nor on searching for other dangerous faults.

Later, Gilbert, in an article published in the prestigious national journal *Science* in 1909, did take a strong stand: "It is the duty of investigators—of seismologists, geologists and scientific engineers—to develop the theory of local danger spots, to discover the foci of recurrent shocks, to develop the theory of earthquake-proof construction. It is the duty of engineers and architects so to adjust construction to the character of the ground that safety shall be secured. It should be the policy of communities in the earthquake district to recognize the danger and make provision against it."

Too late. The scientists had had their chance—their "teachable moment," as one of my students calls it. In 1906, a strong message might have made a difference. In 1909, San Francisco had moved on, repairing the damage, and the disaster was clearly a fire, not an earthquake. The boosters had won. Shortly afterward, Gilbert was felled by a stroke and his wise counsel was lost to science.

Ironically, the San Francisco Bay Area would not be struck by another severe earthquake for more than eighty years, when in 1989 an earthquake in the Santa Cruz Mountains would create havoc once again in San Francisco. And to this day, the San Andreas Fault has not had an earthquake as large as the 1906 event.

An outgrowth of the earthquake was the organization of a professional group dedicated to the study of earthquakes, the Seismological Society of America, which issued its first formal publication in 1911. John C. Branner of Stanford envisioned it as a large tent, encompassing not only geologists and seismologists but also astronomers, engineers, and architects, a larger community that would focus on analyzing earthquakes. Branner's concern, like Gilbert's, was for public safety, but as the Seismological Society evolved it attracted a number of research physicists interested not in earthquake hazards but in the structure of the Earth based on seismic waves.

Seismographs had been in use for more than two decades. By the time of the San Francisco Earthquake, newer versions could record a large earthquake thousands of miles away, on a different continent, even on the opposite side of the Earth. If the travel time of the seismic wave through the Earth could be determined precisely by the use of extremely accurate clocks, then a seismograph record would open a window into the hitherto-unknown interior of the Earth. Seismographs of the early twentieth century led to great scientific discoveries. Seismic waves showed that the Earth is made up of a series of concentric shells, like an onion, including a crust, mantle, and nickel-iron core (see Chapter 2). For many seismologists, the internal structure of the Earth was the important research question they wanted to ask of their seismographs, and earthquakes were of interest only because they provided the signal that explored the Earth's interior—like X-rays explore the human body. This conflict between pure and applied seismology would continue for decades, both within and outside the Seismological Society of America.

Branner did not trust seismographs or seismographers, however, and he relied on a large group of observers who would report on the effects of earthquakes at different places in California. One of the most meticulous observers of the San Francisco Earthquake was Alexander G. McAdie, head of the San Francisco office of the U.S. Weather Bureau. McAdie paved the way for Congress in 1914 to authorize the Weather Bureau to make such observations at all its weather stations. Branner had a system in place to investigate earthquakes as they happened.

At this time, the scene shifted from San Francisco to southern California, which was overtaking the San Francisco Bay Area as California's great engine of economic growth. Southern California had considered itself free of earthquakes—which were regarded as a San Francisco problem. But damaging earthquakes struck the southeastern California desert in 1915 and 1918, and Branner—at his own expense— sent scientists to study them. The earthquakes were shown to have struck faults on the opposite side of the Coachella and Imperial Valleys from the San Andreas Fault. But these earthquakes, like the great 1857 and 1872 shocks, struck thinly populated territory and they received little attention from the general public.

The burgeoning city of Los Angeles, home of the new movie industry and center of a vast oil, citrus, and cattle-ranching empire, took no notice of earthquakes, unmindful of the Spanish-era shocks of 1812. However, the earthquakes in the southeastern California desert gained new supporters for Branner, including the head of the engineering department of the city of Los Angeles and a well-connected petroleum geologist, one of Branner's former students.

So investigators, including influential scientists from Los Angeles, were ready for a moderate earthquake on June 21, 1920, which did considerable damage to the business district of Inglewood, a western suburb of Los Angeles. Stephen Taber, a former student of Branner's and at the time a visiting scientist at Stanford, was sent to investigate. Taber found that the Inglewood Earthquake struck the Newport-

Inglewood Fault, which, at the time of the quake, was known by petroleum geologists to contain vast deposits of oil. Oil companies located their wildcat wells on low hills that were atop great oil fields, including Signal Hill overlying the Long Beach Oil Field, Dominguez Hill overlying the Dominguez Field, and the Baldwin Hills overlying the Inglewood Field. Later research would show that these hills had been forced up by tectonic activity on the Newport-Inglewood Fault.

The problem was not the oil fields. The problem was that the fault ran through heavily populated suburbs of Los Angeles. As part of his report, Taber stated that it was "of the utmost importance that all active faults [in the Los Angeles area] be located so that engineers and architects can take precautions in the location and construction of aqueducts, buildings, and other structures."

Then the propaganda machine of California boosters swung into action. The Los Angeles Chamber of Commerce issued a pamphlet reassuring people that the soft sedimentary layers in the city would absorb earthquake waves—which led an astonished Branner to retort that exactly the opposite would happen. Unlike San Francisco in 1906, scientists and engineers were vocal in countering the arguments of the boosters that California had nothing to fear from earthquakes.

Despite the increase in scientific interest in earthquakes, there was no earthquake research center in Los Angeles comparable to Berkeley and Stanford in the Bay Area.

Harry O. Wood had earlier been an instructor at the University of California under Lawson at the time of the San Francisco Earthquake and had participated in the study of that earthquake under the sponsorship of the Carnegie Institution of Washington. After World War I, Wood found a job in Washington with the newly established National Research Council, where he developed important contacts including the director of the Carnegie Institution and George Ellery Hale, head of Carnegie's Mt. Wilson Observatory in Pasadena. In 1921, Wood persuaded the Carnegie Institution to sponsor seismological research in southern California, and he was hired as a research associate, with office space provided by Hale at the Mt. Wilson Observatory.

Another scientist who became interested in the project was Robert Millikan, an internationally renowned physicist and future Nobel laureate who took over the former Throop Institute in Pasadena as the California Institute of Technology. Millikan and Hale shared a goal of making Caltech a world-class scientific institution, and their method was to bring to Pasadena top scientists in a few selected fields, notably physics and chemistry, with the help of private benefactors. Carnegie's support of Wood at its astronomical observatory provided an opening in applied physics, the study of earthquakes.

A recent Stanford graduate, uncertain about his future and employed as a bookkeeper at the warehouse of the California Hardware Company, stopped by Pasadena to hear a lecture by Millikan. The young man was so inspired that he decided to undertake graduate studies in theoretical physics at Caltech. His name was Charles Richter.

Together with John Anderson, an astronomer at the observatory, Wood set about designing a new seismograph that would specialize in local earthquakes instead of the distant earthquakes that so excited other seismologists interested in the structure of the Earth. Funds were secured from the Carnegie Corporation of New York and from Caltech to establish a central seismograph station at Pasadena, followed by outlying stations elsewhere in southern California.

At the same time, Andrew Lawson, with the support of Wood, persuaded members of the California congressional delegation and Secretary of Commerce Herbert Hoover to direct the U.S. Coast and Geodetic Survey to resurvey California to see if crustal deformation had occurred since the 1906 earthquake. Preliminary results showed that since the 1880s, survey benchmarks west of the San Andreas Fault in Santa Barbara County had moved an alarming twenty-four feet northward relative to points east of the fault.

At Stanford, Branner's campaign for earthquake awareness was taken up by Bailey Willis, who came to Stanford after a distinguished career with the U.S. Geological Survey. Willis briskly expanded on Branner's program of applied seismology. He pressed for publication of a map of active faults of California with support from the Carnegie Institution, the Seismological Society of America, and private donations, and this map was published in 1923. Willis promoted earthquake studies and advocated stronger building standards and, at the same time, expanded membership in the Seismological Society of America. In addition to seismologists and geologists, Willis followed Branner's lead by recruiting advocates among engineers and architects.

On June 29, 1925, an earthquake hammered the small resort city of Santa Barbara, destroying much of the downtown area and killing twelve people. The boosters again claimed that earthquakes were an anomaly, not to be concerned about, but this time they were met by sizeable opposition from scientists and engineers. Nevertheless, the boosters carried the day; there was no decrease in the number of people moving to California and the real estate boom of the 1920s continued unabated. Citizens of Santa Barbara complained bitterly that the booster campaign was so effective that it was hard for them to convince charitable organizations that their losses, about $15 million, were serious and that they did indeed need assistance.

Willis and engineer Henry Dewell published a detailed account of the Santa Barbara Earthquake and its damage in the *Bulletin of the*

Seismological Society of America. In addition, he and other scientists and engineers continued to give speeches and write articles about the need to focus on earthquake hazards. These had some effect: the cities of Santa Barbara and Palo Alto passed ordinances upgrading their building codes to protect against earthquakes. The new seismographs designed by Wood and Anderson began to be deployed in the Bay Area. And an earthquake engineering testing laboratory was established at Stanford.

Still, Willis was frustrated by the opposition to earthquake preparedness from the newspapers and business interests, despite the evidence from the damaging Santa Barbara Earthquake. To get their attention, he took a drastic step: he predicted that a catastrophic earthquake would strike southern California within the next ten years! Harry Wood had argued as early as 1920 that southern California had experienced earthquakes in 1769, 1812, and 1857, at approximately forty-five-year intervals, and the absence of any large earthquakes since 1857 meant to him that one was overdue. Willis was also influenced by the resurvey that showed twenty-four feet of northward motion west of the San Andreas Fault relative to the area east of the fault.

Probably because Willis was considered one of the most distinguished scientists in the United States, his prediction was quickly picked up and embellished by the media. *Time* magazine reported that "within the next ten years Los Angeles will be wrenched by a tremor worse than that of San Francisco." In a speech to the National Board of Fire Underwriters in New York City, Willis did not put a specific time on his predicted earthquake, but in answer to a question, he stated that the earthquake "is more likely to come in three years than in ten and more likely to come in five years than in three."

Although California boosters were ignoring the prediction, the insurance industry was not: earthquake insurance rates increased dramatically.

Lawson, frequently at odds with Willis, offered little support for his prediction, but Wood, together with two professors at Caltech, geologist J.P. Buwalda and civil engineer R.R. Martel, stated that the arguments for the prediction were more convincing than the arguments against it. A positive outcome was a concerted effort to upgrade California building codes to protect against earthquakes.

Then the business interests went on the attack. Henry M. Robinson, a Caltech trustee and major financial benefactor, wrote to the Caltech administration stating: "I wonder if you have any idea how much damage this loose talk of these two men [Buwalda and Martel] is doing to the [property] values in Southern California . . . if we . . . can not stop their talk about the earthquake problem I for one am going to see what I can do about stopping the whole seismological game." This threat temporarily silenced Buwalda, Martel, and Wood.

Meanwhile, the Building Owners and Managers Association of Los Angeles attacked Willis and his prediction directly. They hired a petroleum geologist, Robert T. Hill, who had worked for the U.S. Geological Survey many years before, and was now working as a consultant. Hill was engaged as a geologist familiar with California faults to attack Willis's prediction, both in speeches and in print. He also rechecked the Coast and Geodetic Survey's new measurements and found that the preliminary report of twenty-four feet of northward movement west of the San Andreas Fault was incorrect; the actual movement was closer to seven feet in the opposite direction—south, not north. This undercut one of Willis's main arguments for a forthcoming earthquake. In addition, Hill discounted the earlier earthquakes as catastrophic, concluding that there had been no catastrophic earthquake in southern California in more than one hundred fifty years. Hill's conclusions were published in 1928 in a heavily promoted book.

As the controversy over his prediction raged, Willis abruptly found himself undercut as president of the Seismological Society of America, largely due to S.D. Townley, a Stanford astronomer and the secretary of the society. Townley opposed Willis's involving the *Bulletin of the Seismological Society of America* in public education and in political stances regarding earthquake safety, stating that this had no place in a scientific journal. Townley also was unconvinced of the merits of Willis's earthquake forecast. As a result, in the late 1920s, Willis was largely forced out of a leadership role in seismology, except for support of the earthquake engineering laboratory at Stanford.

So the scientists were silenced. Once again, the boosters had won. But Willis, Wood, and others had built an infrastructure that would be able to deal with the earthquakes that followed.

On July 8, 1929, after several foreshocks, a moderate earthquake rattled the cities of Whittier and Norwalk in east Los Angeles, causing considerable damage to the East Whittier School. By this time, the new Seismological Lab at Caltech was in full operation, and among its employees was Charles Richter, who had turned his attention from theoretical physics to seismology. The Whittier Earthquake was felt by Richter at home, and he and Harry Wood described the earthquake in the *Bulletin of the Seismological Society of America* two years later. The earthquake was not a disaster, but it enabled the Seismological Lab to deal with its first local earthquake. It was a trial run for the larger earthquake that followed four years later.

At 5:54 P.M. on March 10, 1933, the Long Beach Earthquake rocked Los Angeles, taking 120 lives and inflicting damages of more than $40 million (more than $400 million in today's dollars). The earthquake was about the same size as the Santa Barbara Earthquake of 1925, but because it shook a densely populated suburb of Los Angeles, it was a much larger-scale disaster. The epicenter was off the coast of Newport Beach in Orange County, but the major losses were in Long Beach, twenty miles to the northwest. The source of the earthquake was the southern end of the Newport-Inglewood Fault, the northern end of which had been the source of the Inglewood Earthquake in 1920.

Some people suggested that this earthquake fulfilled Willis's prediction of a catastrophic earthquake within ten years, but in fact the earthquake was too small to fit his prediction.

As before, the boosters came out in full force, led by the *Los Angeles Times*, to downplay the danger from California earthquakes in comparison to other natural disasters in the country. A representative of the Los Angeles Chamber of Commerce went on a national tour to make the point that earthquakes rarely produced the devastation that severe storms did elsewhere.

But compared to previous earthquakes, the booster response was weak and dispirited. The earthquake struck during the depths of the Great Depression, and the California real estate boom had run out of steam several years before. The business community was in bad straits financially and was unable to mount the attacks that it had done before. In addition, the depressed condition of the California economy meant that only the federal government had the resources to help the stricken communities. But to receive federal assistance, the California congressional delegation had to admit that the earthquake had done a lot of damage and that the state needed help from Washington.

Furthermore, the residents of Los Angeles had had enough. Everyone had felt the earthquake and many had suffered damage. In addition, the earthquake had destroyed fifteen of the thirty-five schools in Long Beach, and many schools elsewhere in Los Angeles were damaged. Because the earthquake had struck after school was already out for the day, few children had died, but it was pointed out that if the earthquake had struck during school hours, thousands of children could have been killed. The *Los Angeles Examiner* published graphic photos of collapsed school buildings, which fueled the outrage of Los Angeles parents. Demands were made that school building contractors be prosecuted for shoddy workmanship.

Engineers and seismologists seized on the public outcry as an opportunity to upgrade the quality of building construction and build on the legacy of Bailey Willis and his predecessors. This time they directed their efforts at legislation. The *Long Beach Press-Telegram* endorsed a call by Harry Wood to regulate building construction, and similar pleas for stricter construction standards from geologist J.P. Buwalda and engineer R.R. Martel of Caltech were published in the *Examiner*. John C. Austin, an architect and former president of the Los

Angeles Chamber of Commerce, added his strong support for upgrading building codes. An inquest by the Los Angeles County coroner on earthquake fatalities turned into a forum during which leading earthquake professionals, questioned by Austin, advocated more stringent construction standards. The coroner's jury recommended that Los Angeles County adopt the earthquake resistance standards of a new building code proposed by the State Chamber of Commerce.

In the month following the earthquake, professional meetings were held in Los Angeles by architects and mechanical engineers, and solutions for the earthquake problem were discussed at length. Harry Wood wrote an article about earthquake preparedness for the *Bulletin of the Seismological Society of America*. The Los Angeles Board of Education convened a panel chaired by Robert Millikan, the Nobel Prize-winning physicist at Caltech. Millikan had persuaded world-renowned seismologist Beno Gutenberg to flee Nazi Germany (Gutenberg was Jewish) and join Charles Richter and Harry Wood at Caltech. Secretarial expenses in preparing the committee's report were covered by none other than that former booster, the Los Angeles Chamber of Commerce.

All of these groups repeated the same theme: the need for better earthquake preparedness. The Millikan report concluded that destructive earthquakes would continue to strike southern California, including the possibility of an earthquake as damaging as the San Francisco Earthquake of 1906. Therefore, "earthquake resistant construction is absolutely necessary in this region in order to avoid great loss of life and heavy damage to property." The Millikan report was even endorsed by the *Los Angeles Times*, which had voiced the boosters' view immediately after the earthquake.

Architects in San Diego, yet to be visited by a damaging earthquake, expressed interest in the recommendations. And in San Francisco, the chief building inspector and a major contributor to setting up the new state building code called for stronger construction standards in the Bay Area, a position advocated by the *San Francisco Chronicle*. On April 18, the twenty-seventh anniversary of the San Francisco Earthquake, a vindicated Bailey Willis was among those advocating higher standards in building construction. Earthquake-resistant building codes were adopted by Los Angeles County and the cities of Los Angeles, Long Beach, Santa Monica, Beverly Hills, and Pasadena.

In Sacramento, Assemblyman C. Don Field, responding to parents' anger over the schools damaged by the earthquake and guided by structural engineers, introduced a bill to make schools safer from earthquakes. The bill gave the State Division of Architecture the power to inspect school construction plans and actual construction to be sure that earthquake-resistant construction was used. The Division of Architecture was also authorized to hire structural engineers to inspect existing school buildings and make sure they met safety standards. This bill was signed into law on April 10, 1933. Enforcement was in the hands of a structural engineer, Clarence H. Kromer, who adopted the earthquake provisions of the State Chamber of Commerce Building Code, which he had helped create.

What about other buildings? Another bill was introduced by the state assemblyman from Long Beach to require that earthquake precautions be taken for all buildings in the state. With strong public support, the Riley Act became law on May 27, 1933. This law was criticized because its enforcement was left in the hands of local building inspectors, many of whom were not trained in earthquake-resistant construction. Many communities, perceiving themselves outside any earthquake danger zone, did not enforce the law.

The Field Act, with enforcement at the state level, became the more valuable of the two laws. Los Angeles cities moved to upgrade existing school buildings, raising money through bond issues with help from the federal government. School officials were prodded into action by a ruling of the Attorney General in November 1933 that school board members could be held personally liable for school injuries or deaths as a result of earthquake damage to school buildings.

The Long Beach Earthquake accomplished what the San Francisco Earthquake had not: it gained the support of major civic groups and newspapers for legislation at the local and state levels. The boosters and developers who had previously managed to deflect any serious discussion about earthquake reinforcement were weakened by the Depression. The earthquake community—including structural engineers, seismologists, geologists, and architects—was better organized and, in contrast to the situation in 1906, they used the earthquake as their "teachable moment" to upgrade building standards in California.

From Long Beach to Sylmar and the National Earthquake Hazard Reduction Program (1933–1977)

After 1933, earthquakes dropped out of the big news for nearly forty years. True, earthquakes did strike California during that period: Imperial Valley in 1940 and the largest quake since 1906 in the southern San Joaquin Valley in 1952. These earthquakes did a lot of damage and produced big headlines, but they were far from the big cities. The general public believed that legislation was now in place to deal with the problem, and there were more pressing matters at hand.

California was growing, even during the Depression, with or without the boosters. Huge projects were underway to deliver water to southern California. World War II brought new military bases and shipyards, and following the War the aircraft industry continued to expand. Hollywood became the movie capital of the world, and the new network of superhighways led to millions of automobiles and to the migration of city-dwellers to the suburbs.

Earthquakes stayed on the scientific agenda as centers of excellence developed at Berkeley, Stanford, and Caltech. Scientific results were published in the *Bulletin of the Seismological Society of America*, which was distributed worldwide, and California became the world leader in earthquake research, eclipsing Japan and Europe, which had been caught up in the chaos of World War II.

The study of earthquakes became more focused on the study of seismograph records, and few geologists stepped forward to take the leadership roles of G.K. Gilbert, Andrew Lawson, John C. Branner, and Bailey Willis. Earthquake investigations, whether by seismologists, geologists, or engineers, were published as scientific research. The calls for social action that characterized the first two decades of the Seismological Society of America became muted after the passage of the Field and Riley Acts.

In 1947, the Coast and Geodetic Survey asked California structural engineers for advice on setting up strong-motion seismographs, used to design buildings to be more resistant to earthquake shaking. The engineers formed an Advisory Committee on Engineering Seismology, which by 1949 became the Earthquake Engineering Research Institute (EERI), forming a link between the Seismological Society of America and professional engineering organizations. This was important because of an ongoing debate among structural engineers between those favoring more earthquake-resistant construction and those concerned about the increased costs of those measures.

The Cold War brought new demands for the services of earthquake specialists. Structural engineers learned that strengthening buildings against earthquakes was similar to protecting them against a nuclear blast. After the increase in underground nuclear testing by both the Soviet Union and the United States, the federal government ramped up funding for new seismographs that could distinguish between natural earthquakes and nuclear explosions. This project, code-named Vela Uniform, resulted in an increase in federal support for seismology from $0.5 million in 1958 to $30 million in 1961. Finally, the Cold War led to the establishment in 1950 of the Federal Civil Defense Administration, which would evolve into the Federal Emergency Management Agency (FEMA). FEMA later became the lead agency in the federal earthquake hazards program.

What about the United States Geological Survey (USGS), the largest Earth science organization in the free world? The USGS was born of Manifest Destiny, and teams of geologists and surveyors had followed the covered wagons and railroads westward to map the mountains and canyons and to explore the mineral and fossil fuel resources that had been acquired by the United States as the country expanded westward. USGS geologists returned from their western expeditions as celebrities, lauded by the eastern media much as astronauts would be a century later. G.K. Gilbert was one of those explorers, and in his travels through the Intermountain West he learned about earthquakes and active faults. Luck would place him in the Bay Area at the time of the San Francisco Earthquake.

The USGS was too large an organization *not* to have an influence on the study of earthquakes. Unlike most federal agencies, the USGS had a long tradition of allowing its senior scientists some latitude in defining their own projects. Individual USGS scientists developed an interest in earthquakes, starting with Gilbert and continuing with reports on a large earthquake that heavily damaged Charleston, South Carolina in 1886 and another that struck southern Alaska in 1899.

In 1909, the USGS hired Levi Noble, an independently wealthy Easterner who was willing to work for a token salary as long as he could select his own research projects. One project presented itself the following year as the result of a wedding present from his in-laws: a fruit ranch at Valyermo astride the San Andreas Fault in the northern foothills of the San Gabriel Mountains. Near Noble's Valyermo ranch, spectacular topography marks the rupture zone of the great 1857 Fort Tejon Earthquake. Taking advantage of the freedom given him by his USGS supervisors, Noble mapped the geology along the fault and pointed out evidence for twenty-four miles of horizontal movement on the fault at a time when the leading geologists, especially Andrew Lawson, insisted that little or no horizontal movement had taken place. Noble's theory met with so much opposition from high places that even he began to doubt it, but his mapping influenced a young graduate student at Caltech named Bob Wallace. Working under J.P. Buwalda, Wallace completed a study of the San Andreas Fault near Palmdale, not far from Noble's field area. After finishing his San Andreas mapping project, Wallace joined the USGS.

Despite the work of Gilbert, Noble, and many others, the official mission of the USGS continued to focus on mineral, fuel, and water resources and on regional geology, as it had in the nineteenth century. However, in the mid-1950s the USGS established a regional office in Menlo Park, south of San Francisco and close to the San Andreas Fault.

The institutional change began as a consequence of a stupendous earthquake—one of the two largest on Earth during the twentieth century—that struck southern Alaska on Good Friday, 1964. The investigation of this earthquake was too large a project for any university, even the developing research centers in California. Alaska was simply too big, and the damaged areas too remote. The USGS was a logical choice to follow up on the earthquake because it was already mapping the geology and mineral resources of Alaska, a twentieth-century follow-up to its mapping in the Lower 48 States in the nineteenth century.

A team of USGS scientists produced a detailed report on the earthquake, following the lead of the Lawson report more than a half century earlier and a report on the 1952 Kern County Earthquake published by the California Division of Mines. Like the Lawson report, the USGS recorded its observations and conclusions as a research study, and, unlike J.C. Branner and Bailey Willis, the USGS did not take a political stand nor advocate earthquake-related legislation.

Even before the Alaska earthquake, individuals within the USGS were advocating a larger federal role in earthquake studies. Bob Wallace and several colleagues submitted a proposal to USGS headquarters for an earthquake-hazards study of the San Andreas Fault. Because their proposal had a $2 million price tag and the money would have had to come out of existing projects, the proposal was turned down.

One problem was that federal responsibility for earthquake research was already vested in another agency. The U.S. Coast and Geodetic Survey, part of the Department of Commerce, had been given the responsibility for seismology in 1925. Even before that, Coast and Geodetic Survey reoccupation of benchmarks after the San Francisco Earthquake had led to the discovery of strain buildup in the Earth's crust preceding the earthquake. A later reoccupation in the 1920s spurred Bailey Willis to make his ill-fated prediction in 1925. By 1947, resurveys had confirmed that strain was once again accumulating across the San Andreas Fault in the Bay Area, building toward the next earthquake. The Coast and Geodetic Survey program in seismology led to establishing the Earthquake Engineering Research Institute.

Yet the USGS had the scientific expertise in geology and seismology to make a major contribution to the understanding of earthquakes. Should the USGS be given an official mandate to work on earthquake problems, in addition to the U.S. Coast and Geodetic Survey? The battle between two federal agencies for an uncertain federal earthquake dollar was about to begin.

In 1965, after publication of a national report advocating a federal program in earthquake prediction, the USGS set up a National Center for Earthquake Research at its regional office in Menlo Park. The Coast and Geodetic Survey countered a month later by establishing an Earthquake Mechanism Laboratory in San Francisco. The Department of Commerce, where the Coast and Geodetic Survey was housed, issued a detailed report on the Alaska Earthquake, paralleling that produced by the USGS, and would produce another detailed report on the 1971

Sylmar Earthquake. The Presidential Science Advisor asked a panel of experts to resolve the problem of two competing agencies, but the director of USGS, Bill Pecora, was made its chairman. Bickering between the two surveys for government funding led to a General Accounting Office report in 1970 pointing out "duplicative and overlapping earthquake research studies along the same portions of the major California earthquake faults."

In 1970, the Coast and Geodetic Survey became part of the National Oceanic and Atmospheric Administration (NOAA), whose senior administrators were more interested in weather and the oceans than in earthquakes. Nonetheless, NOAA fought hard to keep the earthquake program, but a budget cut in 1972 threatening some of NOAA's core programs led to a decision by the Office of Management and Budget in favor of the USGS. Thus ended the interagency dispute, establishing the USGS as the lead agency responsible for earthquake research.

The Alaska Earthquake triggered an effort led by Frank Press, director of the Caltech Seismological Lab, to get the federal government involved on a larger scale, particularly in a program to develop a capability of predicting earthquakes. In 1965, a panel of distinguished scientists commissioned by the President's Office of Science and Technology Policy and chaired by Press recommended a major ten-year program in earthquake prediction. Other reports followed, with structural engineers, seismologists, and geologists arguing over the directions earthquake research should take. Finally, in 1970, a task force of the Office of Science and Technology Policy led by Karl Steinbrugge, a structural engineer who had described the damage from the Kern County Earthquake of 1952, brought the various competing elements together and issued a widely praised report on addressing future losses due to earthquakes.

Even before a national program was established, these reports led to an improved funding climate within the USGS. Seismologists at the Denver office of the USGS were already heavily involved in the Vela Uniform program of nuclear test monitoring. After the Alaska Earthquake, these geophysicists moved to Menlo Park and joined the investigation of that earthquake. In 1968, an earthquake struck the San Jacinto Fault in southeastern California, and USGS geologists and geophysicists swung into action. A geologist, Malcolm Clark, dug a trench across the fault trace and discovered geological evidence for a prehistoric earthquake on the fault that had ruptured in 1968. This was the first paleoseismological trench in the world. The USGS was well positioned for the next big urban earthquake, which would strike three years later in the early morning hours of February 9, 1971.

The California Division of Mines and Geology (DMG), like its federal counterpart, the USGS, also had the problem of a legislative mandate to study mineral resources rather than earthquakes. This began to change with the appointment of a new State Geologist, Ian Campbell, who began to move the DMG into urban hazards research (see Chapter 15). With support from its governing board, which included earthquake scientists Clarence Allen and Karl Steinbrugge, DMG began its own earthquake program, which included analysis of earthquake hazards of proposed major real estate developments.

In the decade before the Sylmar Earthquake, I was a petroleum geologist working for Shell Oil Company in Ventura and Los Angeles. I was not concerned, nor were my coworkers concerned about the possibility of earthquakes in southern California. My work took me to several major faults near Ventura that were important because they were adjacent to large deposits of oil, including the Saticoy oil field beneath the Oak Ridge Fault. I learned that the oil reservoirs at Saticoy were no older than unconsolidated surface sediments in other parts of the country, yet these reservoirs were tectonically tilted up to vertical and even overturned. But the possibility that this tilting was accompanied by earthquakes never crossed my mind.

I became acquainted with Tom Bailey, a groundwater geologist and Ventura city councilman who had mapped the mountain ranges north of Ventura for Shell in the 1930s, following a devastating brush fire that had denuded the landscape. Bailey had found Ice-Age elephant bones in sediments of the same age as the upside-down sandstone oil reservoirs at Saticoy. And he was thinking about earthquakes when he finally convinced me that these sediments were extremely young to be so deformed and faulted.

Local petroleum geologists used to have lunch on Thursdays at the Pierpont Inn in Ventura to swap lies about what each company was finding in the numerous wildcat wells that were being drilled in the Ventura basin. Tom Bailey showed up at one of these lunches with an invitation to take a short field trip to the Santa Monica Mountains to visit a nuclear reactor site proposed by the Los Angeles Department of Water and Power at Corral Canyon, near Malibu. Naturally we jumped at the chance to look at rocks instead of going back to the office on a slow Thursday afternoon.

What we saw at Corral Canyon was shocking. A bulldozer trench had been excavated across the site for the reactor, and the rock in the trench was more intensely gouged, sheared, and fractured than any I had ever seen! I couldn't believe that anyone in his right mind would advocate placing a nuclear power plant so close to a known active fault, the Malibu Coast Fault. Yet some famous engineering geologists had signed off on the project. Bailey was there representing Malibu residents, including Bob Hope and Angela Lansbury, in an effort to stop construction, and he needed our support. He got it.

Concerns about earthquakes and landslides led the Safety and Licensing Board of the Atomic Energy Commission in 1965 to stiffen engineering requirements to resist fault displacement directly beneath the plant—requirements the Department of Water and Power were unable to meet. The project was abandoned.

Elsewhere in the state, the Pacific Gas & Electric Company (PG&E) was planning to construct a nuclear power plant at Bodega Head, north of San Francisco and close to the 1906 break of the San Andreas Fault at the small town of Bodega Bay to the east. This project had been approved by the Atomic Energy Commission and the Sonoma County Board of Supervisors. Arrayed against the power plant was a coalition of local preservationists alarmed at how the power plant would mar the beauty of this section of coastline. They were also concerned that the plant was so close to the San Andreas Fault that a future 1906-type earthquake could lead to catastrophic failure of the reactor. The activists gained the support of Governor Pat Brown and U.S. Senator Claire Engle, and battle lines were drawn.

Experts for PG&E argued that the plant could be engineered against a large earthquake and that the fault zone directly beneath the reactor, which had not ruptured in 1906, was inactive. But other experts, including scientists from USGS, disagreed. Still, the project seemed unstoppable until some activists released helium balloons, labeled "Strontium-90" after a particularly toxic byproduct of radioactive decay, from the nuclear reactor site. The balloons drifted southward and some were found at San Francisco, resulting in embarrassing media attention. In 1965, the Atomic Energy Commission expressed concern about the safety of the site against earthquakes, and PG&E abandoned the project, even though construction had already begun.

Earlier in the century, and early in the explosive growth of California, the state's boosters had considered it necessary to issue soothing statements discounting the earthquake problem. In the postwar years prior to the Sylmar Earthquake of 1971, the boosters simply ignored earthquakes. California was growing too big and too fast, and the promoters and developers ran roughshod over any opposition, including an unsuccessful attempt in 1951 by school officials and builders to gut the school-construction safeguards of the Field Act.

Nowhere was this more obvious than the housing subdivisions that paved over the countryside surrounding Los Angeles, San Francisco, and other major cities. Housing tracts were built over landslides and active faults, including Daly City, a suburb of San Francisco, built directly across the San Andreas Fault. The East Bay cities of Oakland and Hayward sprouted housing developments and shopping malls across the active Hayward Fault that had ruptured in 1868. The active fault map of Bailey Willis was forgotten.

The 1971 Sylmar Earthquake was accompanied by a rupture on the previously unknown San Fernando Fault, cutting across streets, driveways, yards, houses, and freeways and killing sixty-four people. The USGS took charge of the investigation, with major participation by the State Division of Mines and Geology (DMG).

At the time of the Sylmar Earthquake, the Field and Riley Acts were generally believed to provide sufficient protection against earthquakes. But the Sylmar Earthquake ripped through new freeway overpasses like spaghetti. A fire truck at the Lopez Canyon Fire Station bounced around in its garage like a toy in a Cracker Jack box. An electric power station was heavily damaged, and the new Olive View County Medical Center, occupied less than four months, was rendered useless and had to be demolished. Cracks appeared in the Van Norman Dam, and thousands of residents living downstream were evacuated because of fears the dam might fail. This led to passage of legislation in 1971 setting up instruments to measure strong ground shaking, funded by building permits and managed by the DMG.

It was back to the drawing boards. The housing subdivisions damaged by the active San Fernando Fault led to passage in 1972 of the Alquist-Priolo Geologic Hazard Zone Act, requiring special studies of fault zones known to be active prior to allowing development (see Chapter 15). The DMG was given responsibility for identifying fault zones subject to Alquist-Priolo and for a wide range of other earthquake-related activities. Building construction standards were increased. In 1973, the USGS converted the National Center of Earthquake Research in Menlo Park to the Office of Earthquake Studies; this office funded earthquake investigations by Survey scientists and academics such as myself through an external grants program.

But no national earthquake program existed, only increased funding to the USGS and an increased commitment to earthquake hazard mitigation by the State of California. Legislation had been drafted by Sen. Alan Cranston's staff, but it received little support on Capitol Hill. Then Bob Castle of the USGS showed Frank Press a study of highway re-leveling that identified a region of rapid uplift centered on Palmdale, in the Mojave Desert close to the San Andreas Fault. Press discussed this study with Edward Teller at a meeting of a national committee exploring new technological opportunities, and Teller brought it to the attention of Vice President Nelson Rockefeller. After a series of hurried meetings, the USGS and the earthquake engineering research program of the National Science Foundation (NSF) received a substantial increase in funding. A special appropriation for study of the Palmdale uplift (or "bulge," as the press called it) was authorized by President Gerald Ford. (I received some research money from this appropriation to study the Santa Susana Fault on the southern edge of the Palmdale uplift.) Finally, in 1977, six years after the Sylmar Earthquake, Congress authorized and funded the National Earthquake Hazards Reduction Program (NEHRP; see Chapter 14), with major responsibilities given to the USGS, following the plan first outlined by Bob Wallace in the early 1960s and built on by several federal task groups during the next decade, especially the Steinbrugge report. Significantly, the Coast and Geodetic Survey, the legally mandated agency for seismology for nearly half a century, was excluded from the new program.

From Sylmar to Now: Life Under NEHRP

The following years were marked by solid growth in earthquake hazards investigations, stimulated by earthquakes in the Imperial Valley in 1979, beneath Loma Prieta Peak in the Santa Cruz Mountains south of San Francisco in 1989, in Humboldt County and in the Mojave Desert in 1992, and again in the San Fernando Valley in 1994. Many geophysicists, geologists, and engineers are now active in earthquake studies at the USGS, the Division of Mines and Geology, and several universities in addition to Berkeley, Stanford, and Caltech. The media frequently describe the scientific and engineering studies in earthquake hazard reduction. Earthquake drills are held in schools.

Compared to other parts of the United States, California is reasonably far along in its plans for the next 1906-scale earthquake. A state earthquake program was established before NEHRP. Legislation is in place to regulate construction in seismically hazardous areas.

Yet apathy remains. Ventura, my former home, had been struck by a large earthquake in 1812, when it was little more than the San Buenaventura Mission. The city and its suburbs are flanked by three major active faults, but few residents would list an earthquake as a major concern. Northern San Bernardino is spread out across a stretch of the San Andreas Fault that has not ruptured for more than three hundred years, but not many are bothered about an earthquake that could severely damage the city. Active faults have been found in downtown San Diego, and the Rose Canyon Fault comes ashore near La Jolla and extends toward Mission Bay. But few people are worried and, just as earlier in the century, vigorous opposition sometimes arises to doing any more about earthquakes than state law requires.

In the 1980s, Palmdale was one of the fastest-growing cities in the country, jumping from twelve thousand in 1980 to sixty-eight thousand in 1990. The city's boosters describe its "bright, sunny days, slight breeze, and mild winters," and the chamber of commerce points to "its location, labor pool, and land, land, land." Omitted is that much of its "land, land, land" lies next to the San Andreas Fault, which had ruptured in California's largest historical earthquake in 1857, although Realtors are generally aware of the Alquist-Priolo zone covering the fault. The city is spreading amoeba-like along the fault east and west of the Antelope Valley Freeway, providing housing for those who don't mind the two-hour commute to Los Angeles.

Then there's the ski-resort town of Mammoth Lakes in the eastern Sierra Nevada. After a moderate-sized earthquake in 1978 and four more in 1980, the USGS began to monitor seismic and volcanic activity there (see Chapter 6). In the next two years, they detected signs of swelling of an active volcano east of town called the Long Valley Caldera. USGS scientists were particularly concerned because the swelling volcano was growing across the only exit route out of the town. Increases in seismicity, steam venting, and swelling of the volcano led the USGS, in consultation with the Division of Mines and Geology and the Governor's office, to issue a Notice of Potential Volcanic Hazards for the Mammoth Lakes area on May 25, 1982. The warning was mailed to concerned communities that had not been part of the consultations. An enterprising reporter from the *Los Angeles Times* got wind of it and published the warning on the date it was issued, before Mammoth Lakes and Mono County had received the official notification.

What was the local reaction? Outrage! Motel reservations were canceled and tourist business fell off—just before the Memorial Day weekend, one of the biggest of the year. The business community was furious, claiming that government scientists and bureaucrats were destroying the community and devastating real estate values. Unfortunately, the USGS could not place a time on a future eruption, nor even guarantee that an eruption would take place at all (so far it hasn't). A meeting between USGS scientists and local citizens produced a lot of hot-tempered discussion, and two county supervisors eventually lost their seats. Much of the problem was that the local community had not been informed about the hazard and about the tightrope that scientists had to walk in advising the public while trying to avoid scaring people and causing panic.

This is the political climate of California today, and this book is written to help people understand a hazard that is real and potentially catastrophic but not yet understood well enough for scientists and engineers to make a reliable diagnosis. As Clarence Allen of Caltech says, "The next earthquake will be a surprise"—despite all the research we have done to date.

A man I met in a bar in Gorman—next to an off-ramp of Interstate 5 north of Los Angeles and directly on the 1857 break on the San Andreas Fault—told me he had moved to Gorman from Mammoth Lakes "because he was afraid of earthquakes." I've met others who know that California has earthquakes but they don't want to talk about it. Many city councils and county boards of supervisors collectively feel the same way, even though their areas are listed as prime candidates for an earthquake. Today, when the word "earthquake" is mentioned, city boosters and local government officials simply hunker down.

I recently completed a tour of the San Andreas Fault, not to study the geology but to talk to people about the fault and about earthquakes. Earthquakes are rarely mentioned, even though San Jose's professional soccer team is called the Earthquakes. But people know where the fault is, and real estate agents and county assessors can refer to a map from the Division of Mines and Geology that locates active faults. Alquist-Priolo seems to be just another bureaucratic hoop a developer must jump through, but if you build near the fault you need a geologic report on your site attesting to its earthquake safety. Maybe Californians are as blasé about earthquakes as Floridians are about hurricanes.

Average citizens won't read our research papers, nor should they have to. They probably won't even read the public announcements put out by government agencies (with the Mammoth Lakes hazard warning a notable and understandable exception). Maybe they will read this book!

This book tries to tell the California earthquake story in a way that my wife, my neighbor, my Congressman, and my insurance agent can understand and find readable. Even though we can't say when or where the next big California earthquake will strike, we can say where the dangerous places are to build, and we can design a building that will ride out an earthquake without its occupants getting killed. We can do this now, today.

Some claim that the Big One would be like an asteroid impact or a direct hit from a nuclear bomb—"We hope it doesn't happen, but we are helpless to do anything about it if it does." This is not true. We can do a lot about earthquakes, individually and collectively.

But first we must become informed.

Suggestions for Further Reading

Geschwind, C.H. 2001. *California Earthquakes: Science, Risk, and the Politics of Hazard Mitigation, 1906–1977*. Baltimore: Johns Hopkins University Press. In press. A fully referenced account of earthquake awareness from the 1906 San Francisco Earthquake to the establishment of the National Earthquake Hazards Reduction Program.

Goodstein, J.R. 1991. *Millikan's School*. New York: W.H. Norton & Co. 317 p. Chapter 7 describes the establishment of the seismological lab at Caltech.

Hansen, G., and E. Condon. 1989. *Denial of Disaster*. San Francisco: Cameron & Co. The cover-up of the San Francisco Earthquake.

Scott, S., interviewer. 1999. Robert E. Wallace: Connections, the EERI Oral History Series. Earthquake Engineering Research Institute OSH-6.

Sieh, K., and S. LeVay. 1988. *The Earth in Turmoil*. New York: William Freeman & Co. Chapter 7, Mammoth Lakes, and Chapter 13, recent earthquake politics in California.

Thomas, G., and M.M. Witts. 1971. *The San Francisco Earthquake*. New York: Dell Publishing Co. 301 p.

ᔕ Part II ᔕ
Tectonic Plates, Geologic Time, and Earthquakes

No one doubts that the Earth is the most hospitable planet in the solar system. We have a breathable atmosphere and the temperature, as Goldilocks said about the porridge, is "just right." Venus is too hot, Mars is too cold, and the Moon and Mercury have no atmosphere at all to speak of.

But in terms of earthquakes, the other planets could be considered safer places to live than the Earth. That's because the Earth's outer shell is broken up into great slabs called *plates* that jostle and grind against one another like huge ice floes. In the process, all that crunching between plates forces parts of the crust upward to create mountains, causing earthquakes in the process. In contrast, the crust of the other inner planets consists entirely of massive rock that experienced most of its mountain-building activity billions of years ago, soon after the planets were formed. Now the crustal movements on these planets have been stilled. There is no grinding of plates against one another to cause them to shake.

But the Earth has active volcanoes and earthquakes, which are geologic phenomena, and to understand them we need a brief introduction to their geologic setting. This requires us to stretch our minds to think about moving masses of rock that are extremely large, many tens of miles thick and hundreds of miles wide. We also must think of great lengths of time. An astronomer asks us to think of great distances of hundreds of billions of miles, and a geologist asks us to think about thousands or even millions of years. An earthquake can happen in less than thirty seconds, but it is a response to the slow motion of massive tectonic plates on the surface of the Earth, building up strain over many thousands of years.

How do we study earthquakes? We can see the effects of past earthquakes in fault ruptures on the Earth's surface. We can learn about earthquakes as they happen by the squiggles they make on a seismograph record. We can think about future earthquakes by measuring the slow buildup of tectonic strain in the Earth, using orbiting satellites.

∽ 1 ∽
A Concept of Time

"What is time? The shadow on the dial, the striking of the clock, the running of the sand, day and night, summer and winter, months, years, centuries—these are but arbitrary and outward signs, the measure of time, not time itself."

Henry Wadsworth Longfellow, *Hyperion*

"All moons, all years, all days, all winds, take their course and pass away."

Mayan proverb

The Earth's crust seems pretty quiet most of the time. When I look at a map of California showing the locations of earthquakes detected by seismographs, I see lots of black dots, each signifying an earthquake (see Frontispiece). Many of these earthquakes southeast of San Francisco lie on or close to the San Andreas Fault. But you and I can drive from San Francisco to Los Angeles along a route close to the San Andreas Fault and never feel an earthquake.

Americans in nineteenth-century California thought that only San Francisco had damaging earthquakes. Southern California, after earthquakes in 1812 and 1857, had no severe earthquakes for another seventy-eight years, when Santa Barbara was partly destroyed by an earthquake in 1925. If people thought about earthquakes at all during those seventy-eight years, they probably believed that Los Angeles was free of earthquakes. In fact, California was experiencing normal earthquake activity during that time. Strain was building up on various faults for future earthquakes, including big ones at Long Beach in 1933 and in the San Fernando Valley in 1971 and 1994. In other parts of California, the strain is still building up and an earthquake hasn't happened yet. But to envision the earthquake cycle as a geologist does, we have to think in terms of thousands of years.

How long is a long time to a geologist? Table 1-1 shows a series of time scales, each encompassing a longer period of time than the last. The first scale is historical, starting with the arrival of Spanish explorers in California more than four centuries ago. The next two scales are in thousands rather than hundreds of years; the recorded history of California spans only a brief part of the Late Quaternary time scale. The Late Cenozoic scale includes millions of years, and the Older Earth History scale covers four-and-a-half *billion* years.

27

OK, I'm a geologist, and I am supposed to think in these great lengths of time. But I still consider it a long time when I'm stuck in traffic on the Santa Ana Freeway. When I was growing up, I thought it was an unacceptably long time until Christmas or my birthday. You might feel that it's a very long time before you graduate from college, or get your kids raised, or retire, and so it's probably tough to envision even the few hundred years in the Historical Time Scale.

Now that I'm older, I've learned to take a somewhat longer view of time (except when I'm stuck on the freeway). I knew both my grandfathers, who told me stories about the horse-and-buggy days. I enjoy reading about the forty-niners and the California Gold Rush of 150 years ago, which to me seems an unbelievably long time ago.

But in fact, California's recorded history is short. The stretch of the coast from Alaska to California was the last region of the Pacific Rim to receive settlers willing to record their history.

In 1542, Juan Rodríguez Cabrillo, trying to find the Northwest Passage, discovered San Diego Bay instead, and in 1579, Francis Drake spent a few weeks repairing his ship on the northern California coast. But the Californias (Alta and Baja) were off the beaten track for the Manila galleon trade, and so the area was ignored by the Spanish and everybody else for the next two hundred years. Finally, in 1769, Gaspar de Portolá sailed into San Diego Bay, followed by Catholic missionaries who established outposts northward along the coast. So a permanent record of happenings in California—including earthquakes first felt by Portolá in 1769 near the site of the future Los Angeles on his way north from San Diego—began to be kept only in the late 1700s. Missions led to ranchos, fur sealing, beaver trapping, and the Americans, who took over—and the rest, as they say, is history, or at least recorded history (Part I). The late arrival of permanent colonists means that the recorded history of California, including the reporting of earthquakes, covers only the past 230 years along the coast, and less than 200 years in the interior. To a geologist, that is a very short time.

Native Americans were in California for thousands of years before that, of course, but they did not keep written records other than enigmatic and beautiful paintings on rocks. Their rich oral traditions are another matter, though, and some of their stories suggest events that could have been great earthquakes and seismic sea waves.

To a geologist, two centuries is like the blinking of an eye. The Earth is more than four-and-a-half billion years old. Evidence from rocks shows that most of California is much younger than that, and only in a few places like the San Gabriel Mountains of southern California do we find rocks more than a billion years old. The age of the California Coast Ranges, the Los Angeles Basin, and the San Andreas Fault are

continued on page 31

Table 1-1. Different time scales of interest in the study of earthquakes

Time Scales
Historical

2000 A.D.	Age of computers, immigration, freeways, and two big-city earthquakes
1980	Imperial Valley Earthquake; Proposition 13; Medfly infestation
	Sylmar Earthquake in San Fernando Valley; BART opens
1960	Development of freeways and interstates; Watts Riot; Berkeley free-speech movement
	Growth of aerospace industry after World War II
1940	Imperial Valley Earthquake; evacuation of Japanese Americans
	Roaring Twenties followed by Great Depression; growth of movie industry in Hollywood
1920	Roaring Twenties; silent pictures; California water projects
	World War I; eruption of Mt. Lassen; Los Angeles Aqueduct
1900	San Francisco Earthquake
	Stanford University founded
1880	Santa Fe Railroad reaches Los Angeles
	American Civil War; Central Pacific Railroad built; University of California chartered
1860	Comstock Lode discovered; Haywards Earthquake
	Gold discovered in Sierra foothills; California becomes a state
1840	Americans migrate to California; Mexican War; Alta California ceded to United States
	Jedediah Smith makes first crossing of Sierra
1820	Spanish rule ends; California part of Mexico
	Two earthquakes damage missions; Russians build a trading post at Fort Ross
1800	Earthquake destroys mission at San Juan Bautista
	Spain gives up to England all rights on Pacific Coast north of California
1780	Father Serra founds missions on coast. San Francisco and Los Angeles founded
	Gaspar de Portolá founds San Diego; Monterey founded soon after
1760	
1740	
1720	Birth of Junípero Serra on the Island of Majorca
1700	Great earthquake on the Cascadia Subduction Zone
1680	Great earthquake on the southern San Andreas Fault
1660	
1640	Spain has no interest in Alta or Baja California; Native Americans left alone
1620	Sebastián Vizcaíno reaches Monterey Bay
1600	Sebastián Cermeño explores northern California coast
1580	Francis Drake repairs his ship near Pt. Reyes
1560	
1540	Juan Rodríguez Cabrillo discovers San Diego Bay

Late Prehistoric

2000 A.D. Today

Cascadia Subduction Zone earthquake 1700; San Andreas earthquake 1680

1500   Great earthquake on San Andreas Fault around 1480

Native Americans prosper as Stone Age culture due to isolation

1000

Large earthquake on San Andreas Fault; size of other earthquakes not well known

500   Cascadia Subduction Zone earthquake

0   Large earthquake on Santa Monica Fault with surface rupture

Late Quaternary

2000 A.D. Today. We call 1950 A.D. "Present" before nuclear fallout messes up our dating scales. B.P. means Before Present, actually Before 1950

5000 B.P. Same as 3000 B.C., but 5,000 years before 1950 A.D.

Glaciers retreat in High Sierra; large earthquake on Hollywood Fault

10,000   Beginning of Holocene; end of Pleistocene; sea level rising rapidly

15,000   Ice caps melting, sea level rising; Hollywood and Santa Monica faults rupture

20,000   Maximum extent of glaciers; sea level 400 feet lower than today

Late Cenozoic

Age, in thousands of years

0 (Today) Sea level 20 feet higher than today 125,000 years ago

500   500,000 years ago. Several ice advances and retreats; Los Angeles basin becomes dry land

Cataclysmic eruption at Long Valley near Bishop; Earth's magnetic field reverses

1,000   More glacial advances and retreats

Colorado River sediments cover up Imperial Valley spreading center

1,500   Uplift of San Gabriel Mountains and San Bernardino Mountains

Beginning of Pleistocene 1,800,000 years ago

2,000   Pliocene Epoch

Los Angeles and Ventura Basins are thousands of feet below sea level

2,500   First major ice age advance 2,400,000 years ago

Still in the Pliocene, which started about 5,300,000 years ago

Older Earth History

Age in millions of years

0 (Today)

2.4   Beginning of ice ages

4.5   Baja California splits from Mexico, forming Gulf of California and San Andreas Fault

15–18	Volcanoes in southern California, including Los Angeles
30	Pacific Plate first comes into contact with North America Plate in California
66	Asteroid slams into southern Mexico; dinosaurs become extinct
180	Breakup of the supercontinent Pangea
245	Greatest mass extinction of organisms in the history of the Earth
570	Beginning of trilobites and shelled organisms
1,000	Primitive life in the Death Valley region
4,600	Age of the Earth, 4,540,000,000 years

measured in millions rather than billions of years. But that is still an incredibly long time. A geologist can easily *talk* about sixty million years, but it is just as hard for a geologist to *imagine* such a long period of time as it is for anybody else.

Knowing that we have millions of years to work with allows the geologist to explain otherwise unexplainable things. The Colorado River has had time to carve the mile-deep Grand Canyon through layers of rock, one sand grain at a time. The battering of Pacific storm waves has sculpted the precipitous cliffs of the Big Sur coast, an endless battle between the tremendous power of water waves against the slow tectonic uplift of the Coast Ranges. Mt. Shasta cannot have grown in a lifetime, but rather it rose by repeated eruptions of lava over hundreds of thousands of years, carved and molded by glacial ice even as it grew. The hillsides on which California subdivisions grow are battlegrounds between the internal forces of uplift and earthquakes and the erosive power of running water and landslides. The trusting homeowner perched on this evolving, dynamic landscape can only hope for a temporary truce in the geological wars during the few decades that his split-level ranch house takes up its position there. I saw a cartoon that said southern California was the place where hillside homes were moving faster than traffic on the freeway. Art Buchwald once said that sometimes when you go home in California your house meets you halfway. If the length of time geologic processes have operated in California is unimaginably long, the rates of the internal processes are incredibly slow—about as fast as your fingernails grow. If you grow to be six feet tall in twenty years, the rate of your growth is much faster than the rate at which strain accumulates along the San Andreas Fault.

The San Andreas Fault is the boundary between two great tectonic plates, North America Plate and Pacific, but when I talk about how fast North America is moving past the Pacific Plate—a little less than an inch-and-a-half per year—I sometimes lose my audience. We talk about speed limits on the freeway of seventy miles per hour, and this guy is worried about speeds of an inch-and-a-half per year? But even that slow rate has resulted in great earthquakes on the San Andreas Fault in 1812, 1857, and 1906. If this rate of travel continues for five million years, coastal California will move northwest more than eighty miles. Keep that up long enough, and—grab your parka and your mittens—Los Angeles will lose its palm trees and be at the same latitude as southern Alaska! Can you *really* picture that? Neither can I.

The great Fort Tejon Earthquake ruptured the central section of the San Andreas Fault early in the days of American settlement, offsetting the fault as much as thirty to forty feet. Backhoe trench excavations of past earthquakes show that a prehistoric earthquake occurred on this section of the fault about 1480. Should we relax because the time between the 1480 and 1857 earthquakes is nearly 380 years, and it has been less than 150 years since the Fort Tejon Earthquake?

Unfortunately, no—because the repeat time of earthquakes can vary a lot. Before the 1480 earthquake, those same trench excavations reveal evidence of two or three earthquakes between 1250 and 1350. In southern California, a section of the San Andreas Fault ruptured in 1812 and again in 1857, just forty-five years later. Yet more than one hundred forty years have gone by without another major earthquake along that section of the fault. We could have another great earthquake on this part of the San Andreas Fault much sooner—maybe in our lifetime, maybe tomorrow. Excavations farther southeast along the fault found evidence for earthquakes in 1680 and 1480.

Another reason we shouldn't laugh at an inch-and-a-half per year is the massive amount of rock that is building up strain along the San Andreas Fault. The slab of rock on both sides of the fault is about sixty miles thick. On the west side, this slab of rock extends across the Pacific Ocean to Japan and New Zealand, and on the east side it extends all the way across North America into the middle of the Atlantic Ocean. So even though the movement rate is slow, the bodies of rock that are in motion are titanic in scale.

Because the times for geologic processes to work are so ponderously long, geologists have devised time scales (see the Late Quaternary and Late Cenozoic scales in Table 1-1) analogous, perhaps, to historians referring to the Middle Ages or the Renaissance. At first, this was done using fossils, because organisms have changed through time by evolution, and distinctive shells or bones of species that had died out were used to characterize specific time intervals called *periods* and *epochs*. In the past few decades, it has become possible to date rocks directly, based on the extremely regular rate of decay of certain radioactive isotopes of elements such as uranium. These atomic clocks enable us to date the age of the Earth at about four-and-a-half billion years and, in addition, to date the age of trilobites, dinosaurs, and other dominant groups of organisms that are now extinct.

In our study of earthquakes, we do not need to be concerned about most of the geologic periods and epochs, including the ages of trilobites and dinosaurs. We do need to know about the times when the geologic processes that produce today's earthquakes have been operating: the Tertiary and Quaternary periods, together known as the Cenozoic Era. We especially need to know something about the geologic history of the later part of the Tertiary Period, and we are most concerned about the Quaternary, which started 1.8 million years ago (Table 1-1). We divide the Quaternary into the Pleistocene and the Holocene epochs, with the Holocene beginning at ten thousand years ago. The Pleistocene Epoch, covering most of the Ice Ages, saw much of the evolution of human beings, as well as the saber-toothed tigers and mastodons that are so elegantly preserved in the La Brea Tar Pits in Los Angeles.

It is the Holocene—the past ten thousand years—that concerns us the most. During the Holocene, the great ice caps of North America and Europe melted away, and the addition of all that meltwater to the oceans caused sea level to rise hundreds of feet. During the last half of the Holocene, civilizations arose in Mesopotamia, Egypt, and China, and written records began to be kept. If geologists can show that a fault sustained an earthquake during the Holocene, it is placed in a special category of hazard. If it ruptured that recently, it is likely to rupture again and is called an *active fault*. This classification, based on the time of most recent activity, is written into law in California and into regulations by federal agencies such as the U.S. Nuclear Regulatory Commission and the U.S. Army Corps of Engineers.

To learn the ages of earthquakes, we have historical records only since 1769, when settlers arrived and began writing about the events around them. But we can use one of the nuclear clocks to date formerly living organisms for the past twenty- to thirty-thousand years. This is *radiocarbon dating*, based on the natural decay of a radioactive isotope of carbon (carbon 14) into stable carbon (carbon 12). Carbon 14 starts off as ordinary nitrogen, which makes up the greater part of the atmosphere. The stable isotope of nitrogen—nitrogen 14—is bombarded by cosmic rays from outer space, changing it to carbon 14, which is unstable. Organisms (including you and I) take up both the radioactive and stable isotopes of carbon in the same proportions as in the atmosphere. After the organism dies, carbon 14 decays to carbon 12 at a precise rate, so that half the carbon 14 is gone in 5,730 years. In another 5,730 years, half of what's left decays to carbon 12, and half of *that* decays in another 5,730 years, until finally, for samples more than about thirty thousand years old, there is too little radioactive carbon 14 to measure. We say that 5,730 years is the *half life* of the radioactive decay of carbon 14 to carbon 12.

Unfortunately, the radiocarbon clock is not as precise as we would like. Radiocarbon dating cannot get us to the exact year, but only to within a few decades of the actual age. An example of a radiocarbon age is 5,300 ± 60 radiocarbon years, an expression of the laboratory precision in measuring the number of atoms of carbon 14 relative to carbon 12. Radiocarbon years are not the same as "calendar" years because the cosmic radiation that creates carbon 14 is not constant, but has changed over the years. Scientists at the University of Washington have designed a conversion scale that changes radiocarbon years to calendar years, and in most reports today this conversion has already been made, using a computer program.

In addition, the geologist or archaeologist must ensure that the carbon sample being dated (charcoal, shell fragment, bone fragment) is the same age as the deposit in which it is found. The charcoal in a deposit might have been washed in from a dead tree that is hundreds of years older. Or the charcoal might be part of a root from a much younger tree that grew and died long after the deposit was buried by other sediment.

To conclude our discussion of time, we need to think of earthquakes in two ways. On the one hand, an earthquake takes place in a matter of seconds, almost (but not quite) in an instant. But on the other hand, an earthquake marks the release of strain that has built up over hundreds, thousands, or tens of thousands of years. We use radiocarbon dating to learn how long it has taken strain to build up enough to break a large mass of rock in an earthquake over the past thirty thousand years. We can also use tree rings to determine when a particular tree growing along a fault was damaged, such as a fault rupturing its roots or strong shaking knocking off major branches.

To understand the earthquake hazard, it is not enough to figure out *what* will happen in a future earthquake. To make progress in forecasting earthquakes, we need to know *how long* it takes a fault to build up enough strain to rupture in an earthquake, and *how large* that earthquake is likely to be. When? Where? How big? Our ability to respond to the danger of earthquakes and to survive them rests on the answers to those questions.

Suggestions for Further Reading

Pellegrino, C.R. 1985. *Time Gate: Hurtling Backward through History.* Blue Ridge Summit, PA, TAB Books, Inc. 275p. An explanation of time by looking backward through ever-increasing time spans to the very beginning; written for the lay person.

Rogers, J.J.W. 1993. *A History of the Earth.* Cambridge University Press. 312p.

Stanley, S.M. 1989. *The Earth and Life through Time.* New York, J.W. Freeman & Co. 689p.

ᔓ 2 ᔒ

Plate Tectonics

"Like a city planner, the plate motions have created Los Angeles. The plate motions have shaped its setting and its setting's exceptional beauty, raising its intimate mountains ten thousand feet. The mountains are such a phalanx that air flowing in from the west cannot get over them, and as a result is the inversion layer that concentrates smog. Plate motions in Los Angeles folded the anticlines that trapped the oil that rained gold and silver into the streets. Plate motions have formed a basin so desiccated that water must be carried to it five hundred miles. Plate motions have built the topography that has induced the weather that has brought the fire that has prepared the topography for city-wrecking flows of rock debris. Plate motions are benign, fatal, eternal, causal, beneficial, ruinous, continual, and inevitable."

John McPhee, 1994, *New Yorker,* after the Northridge Earthquake

1. The Earth's Crust: Not Very Well Designed

As an engineered structure, the Earth's crust is not up to code. From time to time, its design problems cause it to fail, and the result is an earthquake.

The principal cause of crustal weakness is geothermal heat. Isotopes of radioactive elements within the Earth decay to other isotopes, producing heat that is trapped beneath the surface. Because of this trapped heat, the crust is warmer with increasing depth. Geothermal steam from The Geysers, north of San Francisco, adds to the northern California power grid. Heat from the Earth creates the hot springs near Mammoth Lakes that delight skiers (except for a volcano scare in 1982) and, on rare occasion, causes the eruption of great volcanoes like Mount Lassen and Mount St. Helens.

Just as iron becomes malleable in a blast furnace or hot silica glass becomes soft enough for a glassblower to produce beautiful bowls, rock becomes weak, like saltwater taffy, when the temperature gets high enough (Figure 2-1). Rock that is soft and weak under these conditions is said to be *ductile*. At lower temperatures, rock is *brittle*, meaning it shatters. Increased temperature tends to weaken rock, but on the other hand, increased *pressure* tends to *strengthen* it. With increasing depth, rock is subjected to conditions that work in opposite directions. The strengthening effect of increased pressure dominates at low temperatures within ten to twenty miles of the Earth's surface, whereas the weakening effect of higher temperature kicks in rather abruptly at

35

greater depth, depending on the type of rock. The strength of rock, then, increases gradually with increasing depth, with the strongest rock just above the depth where temperature weakening takes over (Figure 2-1), a depth called the *brittle-ductile transition*.

Think about a bridge with a layer of asphalt and concrete over a framework of steel. If the bridge collapses, it will be because the steel frame fails, not the weaker layers of concrete or asphalt on top. So it is with the Earth's crust. The crust fails when its strongest layer breaks, just above the brittle-ductile transition where temperature begins to weaken its minerals. Earthquakes tend to originate in this strongest layer. When this layer fails, shallower and deeper rock layers fail, too.

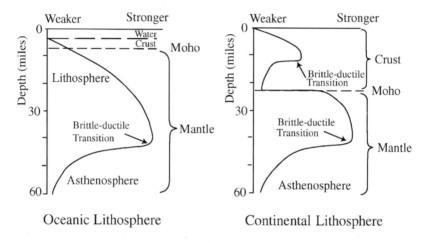

Oceanic Lithosphere   Continental Lithosphere

Figure 2-1. Strength of continental lithosphere (crust and upper mantle) compared to oceanic lithosphere. As rocks get buried, they get hotter due to the Earth's geothermal gradient. They also get stronger—down to a point, where temperature takes over, and they abruptly get weaker, at a level called the brittle-ductile transition. The Mohorovičić discontinuity (Moho for short) marks the boundary between the crust, made up of granite and basalt, and the mantle, made up of peridotite. Temperature softens granite at a much shallower depth than peridotite, so that the lower continental crust is a soft, squishy layer between the brittle upper crust and the brittle upper mantle. Earthquakes are limited to the brittle layers of continental crust, and they tend to nucleate where the crust is strongest, just above the brittle-ductile transition to soft, plastic lower crust below. For oceanic lithosphere, the Moho is so shallow there is no soft layer. The hard lithosphere makes up the tectonic plates. The base of the lithosphere is where peridotite in the mantle becomes soft at high temperature. The soft stuff beneath is called the asthenosphere. From Yeats et al. (1997).

2. Continents and Ocean Basins

Unlike the other inner planets, the surface of the Earth is at two predominant levels, one averaging 2,750 feet (840 m) above sea level, making up the continents where we all live, and the other averaging 12,100 feet (3,700 m) below sea level, making up the ocean basins (Figures 2-2 and 2-3). If you were able to look at the Earth with the water removed, the continents, together with their submerged continental shelves, would appear as gigantic plateaus, with steep slopes down to the ocean basins below.

Imagine yourself flying along the California coast with all the seawater removed. You would look out over a narrow continental shelf, which indeed was dry land at the height of the ice ages when sea level was nearly four hundred feet lower than it is today. Beyond that, the land slopes downward for thousands of feet. The Channel Islands and Santa Catalina Island are revealed as the higher parts of much larger mountain ranges resting on the deep ocean floor. A canyon rivaling the Grand Canyon twists downward from Monterey Bay, and a narrow, linear ridge strikes due west of Cape Mendocino in northern California (Figure 2-4). It's as though people living in California were in Tibet, looking down to the plains of India far below.

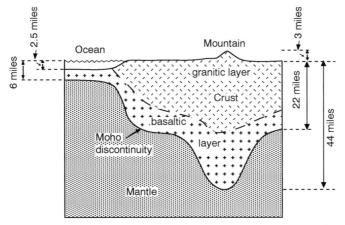

Figure 2-2. Cross section of oceanic crust (left) and continental crust (center and right). Continent is composed of granite, which is lighter, thicker, and more buoyant than oceanic crust, which is underlain by heavier basalt. Both continental and oceanic crust overlie the mantle, composed of peridotite. The top of the mantle is the Mohorovičić discontinuity (Moho for short). The continent stands high with respect to the ocean basin, and for it to be in balance it's underlain by a deep root of lighter crust. Mountain ranges stand above the continent and are underlain by still deeper roots. From Yeats et al. (1997).

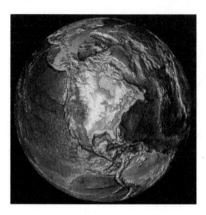

Figure 2-3 (Left) The Earth viewed from space with the water removed. The continents stand high above the ocean basins, with the boundary between the two a steep slope. Computer image by the National Oceanic and Atmospheric Administration. (Right) Plate tectonic subdivision of the Earth. Oceanic crust moves away from a seafloor spreading center (double lines) in the Atlantic Ocean (Mid Atlantic Ridge), causing Europe and Africa to move away from North and South America, forming the North America, South America, Eurasian, and Africa Plates. Oceanic crust also spreads away from the East Pacific Rise, forming small oceanic plates (Nazca, Cocos, Juan de Fuca (J on map) east of the Rise that dive beneath the North America and South America Plates at subduction zones (solid lines with triangles), accompanied by Earth's largest earthquakes. The Pacific Plate—the world's largest—is mainly oceanic, but it is continental in California, where it moves past the North America Plate in a transform fault, which includes the San Andreas Fault and the Queen Charlotte Fault (QC on map).

The reason for the different levels is that the continents and ocean basins are made up of different kinds of rock. Continental rocks are rich in the light-colored minerals quartz and feldspar, which make *granite*, the principal rock in the continent (Figure 2-2). You can find good exposures of granite in the Sierra Nevada, which led John Muir, viewing the pale granite cliffs of Yosemite Valley, to call the Sierra "The Range of Light." Other places to find granite are the mountains in Cleveland National Forest along Interstate 8 between San Diego and El Centro, Mt. San Jacinto towering above Palm Springs, the bouldery slopes around Lake Arrowhead and Big Bear Lake, and the brushy outcrops of Griffith Park near downtown Los Angeles.

Ocean-basin rock, on the other hand, is predominantly *basalt*, which contains the light-colored mineral feldspar but is dark brown to black, because its color is dominated by dark, heavy minerals such as pyroxene and magnetite. Basalt lava characterizes the Columbia Plateau and

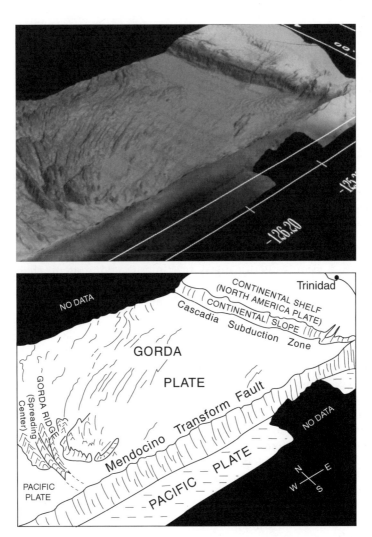

Figure 2-4. Computer image of the Cascadia Subduction Zone and Mendocino Fracture Zone off northern California, viewed from the southwest with water removed. The continental slope marks the transition between buoyant continental crust of California, which rises above sea level, and the oceanic Gorda Plate. The Cascadia Subduction Zone is at the base of the continental slope. The Mendocino Fracture Zone is a ridge extending west from Cape Mendocino that marks the position of the Mendocino Transform Fault. The south side of the ridge is the Mendocino Escarpment, south of which is oceanic crust of the Pacific Plate. Image produced by Chris Goldfinger, Active Tectonics Lab, Oregon State University.

Columbia Gorge of the Pacific Northwest. Basalt makes up the craggy moonscape of Lava Beds National Monument, near the Oregon border in Siskiyou County, where Captain Jack and his Modoc Indians held out against the U.S. Army for nearly two years. Cinder cones of dark basalt, resembling giant anthills, are found in the Mojave Desert— Pisgah Crater near Interstate 40 east of Barstow, and Amboy Crater on the lonely road between Ludlow and Amboy. None of these rocks were formed on an ocean floor, but the dark rocks below the lighthouse at Point Bonita, in Marin County at the western entrance of the Golden Gate, were an ocean floor many millions of years ago. Other examples of ocean-floor basalt are the craggy "knockers" that stick up above the grassy slopes of the Coast Ranges north of San Francisco.

A third type of rock, called *peridotite*, underlies both the continents and the ocean basins and is made up of heavy minerals such as pyroxene and olivine. This dark rock has no feldspar and is heavier than either basalt or granite. Peridotite is brittle and strong at much higher temperatures than either basalt or granite, which accounts for deep earthquakes beneath Del Norte and Humboldt counties in northwestern California.

Peridotite does not form naturally at the Earth's surface. It is found only in special circumstances where great tectonic forces have raised it up to view. As it comes to the surface it absorbs water, and the streaky green rock that results is called *serpentine*. Tectonic forces have been at work throughout California, so that serpentine is found in roadcuts in the Coast Ranges and the foothills of the Sierra. It is the dominant rock in Castle Crags State Park, west of Interstate 5 at Dunsmuir, in outcrops along Highway 101 at San Luis Obispo, and in some of the road cuts in San Francisco. In fact, serpentine is so abundant that it has been designated the California State Rock.

During the four-and-a-half billion years of Earth history, convection currents sweeping at extremely slow speeds through the Earth's interior have resulted in the gradual accumulation of granite and basalt near the surface, much like scum that collects at the top of a large pot of slowly boiling soup. Granite and basalt float on top because they are lower in density than peridotite.

Basalt and granite make up the *crust*, and the underlying heavy peridotite makes up the *mantle*, which extends all the way down to the top of the molten outer core of the Earth at 1,800 miles (2,900 kilometers) depth. The boundary between the crust and the mantle is called the *Moho* (Figure 2-2), shorthand for the name of the Croatian seismologist Andrija Mohorovičić, who discovered it in 1909. The Moho beneath the continents is commonly at depths of twenty to forty miles (thirty-five to seventy kilometers), deepest beneath mountain ranges, whereas the Moho beneath ocean basins might be no more than six miles beneath the sea floor (Figure 2-2).

The continents are made up of granite, which has relatively low density, and they stand higher than the ocean basins underlain by basalt and peridotite for the same reason that icebergs float on the ocean and ice cubes float in a glass of ice tea. And if you look at the ice cubes in your tea, you will see that there is quite a lot of ice below the surface of the tea. This ice of lower density beneath the surface balances and buoys up the ice that sticks up above the water. For the same reason, the granitic crust of the continents extends to depths in the Earth much greater than the basaltic crust of the ocean basins (Figure 2-2). The basaltic crust beneath ocean basins is relatively thin, and its relation to the mantle is more like the water freezing on the surface of a pond.

But how can we use ice and water as a comparison with solid rock? Water is a liquid, and the crust and mantle are solids. How, then, can we speak of convection currents in solid rock?

This comparison can be made for two reasons. First, rock beneath the brittle-ductile transition is weak because it's subjected to blast-furnace temperatures. Second, the tectonic processes that cause continents to rise above ocean basins are extremely slow. We know from experiments that if the temperature is high enough, rock flows as a solid, although it does so very slowly—fractions of an inch per year. This process, well known in metalworking, is called *hot creep*.

We have seen that earthquakes occur in the brittle upper crust, but not in the hot, plastic lower crust, which is too weak to store strain energy that could be released as earthquakes. The reason for this is the abundance in the crust of the light-colored minerals quartz and feldspar, which become soft and weak at relatively low temperature, about 575°F. For this reason, the upper crust beneath the continents is strong, but the lower crust is soft and weak. Oceanic crust, on the other hand, is so thin (Figure 2-2) that *all* of it is strong, and so is the upper mantle. Peridotite, the rock of the mantle, is made up of olivine and pyroxene, minerals that are still very strong at temperatures that prevail below the Moho, as high as 1,400–1,500°F. These temperatures are reached at depths as much as sixty miles (100 kilometers).

The parts of the outer Earth that are brittle and strong are called the *lithosphere* and the weak parts below are called the *asthenosphere*. Beneath the ocean basins, the lithosphere includes the thin crust and part of the upper mantle. Beneath the continents, the upper crust is brittle but the lower crust is not. Below the Moho, the upper mantle might also be brittle and form the lowest layer of continental lithosphere. So the continental crust can be compared to peanut butter between two crackers; both crackers are crunchy (brittle) but the peanut butter is soft (ductile lower crust). For oceanic lithosphere, you don't have any peanut butter, and the crunchy cracker is a lot thicker.

The flow of solid rock in the asthenosphere produces strain in the strong lithosphere. It is the response of the lithosphere to this strain that causes earthquakes. All earthquakes occur within the lithosphere, including slabs of oceanic lithosphere that have penetrated hundreds of miles into the asthenosphere.

3. The Dance of the Plates: We Know the Beat but Not the Tune

The dominant cause of the tectonic activity that takes place at the Earth's surface is the extremely slow flow of rock in the mantle that is solid, yet ductile. This leads us now to a discussion of *plate tectonics.*

We would have no earthquake problems if the lithosphere, sixty miles thick, completely encircled the Earth without any breaks as it does on the other inner planets. Unfortunately, the sixty-mile thickness of the lithosphere on the "third rock from the sun" is not enough to withstand the stresses coming from the slow, roiling currents of the asthenosphere below. The lithosphere is broken up into gigantic *tectonic plates* that grind against one another, producing earthquakes and volcanic eruptions (Figure 2-3). Most of these plates are of continental size. California east of the San Andreas Fault is part of the North America Plate, which extends all the way across the United States and Canada to the middle of the Atlantic Ocean. California west of the San Andreas Fault is part of the Pacific Plate, the world's largest, which underlies most of the Pacific Ocean and reaches to Alaska, Japan, and New Zealand. Other plates are smaller, like the Gorda-Juan de Fuca Plate off the northern coast, which is smaller than California.

Running down the center of the floor of the Atlantic Ocean, like the seam on a baseball, the Mid-Atlantic Ridge (Figure 2-3) is formed by the upwelling of hot material from the asthenosphere, which broke up the granite supercontinent of Pangea, starting about 180 million years ago. North and South America, fragments of Pangea, sailed away from Africa and Europe like great granitic icebergs on a basaltic sea, and the deep Atlantic Ocean floor of basalt began to grow in the widening rift welling up between the continents. The Atlantic Ocean Basin is still widening at slightly less than an inch per year. The Mid-Atlantic Ridge is a ridge because the newly formed oceanic lithosphere is hotter and thus lighter and more buoyant than older oceanic lithosphere closer to the continents. Hot springs—called *black smokers*—bubble up along the ridge, and new basaltic lava flows erupt on the ocean floor at the ridge. All of the Atlantic Ocean floor has been created as basaltic lava in the past 180 million years.

There is also a ridge in the Pacific Ocean called the East Pacific Rise, but this ridge is not at the center of the ocean like the Mid-Atlantic

Ridge. Instead, it lies toward the eastern margin of the Pacific (Figure 2-3). But the origin is the same: oceanic crust rises to the surface and solidifies at the East Pacific Rise, then moves away to the east and west. The portion moving toward the west becomes part of the great Pacific Plate. The portion moving toward the east becomes part of several smaller plates off the west coast of North and South America, including the Juan de Fuca Plate off Oregon and Washington, the Gorda Plate off northern California, and the Cocos Plate off Mexico and Central America (Figure 2-3).

To view an ocean basin in the making, we have only to travel to the Sea of Cortés, the Gulf of California, separating the Baja California peninsula from the rest of Mexico. Five million years ago, Baja was nestled against Mexico. About four-and-a-half million years ago, the East Pacific Rise welled up beneath the continent, breaking off Baja California, which drifted off to the northwest, taking coastal Alta California along with it and leaving new ocean floor in its wake. The deep parts of the Gulf are mini-ocean basins called *spreading centers,* with basalt lava and hot springs like those in the Mid-Atlantic Ridge and East Pacific Rise. The northernmost spreading center, oddly enough, is in the Imperial Valley, where continental crust is being pulled apart, and the gap is being filled by sediments of the Colorado River. In Chapter 4, we will see how the opening of the Gulf of California played a role in the origin of the San Andreas Fault.

But if new crust is being made, then old crust must be destroyed at the same rate somewhere else, because the Earth has remained the same size through time. The destruction of crust takes place at *subduction zones,* where oceanic lithosphere is forced down into the asthenosphere. Most subduction zones are found around the edges of the Pacific Ocean, which leads to the name *Pacific Rim of Fire* because of the abundance of active volcanoes and earthquakes, including the largest earthquakes experienced on Earth. The greatest depths in the oceans, nearly seven miles, are found in deep-sea trenches in the western Pacific, where oceanic lithosphere is being subducted beneath the Philippines and beneath the island of Guam. Volcanoes are erupted through the lithosphere of the plate on top.

One of these subduction zones, the *Cascadia Subduction Zone*, lies off the Pacific Northwest, including northern California, where the Gorda Plate and Juan de Fuca Plate are being driven beneath the North American continent (Figures 2-4, 2-5, 2-6). Mt. Shasta and Mt. Lassen are products of the subduction of the Gorda Plate. This region is discussed further in Chapter 7.

At some plate boundaries, lithosphere is neither created at a mid-ocean ridge nor destroyed at a subduction zone. Instead, two plates crunch and grind past each other, producing earthquakes in the process.

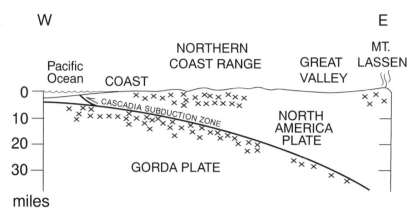

Figure 2-5. Cross section of the Cascadia Subduction Zone in northern California. The oceanic Gorda Plate is subducting beneath the margin of the continent, resulting in earthquakes (marked by Xs) along the subduction zone and in both the underlying Gorda Plate and overlying North America Plate in Humboldt and Del Norte counties. Gorda Plate earthquakes are detected as far east as the northern Sacramento Valley. Farther east, the Mt. Shasta and Mt. Lassen volcanoes are also related to the Cascadia Subduction Zone.

These boundaries are called *transform faults,* and on the ocean floor they are called *fracture zones.* The best-known transform fault on Earth is the San Andreas Fault, where the Pacific and North American plates grate past each other. Off the Pacific Northwest, part of the boundary between the Juan de Fuca-Gorda and Pacific Plates is the Blanco Fracture Zone, separating the Gorda and Juan de Fuca Ridges (Figure 2-6). Both the San Andreas Fault and the Blanco Fracture Zone have earthquakes.

During the past two decades, scientists have been able to determine the rates at which the plates move with respect to one another. This is done by observing changes in the Earth's magnetic field preserved in oceanic crust and by drilling core holes in the deep-ocean floor to determine the age of the oldest sediment overlying the basaltic crust in various parts of the oceans. In the past few years, these rates have been confirmed by direct measurements using space satellites through the Global Positioning System (GPS) and by the relative motion of radio telescopes with respect to quasar signals from outermost space (see Chapter 3). All our information about relative plate motion can be fed into a computer model that tells us the motion of any given plate with respect to any other. We can even predict with some confidence the plate configuration of the Earth millions of years from now, which allows us to forecast that coastal California, including Los Angeles, is moving slowly but inexorably toward Alaska.

However, we have no underlying theory that explains *why* the plates move as they do, which leads to our description of the dance of the plates: we know the beat, but we don't know the tune.

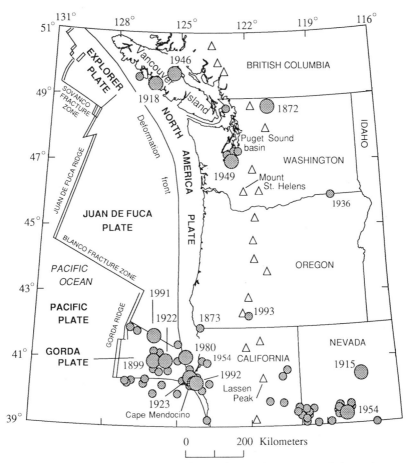

Figure 2-6. Plate tectonics of the Pacific Northwest. Oceanic crust is formed at the Juan de Fuca and Gorda ridges, adding to the size of the Pacific Plate to the west and the Gorda and Juan de Fuca Plates to the east. The plates east of the spreading center are carried beneath North America at the Cascadia Subduction Zone (Figure 2-5), where they give rise to the Cascade volcanoes (open triangles). Shaded circles locate large earthquakes. From USGS.

Near the tiny settlement of Petrolia in Humboldt County, the Pacific, North America, and Gorda plates come together in a seismically active place called the *Mendocino Triple Junction*. North of the triple junction, the Gorda Plate is driving beneath the North American continent (Figures 2-4 and 2-5). Southeast of the triple junction, North America is sliding southeast against the Pacific Plate along the San Andreas Transform Fault. West of the triple junction, the Pacific Plate is sliding westward against the Gorda Plate along an oceanic transform fault called the Mendocino Fracture Zone (Figure 2-4). We know the rates at

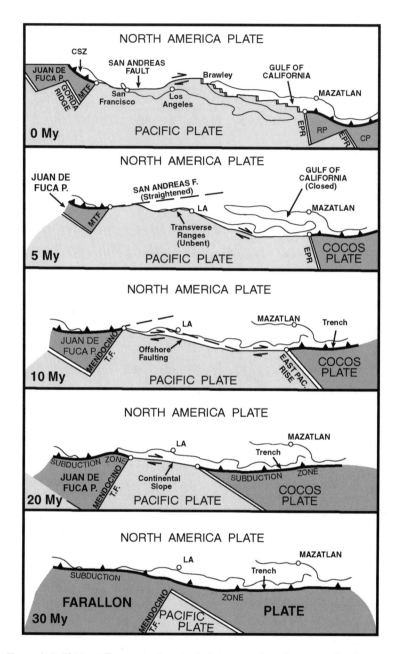

Figure 2-7. Thirty million years (m.y.) of plate tectonics off western North America. (Bottom diagram): At 30 m.y., the oceanic Farallon Plate was subducting under the North America Plate. The double line marks the East

caption continues on facing page

which these processes are taking place, so we can reconstruct California's plate tectonic history backward for the past thirty million years.

4. A Brief, 30-Million-Year History of California

Using sophisticated computer models, it's fairly straightforward to work out the plate-tectonic history of the Earth for hundreds of millions of years. What did California look like thirty million years ago?

At that time, the oceanic crust west of North America formed part of the Farallon Plate, not the Pacific Plate (Figure 2-7), and the Farallon Plate was being subducted beneath North America, including all of California. The Farallon Plate and Pacific Plate were separated by the East Pacific Rise, part of the world-encircling mountain system that marks where new oceanic crust is formed and spreads away, and the Mendocino Transform Fault, which at that time was west of what would later be Los Angeles (Figure 2-7). The Baja California peninsula was part of the Mexican mainland, with no Gulf of California in between.

Sea-floor spreading on the Mid-Atlantic Ridge had been forcing North America westward, away from Europe and toward the East Pacific Rise (Figure 2-3). The Farallon Plate was being slowly destroyed by subduction beneath North America, and active volcanoes erupted through the Coast Ranges and Baja California. As the Farallon Plate continued to be slowly consumed, the Pacific Plate came into contact with the North America Plate. But the Farallon Plate had been moving eastward, toward the continent, whereas the Pacific Plate was moving

Pacific Rise, where the Pacific and Farallon plates were moving apart by sea-floor spreading. The single line at left marks the Mendocino Transform Fault (MTF), which at that time was west of the future location of Los Angeles (LA). The Pacific Plate was moving northwest at the same time that North America was being driven westward by sea-floor spreading on the Mid-Atlantic Ridge. By 20 m.y., the Pacific and North America plates had met at a transform fault at the base of the continental slope. This transform fault widened with time (10m.y., 5 m.y.) as more and more of the Pacific Plate came into contact with North America. (The Queen Charlotte Fault, off British Columbia and southern Alaska, is a modern-day example of a transform fault at the base of the continental slope; see Figure 2-3.) The Mendocino Transform Fault moved northward relative to California. Between 5 m.y. and today, the transform fault at the base of the continental slope shifted position inland, slicing off Baja California and part of Alta California as part of the Pacific Plate. Since then, this continental slice has been moving past the rest of North America, accompanied by large earthquakes. The San Andreas Fault is a transform fault because it separates spreading centers at the Gorda and Juan de Fuca ridges from the spreading centers in the Gulf of California and Imperial Valley. CP, Cocos Plate; RP, Rivera Plate.

northwest, parallel to the continental edge. So after the plates came into contact, the Pacific Plate moved northwest past North America along a new transform fault at the base of the continental slope, a forerunner to the San Andreas Fault (Figure 2-7). The Mendocino Triple Junction moved northwest, too, and the San Andreas ancestor grew in length as the former Farallon Plate broke up into the Juan de Fuca Plate off northern California, Oregon, and Washington, and the Cocos Plate off Mexico and Central America.

About four-and-a-half million years ago, the transform fault shifted inland to its present position within the continent as the San Andreas Fault, and Baja California broke away from Mexico to form a new ocean basin, the Gulf of California, in its wake. The Juan de Fuca Plate is breaking off the Gorda Plate along the Blanco Transform Fault, and the Rivera Plate, part of the former Cocos Plate, has appeared at the mouth of the Gulf of California. Subduction still continues today, accompanied by active volcanoes, off northern California and off Mexico south of the Gulf.

Visualization of these examples of plate tectonics stretches the imagination until we recall that this has taken thirty million years—a length of time that overwhelms comprehension. We are forced to put our imagination of natural processes into ultra-high speed so that lifetimes flash by in a couple of seconds, and we would get a plate-boundary subduction-zone earthquake at Cascadia every fifteen seconds. Even at that rate, the disappearance of the Farallon Plate would seem extraordinarily slow. If you were watching it as you would a movie, you'd have to bring lots of popcorn. In fact, you *can* watch it: Tanya Atwater of the University of California-Santa Barbara, a pioneer in working out the plate tectonics of California, has created an animated video of the past thirty million years, depicting the plate tectonics shown in Figure 2-7.

Suggestions for Further Reading

Glen, W. 1982. *The Road to Jaramillo*. Stanford: Stanford University Press. An account of the plate tectonics revolution.

Kearey, P., and F.J. Vine. 1990. *Global Tectonics*. London: Blackwell Scientific Publications. 302p.

Lillie, R.J. 1999. *Whole-Earth Geophysics*. Englewood Cliffs, N.J.: Prentice-Hall. 361p.

↜ 3 ↜
Earthquake Basics

1. Introduction

The problem is that earthquakes start out many miles beneath the surface, too deep for us to observe them directly. So we study them from afar by (1) observing the geological changes at the ground surface, (2) analyzing the symphony of earthquake vibrations recorded on seismographs, and (3) monitoring the tectonic changes in the Earth's crust by surveying it repeatedly, at first using land survey techniques and now using satellites. In addition, we have laboratory experimental results on how rocks behave at the depths and temperatures where earthquakes form, which helps in understanding what happens during an earthquake. One of the important things to recognize is that rocks, like rubber bands, are elastic.

2. Elastic Rocks: How they Bend and Break

If you blow up a balloon, the addition of air causes the balloon to expand. If you then squeeze the balloon with your hands (Figure 3-1, left), the balloon will change its shape. Removing your hands causes the balloon to return to its former shape (Figure 3-1, lower left). If you take a thin board and push the ends toward each other (Figure 3-1, right), the board will bend. If you let the board go, it will straighten out again. This is called *elasticity*. When air is blown into the balloon, when the balloon is squeezed, or when the board is bent, strain energy

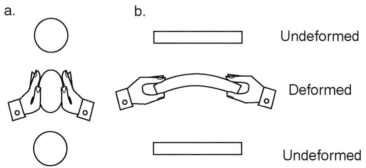

Figure 3-1. Elasticity. (a) An inflated balloon is squeezed between two hands, changing its shape. If the hands are removed, the balloon returns to its earlier shape. (b) A thin board is bent into a curved shape. If the hands bending the board are removed, the board returns to its original shape. The balloon and board are both elastic.

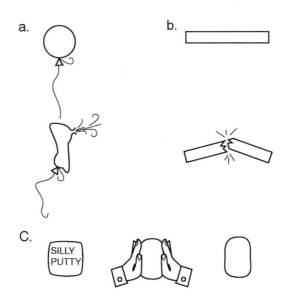

Figure 3-2. (a) When the balloon is squeezed too hard, it pops. (b) When the board is bent too much, it breaks. These are examples of brittle fracture. (c) When a piece of bubble gum or Silly Putty is squeezed between two hands, it deforms. When the hands are removed, it stays in the same deformed shape. This is called ductile deformation.

is stored up inside the rubber walls of the balloon and within the board. When the balloon is released, or the board is let go, the energy is released as balloon and board return to their former shapes.

But if the balloon is blown up even further, it finally reaches a point where it can hold no more air and it bursts (Figure 3-2, left). The strain energy is released in this case, too, but it is released abruptly, with a pop. Instead of returning to its former size, the balloon breaks into tattered fragments. In the same way, if the small board is bent too far, it breaks with a snap as the strain energy is released (Figure 3-2, right).

It isn't quite as easy to picture rocks as being elastic, but they are. If a rock is squeezed in a laboratory rock press, it behaves like a rubber ball, changing its shape slightly. When the pressure of the rock press is released, the rock (or the rubber ball) returns to its former shape, just as the balloon or the board does, as shown in Figure 3-1. But if the rock press continues to bear down on the rock with greater force, ultimately the rock will break, like the balloon or the board in Figure 3-2.

After the great San Francisco Earthquake of 1906 on the San Andreas Fault, Professor Harry F. Reid of Johns Hopkins University, a member of Andrew Lawson's State Earthquake Investigation Commission (see Part I), compared two nineteenth-century land surveys on both sides of the fault with a new survey taken just after the earthquake. These survey comparisons showed that widely separated survey benchmarks on opposite sides of the fault had moved more than ten feet with respect to each other even *before* the earthquake. This slow movement was in the same direction as the sudden movement *during* the earthquake. This led Reid to propose his *elastic rebound theory*, which states that the

Earth's crust acts like the bent board mentioned earlier (Figure 3-3). Strain accumulates in the crust until it causes the crust to rupture in an earthquake, like breaking the board and popping the balloon.

Another half century would pass before we understood *why* the strain had built up in the crust before the San Francisco Earthquake. We know now that it is due to plate tectonics. The Pacific Plate is slowly grinding past the North America Plate along the San Andreas Fault. But the San Andreas Fault is stuck, so the crust deforms elastically as a result, like bending the board. The break is along the San Andreas Fault because it is relatively weak compared to other parts of the two plates that haven't been broken repeatedly by faults. A section of the fault that is slightly weaker than other sections gives way first, releasing the plate-tectonic strain as an earthquake.

If we knew the crustal strengths of various faults, and if we knew the rate at which strain is building up in the crust at these faults, we could then forecast when the next earthquake would strike—an idea that occurred to Harry Reid. We are beginning to understand the rate at which strain builds up on a few of our most hazardous faults, like the San Andreas Fault. But we have very little confidence in our knowledge of the crustal strength that must be overcome to produce an earthquake. Crustal strengths are different for different parts of the crust, and are probably different on the same part of a fault at different times in its history. This makes it difficult to forecast when the next earthquake will strike the San Andreas Fault.

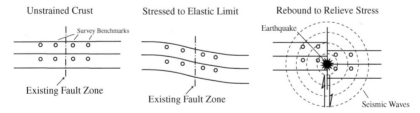

Figure 3-3. Illustration of elastic rebound theory of Harry F. Reid. The maps show the San Andreas Fault, and the small circles represent land survey markers. The horizontal lines are roads or rows of trees crossing the fault. (Left) A land survey taken in the nineteenth century. (Center) A later land survey taken just before the 1906 San Francisco Earthquake shows that the position of the land survey markers have changed with respect to one another. Reid saw that this represented elastic strain building up in the crust. (Right) A survey taken after the San Francisco Earthquake. The markers have rebounded, releasing their elastic strain energy, and the horizontal lines are now displaced across the San Andreas Fault. As noted in Part I, the U.S. Coast and Geodetic Survey was given the job in the 1920s of remeasuring the survey markers to determine whether the strain was building up again in the crust toward the next earthquake.

3. A Classification of Faults

Most damaging earthquakes form on faults at a depth of five miles or more in the Earth's crust, too deep to be observed directly. But most of these faults are also exposed at the surface, where they can be studied by geologists. Larger earthquakes may be accompanied by surface movement on these faults, damaging or destroying human-made structures under which they pass.

Some faults are vertical, so that an earthquake at ten miles depth is directly beneath the fault at the surface. Other faults dip at a low angle, so that the fault at the surface might be several miles away from the *epicenter*, the point on the Earth's surface directly above the earthquake (Figure 3-4). Where the fault has a low dip or inclination, the rock above the fault is called the *hanging wall*, and the rock below the fault is called the *footwall*. These are terms that were first coined by miners and prospectors. Valuable ore deposits are commonly found in fault zones, and miners working underground along a fault zone find themselves standing on the footwall, with the hanging wall over their heads.

If the hanging wall moves up or down during an earthquake, the fault is called a *dip-slip fault* (Figure 3-4). If the hanging wall moves sideways, parallel with the Earth's surface (as shown in Figures 3-3, 3-5, and 3-6), the fault is called a *strike-slip fault*.

There are two kinds of strike-slip fault: *right-lateral* and *left-lateral*. If you stand on one side of a right-lateral fault, objects on the other side of the fault appear to move to your right during an earthquake (Figures 3-5a and b). The San Andreas Fault is the world's best-known right-

Figure 3-4. A cross section of the Earth's crust. The focus or hypocenter is that point within the crust where the earthquake nucleates. The epicenter is on the Earth's surface directly above the focus. The focal depth is the depth

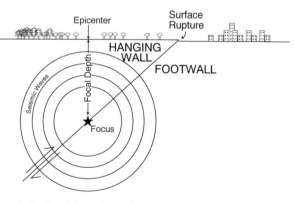

of the earthquake beneath the Earth's surface. The earthquake fault has a low dip angle so that the surface trace of the fault, where surface rupture may be expected, is displaced horizontally from the epicenter. The block above the fault is the hanging wall, and the block below the fault is the footwall.

Figure 3-5a. Right-lateral strike-slip fault. Aerial view of San Andreas Fault in Carrizo Plain, California. Fault is marked by a linear zone that can be traced from left to right across photo. Two streams crossing the fault have been deflected to right. The most recent rupture was during the Fort Tejon Earthquake of 1857. Photo by U.S. Geological Survey.

Figure 3-5b. Right-lateral strike-slip fault. Offset furrows in a cultivated field near El Centro, California during an earthquake on October 15, 1979. Photo credit: University of Colorado, as reproduced in National Oceanic and Atmospheric Administration Natural Hazards Slide Set: Earthquakes in Southern California 1979–1989.

Figure 3-6. Road displaced to the left during an earthquake in 1990 on a left-lateral strike-slip fault on the Island of Luzon in the Philippines. Photo by T. Nakata, Hiroshima University.

Figure 3-7. Normal fault scarp at margin of Pleasant Valley, south of Winnemucca, Nevada formed during an earthquake in 1915 raising the hills on the left with respect to the terrain on the right. Fault dips (slopes) toward the right. Truck is parked on hanging wall of fault; left skyline

is part of the footwall. Photo by Robert Wallace, U.S. Geological Survey.

lateral fault (Figure 3-5a). At a left-lateral fault, objects on the other side of the fault appear to move to your left (Figure 3-6). The Garlock Fault, separating the Mojave Desert from the Tehachapi Mountains and southern Sierra Nevada, is a left-lateral fault. Strike-slip faults tend to dip nearly vertically, but there are exceptions.

In dip-slip faults, if the hanging wall moves down with respect to the footwall, it's called a *normal fault* (Figure 3-7). This happens when the crust is being pulled apart, as in the case of faults in northeastern California, western Nevada, or at seafloor spreading centers. If the hanging wall moves up with respect to the footwall, it's called a *reverse fault* (Figure 3-8). This happens when the crust is jammed together. The Cascadia Subduction Zone, where the Gorda Oceanic Plate is driving beneath northern California, is a very large-scale reverse fault (Figure 2-5). The 1971 Sylmar Earthquake ruptured the San Fernando Reverse Fault, buckling sidewalks and raising the ground, as shown in Figure 3-8a. The 1999 Chi-Chi, Taiwan, earthquake was accompanied by surface rupture on a reverse fault, including the rupture across a running track at a high school (Figure 3-8b). Where the dip of a reverse fault is very low, it's called a *thrust fault*.

The 1983 Coalinga Earthquake in the central Coast Ranges and the 1994 Northridge Earthquake in the San Fernando Valley struck reverse faults that didn't reach the surface. Reverse faults that don't reach the surface are called *blind faults*, and if they have low dips, they're called *blind thrusts*. In most cases, such faults are expressed at the Earth's surface as folds in rock. An upward fold in rock is called an *anticline* (Figure 3-9) and a downward fold is called a *syncline*. Before these two earthquakes, geologists thought that anticlines and synclines form slowly and gradually and are not related to earthquakes. Now it's known that they can hide blind faults that are the source of earthquakes. Folds

Figure 3-8a. Reverse fault in the San Fernando Valley, California, formed during the Sylmar Earthquake of February 9, 1971. Fault extends from left to right. Buckling of sidewalk indicates compression; fault dips away from viewer. Hanging wall (in background) was at same level as footwall (in foreground) before the earthquake. Ruined building in left background was part of a convalescent home in which several people died.

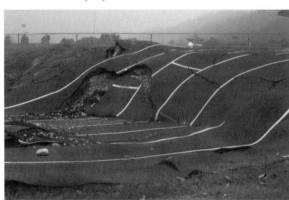

Figure 3-8b. Reverse fault across a running track at Kuangfu High School in central Taiwan, formed during the Chi-Chi Earthquake of September 21, 1999. Photos by Robert Yeats.

Figure 3-9. Ventura Avenue Anticline in oil field north of Ventura, California. Folded rock layers were formerly horizontal, deposited on the floor of the ocean. Folding is controlled by displacement on a deeply buried reverse fault called a blind thrust. Photo by Robert Yeats.

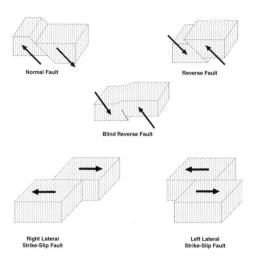

Figure 3-10. Diagrammatic representation of the four types of faults that produce earthquakes, shown as block diagrams: left-lateral strike-slip fault, right-lateral strike-slip fault, normal fault, and reverse fault. Center diagram is a blind reverse fault, in which the fault does not reach the surface but is manifested by a warp or fold of the surface. Arrows show relative movement of each side of the fault.

cover blind faults in the northern Los Angeles Basin, the Ventura Avenue Anticline in Ventura County (Figure 3-9), and the low hills at the western edge of the San Joaquin and Sacramento Valleys.

Figure 3-10 is a summary diagram showing the four types of faults that produce earthquakes—left-lateral strike-slip fault, right-lateral strike-slip fault, normal fault, and reverse fault—and a blind-thrust fault, the special type of reverse fault that does not reach the surface but is manifested at the surface as an anticline or a warp.

4. Slip Rates and Earthquake Recurrence Intervals

Major earthquakes are generally followed by aftershocks—some large enough to cause damage and loss of life on their own. Aftershocks are part of the earthquake that just struck, like echoes but lasting sometimes for months or even years. But if you have just suffered through an earthquake, the aftershocks cause you to ask: When will the next earthquake strike? Let's restate the question: When will the next earthquake strike *the same section of fault?*

The San Fernando Valley had an earthquake in 1994, twenty-three years after an earlier one in 1971. But these earthquakes were on different faults, so my question is the same one asked by residents of San Francisco after their calamity of 1906: When will another shock like the 1906 earthquake strike this part of the San Andreas Fault and again put San Francisco to the test? Of all the members of the State Earthquake Investigation Commission, Harry Reid gave the most thought to this question.

To answer this question, the geologist determines the *slip rate*, the rate at which one side of a fault moves past the other side over many thousands of years and many earthquakes. This is done by identifying and then determining the age of a feature such as a river channel that was once continuous across the fault but is now offset by it.

The San Andreas Fault has split an ancient volcano, 23.5 million years old, in half. The half of the volcano west of the fault forms the Pinnacles National Monument in the Coast Ranges southeast of Salinas. On the east side, the other half is at the edge of the Mojave Desert east of Tejon Pass, where the rocks are called the Neenach Volcanics. These are now separated by 195 miles (315 kilometers). If we assume that strike slip began just after the volcano erupted, then we divide the distance between the two halves of the volcano by the age of the volcano and get a slip rate of about one-half inch (13.4 mm) per year.

However, this requires us to assume that the San Andreas Fault started just after the volcano erupted and has been rupturing by means of earthquakes in exactly the same way ever since. But in southern California, the San Andreas Fault began in its present location less than five million years ago, when the Pacific Plate-North America Plate boundary shifted from the base of the continental slope to where it is today.

A better idea is to use little gullies that used to flow straight across the fault, but are now offset by strike slip (Figure 3-5a). For example, Wallace Creek is offset 420 feet (130 meters) across the San Andreas Fault in the Carrizo Plain. Sediments deposited in the channel of Wallace Creek prior to its offset are 3,700 years old, based on radiocarbon dating of charcoal in the deposits. The slip rate is the amount of the offset— 420 feet—divided by the age of the channel that is offset—3,700 years— a little less than 1.4 inches (35 mm) per year.

Wallace Creek, named for Bob Wallace of the USGS (see Part I), is in the Carrizo Plain, where offset during the great Fort Tejon Earthquake of 1857 was thirty to forty feet. How long would it take for the fault to build up as much strain as it released in 1857? To find out, divide the 1857 slip—thirty to forty feet—by the slip rate—1.4 inches per year— to get 260 to 340 years, an estimate of the *earthquake recurrence interval* for this part of the fault. (I round off the numbers because the age of the offset Wallace Creek, 3,700 years, and the amount of its offset are not precisely known.) Paleoseismologic studies of backhoe excavations show that the last earthquake to strike this part of the fault prior to 1857 was around the year 1480, an interval of 370 to 380 years, which agrees with our calculations within our uncertainty of measurement. This is reassuring because the lowest estimate of the recurrence interval, 260 years, won't end until after the year 2100.

Most California faults have much slower slip rates, so the earthquake recurrence times are much longer. Say that a reverse fault in the Ventura Basin has a slip rate of one-twenty-fifth inch (one millimeter) per year, and shows in a backhoe trench excavation across the fault that an earthquake on the fault will cause it to move ten feet (120 inches). The return time would be three thousand years. Some faults, such as the Hollywood Fault and Santa Monica Fault in the northern Los Angeles Basin, have even slower slip rates and estimated earthquake return times of eight thousand to more than ten thousand years.

Unfortunately, working out the recurrence interval is not so simple because the faults and the earthquakes they produce are not very orderly. For example, the 1812 and 1857 earthquakes on the same section of the San Andreas Fault ruptured different lengths of the fault, and their offsets were different. Displacements on the same fault during the same earthquake differ from one end of the rupture to the other. The recurrence intervals differ as well. We were reassured by the recurrence interval of 370 to 380 years between the 1857 earthquake and a prehistoric event around 1480, but the earthquake prior to 1480 struck around 1350, a recurrence interval of only 130 years.

We can give a statistical likelihood of an earthquake striking a given part of the San Andreas Fault in a certain time interval after the last earthquake, but we can't nail this down any closer because of the poorly understood variability in strength of fault zones, variability in time, and position on the fault. Another difficulty is in our clock— radiocarbon dating. Charcoal might be rare in prehistoric sediments deposited in California's semiarid climate. And radiocarbon doesn't actually date an earthquake; it dates the youngest sediments cut by a fault and the oldest unfaulted sediments overlying the fault—assuming that these sediments have charcoal suitable for dating.

5. What Happens During an Earthquake?

Crustal earthquakes in California start at depths of five to twelve miles, typically in that layer of the Earth's crust that is strongest due to burial pressure, just above the brittle-ductile transition, the depth below which temperature weakening starts to take effect (Figure 2-1). This is too deep for us to study directly by deep drilling, so we have to base our understanding on indirect evidence. We do this by studying the detailed properties of seismic waves that pass through these crustal layers, or by subjecting rocks to laboratory tests at temperatures and pressures expected at those depths. And some ancient fault zones have been uplifted and eroded in the millions of years since faulting took place, allowing us to observe them directly at the surface and make inferences on how earthquakes may have occurred on them.

An earthquake is most likely to rupture the crust where it previously had been broken at a fault, because a fault zone tends to be weaker than unfaulted rock around it. The Earth's crust, like a chain, is only as strong as its weakest link. Strain has built up elastically, and now the strength of the faulted crust directly above the zone where temperature weakening occurs is reached. Suddenly this strong layer fails and the rupture races sideways and upward toward the surface, breaking the weaker layers above it. The motion produces friction, which generates heat that might be sufficient to melt the rock in places. In cases where the rupture extends for only a mile or so, the earthquake is a relatively minor one, like the Sierra Madre Earthquake north of the San Gabriel Valley in 1991. But in rare instances the rupture keeps going for hundreds of miles, resulting in a great earthquake like the 1906 San Francisco Earthquake. Scientists can't say why one earthquake stops after only a small segment of a fault ruptures, but another earthquake results from rupture on a fault for hundreds of miles.

The rupture causes the sudden loss of strain energy that the rock had built up over hundreds of years, equivalent to the snap of the board or the pop of the balloon. The shock radiates out from the rupture as seismic waves, which travel to the surface and produce the shaking we experience in an earthquake (Figure 3-11). There are three basic types: *P waves* (primary waves), *S waves* (secondary or shear waves), and *surface waves*. P and S waves are called *body waves* because they pass directly through the Earth, whereas surface waves travel along the surface like the ripples in a pond when a stone is thrown into it.

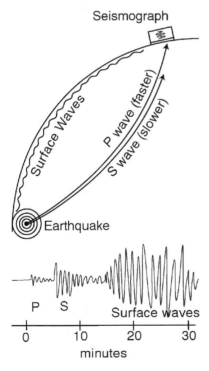

Seismograph

Figure 3-11. An earthquake produces P waves, or compressional waves, that travel faster and reach the seismograph first; and S waves, or shear waves, that are slower. Both are transmitted within the Earth and are called body waves. Even slower are surface waves that run along the surface of the Earth and do a lot of the damage. The earthquake focus is the point within the Earth where the earthquake originates. The epicenter is a point on the surface directly above the focus. The diagram below is a seismogram, reading from left to right, showing that the P wave arrives first, followed by the S wave and then by surface waves.

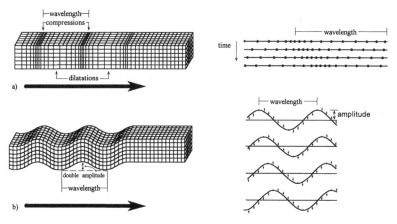

Figure 3-12. Two views of P waves (a) and S waves (b), all moving from left to right. A P wave moves by alternately compressing and dilating the material through which it passes, somewhat like stop-and-go traffic on the freeway during rush hour. An S wave moves by shearing the material from side to side, a bit like flipping a clothesline. Note the illustration of wavelength for P and S waves and amplitude for S waves. The number of complete wavelengths to pass a point in a second is the frequency.

P and S waves are fundamentally different (Figure 3-12). A P wave is easily understood by a pool player, who "breaks" a set of pool balls arranged in a tight triangle, all touching. When the cue ball hits the other balls, the energy of striking momentarily compresses the next ball elastically. The compression is transferred to the next ball, then to the next, until the entire set of pool balls scatters around the table. P waves pass through a solid, such as rock, and they can also pass through water or air. When earthquake waves pass through air, sometimes they produce a noise.

To illustrate an S wave, tie one end of a clothesline to a tree. Hold the line tight and shake it rapidly from side to side. You can see what looks like waves running down the clothesline toward the tree, distorting the shape of the clothesline. Similarly, when S waves pass through rock they distort its shape. S waves cannot pass through liquid or air, and you would not feel them aboard a ship at sea.

S waves are slower than P waves, and the seismologist uses this fact to tell how far it is from the seismograph to the earthquake (Figure 3-13). The seismogram records the P wave first, then the S wave. If the seismologist knows the speed of each wave, then by knowing that both waves started at the same time it's possible to work out how far the earthquake waves have traveled to reach the seismograph. If we can determine the distance of the same earthquake from several different seismograph stations, we are able to locate the *epicenter*, the point on

Figure 3-13. How to locate an earthquake. (a) Both P and S waves leave the focus at the same time, but the P wave travels faster. We know the speed of both P waves and S waves, so we can use the time between the P wave arrival and the S wave arrival at the Wood-Anderson seismograph to determine the distance the seismograph station is from the earthquake, although we still don't know the direction to the earthquake. (b) We plot the distance as the radius of a circle with the seismograph station at its center. With a minimum of three seismograph stations, each with their circles based on the delay between P and S waves, we locate the epicenter, which is the only point common to all three circles.

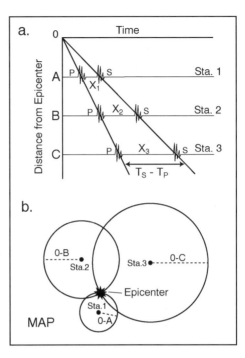

the Earth's surface directly above the earthquake *focus*. The focus or *hypocenter* is the point beneath the Earth's surface where the crust or mantle first ruptures to cause an earthquake (Figure 3-4). The depth of the earthquake below the surface is called its *focal depth*.

The surface waves are more complex. After reaching the surface, much earthquake energy will run along the surface, causing the ground to go up and down or sway from side to side. Some people caught in an earthquake have reported that they could actually *see* the ground moving up and down, like an ocean wave, but faster.

An earthquake releases a complex array of waves, with great variation in *frequency*, which is the number of waves to pass a point in a second. A guitar string vibrates many times per second, but it takes successive ocean waves many seconds to reach a waiting surfer. The ocean wave has a low frequency, and the guitar string vibrates at a high frequency. An earthquake can be compared to a symphony orchestra, with cellos, bassoons, and bass drums producing sound waves that vibrate at low frequencies, and piccolos, flutes, and violins that vibrate at high frequencies. It is by using high-speed computers that a seismologist can separate out the complex vibrations produced by an earthquake and begin to read and understand the music of the spheres.

Low-frequency body waves of large earthquakes travel on a curving path through the Earth for thousands of miles to reach seismographs around the world. I pointed out earlier that only the outermost parts of the Earth are elastic. How can the mantle, which is capable of the slow plastic flow that drives plate tectonics, also behave as an elastic solid when earthquake waves pass through it?

To explain this, I turn to the geologist's favorite toy, Silly Putty. Silly Putty is a soft ball the color of bubble gum that can be stretched out when pulled slowly. Hang a piece of Silly Putty over the side of a table and it will slowly drip to the floor under its own weight, like soft tar (ductile flow). Yet it also can bounce like a ball, indicating that it can be elastic. If Silly Putty is stretched out suddenly, it will break—sometimes into several pieces (brittle fracture).

The difference is whether the strain is applied suddenly or slowly. When strain is applied quickly, Silly Putty will absorb strain elastically (it'll bounce), or it'll shatter, depending on whether the strain takes it past its breaking point. Earthquake waves deform rock very quickly, and like Silly Putty, the rock behaves like an elastic solid. If strain is applied slowly, Silly Putty flows, almost like tar. This is the way the asthenosphere and lower crust work. The internal currents that drive the motion of plate tectonics are extremely slow, inches per year or less, and at those slow rates, rock flows.

6. Measuring an Earthquake

a. Magnitude

The chorus of high-frequency and low-frequency seismic waves that radiate from an earthquake indicates that no single number can characterize an earthquake, just as no single number can be used to describe a Napa Valley wine or a sunset view of Yosemite.

The size of an earthquake was once measured largely on the basis of how much damage was done. This was unsatisfactory to Caltech seismologist Charles Richter, who wanted a more quantitative measure of earthquake size, at least for southern California. Following up on earlier work done by the Japanese, Richter in 1935 established a *magnitude* scale based on how much a seismograph needle was deflected by a seismic wave generated by an earthquake about sixty miles (100 kilometers) away (Figure 3-14). Richter used a seismograph specially designed by Harry Wood and John Anderson to record local southern California earthquakes (see Part I). This seismograph was best suited for those waves that vibrated with a frequency of about five times per second, which is a bit like measuring how loud an orchestra is by how loud it plays middle C. Nonetheless, it enabled Richter and his colleagues to distinguish large, medium, and small earthquakes in

California, which was all they wanted to do. Anderson was an astronomer, and the seismograph was built at the Mt. Wilson Observatory—which might account for the word *magnitude*, which also expresses how bright a star is.

Complicating the problem for the lay person is that Richter's scale is logarithmic, which means that an earthquake of magnitude 5 would deflect the needle of the Wood-Anderson seismograph ten times more than an earthquake of magnitude 4 (Figure 3-14). And an increase of one magnitude unit represents about a thirty-fold increase in release of stored-up seismic strain energy. So the Hector Mine Earthquake of magnitude 7 in the Mojave Desert on October 16, 1999 would be the equivalent of about thirty earthquakes the size of the Whittier Narrows Earthquake of October 1, 1987, which was magnitude 6.

Richter never claimed that his magnitude scale, now called *local magnitude* and labeled M_L, was an accurate measure of earthquakes. Nonetheless, the Richter magnitude scale caught on with the media and the general public, and it is still the first thing a reporter asks a professional about an earthquake: "How big was it on the Richter scale?" The Richter magnitude scale works reasonably well for small to moderate-size earthquakes, but it works poorly for very large earthquakes, the ones we call great earthquakes. For these, other magnitude scales are necessary.

To record earthquakes at seismographs thousands of miles away, seismologists had to use long-period (low-frequency) waves, because

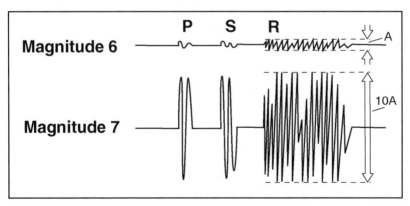

Figure 3-14. Richter's concept of magnitude. The delay between the P wave and the S wave is the same in both seismograms, so the two earthquakes are the same distance from the seismograph. The larger magnitude has a greater amplitude of deflection of the seismic waves. Richter used those earthquake waves with a frequency of about five wavelengths per second. In the figure, A is twice the amplitude. The magnitude 7 earthquake has a value of A ten times that of the magnitude 6 earthquake.

the high-frequency waves recorded by Richter on the Wood-Anderson seismographs die out a few hundred miles away from the epicenter. To understand this problem, think about how heavy metal music is heard a long distance away from its source, a live band or a boom box. Sometimes when my window is open on a summer evening I can hear the stereo playing in a passing car, but all I can make out are the very deep, or low-frequency, tones of the bass guitar, which transmit through the air more efficiently than the treble (high-frequency) guitar notes or the voices of the singers. In this same way, low-frequency earthquake waves can be recorded thousands of miles away from the earthquake source and used to study the internal structure of the Earth. A commonly used earthquake scale is the *surface wave magnitude scale*, or M_s, which measures the largest deflection of the needle on the seismograph for a surface wave that takes about twenty seconds to pass a point (about the same frequency as some ocean waves).

The magnitude scale most useful to professionals is the *moment magnitude scale*, or M_w, which comes closest to measuring the true size of an earthquake, particularly a large one. This scale relates magnitude to the area of the fault that ruptures and the amount of slip that takes place on the fault. For large earthquakes, this can be done by measuring the length of the fault that ruptures at the surface and figuring out how deep the zone of aftershocks extends, thereby calculating the area of the rupture. The amount of slip can be measured at the surface as well. The seismologist can also measure M_w by studying the characteristics of low-frequency seismic waves, and the surveyor or geodesist can measure it by remeasuring the relative displacement of survey benchmarks immediately after an earthquake to work out the distortion of the ground surface and envisioning a subsurface fault that would produce the observed distortion (see below).

For small to intermediate-size earthquakes, the magnitude scales are designed so that there is relatively little difference between Richter magnitude, surface-wave magnitude, and moment magnitude. But for very large earthquakes, the difference is dramatic. For example, both the 1906 San Francisco Earthquake and the 1964 Alaska Earthquake had a surface-wave magnitude of 8.3. However, the San Francisco Earthquake had a moment magnitude of only 7.7, whereas the Alaska Earthquake had a moment magnitude of 9.2, which made it the second-largest earthquake of the twentieth century.

b. Intensity

Measuring the size of an earthquake by the energy it releases is all well and good, but it's still important to measure how much damage it does at critical places (such as where you or I happen to be when the earthquake strikes). This measurement is called earthquake *intensity*,

Table 3-1. Abridged Modified Mercalli (MM) Intensity Scale. Masonry A: good workmanship, mortar, and design; reinforced, especially laterally, and bound together using steel, concrete, etc. Masonry B: good workmanship and mortar, reinforced, but not designed in detail to resist lateral forces. Masonry C: ordinary workmanship and mortar, no extreme weakness like failing to tie in at corners, but neither reinforced nor designed against horizontal forces. Masonry D: weak materials such as adobe; poor mortar, low standards of workmanship, weak horizontally. From Richter (1958).

Modified Mercalli Intensity Scale

Intensity	Description and Peak Ground Acceleration in percent g
I	Not felt except by a very few under especially favorable circumstances.
II	Felt only by a few persons at rest, especially on upper floors of buildings. Delicately suspended objects may swing.
III	Felt quite noticeably indoors, especially on upper floors of buildings, but many people do not recognize it as an earthquake. Standing automobiles may rock slightly. Vibrations like passing of truck.
IV	During the day, felt indoors by many, outdoors by few. At night, some awakened. Dishes, windows, doors disturbed; walls make creaking sound. Sensation like heavy truck striking building. Standing automobiles rocked noticeably. 0.015–0.02g
V	Felt by nearly everyone, many awakened. Some dishes, windows, etc. broken; cracked plaster in a few places; unstable objects overturned. Disturbances of trees, poles, and other tall objects sometimes noticed. Pendulum clocks might stop. 0.03–0.04g
VI	Felt by all, many frightened and run outdoors. Some heavy furniture moved; a few instances of fallen plaster and damaged chimneys. Damage slight; masonry D cracked. 0.06–0.07g
VII	Everybody runs outdoors. Damage negligible in buildings of good design and construction; slight to moderate in well-built ordinary structures; considerable in poorly built or badly designed structures (masonry D); some chimneys broken. Noticed by persons driving cars. 0.10–0.15g
VIII	Damage slight in specially designed structures; no damage to masonry A, some damage to masonry B, considerable damage to masonry C with partial collapse. Panel walls thrown out of frame structures. Fall of chimneys, factory stacks, columns, monuments, walls. Frame houses moved off foundations if not bolted. Heavy furniture overturned. Sand and mud ejected in small amounts. Changes in well water. Persons driving cars disturbed. 0.25–0.30g
IX	Damage considerable in specially designed structures; well-designed frame structures thrown out of plumb; great in substantial buildings, with partial collapse. Masonry B seriously damaged, masonry C heavily damaged, some with partial

	collapse, masonry D destroyed. Buildings shifted off foundations. Ground cracked conspicuously. Underground pipes broken. 0.50–0.55g
X	Some well-built wooden structures destroyed; most masonry and frame structures destroyed with foundations; ground badly cracked. Rails bent. Landslides considerable from river banks and steep slopes. Shifted sand and mud. Water splashed, slopped over bank. Greater than 0.60g
XI	Few, if any, masonry structures remain standing. Bridges destroyed. Broad fissures in ground. Underground pipelines completely out of service. Earth slumps and land slips in soft ground. Rails bent greatly.
XII	Damage total. Waves seen on ground surface. Lines of sight and level distorted. Objects thrown into the air.

which is measured by a Roman numeral scale (Table 3-1). Intensity III means no damage, and not everybody feels it. Intensity VII or VIII involves moderate damage, particularly to poorly constructed buildings. Intensity XI or XII is characterized by nearly total destruction.

Earthquake intensities are based on a post-earthquake survey of a large area: damage is noted, and people are questioned about what they felt (Figure 3-15). An intensity map is a series of concentric lines, irregular rather than circular, in which the highest intensities are generally (but not always) closest to the epicenter of the earthquake. For illustration, an intensity map is shown for the 1989 Loma Prieta Earthquake in the San Francisco Bay Area (Figure 3-15). High intensities were recorded near the epicenter, as expected. But intensity can also be influenced by the characteristics of the ground. Buildings on solid rock tend to fare better (and thus are subjected to lower intensities) than buildings on thick soft soil. The Marina District of San Francisco and the Oakland end of the San Francisco Bay Bridge suffered intensities of IX, even though they were far from the epicenter. This problem is discussed further in Chapter 9.

Table 3-1 relates earthquake intensity to the maximum amount of ground acceleration (*peak ground acceleration*, or PGA) that is measured with a special seismograph called a strong-motion accelerograph. Acceleration is measured as a percentage of the Earth's gravity. A vertical acceleration of one g would be just enough to lift you (or anything else) off the ground. Obviously, this would have a major impact on damage done by an earthquake at a given site. As pointed out above, Intensities VII and VIII can result in major damage to poorly constructed buildings, whereas well-constructed buildings should ride out those intensities with much less damage. This points out the importance of earthquake-resistant construction and strong building codes (discussed further in Chapters 12, 13, and 15). Nearly all buildings will ride out

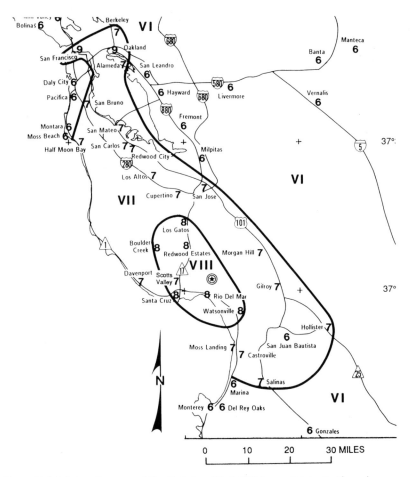

Figure 3-15. Intensity map of the October 17, 1989 Loma Prieta Earthquake. The highest intensities are generally closest to the epicenter (star and double circle), but high intensities of 9 in the Marina District of San Francisco and the Oakland end of the Bay Bridge were caused by ground conditions. From U.S. Geological Survey.

intensities of VI or less, even if they are poorly constructed. For the rare occasions when intensities reach XI or XII, many buildings will fail even if they are well constructed. But for the more common intensities of VII through X, earthquake-resistant construction will probably mean the difference between collapse of the building, with loss of life, and survival of the building and its inhabitants.

c. Fault-Plane Solutions

In the early days of seismography, it was enough to locate an earthquake accurately and to determine its magnitude. But seismic waves contain much more information, including the type of faulting. The seismogram shows that the first motion of an earthquake P wave is either a push toward the seismograph or a pull away from it. With the modern networks in California, it's possible to determine the push or pull relationship at many stations, leading to information about whether the earthquake is on a reverse fault, a normal fault, or a strike-slip fault. Many earthquakes are not accompanied by surface faulting, so the *fault-plane solutions* are the best evidence of the type of fault causing the earthquake. In cases like the 1992 Landers Earthquake, the fault-plane solution matched the surface rupture. But the 1989 Loma Prieta Earthquake did not produce surface rupture, and the fault-plane solution was not on the San Andreas Fault, as expected, but on a hitherto-unknown reverse fault with some strike-slip component. By recording seismic waves digitally, these waves can be analyzed to show that an earthquake can consist of several ruptures within a few seconds of each other, some with very different fault-plane solutions.

6. Measuring Crustal Deformation Directly —Tectonic Geodesy

As stated at the beginning of this chapter, Harry F. Reid based his elastic rebound theory on the displacement of survey benchmarks relative to one another. These benchmarks recorded the slow elastic deformation of the Earth's crust prior to the 1906 earthquake, and after the earthquake the benchmarks snapped back, thereby giving an estimate of tectonic deformation independent of seismographs or of geological observations. Continued measurements of the benchmarks record the accumulation of strain toward the next earthquake. If geology records past earthquakes, and seismographs record earthquakes as they happen, measuring the accumulation of tectonic strain says something about the earthquakes of the future.

Reid showed that a major contribution to earthquake science could be made by a branch of civil engineering called surveying—land measurements of the distance between survey markers (*trilateration*), the horizontal angles between three markers (*triangulation*), and the difference in elevation between two survey markers (*leveling*).

Surveyors need to know about the effects of earthquakes on property boundaries. Surveying implies that the land stays where it is. But if an earthquake is accompanied by a ten-foot strike-slip offset on a fault crossing your property, would your property lines be offset, too? In Japan, where individual rice paddies and tea gardens have property boundaries that are hundreds of years old, property boundaries *are* offset. A land survey map of part of the island of Shikoku shows rice paddy boundaries offset by a large earthquake fault in 1596.

The need to have accurate land surveys leads to the science of *geodesy*, the study of the shape and configuration of the Earth. *Tectonic geodesy* is the comparison of surveys done at different times to reveal deformation of the crust between the times of the surveys.

Following Reid's discovery, the U.S. Coast and Geodetic Survey (now the National Geodetic Survey) took over the responsibility for tectonic geodesy, which led them into strong-motion seismology. For a time, the Coast and Geodetic Survey was the only federal agency with a mandate to study earthquakes (see Part I).

After the great Alaska Earthquake of 1964, the USGS began to take an interest in tectonic geodesy as a way to study earthquakes. The leader in this effort was a young geophysicist named Jim Savage, who compared surveys before and after the earthquake to measure the crustal changes that accompanied the earthquake. The elevation changes were so large that along the coastline they could be easily seen without surveying instruments: sea level appeared to rise suddenly where the land went down, and it appeared to drop where the land went up.

Up until the time of the earthquake, some scientists believed that the faults at deep-sea trenches were vertical. But Savage, working with geologist George Plafker, was able to use the differences in surveys to show that the great subduction-zone fault generating the earthquake dipped gently northward, underneath the Alaskan landmass. Savage and Plafker then studied an even larger subduction-zone earthquake that had struck southern Chile in 1960 (M_w 9.5, the largest earthquake of the twentieth century) and showed that the earthquake fault in the Chilean deep-sea trench dipped beneath the South American continent. Seismologists, using newly established, high-quality seismographs set up to monitor nuclear weapons testing, confirmed this by showing that earthquakes defined a landward-dipping zone that could be traced hundreds of miles beneath the surface. All these discoveries were building blocks in the emerging new theory of plate tectonics.

Savage then turned his attention to the San Andreas Fault, close to his USGS office in Menlo Park. There were several reasons to focus on the San Andreas and related faults: (1) tectonic creep was being recorded on these faults at Hayward, Hollister, and elsewhere (see Chapter 4), (2) a high-quality seismograph network operated by the University of California at Berkeley was already in place, (3) a large population in the San Francisco Bay Area was at risk from earthquakes, and finally, (4) Harry Reid had already laid out the problem to be solved. The USGS could not rely on the routine surveys done for local government or property owners or even surveys done by the Coast and Geodetic Survey.

They needed specialized and more frequent resurveys over longer baselines, and they developed instruments that used lasers to determine distance.

Soon the San Andreas, Hayward, and Calaveras faults were spanned by a spider web of line-length measurements between benchmarks on both sides of these faults. Resurveys were done once a year, more frequently later in the project. The results confirmed the elastic-rebound theory of Reid, and the large number of benchmarks and the more frequent surveying campaigns added precision that was lacking before. Not only could Savage and his coworkers determine how fast strain is building up on the San Andreas, Hayward, and Calaveras faults, they were even able to determine how deep within the Earth's crust the faults are locked.

After the 1971 Sylmar Earthquake in the San Fernando Valley, Savage re-leveled survey lines that crossed the surface rupture. He was able to use the geodetic data to map the fault dipping beneath the San Gabriel Mountains, just as he had done for the Alaska Earthquake fault seven years before. The depiction of the source fault based on tectonic geodesy could be compared with the fault as illuminated by aftershocks and by the surface geology of the fault scarp. This would be the wave of the future in the analysis of California earthquakes.

Still, the land survey techniques were too slow, too cumbersome, and too expensive. A major problem was that the baselines were short, because you had to see from one to the other to make a measurement.

The answer to the problem came from space.

First, scientists from the National Aeronautical and Space Administration (NASA) discovered mysterious, regularly spaced radio signals from quasars in deep outer space. By analyzing these signals simultaneously from several radio telescopes as the Earth rotated, the distances between radio telescopes could be determined to great precision. And these distances changed over time. Using a technique called Very Long Baseline Interferometry (VLBI), NASA could determine the motion of radio telescopes on one side of the San Andreas Fault with respect to telescopes on the other side. These motions confirmed Savage's observations, even though some of the radio telescopes being used were hundreds of miles away from the San Andreas Fault.

Length of baseline ceased to be a problem, and the motion of a radio telescope at Vandenberg Air Force Base could be compared to a telescope in the Mojave Desert, in northeastern California, in Hawaii, in Japan, in Texas, or in Massachusetts. Using VLBI, NASA scientists were able to show that the motions of plate tectonics measured over time spans of hundreds of thousands of years were at the same rate as motions measured for only a few years—plate tectonics in real time.

But there were not enough radio telescopes to equal Savage's dense network of survey stations across the San Andreas Fault. Again, the solution came from space, this time from a group (called a *constellation*) of NAVSTAR satellites that orbit the Earth at an altitude of about twelve thousand miles. This became the Global Positioning System, or GPS.

GPS was developed by the military so that "smart bombs" could zero in on individual buildings in Baghdad or Belgrade, but a degraded form of the military signal (called Selected Availability) was made available for civilian use. Low-cost GPS receivers allow hunters to locate themselves in the mountains and sailors to locate themselves at sea. You can install one on the dashboard of your car to find where you are in a strange city. GPS is now widely used in routine surveying.

The degraded signal released by the military could be used for earthquake studies because it doesn't really matter where we are *exactly*, but only where we are *relative to the last time we measured*. This allows us to measure small changes of only a fraction of an inch, which is sufficient to measure strain accumulating across major California faults. As of May 2000, the signal is no longer degraded, which should allow even greater accuracy in measurements.

Uncertainties about variations in the troposphere high above the Earth mean that GPS does much better at measuring horizontal changes than it does vertical changes; leveling using GPS is less accurate than leveling based on ground surveys.

NASA's Jet Propulsion Lab at Pasadena, together with scientists at Caltech and MIT, began a series of survey campaigns in southern California in the late 1980s, and again they confirmed the earlier ground-based and VLBI measurements. GPS campaigns could be done quickly and inexpensively, and like VLBI, it was not necessary to see between two adjacent ground survey points. It was only necessary for all stations to lock onto one or more of the orbiting NAVSTAR satellites. One of the discoveries was the rate at which the mountains north of the Santa Barbara Channel, Ventura Basin, and Los Angeles Basin are closing in on mountains to the south, squeezing these lowlands together like a vise (see Chapter 5).

In addition to measuring the long-term accumulation of elastic strain, GPS was able to measure the release of strain in the 1992 Landers Earthquake in the Mojave Desert and the 1994 Northridge Earthquake in the San Fernando Valley. The survey network around the San Fernando Valley was dense enough that GPS could determine the size and orientation of the source fault plane and the amount of displacement during the earthquake. This determination was independent of fault source measurements made from seismographs.

By the time of the Landers Earthquake, tectonic geodesists recognized that campaign-style GPS, in which teams of geodesists went to the

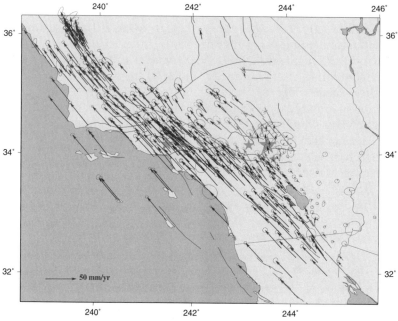

Figure 3-16. Accumulation of strain across the San Andreas Fault System in southern California based on the deformation of survey markers measured by the Global Positioning System (GPS). Base of each arrow locates the GPS survey station, and the length and direction of each arrow give the motion of the station relative to the North America Plate (upper right corner of map). Stations on the coast and on offshore islands are moving about 50 mm (2 inches) per year relative to North America. Circles and ellipses at arrow tips give the uncertainty in measurement. Thin curved lines show active faults. The locations of large earthquakes since 1990 are shown as stars, with the size of the star proportional to magnitude. Prepared at UCLA for the Southern California Earthquake Center; image courtesy of Kenneth W. Hudnut, USGS and Southern California Integrated GPS Network.

field several times a year to remeasure their ground survey points, was not enough. The measurements needed to be more frequent, and the time of occupation of individual sites needed to be longer to increase the level of confidence in measured tectonic changes and to look for possible short-term geodetic changes that might precede an earthquake. So permanent GPS receivers were installed at critical localities that were shown to be stable against other types of ground motion unrelated to tectonics, such as ground slumping or freeze-thaw. The permanent network was not dense enough to provide an accurate measure of either the Landers or the Northridge Earthquake, but the changes they recorded showed great promise for the future.

After Northridge, a group of scientists organized the Southern California Integrated GPS Network (SCIGN), which will have more than one hundred permanent GPS receivers monitoring crustal change in southern California, with special attention to the Los Angeles metropolitan area. An example of strain measurements across the San Andreas Fault System is shown in Figure 3-16. Figure 3-17 shows a GPS receiver measuring deformation accompanying the 1999 Hector Mine Earthquake. Other networks of permanent GPS receivers are being installed in northern California (the BARD array); the Great Basin, including Nevada and Utah (the BARGEN network); and the Pacific Northwest (PANGA). The permanent arrays are augmented by GPS campaigns where it's necessary to obtain more dense coverage than can be obtained with permanent stations.

The Landers Earthquake produced one more surprise from space. A European satellite had been obtaining radar images of the Mojave Desert before the earthquake, and it took more images afterwards. Radar images are like regular aerial photographs, except that the image is based on sound waves rather than light waves. Using a computer, the before and after images were laid on top of each other, and where the ground had moved during the earthquake it revealed a striped pattern, called an *interferogram*. The displacement patterns close to the rupture and in mountainous terrain were too complex to be seen, but farther away the radar interferometry patterns were simpler, revealing the amount of deformation of the crust away from the surface rupture. The displacements matched the point displacements measured by GPS, and as with GPS, radar interferometry provided still another independent method to measure the displacement produced by the earthquake. The technique was even able to show the deformation pattern of some of the larger aftershocks. Interferograms were created for the Northridge and Hector Mine Earthquakes; they have even been used to measure the slow accumulation of tectonic strain east of San Francisco Bay.

Figure 3-17. A GPS survey station installed southwest of Ludlow in the Mojave Desert by Aris Aspiotis to measure the amount of geodetic change caused by the Hector Mine Earthquake. GPS antenna is on a post anchored in bedrock; solar panel to right. Photo taken on October 17, 1999 by John Galetzka, Southern California Integrated GPS Network coordinator.

7. Summary

Earthquakes result when elastic strain builds up in the crust until the strength of the crust is exceeded, and the crust ruptures along a fault. Some of the fault ruptures do not reach the surface and are detected only by seismographs, but many larger earthquakes are accompanied by surface rupture, which can be studied by geologists. Reverse faults are less likely to rupture the surface than strike-slip faults or normal faults. A special class of low-angle reverse fault called a blind thrust does not reach the surface, but does bend the rocks at the surface into a fold. Paleoseismology extends the description of contemporary earthquakes back into prehistory, with the objective of learning the slip rate and the recurrence interval of earthquakes along a given fault.

In the last century, earthquakes have been recorded on seismographs, with the size of the earthquake, its magnitude, expressed by the amplitude of the earthquake wave recorded at the seismograph. A problem with measuring earthquake size in this way is the broad spectrum of seismic vibrations produced by the earthquake symphony. A better measure of the size of large earthquakes is the moment magnitude, calculated from the area of fault rupture and the fault displacement during the earthquake. In addition to magnitude, a seismograph measures earthquake depth and the nature and orientation of fault displacement at the earthquake source. Earthquake intensity is a measure of the degree of strong shaking at a given locality, important for studying damage.

Tectonic geodesy, especially the use of GPS, allows the measurement of long-term buildup of elastic strain in the crust and the release of strain after a major earthquake. If geology records past earthquakes and seismograph records earthquakes as they happen, tectonic geodesy records the buildup of strain toward the earthquakes of the future.

Suggestions for Further Reading

Bolt, B.A. 1999. *Earthquakes: 4th Edition*. New York: W.H. Freeman & Co. 366p.

Brumbaugh, D.S. 1999. *Earthquakes: Science and Society*. Upper Saddle River, NJ: Prentice-Hall.

Carter, W.E., and D.S. Robertson. 1986. Studying the Earth by very-long-baseline interferometry. *Scientific American*, v. 255, no. 5, pp. 46-54.

Lillie, R.J. 1999. *Whole-Earth Geophysics*. Englewood Cliffs, N.J.: Prentice-Hall. 361p.

Scholz, C. 1990. *Mechanics of Earthquakes and Faulting*. Cambridge University Press. 439p. A technical treatment of how rocks deform and produce earthquakes.

Yeats, R.S., K.E. Sieh, and C.R. Allen. 1997. *The Geology of Earthquakes*. New York: Oxford University Press. 568p.; chapters 2, 3, 4, and 5, pp. 17–113.

~ 4 ~
The San Andreas Fault System:
The Big One

"Where can we go, when there's no San Francisco? Better get ready to tie up the boat in Idaho."

Calypso song from "Day by Day."

"The much publicized fact . . . that the San Andreas system is not just one trace but a whole family of faults in a stepped and splintering band a great many miles wide . . . has done nothing to discourage the expanding populace from creating new urban shorelines and new urban skylines and so crowding the faults themselves that the faults' characteristic landforms are obscured beneath tens of thousands of buildings and homes."

John McPhee, *Assembling California.*

Introduction

The California landscape is cut by many faults capable of making earthquakes, but one of these, the San Andreas Fault, is more important than all the others. It is the principal boundary between the Pacific Plate and North America Plate, and its displacement rate is the highest of all California faults—more than one inch per year. Two of the greatest earthquakes in the history of California, the 1857 Fort Tejon Earthquake and the 1906 San Francisco Earthquake, resulted from slippage along this fault. San Andreas earthquakes caused great damage many miles away from the fault; the San Juan Capistrano Mission on the coast south of Los Angeles was destroyed by a San Andreas earthquake in 1812. In evaluating the earthquake danger to Los Angeles, the distant San Andreas Fault must be considered in addition to local faults directly beneath the city.

The San Andreas Fault is linked genetically to other faults, even those many miles away. West of Bakersfield in southern California, the San Andreas bends to the left to follow a more east-west trend, so that the Pacific Plate drives obliquely into the North America Plate to raise the Transverse Ranges and their attendant thrust faults in the Ventura, Los Angeles, and San Gabriel basins (see Chapter 5).

This chapter analyzes the San Andreas Fault and others related to it, first tracking these faults across California where they affect the cultures of the communities they pass beneath, innocently quiet most of the time, potential Swords of Damocles. Scientists are introduced who

Figure 4-1. Important localities along the San Andreas Fault (SAF) and boundaries of earthquake segments. Brawley Seismic Zone refers to spreading center (double lines) at east edge of Salton Sea. SJF, San Jacinto Fault; CF, Calaveras Fault; RCF, Rodgers Creek Fault. Modified from a drawing by Clarence R. Allen, Caltech.

contributed in a major way to our understanding of the fault. Study of the San Andreas Fault has helped in the study of similar, less well-understood faults elsewhere in the world, such as the North Anatolian Fault, which took the lives of more than fifteen thousand people in two earthquakes in Turkey in 1999. The chapter closes with a discussion of how scientists work out the earthquake history of the fault, especially where the fault traverses heavily populated regions such as the San Francisco Peninsula and the San Bernardino Inland Empire.

The Path of the San Andreas Fault through California

The Most Famous Fault in the World divides California in two (Figure 4-1), cleaving it from northwest to southeast, with the Klamath and Siskiyou Mountains, the Sierra Nevada, the Great Valley, the Mojave Desert, and San Francisco on the North America Plate; and the Peninsular Ranges, the Los Angeles and Ventura Basins, the offshore

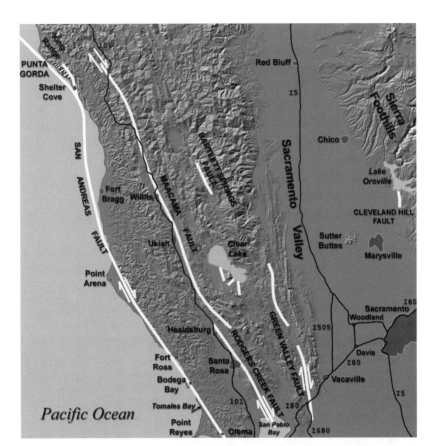

Figure 4-2. Computer-generated topographic map of northern Coast Ranges showing active strike-slip faults, including the northern San Andreas Fault. In the Sierra foothills, the Cleveland Hill Fault ruptured during an earthquake in 1975 possibly related to filling of Lake Oroville (see Chapter 6).

islands, and most of the Coast Ranges, including the San Francisco Peninsula west of Interstate 280, on the Pacific Plate.

The northern end of the fault is the Triple Junction between the Pacific, North America, and Gorda Plates (Figure 2-6), officially placed at the isolated village of Petrolia in Humboldt County (Figure 4-1), epicenter of a large earthquake in 1992. South of Petrolia, the fault skirts the Lost Coast of the King Range, a fir-clad wilderness so remote that it is little changed since it was first observed by Bartolomé Ferrelo in 1543. The fault is out of sight on the sea floor and in the wilds of the King Range except at the coastal settlement of Shelter Cove (Figure 4-2), where a geologist, François Matthes, found the northernmost evidence of ground rupture from the 1906 San Francisco Earthquake.

Shelter Cove is the hardest to reach of any populated part of the San Andreas Fault. You turn off Highway 101 at Garberville and wind past redwood groves and cross the rugged, tree-clad King Range, emerging into curving residential streets, part of the 4,000-lot Shelter Cove real estate development. Shelter Cove, next to Point Delgada, is a foggy and windy plateau protruding into the sea, separated from the King Range by the 1906 break of the San Andreas Fault. Point Delgada is the present location of the Cape Mendocino Lighthouse, relocated to Shelter Cove as a tourist attraction. Because of thick vegetation, the San Andreas Fault is not easy to see at Shelter Cove, and no signs point it out, although geologists have confirmed that the surface rupture mapped by Matthes in 1906 is an active fault, not a landslide.

From Shelter Cove, the fault lies just off the Mendocino coast, including Fort Bragg, which was heavily damaged in the 1906 earthquake. The fault makes landfall near Point Arena at Alder Creek. An aerial view southeast from Point Arena would show the ruler-straight valley of the Garcia River and, farther south, the Gualala River in Sonoma County, beyond which the fault again strikes offshore south of Fort Ross, the former outpost of the Russian-American Fur Company.

Figure 4-3. Space shuttle photo of San Francisco Bay Area showing San Andreas Fault as linear band from left (northwest) to right. Two promontories at left are Bodega Head and Point Reyes; San Andreas follows dark band of vegetation east of Point Reyes. The fault crosses the San Francisco Peninsula and, near the east edge of the photograph, bends to the left. The Santa Cruz Mountains are the dark patch of forested area west of the fault. East of San Francisco Bay, another linear band marks the active Hayward Fault.

The Fort Ross Visitors' Center makes no mention of the nearby San Andreas Fault, although the fort was knocked down during the 1906 earthquake.

Bodega Head gives evidence that it is on a plate boundary. Light-colored continental granite, scarred by attempts to place a nuclear power plant there (discussed in Part I), lies seaward of dark ocean-floor sedimentary rock of the Franciscan Formation, exposed in the hills above the fishing village of Bodega Bay (Figure 4-3). Bodega Bay's main claim to fame is that Alfred Hitchcock's movie *The Birds* was filmed there; no one points out the churning and displacement of soft sediment that accompanied the 1906 earthquake. In Marin County, the fault forms a narrow fjord, Tomales Bay, and at the Bear Valley Visitors' Center for the Point Reyes National Seashore at Olema, an earthquake loop trail 0.7 miles long celebrates the rupture across a dairy farm, preserving a sixteen-foot right-lateral offset of a picket fence. At Point Reyes and west of Tomales Bay, continental granite like that at Bodega Head sheds light-colored sediment, forming white cliffs that might have reminded Francis Drake of the cliffs of Dover in his native England when he overhauled his ship at Drakes Bay in 1579. The fault heads out to sea at Bolinas and Stinson Beach, enroute to San Francisco.

The San Andreas Fault makes its southernmost landfall at Daly City, on the San Francisco Peninsula in San Mateo County, not quite in line with its straight trace in Marin County. The fault trace sidesteps west of the Golden Gate at the epicenter of the 1906 earthquake, which started there and raced along the fault both to the north and south. The epicenters of the 1812 San Juan Capistrano and 1857 Fort Tejon earthquakes (discussed below), are far from the damaged places that gave them their names, but the 1906 earthquake *really is* the San Francisco Earthquake. Its epicenter was closer to San Francisco than to any other town. A smaller earthquake in 1957—an echo of 1906—was located at the same spot.

Faulting in 1906 had climbed the landslide-ravaged cliffs onto farmland, cutting a furrow fifteen miles long in what would become Daly City as San Franciscans burst from the city and headed for the suburbs after World War II. The 1957 earthquake, only M 5.5, had buckled sidewalks, cracked buildings, and sent people running into the streets. The wake-up call was not enough to save Daly City from becoming suburbia in the 1960s, with look-alike houses and streets covering the barren hills and the San Andreas Fault, leaving only the landslides in the sea cliffs as a reminder that geology always plays the last card (Figure 4-4). The fault is close to Skyline Drive, parallel to San Andreas Lake (Figure 4-5), which gave its name to the Most Famous Fault in the World, thanks to Professor Andrew Lawson. (Maybe Lawson named the fault after himself, *Andreas* being Spanish for *Andrew*.) San

Figure 4-4. View southeast along the San Andreas Fault at Daly City. Houses have been destroyed above the landslide-ravaged beach cliffs in foreground. In far distance is San Andreas Lake. Photo by Robert Wallace, U.S. Geological Survey.

Andreas Lake and the Crystal Springs Reservoir, with their cargo of water from the Sierra Nevada, are flanked by Interstate 280, the Junipero Serra Freeway. The undeveloped area around the reservoirs is part of the San Francisco Fish and Game Refuge; the absence of housing developments is in stark contrast to urbanized areas along the fault to the north. The next earthquake could break through the dams holding back the water and cause flooding downstream, although these dams did not fail in the 1906 or 1989 earthquakes. North of the Golden Gate, right-lateral displacement in 1906 was as much as sixteen feet, but from Daly City southward displacements were much smaller. The reason could be that parts of the fault might have ruptured in earthquakes in October 1800, during Spanish rule, and in June 1838, during the last years of Mexican rule.

South of Upper Crystal Springs Reservoir, the San Andreas Fault cuts across the formal gardens of the Filoli Mansion, a National Trust Historic Site where the saga of the wealthy Carringtons was played out in the television soap opera *Dynasty*. The fault bends to the left, past Woodside and Saratoga, across Stanford University land, where the fault is a little too close to the Stanford Linear Accelerator. The plate motion is parallel to the fault north of Stanford, but the left bend causes the North America Plate to jam into the Pacific Plate in its efforts to slide past it,

Figure 4-5. View southeast along San Andreas Lake (foreground) and Crystal Springs Reservoir, both of which follow the San Andreas Fault. Photo by Robert Wallace, U.S. Geological Survey.

like a warped and stuck door. This converts the pure strike slip farther north to both strike slip and reverse slip adjacent to the southern Santa Cruz Mountains. In the 1980s, earthquake forecasters suspected that this segment of the fault, because of the small displacement in 1906, might be the site of the next big earthquake (see Chapter 8). Sure enough, on October 17, 1989, a M 6.9 earthquake rumbled through the mountains beneath Loma Prieta Peak, with severe damage as far away as the Oakland Bay Bridge and the Marina District of San Francisco.

But the search for Loma Prieta surface rupture proved to be frustrating. In contrast to the 1906 earthquake, the 1989 earthquake was not accompanied by any significant surface rupture on the San Andreas Fault. Instead, the southern Santa Cruz Mountains were pushed up along a blind fault, with displacement in part by reverse faulting, according to the analysis of seismograms. The aftershocks were in the general vicinity of the San Andreas Fault, but apparently a previously unknown reverse fault adjacent to the San Andreas had broken, part of the overall fault system but not the main fault itself.

The San Andreas Fault continues southeast in the Santa Cruz Mountains above Silicon Valley in Santa Clara County past Los Gatos. The fault cuts across an abutment of the dam at Lexington Reservoir and is traced to the San Juan Bautista Mission, founded by the

Figure 4-6. Culvert at Almaden-Cienega Winery near Paicines offset by creeping movement along San Andreas Fault. Photo by Robert Yeats in April 1978.

Franciscans in 1797 and thrown down by an earthquake three years later, in October 1800. The San Andreas Fault lies just to the east of the mission, forming a scarp separating the mission grounds from low-lying farmland farther east. The southern end of surface faulting in 1906 was recorded a short distance northwest of San Juan Bautista, and the mission was severely damaged in that earthquake. Kim Novak and Jimmy Stewart played out the climactic scenes of Alfred Hitchcock's film *Vertigo* within the mission; one wonders whether Hitchcock sensed the drama of filming on a plate boundary.

A strange thing happens at the Almaden-Cienega winery on Cienega Road, south of Hollister and west of Paicines. The fault moves without causing earthquakes—or large ones, anyway. The USGS set up sensors in the winery building many years ago to measure the slow deformation, called *fault creep*. The wine storage building with its fermenting tanks and a culvert outside (Figure 4-6) are slowly being displaced sideways as the Pacific Plate moves past the North America Plate beneath the building. A wooden tank behind the tasting room has been thrown out of line. The winery was closed when I visited it in the spring of 2000; it was not clear whether the fault had caused the closure.

Fault creep occurs where the crust is too weak to build up enough strain to release in a proper earthquake. The tectonic plates simply slide past each other smoothly, without any serious shaking.

Within the Coast Ranges farther southeast, State Highway 35 follows a valley formed by the fault. Its trace is easily seen from an airplane window as it displaces streams and produces sagponds and pressure ridges (Figures 4-7 and 4-8). It passes by the tiny community of Bitterwater, and a one-well oil field produces oil that apparently was trapped by the San Andreas Fault.

Beyond Bitterwater, the fault is traced to the isolated backcountry village of Parkfield, population thirty-seven.

Parkfield became famous due to a M 5.5 earthquake on June 27, 1966. Geologists and seismologists from Caltech and the USGS converged on the scene and found that the center stripe of Highway 46 at Cholame had been offset right laterally about two inches. When the Caltech and USGS groups compared notes, they found that about half the offset had taken place not during but after the earthquake. In a field trip eleven days before the earthquake, Clarence Allen of Caltech and a group of Japanese scientists had observed ground cracks that turned out to be at exactly the same place in the road as the subsequent

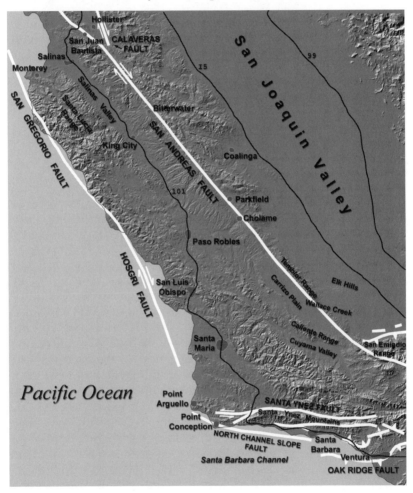

Figure 4-7. Computer-generated topographic map of southern Coast Ranges showing San Andreas, San Gregorio, and Hosgri faults and faults of the western Transverse Ranges of the lower Santa Clara Valley near Ventura and the Santa Barbara coast (see Chapter 5).

Figure 4-8. Sagpond along San Andreas Fault in Peachtree Valley north of Parkfield. Photo by Robert Yeats.

June 27 offset. A water pipeline crossing the fault had ruptured about nine hours before the earthquake. Not only did faulting occur during the earthquake, it occurred before and after as well.

Things got even more interesting when a rancher, Herb Durham, took Bob Wallace of the USGS to Turkey Flat Road, which had been offset during the earthquake. Durham pointed out that the road previously had been broken during an earthquake in 1934. When the Berkeley seismogram of the 1966 event was laid over the record for 1934, the squiggles were almost identical, and they also matched those of a still earlier earthquake in 1922. Newspaper accounts identified even earlier earthquakes in 1901, 1881, and 1857.

The near-periodic recurrence of earthquakes on this comparatively weak section of the San Andreas Fault suggested that Parkfield would be a good place to set up instruments to get a detailed record of the next earthquake and possibly forecast it. According to past performance, the next earthquake was due in 1988. (The Parkfield forecast, still unfulfilled, is discussed further in Chapter 8.) This led to celebrity status for Parkfield. A sign on the water tower next to the Parkfield Café identifies it as the "Earthquake Capitol of the World. Be here when it happens!" (Figure 4-9). Business improved as journalists dropped by to do stories about the "earthquake capitol." A display inside the café highlights Parkfield's last earthquake, and a California fault map decorates one wall. USGS scientists make frequent visits to monitor their seismometers, laser Geodimeters, and magnetometers, and university field-trippers and international earthquake scientists include Parkfield on their itineraries. The earthquakes are frequent enough that some old-timers remember both the 1966 and 1934 earthquakes, and here, more than any other place in California, earthquakes are a part of everyday life and are even good for business.

Figure 4-9. Parkfield, the "Earthquake Capitol of the World," according to sign on water tower outside the Parkfield Café. Photo by Robert Yeats.

Southeast of Parkfield, the fault line is so straight that it looks like the result of human rather than earthquake activity, and it passes through the most barren wasteland of the Coast Ranges. Near Cholame, the fault crosses the intersection of State Highways 41 and 46 in San Luis Obispo County, where actor James Dean died when his Porsche Spyder collided with a Ford; a memorial to Dean is nearby on the grounds of the Jack Ranch Café. The area is so desolate that Alfred Hitchcock used it for a scene in *North by Northwest* (what was it about the San Andreas Fault that attracted Hitchcock?).

The fault is so fresh in the Carrizo Plain that it appears to have ruptured yesterday (Figures 3-5a, 4-10, and 4-11), and in a geological sense, it had. On the morning of January 9, 1857, the fault broke from Cholame to Cajon Pass, near San Bernardino, during an earthquake of M 7.9. This was the largest earthquake in California history, larger than the San Francisco Earthquake of 1906. But in 1857 nobody lived on the part of the fault that broke, except for a military detachment at Fort Tejon, on the Grapevine Route between Los Angeles and Bakersfield. Every building at Fort Tejon was damaged and trees were thrown down nearby, so the earthquake became known as the Fort Tejon Earthquake. The Carrizo Plain northwest to Cholame was uninhabited, although a cowboy stated later that he spotted a round sheep corral that had been offset to form the shape of an S. (The corral has never been located.) Most of the contemporary accounts of shaking

Figure 4-10. The San Andreas Fault in Carrizo Plain from the Los Angeles to San Francisco Shuttle in late afternoon. View is east across the Temblor (Earthquake) Hills toward San Joaquin Valley. Photo by Robert Yeats.

came from populated regions, including Los Angeles, San Diego, San Francisco, and the Great Valley as far north as Marysville.

The epicenter was actually almost a hundred miles away in the central Coast Ranges. The great earthquake might have been triggered by a Parkfield earthquake a hundred times smaller. If this is true, then Parkfield gains a much greater significance: a Parkfield earthquake could set off another Big One on the San Andreas Fault.

The preservation of the fault breaks in Carrizo Plain is due to the near-desert climate. The pristine tectonic features led Bob Wallace to a right-laterally offset stream that eventually became named Wallace Creek, in honor of his research on the 1857 rupture and his discovery of evidence of still-earlier ruptures that produced larger stream offsets. To get to Wallace Creek, take State Highway 58 east of California Valley about six miles; if coming from Bakersfield, cross the main Coast Range summit for about three miles. Turn south onto 7 Mile Road (toward a white salt flat) for 0.3 miles, then turn left onto Elkhorn Road (gravel) for about four miles to a gravel parking lot on the left side of the road. A short interpretive trail leads to the San Andreas Fault and explains the offset stream and an excavation that preserves evidence for earlier fault offsets.

Southeast of Carrizo Plain, the fault makes a sweeping left bend, much larger than the bend at the Santa Cruz Mountains, and climbs into pine-clad highlands with the San Emigdio Range to the north and Mt. Abel and Frazier Mountain to the south. The fault strikes east-southeast, and between the resort villages of Lake of the Woods and

Figure 4-11. Right-lateral stream offset along the San Andreas Fault in Carrizo Plain. Drainage flows from right to left in foreground, is deflected at the point where two people are standing, and turns again to left in middle distance. Photo by Robert Yeats.

Frazier Park, it strikes due east. This orientation causes the Pacific Plate to pile up against the North America Plate, but on a much larger scale than in the Santa Cruz Mountains. The result is a series of east-west mountain ridges called the Transverse Ranges (Figure 4-7), including the San Gabriel and San Bernardino Mountains, with the highest elevations in southern California (discussed further in Chapter 5). Only southeast of San Bernardino does the fault turn back into its southeast strike, sub-parallel to the Pacific-North America plate motion.

Interstate 5 crosses the fault at Tejon Pass, the top of the Grapevine, and follows the fault past Gorman, built entirely within the fault zone. A county road runs parallel to the fault trace along the northern foothills of the San Gabriel Mountains, past Lake Hughes and Leona Valley to Highway 14, the Antelope Valley Freeway, and Palmdale.

The freeway road cut south of Motel Row on Palmdale Boulevard exposes contorted lake sediments in the fault zone (Figure 4-12). The fault itself is the zone of disturbed ground at the southern end of this road cut (Figure 4-13). The road cut is spectacular but no sign marks the San Andreas Fault. Because it is on a freeway, the road cut can be viewed only from a car driving along the freeway.

Palmdale is so caught up in land development accommodating the urban commuter spillover from Los Angeles that few people think about the earthquake hazard of the San Andreas Fault. The Pearblossom Highway connects Palmdale with Interstate 15, the road to Las Vegas, which crosses Cajon Pass, a low divide between the San Gabriel Mountains and the San Bernardino Mountains. South of Pearblossom,

Figure 4-12. Freeway roadcut on State Highway 14 south of Palmdale, showing contorted lake deposits near the San Andreas Fault. Photo by Robert Wallace, U.S. Geological Survey.

Figure 4-13. Aerial view of same roadcut shown in Figure 4-12; San Andreas Fault is shown as linear band from lower left to upper right. City of Palmdale in distance. Photo by Robert Wallace, U.S. Geological Survey.

the road to Devils Punchbowl County Park passes by Pallett Creek, a small stream that takes a right jog at the San Andreas Fault. This creek has eroded down through its own organic marsh deposits, revealing nearly two thousand years of earthquake history on the fault, described in trench excavations by Kerry Sieh, then a Stanford graduate student and now a geology professor at Caltech.

Farther southeast, near the ski resort of Wrightwood, another trench excavation by the USGS revealed evidence of not only the 1857

Figure 4-14. Computer-generated topographic map of southeastern section of San Andreas Fault in southeastern California. Fault ends at Bombay Beach on the Salton Sea at a spreading center (Brawley Seismic Zone), now covered by sediments of the Colorado River. To the west, in the Peninsular Ranges, are other strike-slip faults: the San Jacinto, Elsinore, and Newport-Inglewood faults. At the northern edge of the map, the San Gabriel and San Bernardino Mountains are part of the Transverse Ranges (see Chapter 5). Farther north in the Mojave Desert are faults that ruptured during the Landers Earthquake in 1992.

earthquake but another one slightly older. Damaged trees along the fault gave a tree-ring date of around 1812, the year of two devastating earthquakes during the Spanish period. One of these earthquakes was somewhere in the Santa Barbara Channel, but the other one had destroyed the mission at San Juan Capistrano on December 8. Even though it is known as the San Juan Capistrano Earthquake, we know now that the earthquake actually was on a then-uninhabited section of the San Andreas Fault. The disconcerting fact about this conclusion is that the 1812 earthquake was followed only forty-four years later by the 1857 earthquake, yet no earthquake has struck here in nearly one hundred fifty years since then.

Even more disconcerting is the earthquake history of the rest of the fault trace, which extends from Cajon Pass through Devore and the northern suburbs of San Bernardino at Highland, then east-southeast across the low San Gorgonio Pass past the rows of windmills on both sides of Interstate 10 to the eastern edge of the Coachella Valley (Figures 4-14, 4-15). This section of the fault has not produced a major earthquake since the time people began keeping records, and paleoseismology shows no earthquake for at least three hundred years.

However, on July 8, 1986, cracks appeared along a small section of the fault zone, locally named the Banning Fault, during an earthquake of M 5.9 along Dillon Road, west of the dusty settlement of North Palm Springs, culturally a world away from Palm Springs, its glamorous neighbor five miles to the south.

From North Palm Springs, the fault runs just north of Thousand Palms and along the low hills in Riverside County east of Indio to the

Figure 4-15. San Andreas Fault in the Coachella Valley east of Thousand Palms. Palm trees tap water coming up along the active fault. Photo by Robert Yeats.

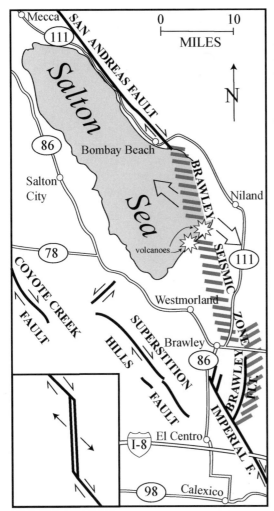

Figure 4-16. San Andreas Fault as a transform fault at the Salton Sea and Imperial Valley. The Brawley Seismic Zone is a spreading center where crust moves away to the northwest and southeast. The spreading center is bounded by transform faults: the San Andreas Fault on the north and the Imperial Fault on the south.

shore of Salton Sea, east of a windswept huddle of trailers and small houses named Bombay Beach (Figure 4-14). At Bombay Beach, the active fault ends—or appears to end. A long, straight subsurface fault underlies the sand hills parallel to the railroad tracks in the direction of Yuma, Arizona, but this fault does not appear to be active.

The reason the active San Andreas Fault appears to end is that it is a plate boundary, a transform fault (see Chapter 2). At the southeast end of the Salton Sea, it joins a spreading center, a zone of intense seismicity called the Brawley Seismic Zone that cuts southward along the eastern edge of the Salton Sea (Figure 4-16). This spreading center is unusual because it is not on the ocean floor but on dry land.

The Gulf of California opened up four or five million years ago, separating Baja California from the rest of Mexico (Figure 2-7). The Gulf has been widening diagonally on spreading centers separated by transform faults, moving Baja California northwestward as new basaltic lava welled up on the sea floor in its wake.

The true northern end of the Gulf of California lies beneath the irrigated fields of the Imperial Valley, filled with sediments of the Colorado River Delta, more than ten thousand feet thick near El Centro. The Brawley Seismic Zone is the northernmost Gulf of California spreading center, and it connects the San Andreas plate-boundary fault with the Imperial Fault, the next transform fault to the south.

Like the spreading centers in the Gulf, the Brawley Seismic Zone has high geothermal temperatures, and it has been associated with small volcanic eruptions. About sixteen thousand years ago, Obsidian Butte, a low, rocky volcanic dome, burst through the Colorado River Delta deposits on the southeast shore of Salton Sea, now a wildlife refuge with a profusion of water birds. The ground along the shore is strewn with volcanic glass and lava, in sharp contrast with the Colorado River silts found elsewhere. This is also the location of the Salton Sea Geothermal Field, still under development. So the San Andreas Fault ends by shifting its plate-boundary role southward to the Brawley Seismic Zone/Spreading Center and the Imperial Fault.

Other Faults of the San Andreas System

Introduction

Plate tectonic theory states that the Earth's crust is made up of moving plates, like shells, giving the impression that the edges of these shells are very narrow and very sharp. If this were true, the earthquake hazard in California would be restricted to the San Andreas Fault, where the greatest displacement has taken place. The first clue that this is not so comes from earthquake geology, which shows that the long-term slip rate on the San Andreas Fault is quite a bit less than the rate at which the Pacific Plate is moving northwest past the North America Plate. This means that part of the relative motion is being taken up along other faults, and these faults must be considered dangerous, too.

The problem is that the continental crust of California, ravaged by faulting over two hundred million years, is riddled with structural flaws and is not strong enough to act as a rigid plate. Faults millions of years old are re-broken by present-day crustal stresses. Geodetic measurements from space show that the Pacific Plate is rigid only on the deep ocean floor west of California, and the North America Plate is rigid only east of Salt Lake City, Utah, in the Colorado Plateau and Great Plains. Stated this way, all of California and Nevada and parts of

Utah and Oregon are within the plate boundary zone and are, to a greater or lesser degree, at risk from earthquakes. Large earthquakes have been recorded off the coast of southern California, east of the Sierra Nevada, in the Central Nevada Seismic Zone, and the Wasatch Fault at Salt Lake City. Microearthquakes recorded on seismographs span this entire region as well.

Earthquakes in the Transverse Ranges, largely west of the San Andreas Fault, and in the desert ranges east of the fault in California and western Nevada are described in the following two chapters. The discussion here is limited to faults that are close to the San Andreas Fault and also strike northwest and, for the most part, are characterized by right-lateral strike slip, like the San Andreas. These faults make up the *San Andreas System*, a broader zone than the *San Andreas Fault* traced above. The fault system south of the Transverse Ranges is described first, followed by the system to the north, including those faults posing an immediate threat to the cities east of San Francisco Bay.

Southern California

The Imperial Fault strikes southeast from the spreading center marked by the Brawley Seismic Zone and crosses the All American Canal into Mexico for at least twenty miles (Figure 4-16). It crosses diagonally the grid of roads serving the irrigated farms of the tabletop-flat floodplain of the Colorado River in the Imperial Valley, and it was only recognized as a fault when the floodplain was churned up along a linear zone during the May 19, 1940, Imperial Valley Earthquake of M 7.1 (Figure 4-17). The northern end of the fault was re-ruptured during a smaller earthquake of M 6.4 on October 15, 1979 (Figure 3-5b). A still-smaller earthquake in the region in 1915 was described by J.C. Branner of Stanford in the early days of earthquake investigations in southern California.

In Baja California, the Imperial Fault ends where the Cerro Prieto Fault takes up to the southwest, another transform fault that accounts for Mexico's Cerro Prieto Geothermal Field. The Cerro Prieto Fault is traced across the lower Colorado River to the Gulf of California in westernmost Sonora. An earthquake of M 7.1 on December 31, 1934 was accompanied by surface rupture on this fault.

At its northwestern end south of Brawley, the Imperial Fault steps westward to the San Jacinto Fault (Figure 4-16) At the southern end of the San Jacinto Fault, the Superstition Hills Fault and the Wienert Fault, in part underlying the flat Imperial Valley farmland like the Imperial Fault does, ruptured in an earthquake of M 6.6 on November 24, 1987. The San Jacinto Fault extends all the way to Cajon Pass near San Bernardino (Figure 4-14). Unlike the historically silent San Andreas Fault on the east side of the Coachella Valley, the San Jacinto Fault has

Figure 4-17. Orange trees offset by the Imperial Fault during an earthquake in 1940. Locality is in Imperial Valley about one-and-a-half miles north of the Mexican border. Photo by Clarence Allen, Caltech, in 1959; orange grove was removed in the early 1960s.

had so many earthquakes in the past hundred years that it is regarded as the most seismically active fault in onshore California today. Fortunately, most of the fault runs through sparsely inhabited desert valleys and ranges west of the Salton Sea, but at its northwestern end it passes through the rapidly growing desert community of Hemet, through the Moreno Valley east of Riverside, and finally across the densely populated southern suburbs of San Bernardino to a junction with the San Andreas Fault near Cajon Pass. On Christmas Day 1899, the northern reach of the San Jacinto Fault sustained an earthquake of M 7.1, collapsing brick buildings in Hemet and San Jacinto and shifting wood-frame buildings off their foundations. Because of the rapid growth of population in the Inland Empire, an earthquake that large and at that location would be a major disaster if it happened today.

The slip rate on the San Jacinto Fault is about a half-inch per year in its northern section, a rate slower than that on the Imperial Fault, reflecting the role of the Imperial Fault as the main plate boundary southeast of the Salton Sea. The San Jacinto slip rate is also less than that on the San Andreas Fault to the east, which has sustained no large earthquakes since the start of record keeping. This is a heads-up warning that the large number of earthquakes on the San Jacinto Fault in the past hundred years might not be representative of its long-term behavior. San Andreas earthquakes might be fewer, but when they do happen, they are likely to be larger and more destructive.

West of the San Jacinto Fault, the Elsinore Fault extends from northern Baja California through the eastern Peninsular Ranges to more densely populated valleys to the northwest, including the cities of Temecula, Lake Elsinore, and Corona (Figure 4-14). At Corona, where the Santa Ana River separates the Peninsular Ranges from the Puente Hills of the Los Angeles Basin, the Elsinore Fault divides into two: the Whittier Fault, which cuts through the Los Angeles suburbs of Yorba Linda, Brea, and Whittier on the south side of the Puente Hills, and the Chino Fault on the east side of the Puente Hills between Corona and Pomona. The northwestern end of the Whittier Fault has been traced across the San Gabriel River at Whittier Narrows. The fault cuts off the east end of the Montebello Hills, and it generated the largest aftershock of the 1987 Whittier Narrows Earthquake farther north beneath the Los Angeles suburb of South San Gabriel. South of the border, the Laguna Salada Fault was the source of an earthquake of M 7 on February 24, 1892, resulting in damage in San Diego. The Elsinore Fault could have been the source of the earthquake felt by the Portolá expedition near the Santa Ana River (Río de los Temblores) on July 28, 1769, although other faults are also candidate sources of that earthquake. The slip rate on the Elsinore Fault is about one-fifth inch (4-6 mm) per year; it is somewhat less on the Laguna Salada Fault in Baja California and on the Whittier Fault in the Los Angeles Basin.

The next fault to the west is the Newport-Inglewood Fault in the western Los Angeles Basin, marked by a row of tectonic hills including the Baldwin Hills at Culver City, Dominguez Hill east of Los Angeles International Airport, Signal Hill at Long Beach, and Huntington Mesa at Huntington Beach. The fault was the source of an earthquake of M 6.4 on March 11, 1933 off the coast at Newport Beach. So much of the damage was concentrated in Long Beach, the largest city on the fault more than fifteen miles to the northwest, that it became known as the Long Beach Earthquake. Smaller earthquakes near the fault caused damage to Inglewood on June 21, 1920 and to Torrance on November 14, 1941.

North of Culver City and Beverly Hills the fault terminates against the Santa Monica Mountains, but at Newport Beach in Orange County, the fault angles offshore west of San Juan Capistrano, San Clemente, the San Onofre nuclear power plant, and Oceanside in San Diego County (Figure 4-14). In San Diego, the fault crosses the coastline east of La Jolla and Mount Soledad where it is called the Rose Canyon Fault, which continues east of Mission Bay. In San Diego, yet to suffer major damage from a local earthquake, the fault breaks up into several structures at Old Town, at the entrance to San Diego Bay, and at Coronado, south of which the active structures continue offshore across the Mexican border. Farther southeast in Baja California are other strike-slip faults, one of which—the San Miguel Fault—was the source of an earthquake of M 6.9 on February 9, 1956, an earthquake strongly felt in San Diego.

Other strike-slip faults are mapped west of the Newport-Inglewood and Rose Canyon faults. The most important of these is the Palos Verdes Fault, which follows the northeastern front of the Palos Verdes Hills between Redondo Beach and San Pedro. Northwest of the Palos Verdes Hills the fault has been mapped on the sea floor in Santa Monica Bay, and southeast of San Pedro the fault has been mapped offshore in San Pedro Channel west of Los Angeles Harbor. Off San Diego, the continuation of the Palos Verdes Fault is called the Coronado Bank Fault, which has been traced on the sea floor into Baja California.

Where the fault strikes northwest-southeast, parallel to the slip between the Pacific Plate and North America Plate, its motion is pure strike slip, but west of Redondo Beach, the fault strikes more toward the west so that the crust to the south presses up against the fault rather than sliding past. This pileup expresses itself in the uplift of the Palos Verdes Hills. The Pacific Ocean surf erodes the sea cliffs along Palos Verdes Drive South, below the expensive homes of Rancho Palos Verdes and Palos Verdes Estates. Hundreds of thousands of years ago the Palos Verdes Hills were ocean floor, and the crustal collision along the Palos Verdes Fault slowly forced the hills upward, leaving evidence of former wave-cut beach cliffs high in the hills giving a stair-stepped silhouette. Although no damaging earthquakes have been attributed to the fault since Los Angeles was settled, its slip rate of one-eighth inch (3 mm) per year and its course past heavily industrialized parts of Torrance and Wilmington and Los Angeles port facilities at San Pedro make the fault one to watch carefully.

Even farther west are strike-slip faults of the submerged California Continental Borderland, including the San Diego Trough Fault at the foot of the continental escarpment west of San Diego, and the San Clemente Fault east of San Clemente Island. The San Diego Trough Fault comes ashore south of Ensenada, Baja California, as the Agua Blanca Fault, and others continue southward off the Baja California coast.

What can be said about these faults as a group? All of them pile up against the Transverse Ranges to the north: the San Gabriel and Santa Monica mountains onshore and the northern Channel Islands offshore. Only the San Andreas Fault itself crosses the Transverse Ranges. All the faults are west of the San Andreas Fault. Slip rates are highest on the San Andreas Fault and progressively lower on faults farther away. The slip rate on the San Andreas Fault is more than an inch (30 mm) per year at Indio; on the San Jacinto Fault it's less than a half inch (6 to 13 mm) per year south of San Bernardino; on the Elsinore Fault it's about a quarter inch (6 mm) per year between Corona and Elsinore, and on faults farther west, it is one-fourth inch (6 mm) per year or less. The western faults, especially the Newport-Inglewood and Palos Verdes faults, are of great concern because they traverse heavily populated suburbs of Los Angeles. Indeed, it was the 1933 earthquake on the Newport-Inglewood Fault that had a dramatic impact on earthquake awareness in general and on upgrading school construction standards in particular, as recounted in Part I.

The northern ends of the Elsinore and San Jacinto faults are more dangerous for the same reason: between Los Angeles and San Bernardino, they underlie heavily populated cities of the San Gabriel Valley and Inland Empire that are only dimly aware of their presence. The days of reckoning with these faults still lie ahead.

Central California

The San Andreas Fault dominates the earthquake hazard in central California north of the Transverse Ranges, but two additional structures pose an additional—although poorly understood—threat (Figure 4-7).

A fault off the central California coast was discovered in the 1960s as oil companies were conducting detailed geophysical surveys in preparation for competitive bidding on offshore federal leases. Two of my fellow geologists in Shell Oil Company, Ernie Hoskins and John Griffiths, were asked by the American Association of Petroleum Geologists to write a scientific paper on the oil prospects of the central California offshore region. Their paper, published in 1971, identified a major offshore fault extending from Point Arguello, southwest of Santa Maria, north to the ocean floor off the Big Sur coast. This fault was not named by Hoskins and Griffiths, but it was soon connected by others to the San Simeon Fault west of Hearst Castle in San Luis Obispo County, the Sur Fault west of Big Sur in Monterey County, and the San Gregorio Fault at Ano Nuevo Point northwest of Santa Cruz and at Seal Cove and Moss Landing in San Mateo County. The fault appears to join the San Andreas Fault west of the Golden Gate at San Francisco.

Geologists were unwilling to use the name of any of the faults skimming the coastline to refer to the entire fault, so they took the first three letters of Hoskins and Griffiths and called the southern part of the fault, which is completely offshore, the Hosgri Fault, a name that stuck. An earthquake in 1927 offshore from Lompoc might have been on the Hosgri Fault, but other sources are also possible (see Chapter 5). The Hosgri Fault gained a lot of attention because of its proximity to the proposed Diablo Canyon nuclear power plant on the coast near San Luis Obispo, leading some frustrated nuclear-power advocates to complain that the Hosgri Fault, entirely offshore in this region, had been "invented" to stymie the nuclear-power industry. Even though the Hosgri Fault is active, its slip rate is low, a tenth of an inch (2.5 mm) per year. The low slip rate permitted the Diablo Canyon nuclear plant to be completed with what are hoped to be adequate engineering safeguards against earthquakes. The San Gregorio Fault to the north has a slip rate of about one-fifth inch (5 mm) per year, a rate based mainly on the lower slip rate on the San Andreas Fault south of the Golden Gate compared to its rate to the north.

The low, grassy foothills of the southern and central Coast Ranges next to the San Joaquin Valley are underlain by a series of broad anticlines that house great oil fields that are still productive today. On May 2, 1983, an earthquake of M 6.7 originated on a blind thrust beneath the Coalinga Anticline, nearly flattening the dusty oil town of Coalinga and causing more than $10 million in damage. Two years later, an earthquake of M 6 was caused by a rupture of a blind thrust beneath the North Kettleman Hills Anticline, southeast of Coalinga. During the Coalinga Earthquake, the Coalinga Anticline rose more than a foot-and-a-half, evidence that the anticline had grown during hundreds of similar earthquakes during the past few hundred thousand years. Coalinga and Kettleman Hills caused earthquake geologists to look more critically at anticlines, including those in the Transverse Ranges (discussed in Chapter 5).

Most displacement in the Coast Ranges is by strike slip in which the crust closer to the coast moves northwest with respect to the San Joaquin Valley. But during the Coalinga and Kettleman Hills earthquakes, the seaward block moved *northeast*, at right angles to strike slip on the San Andreas and other faults. The reason is not entirely clear. Earthquake experts call it *strain partitioning*, meaning that sometimes you have strike-slip earthquakes and sometimes blind-thrust earthquakes. Some geophysicists believe that this is evidence that the San Andreas Fault is much weaker than believed earlier. A possible linkage between the Coalinga Earthquake and the Parkfield Earthquake forecast on the San Andreas Fault is explored in Chapter 8.

San Francisco Bay Area and Northern Coast Ranges
Northwest of Parkfield, the "Earthquake Capitol of the World," the San Andreas Fault slices a narrow gash through the oak-studded back country of the Diablo Range between Monterey and San Benito counties. This is one of the easiest places in California to see the fault. The country is largely unmodified by human activity, and some of the fault displacement is by fault creep, unaccompanied by strong ground shaking. The slip rate is as high as it is anywhere in California, more than an inch (up to 34 mm) per year.

But close to Hollister, the slip rate abruptly falls to half its rate at Parkfield, less than two-thirds of an inch (14 to 17 mm) per year. The reason for this is the Calaveras Fault, which starts parallel to and close to the San Andreas Fault along State Highway 25 south of Paicines, and then turns northward through the city of Hollister itself, where the fault creeps at about the same rate as the San Andreas at San Juan Bautista to the west, about a half inch (15 mm) per year.

Because the fault is creeping in Hollister, it is immediately noticeable in the shady neighborhood of old houses north of Dunne City Park, especially to the Hollister Street Department (Figures 4-18 and 4-19). The fault passes beneath a garage, jamming its doors, and sidewalks and curbs are skewed to the right. The fault cuts diagonally across the intersections of Powell Street and Locust Avenue, continually re-breaking the asphalt surface, and angles up Park Hill north of town. The rate of creep on the Calaveras Fault is nearly as large as its predicted slip rate based on geology, and one might hope that all the slip would be taken up by creep and the fault would not be a source of large earthquakes. However, the Morgan Hill Earthquake (M 6.2) struck a section of the fault north of Hollister in 1984—evidence that the creeping section of the fault can generate moderate-size earthquakes, although probably not large ones.

At Calaveras Reservoir at the Santa Clara-Alameda County line northeast of Milpitas, the Calaveras Fault approaches the Hayward Fault, which angles to the northwest, taking more than half of the southern

Figure 4-18. Street map of part of Hollister near Dunne Park showing streets offset by fault creep on Calaveras Fault.

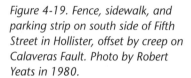

Figure 4-19. Fence, sidewalk, and parking strip on south side of Fifth Street in Hollister, offset by creep on Calaveras Fault. Photo by Robert Yeats in 1980.

Calaveras slip rate with it. The Hayward Fault leaves the foothills of the Diablo Range, passes beneath Interstate 680, and underlies the East Bay cities of Fremont, Hayward, San Leandro, Oakland, Berkeley, El Cerrito, and San Pablo, reaching San Pablo Bay at Pinole Point. Fault creep at a rate of a quarter-inch per year affects Hayward city streets just as at Hollister. In Berkeley, the fault crosses the University of California campus, passing beneath Memorial Stadium.

The Hayward Fault caused California's first great urban earthquake of M 7.1 in 1868, and forty years later it was tracked, along with the San Andreas Fault, by Andrew Lawson's State Earthquake Investigation Commission. The proximity of the Hayward Fault to Lawson's campus office undoubtedly added to his interest in studying the Hayward Earthquake as well as the San Francisco Earthquake.

North of its intersection with the Hayward Fault, the Calaveras Fault, with a diminished slip rate of a quarter inch (6 mm) per year, runs close to Interstate 680 near Pleasanton, Dublin, and San Ramon; this section of the fault sustained an earthquake of M 5.8 in 1861. Faults have been mapped northwest of San Ramon to Walnut Creek, but these faults are not clearly active. Instead, a zone of microearthquakes shifts northeast to the Concord Fault, which runs beneath Concord and Martinez and reaches Suisun Bay just east of the Benicia-Martinez Toll Bridge on Interstate 680.

Other active faults are mapped farther east, including the Greenville Fault and Ortigalita Fault, but slip rates are much lower. The easternmost foothills of the Diablo Range are made up of anticlines hiding blind thrusts, similar to those at Coalinga and Kettleman Hills. These blind thrusts were the source of the Vacaville-Winters earthquakes in 1892. An earthquake of M 6.5 on April 19, 1892 was followed by a M 6.2 aftershock on April 21 and a M 5.5 aftershock near Davis on April 30.

What happens to the Hayward and Calaveras faults north of San Pablo Bay and Suisun Bay?

The Rodgers Creek Fault (Figure 4-2) is the northern continuation of the Hayward Fault, although it is offset about three miles from a straight-line projection of the Hayward Fault across San Pablo Bay. This fault passes beneath Santa Rosa and ends southeast of Healdsburg in wine country. The slip rate of one-third inch (9 mm) per year for the Hayward Fault is used for the Rodgers Creek Fault as well. The Rodgers Creek Fault is locked, but its offset continuation, the Maacama Fault, has a creep rate slightly greater than a quarter inch (7 mm) per year at Willits, in Mendocino County. The Maacama Fault is marked on earthquake maps by a linear band of microearthquakes. High strain rates appear to be present along faults near Garberville in Humboldt County; these faults are hard to follow because of thick vegetation.

Farther east in the northern Coast Ranges, the Calaveras and Concord faults are traced across Suisun Bay to the Green Valley Fault and other faults in Napa County and Lake County. These faults are presumed to be active but their earthquake potential is poorly known. On September 3, 2000, at 1:30 a.m., an earthquake of M 5.2 struck a previously unknown strike-slip fault three miles southwest of Yountville in the Napa Valley, halfway between the Rodgers Creek and Green Valley faults. Twenty-five people were injured, one critically, and damage was estimated at more than $50 million. Governor Gray Davis declared this region a disaster area. Still farther east, at the west edge of the Sacramento Valley, large anticlines mask blind thrusts, as they do farther south at Coalinga.

The strike-slip faults of the northern Coast Ranges are subparallel to the San Andreas Fault, with lower slip rates and a less well defined hazard. The San Andreas Fault turns west at the Triple Junction near Cape Mendocino, but the fault zones farther east might continue north past Cape Mendocino east of Eureka (see Chapter 7).

San Andreas Fault Pioneers

Before discussing how we assess the earthquake hazard of faults of the San Andreas System, it's useful to consider some of the individuals who contributed to our understanding of the San Andreas Fault. The list of contributors is long and growing; I limit my discussion here to four geologists and two geophysicists who stand out in my mind.

The first was Andrew C. Lawson. Lawson was a pipe-smoking Canadian field geologist who established his professional reputation in the ancient rocks of western Ontario before moving to Vancouver, B.C. as a consultant. At the end of the 1890 field season, he received two job offers—one from G.K. Gilbert of the USGS, which he turned down, and another from the University of California, which he accepted. Tall and athletic, with a walrus mustache and short, dark beard, Lawson began to take graduate students on grueling field-mapping projects from his base at Berkeley, peppering them with questions about the rocks they were studying. Among his students, Lawson was known as "the King," and in his domain he was an absolute monarch. In 1893, he and his students discovered the great "rift" that transects the San Francisco Peninsula and named it after the San Andreas Reservoir through which it passes.

After the 1906 earthquake, "the King" was the natural choice to head up an investigation, which set the standard for scientific reporting on earthquakes from then to now. Lawson was a strong advocate for establishing the Seismological Society of America. Argumentative and temperamental, he was a stickler for clear scientific thinking and for the importance of geological field work. In later years he would become engaged in a long-running and colorful debate with Bailey Willis of Stanford University. After Lawson's wife died, he married a young woman and fathered a child at the age of eighty-seven, a time when he was establishing a separate reputation as a home builder. He was ninety when he died.

Grove Karl Gilbert of the USGS, a towering figure in American science, was in his sixties, nearly twenty years older than Lawson, when he found himself in Berkeley at the time of the San Francisco Earthquake. Although he was there on another assignment, he immediately began mapping the ground broken along the San Andreas Fault. Prior to 1906, only Gilbert had seen the geological results of a California earthquake: the 1872 Owens Valley Earthquake, which, like the San Francisco Earthquake, provided evidence that the crust on one side of the fault had moved right laterally with respect to the crust on the other side. Gilbert was a leader in structural geology and in the evolution of landforms, thereby combining geology and geography, and his background in mathematics and physics qualified him as an engineer. Gilbert mapped the surface rupture in the field and described the tortured terrain near Olema, in Marin County, that had been churned up in 1906. His descriptions are as applicable today in mapping the rupture of the 1999 Izmit, Turkey, Earthquake on the North Anatolian Fault as they were in 1906.

Yet both Lawson and Gilbert missed the main lesson of the San Francisco Earthquake—that the San Andreas Fault had moved horizontally many miles in its geologic past. They recognized that the 1906 earthquake had displaced the ground horizontally, but Lawson, especially, would continue to insist that the long-term motion on the fault was up and down, not side to side. Scientists such as Levi Noble of the USGS and Harry Wood and J.P. Buwalda of Caltech, who found evidence for large amounts of strike slip on sections of the San Andreas Fault, were shouted down.

The main problem was that most of California was still unmapped by geologists, so the significance of continental granite west of oceanic sediment, serpentine, and basalt was not fully appreciated. Into the breach stepped a tall, shy Stanford graduate from the Santa Maria area named Tom Dibblee. All Dibblee asked of life was to be able to do geologic field work, beginning with his pioneer family's Spanish land grant, Rancho San Julian, in western Santa Barbara County. Then he was hired by Richfield Oil Company to map the Coast Ranges, especially the Cuyama Valley west of Bakersfield, which his Richfield partner and mentor, Mason Hill, thought might contain undiscovered oil. Dibblee was rarely in the office. Most of the time, he was hiking over the chaparral- and mesquite-covered hills with a loaf of bread and some salami and cheese, mapping the geologic formations he found on the way. Many nights, he would roll out a sleeping bag beside his field vehicle. His field expenses were so small that other oil geologists who preferred motels and restaurants began to complain.

Field mapping is what a geologist will tell you he or she loves to do most. It's the equivalent of combat experience for an infantryman or flight time for a pilot. But few of us spend much time actually doing it, and when Dibblee was able to devote his life to making geologic maps in the field, he became the geologist's folk hero, mapping more California geology than any geologist before or since.

And mapping brought results. Despite one wildcatter's sneer that he could drink every drop of oil found in the Cuyama Valley, Richfield brought in two big oil fields in 1948 at the foot of Caliente Mountain, and the Elkhorn Café, a rancher's hangout in New Cuyama, blossomed into an oil-finder's watering hole. One of the reservoir sands was named the Dibblee Sand in honor of its discoverer.

But Dibblee and Hill had more to say, because in Dibblee's mapping in the Carrizo Plain east of the Cuyama Valley he had observed the mismatch of sedimentary rocks across the San Andreas Fault. He ranged along the entire San Andreas Fault from Point Arena to the Salton Sea, and in his mapping, he and Hill were able to match the rocks on the west side with those on the east. In 1953 they published a paper claiming that the displacement on the fault totaled hundreds of miles, leading to the conclusion that the right-lateral movements in 1857 and 1906 were only the latest in many hundreds of movements over millions of years. For the first time, Levi Noble (discussed in Part I), who had long advocated large-scale strike slip on the San Andreas Fault north of the San Gabriel Mountains, began to be taken seriously.

The Hill and Dibblee paper was published before plate tectonics came into fashion, and most geologists—including those in senior positions with my employer, Shell Oil Company, some of whom had studied at Berkeley—thought the idea was farfetched, even bizarre. But in the next fifteen years, plate tectonics became accepted by geologists and geophysicists, and the San Andreas was revealed as a great transform fault. A wild, crazy idea of the 1950s became the paradigm of the 1970s and still is today.

Part of the change was a field geologist's maxim: "The best geologist is the one who has seen the most rocks." Dibblee, now in his eighties and continuing his marathon mapping project as part of his Dibblee Foundation in Santa Barbara, has no peer. He has seen the most rocks.

It was clear that the San Andreas Fault had a long geologic history, but the human historical record is too short, less than two hundred years. How could the earthquake record be carried back into the geologic past to allow the past to foretell the future? As an undergraduate at the University of California at Riverside, Kerry Sieh had heard a talk by an engineering-geology consultant showing how backhoe excavations along the Hayward Fault in the Bay Area could locate the active fault precisely. After completing an undergraduate project on the nearby San Jacinto Fault, Sieh enrolled as a graduate student at Stanford University and spent a summer working on earthquake faults crossing the Alaska Pipeline route along with Gary Carver (of whom more will be said in Chapter 7). Later, Sieh found a small stream crossing the 1857 earthquake rupture on the north side of the San Gabriel Mountains—a stream named Pallett Creek, which had cut down through faulted peat deposits along the San Andreas Fault. Was it possible to study these deformed sediments like an archaeologist excavating a burial mound to identify past earthquakes before a historical record existed?

Sieh floated this idea with his faculty advisors at Stanford. Could he get a Ph.D. by mapping an area smaller than the Stanford Quad, studying soft sediments rather than hard rocks as most geologists did? Not likely, they said—except the dean of the School of Earth Sciences, Richard Jahns, an engineering geologist used to backhoe excavations in studying building foundations. Go for it, said Jahns.

And so, with a backhoe as his geology hammer, Sieh began to carve back the Pallett Creek excavations, slicing away layers like burial levels at an ancient city, collecting samples from buried peat bogs for radiocarbon dating. In the mid-1970s, I attended a meeting at Mammoth Lakes where Sieh displayed his bedsheet-sized trench logs on the wall, with detailed, inch-by-inch drawings of each layer showing faults cutting some layers and overlain by others, and vertical injections of sand that had been liquefied by strong shaking during prehistoric earthquakes (Figure 4-20). Sieh extended the San Andreas earthquake record from less than two centuries to more than fifteen hundred years, with fault ruptures providing evidence for at least nine earthquakes at Pallett Creek (Figure 4-21). The historical earthquakes could now be placed into a longer, more representative prehistoric perspective. The science of paleoseismology, envisioned along the Wasatch Fault in Utah by G.K. Gilbert almost a century earlier, had come to the San Andreas, and Pallett Creek was its Rosetta Stone.

All the people I have written about are geologists, yet geophysicists are now major players in earthquake investigations on the San Andreas and other faults. But at the time of the San Francisco Earthquake, geophysics was simply applied physics. Physicists invented the modern seismograph to measure earthquake waves and to learn about the internal structure of the Earth. Other instruments measured slight changes in the Earth's gravity and magnetic field. The object of geophysics was and is to apply the laws of physics to the Earth, and to quantify what had largely been a descriptive science.

The most important geophysicist in the early study of the San Andreas Fault was Harry Fielding Reid, whom Andrew Lawson described as the "first American geophysicist." Reid was born in Baltimore, Maryland, received his education at the new Johns Hopkins University

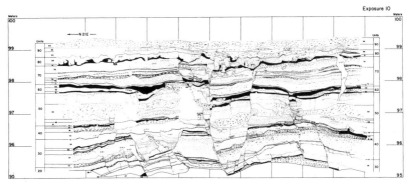

Figure 4-20. Sketch of part of a trench log at Pallett Creek drawn by Kerry Sieh, Caltech. Black layers are organic deposits suitable for radiocarbon dating. Faults are terminated upward by sediments deposited across them after an earthquake, permitting the earthquake caused by the faulting to be dated. Can you find evidence of eight earthquakes in this trench log? Reproduced with permission of American Geophysical Union.

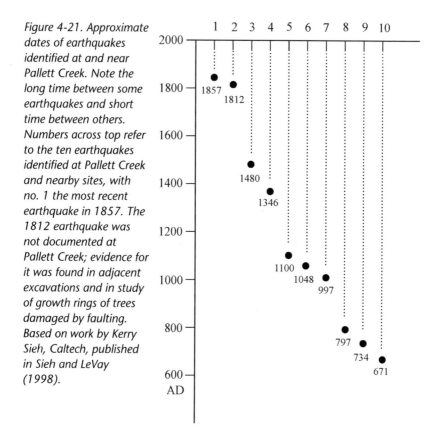

Figure 4-21. Approximate dates of earthquakes identified at and near Pallett Creek. Note the long time between some earthquakes and short time between others. Numbers across top refer to the ten earthquakes identified at Pallett Creek and nearby sites, with no. 1 most recent earthquake in 1857. The 1812 earthquake was not documented at Pallett Creek; evidence for it was found in adjacent excavations and in study of growth rings of trees damaged by faulting. Based on work by Kerry Sieh, Caltech, published in Sieh and LeVay (1998).

in Baltimore, and spent most of his professional life there. But a boyhood sojourn in Switzerland changed his life: he became a mountain climber. Mountaineering led him to study glaciers in the Alps, in the Pacific Northwest, and in Alaska. He wrote about an expedition to the Muir Glacier in Alaska in the *National Geographic*.

Like Gilbert, Reid was a physicist, a mathematician, and a geologist. He became interested in earthquakes as early as 1902, when he was put in charge of earthquake recordkeeping at the USGS. He was a natural choice for the State Earthquake Investigation Commission studying the San Francisco Earthquake. Among other things, Reid analyzed the seismograms of the 1906 earthquake, and in the final report on that earthquake he described the theory of the seismograph, the first paper on that subject published in the United States.

It isn't clear why Reid decided to compare geodetic surveys on both sides of the San Andreas Fault taken prior to the earthquake and afterward, but in doing so Reid went beyond describing the geology and the damage. He sought out the cause of the earthquake. A comparison of two nineteenth-century surveys showed crustal deformation in the same sense as the fault displacement during the earthquake. The meaning was clear: the crust was deforming elastically, building up strain that would be released ultimately in the 1906 earthquake. Perhaps the most important contribution to the State Earthquake Investigation Commission report was Reid's formulation of the elastic rebound theory of earthquakes. More than half a century before the theory of plate tectonics was generally accepted, Reid understood that great crustal blocks on both sides of the fault were moving inexorably, building up strain on the fault, and he thought this could lead to a forecast of the time of the next earthquake. Because the crustal blocks moved horizontally, Reid undoubtedly would have disagreed with Lawson that the long-term movement on the San Andreas Fault was up and down rather than sideways.

Seismologists would have made more important contributions to the study of the San Andreas Fault, but the 1906 earthquake was the last major earthquake on the fault, except for the moderate-sized earthquakes at Parkfield and small earthquakes on faults in the San Francisco Bay Area. A seismograph network operated by Perry Byerly of the University of California at Berkeley in northern California recorded the 1934 Parkfield Earthquake on the San Andreas Fault as well as other earthquakes on weaker parts of the San Andreas, Calaveras, and Hayward faults, so that these faults began to be illuminated by earthquake epicenters based on seismograph records in addition to being mapped in the field. Byerly was able to use the earthquake first motions in seismograms from several stations of the Berkeley network to prove that the 1934 Parkfield Earthquake was produced by strike slip on a northwest-striking fault, confirming the observations of the geologists. In so doing, Byerly showed that the seismologist could not only locate an earthquake and determine its size, but also learn about how the rupture takes place.

Paleoseismology and Segmentation of the San Andreas Fault

If the entire San Andreas Fault were to rupture at the same time, the resulting earthquake would be truly humongous, well over M 8. But no reputable scientist believes that this will happen, mainly because the central part of the fault is so weak (Figure 4-1). From San Juan Bautista to Parkfield and Cholame, the fault yields by fault creep or by small earthquakes like those at Parkfield. In contrast, the rupture zone of the 1857 Fort Tejon Earthquake from Cholame to Cajon Pass has almost no microseismicity (see Frontispiece), indicating that plate-tectonic strain is building up along the fault. Also, most of the rupture zone of the 1906 San Francisco Earthquake has essentially no microearthquakes, and here, too, the fault is building up strain toward the next earthquake. There seems to be no way that an earthquake relieving strain on either the 1906 section or 1857 section of the fault could propagate through the central weak section of the fault. Strain is not allowed to build up because the fault has been creeping, or it has been releasing strain in smaller, Parkfield-size earthquakes.

The goal of establishing segment boundaries on the fault is to limit the predicted size of an earthquake on any given section of the fault. Based on its seismicity, the San Andreas Fault can be divided into a locked 1906 segment, a weak central segment, a locked 1857 segment, and a southern segment southeast of Cajon Pass that hasn't suffered an earthquake in at least three hundred years (Figure 4-1).

Paleoseismology and the historical record suggest that the 1906 segment can be further divided into two segments. The last prehistoric earthquake on the fault north of San Francisco took place after 1650 A.D., less than two hundred fifty years before the 1906 earthquake. This was after Francis Drake and several Spanish explorers reconnoitered the north coast but before anyone keeping records lived there. An earlier earthquake struck between 1270 and 1450 A.D., and at Point Arena at least five surface-rupturing earthquakes have occurred in the past two thousand years, including the 1906 earthquake.

But in the San Francisco Peninsula and Santa Cruz Mountains, the displacement in 1906 was much less than it was farther north, suggesting that not all the built-up strain in this area was released in 1906 and that perhaps other, smaller earthquakes might release this added strain. The Loma Prieta Earthquake did indeed strike the Santa Cruz Mountains in 1989, although it did not occur on the San Andreas Fault itself. A previous historical earthquake in June 1838, also might have occurred on this section of the fault system, but it isn't clear that this earthquake took place on the San Andreas Fault. Farther south, the three-year-old mission at San Juan Bautista was destroyed by an earthquake in October, 1800. This same area was struck by an earthquake of M 6 on April 24, 1890, throwing a railroad bridge across the Pajaro River out of line about one-and-a-half feet near the San Andreas Fault. This earthquake probably struck the fault north of San Juan Bautista. So the return times of historical earthquakes on this southern section of the fault have been less than a hundred years (keeping in mind that the earlier earthquakes might have occurred on faults other than the San Andreas itself), whereas the last two earthquakes north of the Golden Gate were separated by as much as two hundred fifty years. The conclusion is that 1906-type earthquakes rupture the entire fault from north of San Juan Bautista to Point Arena and beyond, whereas shorter sections of the fault south of San Francisco rupture more frequently in intervals of less than a hundred years.

The weak part of the fault south of the Santa Cruz Mountains may be subdivided into a creeping section between San Juan Bautista and Parkfield and a section from Parkfield to Cholame that ruptures every few decades, the last times in 1922, 1934, and 1966. The general idea behind these segmentation schemes is that the San Andreas Fault is weakest north of Parkfield, stronger at Parkfield and the Santa Cruz Mountains, and strongest north of San Francisco and south of Cholame. Where the fault is weakest, it ruptures by fault creep or small earthquakes. Where it is strongest, more strain builds up before the earthquake, so that the recurrence interval between successive earthquakes is longer. When the earthquake finally strikes, it has more strain to release, so it's larger and more destructive.

If we could classify segments in this way, the maximum earthquake size in any given segment of the fault could be predicted. Such an earthquake would be *characteristic* of this section of the fault. Displacements on successive earthquakes would be the same, and the boundaries between segments would be the same through several earthquake cycles.

But paleoseismic investigations of backhoe trenches across the 1857 segment and the segment farther southeast that has not ruptured historically give a more complicated picture (Figure 4-22). In the Carrizo Plain, Lisa Grant of the University of California at Irvine and Kerry Sieh have shown that the return times between successive earthquakes are variable. Northwest of Cajon Pass, where a prehistoric earthquake record has been obtained at other sites beside Pallett Creek and Wrightwood, earthquake ruptures terminate at different places. The 1812 earthquake was accompanied by rupture of a smaller stretch of the fault than the 1857 earthquake, and the two earthquakes started and stopped at different places. Those two earthquakes were separated by only forty-five years, yet more than one hundred forty years have elapsed without another earthquake in that region.

From San Bernardino southeastward, the last earthquake struck around 1680 A.D., but at one trench site near San Bernardino even the 1680 earthquake cannot be identified. This earthquake, and perhaps an earlier one around 1480, might have struck the Coachella Valley segment southeast of San Bernardino as well as part of the 1857 segment, even though one trench site finds no evidence for the 1680 earthquake (Figure 4-22).

Paleoseismologists from the Southern California Earthquake Center and the USGS have been trying to resolve these problems, which requires that they agree on an earthquake chronology all along the fault, continuing the project begun by Kerry Sieh at Pallett Creek twenty-five years ago. If the paleoseismic history for each part of the fault were better known, the future behavior of the fault could be forecast more accurately.

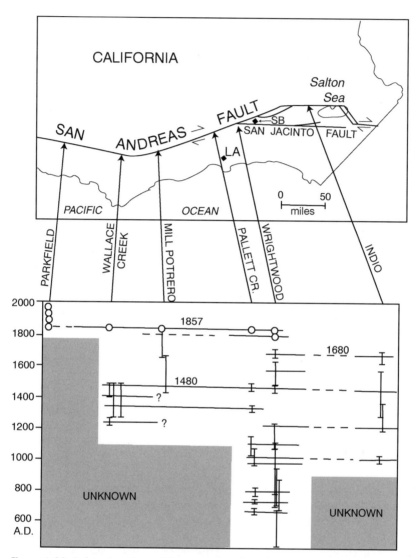

Figure 4-22. Paleoseismology of the central and southern San Andreas Fault. Earthquake history based on a few trenching sites where paleoseismological evidence is available, including Wallace Creek, Pallett Creek, Wrightwood, and Indio (located on map at top. Earthquakes at Parkfield and in 1857 and 1812 are historical (circles); others based on radiocarbon dates, with I-symbols giving the uncertainty in radiocarbon dating. Earthquakes shown as 1680 and 1480 could represent more than one event too closely spaced to discriminate with radiocarbon dating. Shaded area: no data. LA, Los Angeles; SB, San Bernadino. Based on work by Lisa Grant, University of California Irvine; Kerry Sieh, Caltech; and Ray Weldon, University of Oregon.

The problem is difficult for three reasons: (1) trenches along the fault might not show evidence for all the prehistoric earthquakes; (2) earthquakes must be bracketed in time by radiocarbon dates of the youngest faulted carbon-bearing layer and the oldest unfaulted layer, and in California's dry climate, charcoal or peat may be absent; and (3) uncertainties in radiocarbon dating limit the dating of any earthquake closer than a few decades, which means that the correlation between earthquakes at different paleoseismic sites along the fault is uncertain.

In the Carrizo Plain, the last earthquake prior to 1857 struck around 1480 A.D., and an earthquake of about this age has been recorded at Pallett Creek, at Wrightwood, and at Indio near the Salton Sea. If this represents a single earthquake extending all the way from the Carrizo Plain to Indio, it would have a magnitude of at least M 8, about twice the size of the 1857 shock. But a sequence of earthquakes along the North Anatolian Fault in Turkey keeps us from jumping to this conclusion. An earthquake of M 7.8 struck the eastern end of the North Anatolian Fault in 1939, and every few years another earthquake would be produced by rupture of the next segment of the fault to the west, with what was thought to be the last earthquake in 1967. But after a lapse of thirty-two years, a M 7.4 earthquake ruptured the next segment to the west on August 17, 1999, killing more than fifteen thousand people. The next segment still to rupture is close to Istanbul, Turkey's largest city, with a population of ten million people.

Suppose that this sequence of earthquakes had struck five hundred years earlier, from 1439 to 1499 A.D., but we could only estimate the ages from radiocarbon dating. Even assuming that each earthquake could be closely bracketed by radiocarbon dates, the uncertainties in these dates could make it look like a single earthquake had ruptured one end of the fault to the other. Very likely the 1480 A.D. "earthquake" was not a single monster event but a series of smaller earthquakes, rupturing the fault like ripping the buttons off a shirt.

Reid's elastic rebound theory predicts that when the strain builds up, an earthquake follows. We think that the strain accumulates at a constant rate based on plate tectonics. If this is so, then the earthquakes should reappear at regular intervals, like Halley's Comet. But at Indio, the 1680 A.D. event was preceded by earthquakes at around 1480, 1350, and 1000 A.D., with return times varying from 130 to more than 300 years. At Pallett Creek, about 330 earthquake-free years preceded the two historical earthquakes of 1812 and 1857, but only 130 years separated the 1480 and 1350 events. Before that, there were clusters of three earthquakes between 700 and 800 A.D. and between 1000 and 1100 A.D. The earthquake history for Pallett Creek, Wrightwood, and Pitman Canyon, sites that are relatively close together with a well-preserved record, is astonishingly different.

So the more we learn from paleoseismology and the closer we get to the truth, the more questions we raise about earthquake size and recurrence intervals. The section of the San Andreas Fault north of San Francisco ruptures at about two hundred fifty-year intervals, and less than a hundred years has elapsed since the 1906 earthquake. Does this mean that this section of the fault is not close to sustaining another earthquake? The Carrizo Plain had not had an earthquake for about three hundred seventy years before the Fort Tejon Earthquake of 1857. Is it relatively unlikely that another earthquake will occur there soon, nearly one hundred fifty years after Fort Tejon, even though there was a cluster of three earthquakes there between 1250 and 1350 A.D.?

From Cajon Pass southward, no earthquake has struck the Coachella Valley and Indio segments of the San Andreas Fault since 1680 A.D., more than three hundred years ago. The recurrence intervals before 1680 A.D. were 200, 130, and 350 years, so the time since the last earthquake is getting close to the maximum recurrence interval for the last four earthquakes. In addition, the 1992 Landers Earthquake (M 7.3) in the Mojave Desert north of the San Andreas Fault might have increased the stress on the San Andreas Fault, leading to a domino effect. If we have learned anything from our studies, we should get ready for a large earthquake on the fault between Cajon Pass and the Salton Sea.

Paleoseismology and Segmentation of Other Faults in the San Andreas Fault System

The San Jacinto Fault has been divided by the Southern California Earthquake Center into seven segments, based on the high seismicity and structural variability of the fault zone. The San Bernardino Valley and San Jacinto Valley segments were shaken by an earthquake of M 6.4 on July 22, 1899, followed five months later by an earthquake on Christmas Day of M 7.1—which would have been catastrophic with today's population. The same area was shaken by an earthquake of M 6.8 on April 21, 1918; this earthquake was investigated by J.C. Branner of Stanford (see Part 1). Another earthquake of M 6.2 struck this area on July 23, 1923. Several separate faults make up the San Jacinto Fault Zone at its northern end, and the 1899 and 1918 earthquakes might have ruptured different faults. None of these earthquakes has been identified in paleoseismic trenches or at the surface. Was this a cluster of earthquakes to be followed by a long period of quiescence, or is the large number of earthquakes a cause for alarm?

Farther southeast, the fault is in barren desert terrain. The Anza segment has not been the source of a large historical earthquake, but paleoseismic investigations show earthquakes there in 1210, 1530, and 1750 A.D., separated by 320 and 220 years, respectively, with no earthquake for the past 250 years. The next segment is Borrego Mountain, with a surface-rupturing earthquake on April 9, 1968 that was studied in detail by the USGS. Malcolm Clark of the USGS dug a paleoseismic trench—the world's first—along the fault and worked out a recurrence interval of about two hundred years, based on offset of sediment deposited in Lake Cahuilla, a prehistoric and larger version of the modern Salton Sea. The Working Group on California Earthquake Probabilities decided at a meeting on November 23, 1987 that the southern end of the San Jacinto Fault was too poorly known to estimate the probability of an earthquake on that segment. The next day, as working-group members were returning to their homes, the Superstition Hills segment of the fault produced two earthquakes—the Elmore Ranch Earthquake of M 6.2 and the Superstition Hills Earthquake of M 6.6 (Figure 4-16). Paleoseismic trenches revealed earlier earthquakes with recurrence intervals of one hundred fifty to three hundred years.

The Elsinore Fault has also been divided into several segments. The Coyote Mountain segment just north of the Mexican border sustained earthquakes about four hundred, twelve hundred, and two thousand years ago, a longer interval than for any paleoseismic sites along the San Jacinto or San Andreas faults. Farther north, the Glen Ivy segment near the city of Elsinore has evidence for five or six earthquakes since 1060 A.D., with the most recent the M 6 Temescal Valley Earthquake in May 1910. This recurrence interval of one hundred fifty to two hundred years is comparable to those on the San Andreas Fault. The Whittier segment, with its lower slip rate, sustained an earthquake between fourteen hundred and twenty-two hundred years ago and an earlier earthquake between three thousand and thirty-one hundred years ago—a recurrence interval of about fifteen hundred years.

Not enough paleoearthquake data are available for strike-slip faults west of the Whittier-Elsinore Fault Zone. Slip rates are low, and the return time for earthquakes at any given site is expected to be many thousands of years. This has an advantage in that radiocarbon dating in trenches would be unlikely to confuse one earthquake with another, as is the case for the San Andreas Fault where successive earthquakes might be separated by less than a hundred years.

The paleoseismic history of the faults east of San Francisco Bay is less well-known than it is in southern California, despite the perception that the Hayward and Calaveras faults have a fairly high probability of rupture in the next thirty years (see Chapter 8). Part of the problem is that these faults move in part by earthquakes and in part by fault creep, and separating these modes of slip in a paleoseismic excavation can be difficult. The Hayward Fault ruptured in 1868, probably as far north as Oakland. The northern end of the fault ruptured prior to the time of recordkeeping (prior to 1776 A.D.) in a still-larger earthquake, leading to a high probability of another earthquake in the near future on that part of the fault.

The Calaveras Fault can be divided into southern, central, and northern segments. The southern segment, which includes the city of Hollister, is largely creeping and has relatively low microseismicity. The central segment is also creeping, but it also accounted for several moderate-size earthquakes, the largest of which were the 1979 Coyote Lake Earthquake (M 5.9) and the 1984 Morgan Hill Earthquake (M 6.2). The northern segment, north of Calaveras Reservoir, has relatively little microseismicity but was the source of an earthquake of M 5.6 in 1861 in the San Ramon Valley. Paleoseismic trench investigations near the southern end of this segment show evidence for five or six earthquakes in the past twenty-five hundred years, an average recurrence interval of five hundred years.

The limited amount of paleoseismic data has led to the Bay Area Paleoseismology Experiment (BAPEX), led by Dave Schwartz of the USGS and including several consulting firms and university scientists. BAPEX is excavating trenches at a large number of sites to work out the earthquake history for the past several thousand years.

Summary and the Future

This chapter has shown where the San Andreas Fault and other faults of the San Andreas System are located so that you can understand where these faults are and perhaps visit them, just as one might visit active volcanoes such as Mount Shasta or Mount Lassen. Even though the San Andreas Fault is as much a part of the personality of the state as golden beaches, vineyards, spectacular mountains, and the movie industry, the fault is rarely mentioned in tourist brochures or the Chamber of Commerce (see Part 1). Yet the landscape formed by the San Andreas Fault has a raw beauty to it, and I'd like to think that one doesn't have to be a geologist to appreciate it. Any flight to San Francisco, Los Angeles, or San Diego from distant cities, as well as the San Francisco-Los Angeles Shuttle (Figure 4-10), allows an opportunity to view the fault on a clear day, either as a linear belt of furrowed ground or as a sharply linear valley or bay, such as the Gualala River or Tomales Bay. In the central Coast Ranges, the fault shows up best in early morning or late afternoon flights, when the sun angle is low and emphasizes ground shadows (Figure 4-10). The fault is obscured where it is covered by houses or shopping centers, but some day it will reassert itself in another earthquake.

We know quite a lot about the San Andreas Fault and somewhat less about its satellite faults. The slip rate is fairly well known, and variations in slip rate can be explained by slip being taken up on branching faults such as the Hosgri, Calaveras, or San Jacinto. But we know less about the earthquake prehistory: too few sites, ambiguity in interpretation, and uncertainties in our geologic clock, radiocarbon dating. Because of this, we are hampered in advising the public on what to expect on a given fault in the next thirty years or so. We couch our forecasts in terms of uncertainty, and this annoys people, but at least we are honest in saying what we don't know.

Much has been learned about the San Andreas Fault since a focused research program was started by the federal and state governments in the 1970s. Discoveries early in the twentieth century were dominated by geologists, but as seismic instruments have become highly sophisticated and have been supplemented by space geodesy using the Global Positioning System, geophysicists are making major contributions, especially in interpreting the environment where earthquakes start and stop, miles below the Earth's surface. A proposal has been made to drill holes in the fault zone to get closer to the action. Drilling would be extremely expensive, but there's no substitute for actually sampling the rocks at depths and temperatures where an earthquake will ensue when those rocks break.

The science is still in its early stages. Each new earthquake is still a surprise, but seismic and geodetic arrays in place at the time of the next earthquake will ensure that more will be learned from that earthquake than from earthquakes that struck even twenty years ago. The scientific community is waiting (along with the rest of the population of California) for the next large San Andreas Fault earthquake; the last one was in 1906. For this reason, many California scientists went to Turkey to study the Izmit Earthquake on the North Anatolian Fault, in hopes that lessons learned there can be applied to the San Andreas Fault in advance of the next, inevitable earthquake.

Suggestions for Further Reading

Clarke, T. 1996. *California Fault*. New York: Ballantine Books. 417p.

Hill, M.L. 1981. San Andreas Fault: History of concepts. *Geological Society of America Bulletin*, v. 92, pp. 112-31.

Sieh, K., and S. LeVay. 1998. *The Earth in Turmoil*. New York: W.H. Freeman. 324p. Chapters 3, 4, and 5 discuss the San Andreas Fault; Chapter 4 is Sieh's personal account of his research on the fault.

Wallace, R.E., editor. 1990. *The San Andreas Fault System, California*. U.S. Geol. Survey Prof. Paper 1515. 293p. Estimates magnitude and recurrence interval for active faults in region, including evidence for slip rate and paleoearthquakes, where available. Contains maps locating the San Andreas Fault.

❦ 5 ❦
The Transverse Ranges: LA in the Squeeze

"The extraordinary and horrifying earthquake which this mission suffered on the memorable day of the glorious Apostle Saint Thomas completely ruined the church. It destroyed the nave, several statues and paintings, and ruined most of the adornments . . . Some of the buildings have been flattened to the ground . . . A hundred of the neophytes' houses and the pozolera (?) kitchen, buildings of adobe(?) and roofed with tile cannot be used; even the adobe wall of the garden, covered with tile, has either fallen down or is out of line to such an extent that the damaged parts will provide scarcely any material which may be used for later reconstruction."

Fray Mariano Payeras and Fray Antonio Ripoll, 31 December 1812, Annual Report from Misión Purísima Concepción for 1812: Santa Barbara Mission Archives Document CMD 941.

Prelude

The Alta California settlements north of Misión San Gabriel Arcángel were despondent as winter began in December, 1812. Aside from the Franciscan missionaries, nobody wanted to live in Alta California, and some of the Europeans were there to avoid serving a jail sentence in Mexico. Contacts with the outside world withered. Mexico was in revolt, and Spain itself was struggling against a puppet monarch installed by the French emperor, Napoleon. There was no time for Spain's most distant and least-promising colony.

The colonial cultural centers were the five Franciscan missions: San Buenaventura and Santa Barbara, founded by Fray Junípero Serra, along with a presidio at Santa Barbara; La Purísima Concepción and San Fernando Rey de España, founded a few years after his death; and Santa Inés, founded in 1804. The missions thrived because of the use of the Chumash Indians as a labor force under harsh conditions. Resettlement of the Chumash from their villages and *temescales* in the countryside to crowded, unsanitary *rancherías* surrounding the mission buildings decimated their numbers from European diseases. Still, the construction of church buildings continued; vineyards were planted; and wheat, corn, and vegetables were grown in nearby fields. Earthquakes in 1800 and 1806 had caused little damage.

On the morning of December 8, an earthquake destroyed the church at San Juan Capistrano only six years after it was completed, burying forty Indians in the rubble. Buildings at San Gabriel and San Fernando were also damaged. The earthquake was also felt in the San Bernardino Valley, of interest because many years later it would be learned that this earthquake actually originated not in the Los Angeles Basin but on the San Andreas Fault northwest of San Bernardino (see Chapter 4).

Less than two weeks later, at about 10 A.M. on December 21, a massive earthquake struck the coastal region from San Fernando to La Purísima in the Santa Maria Valley, followed by a second, possibly stronger shock fifteen minutes later. The mission and presidio at Santa Barbara were severely damaged, as well as the Ranchería Mescaltitan, causing the Indians to flee. The missions at La Purísima and San Buenaventura also suffered damage, and the earthquake was also felt as far as Santa Inés and San Fernando.

On the heels of the earthquake, a great wave, or tsunami, struck Santa Barbara, carrying a ship up a coastal canyon and leading to the evacuation of the Mescaltitan ranchería. The earthquake probably originated on a reverse fault in the Santa Barbara Channel, with the tsunami generated by the earthquake or by a submarine landslide.

Despite this violence early in its history, the coastal Santa Barbara, Ventura, and Los Angeles regions expanded under U.S. rule without any consideration of earthquake hazard—Santa Barbara as a resort community, Ventura as an agricultural and petroleum center, and Los Angeles as the center of growth in southern California. The Santa Barbara Earthquake of 1925 (see Part I) was only a temporary deterrent to growth, and only with the Sylmar Earthquake of 1971 did Angelenos finally recognize that earthquakes—along with brush fires, landslides, smog, and winter storms—were a threat to the California golden dream.

The coastline from Ventura to Point Conception beyond Santa Barbara is unusual in that it faces south, not west, toward the mountainous Northern Channel Islands, a submerged mountain range that projects westward from the Santa Monica Mountains north of Los Angeles (Figure 4-7). The Santa Ynez Range and Topa Topa Mountains rise north of Santa Barbara and Ventura, and farther east are the San Gabriel and San Bernardino Mountains, raised up because the Big Bend of the San Andreas Fault causes continental crust of the North America Plate to collide with crust of the Pacific Plate (Figures 5-1 and 4-14). These are collectively known as the Transverse Ranges, so called because they are transverse to the normal north-south trend of ranges along the Pacific margin of North America.

The mountain ranges are raised to the highest elevations in southern California, and between them the crust is dropped down to depths of many miles—although this fact is hidden by great thicknesses of sediment beneath the valleys, including the world's thickest deposits of Pleistocene age in the Santa Clara Valley south of Fillmore. From

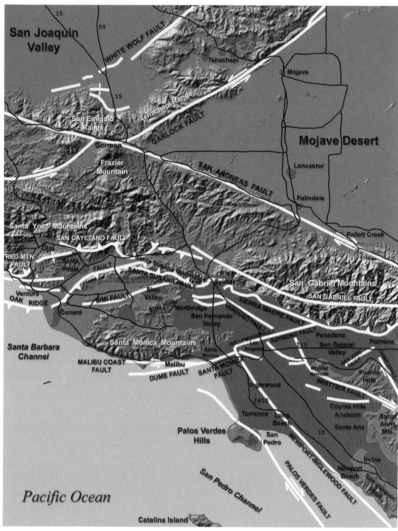

Figure 5-1. Computer-generated topographic map of central Transverse Ranges, including Ventura Basin, San Fernando Valley, Los Angeles Basin, and San Gabriel Valley. Mountains flanking these lowlands (Santa Ynez, Santa Monica, and San Gabriel mountains) trend east-west, leading to their designation as Transverse Ranges. East-west faults in the Transverse Ranges are characterized by left-lateral strike slip and by reverse displacement. The Red Mountain, Oak Ridge, San Cayetano, Santa Susana, and Sierra Madre reverse faults pose a major threat to the Los Angeles metropolitan region. The San Andreas Fault strikes west-northwest, part of its Big Bend across the Transverse Ranges. The northwest-striking Palos Verdes, Newport-Inglewood, and Whittier faults in the Los Angeles Basin are right-lateral strike-slip faults of the Peninsular Ranges, including the Santa Ana Mountains.

west to east, these thick basins of sediment include the Santa Barbara Channel, the Ventura Basin, the San Fernando Valley, the Los Angeles Basin, and the San Gabriel and San Bernardino valleys.

Great thicknesses of sediment resulted in vast accumulations of oil and gas in the Ventura and Los Angeles basins and in the Santa Barbara Channel, adding to the wealth of southern California. In the first few decades of the twentieth century, Los Angeles was the Saudi Arabia of world oil; a new discovery would depress the price of crude oil throughout the world. The wildcat wells and seismic profiles used by the petroleum industry to define the subsurface wealth of southern California now serve an additional purpose: they help define earthquake faults, often to depths of several miles.

This chapter considers the earthquake hazard of the Transverse Ranges, which is dominated not by San Andreas-type strike-slip faults but by reverse faults, in which one block rides up over the other. As a result, the Transverse Ranges are being squeezed together so that the central Coast Ranges and San Joaquin Valley are being forced closer to the Peninsular Ranges south of Los Angeles by about a quarter inch (5–8 mm) per year (Figure 5-2). Right-lateral strike-slip faults west of the San Andreas Fault pose an additional hazard. One of these was the source of the 1933 Long Beach Earthquake (Part I and Chapter 4). In addition, active left-lateral faults are found in the Santa Monica Mountains and on the Northern Channel Islands, although none of these faults has produced a severe earthquake in historic time.

Coping with Reverse Faults

The San Andreas Fault is easy to see from an airplane as a long, narrow furrow of disturbed ground. Reverse faults are harder to see because they generally are strongly curved in map or aerial view, following the base of a mountain. For example, the hills between Fillmore and Piru north of the Santa Clara Valley are underlain by contorted sedimentary rocks that are five to twenty million years old. Yet the Santa Clara Valley itself is underlain by a great thickness of flat-lying Pleistocene sediments, with much of these deposits less than a million years old. East of Fillmore, State Highway 126, on the northern edge of the valley, runs along the trace of the active San Cayetano Fault, probably the fastest-moving reverse fault in southern California. But the fault itself is difficult to see, in part because it is partly buried by landslides that might have been triggered by prehistoric earthquakes. On its south side, the valley is separated from Oak Ridge by another great reverse fault, the Oak Ridge Fault, also marked by massive landslides. The Santa Clara Valley is in the footwall of both the San Cayetano Fault and Oak Ridge Fault, and the mountains on both sides are in the hanging walls of these faults (Figure 5-3).

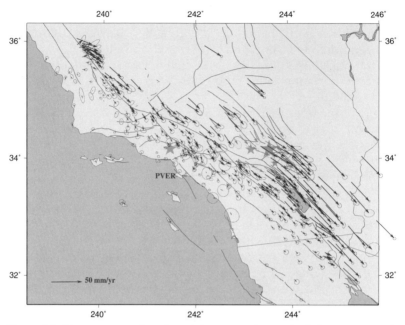

Figure 5-2. Measurement of motion of the mountains north of the Ventura and Los Angeles Basins relative to Palos Verdes Hills (PVER), which is assumed to be stationary. This is the only difference between this plot and Figure 3-16, which shows motion relative to the North America Plate. Both are based on the Global Positioning System. Base of each arrow locates the survey station, and the length and direction of each arrow give the motion of the station relative to PVER. Circles and ellipses at arrow tips give the uncertainty in measurement. Thin, curved lines show active faults. The locations of large earthquakes since 1990 are shown as stars, with the size of the star proportional to magnitude. The stations north and northwest of PVER are moving toward PVER at a rate of a quarter inch (5–8 mm) per year. Shortening is also taking place across the Santa Barbara Channel and Ventura Basin. Image prepared at UCLA for the Southern California Earthquake Center and provided courtesy of Kenneth W. Hudnut, USGS and Southern California Integrated GPS Network (SCIGN).

Because the Ventura Basin has been subjected to an intensive oil drilling campaign lasting more than a hundred years, wildcat wells have punched through the ancient Tertiarydeposits and crossed the San Cayetano Fault into flat-lying Pleistocene deposits beneath. Oil fields have been discovered in Pleistocene deposits beneath the Oak Ridge Fault. The Oak Ridge and San Cayetano faults are not vertical like the San Andreas, but they dip gently south and north, away from the Santa Clara Valley. So the Santa Clara Valley, narrow at the surface, is many miles wide beneath the surface, squeezed together by north-south crustal compression and displacement on the Oak Ridge and San Cayetano faults, acting collectively as a nutcracker (Figure 5-3).

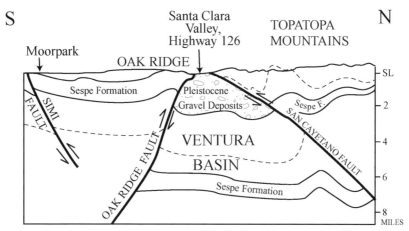

Figure 5-3. The Ventura Basin is being squeezed together by two reverse faults, the Oak Ridge Fault on the south and the San Cayetano Fault on the north, which are acting together like a giant nutcracker. GPS measurements show that the Topatopa Mountains are moving toward Oak Ridge and Moorpark at about a quarter inch (5–8 mm) per year. The absence of major earthquakes on these faults in recorded history leads to a lack of concern by local residents about a local earthquake on one of these faults. However, evidence from backhoe excavations shows that the San Cayetano Fault experienced a large, surface-rupturing earthquake shortly before the establishment of Spanish missions.

The San Cayetano Fault is hard to detect at the surface without oil-well data, but blind thrusts are even harder to pick up. The Whittier Narrows Earthquake of October 1, 1987 ruptured a blind thrust that is miles beneath the surface, beneath the deepest oil wells. Its surface expression is the Montebello Hills of east Los Angeles, raised up by compression into an anticline that houses a giant oil field (Figure 5-4). This fold, like the Coalinga Anticline associated with the May 1983 Coalinga Earthquake (Chapter 4), grew by successive earthquakes on a blind thrust. It's possible to map this thrust only indirectly by studying the folded rocks above it and by studying the geodetic changes from surveyors' monuments that moved relative to one another during the earthquake. With more careful analysis, the Whittier Narrows Fault has been imaged by the distribution of earthquake aftershocks and by seismic profiles obtained by the petroleum industry in the search for oil and gas. But these methods, although useful, are not quite the same as standing directly on the San Andreas Fault, with its obvious effect on the countryside. As a result, different scientists, like the proverbial blind Hindus feeling different parts of an elephant, have different views of the hidden fault. Reverse faults pose an additional hazard. The hanging wall, the block of rock on top of the fault that moves relatively upward, seems to suffer greater damage than the footwall. In the Chi-

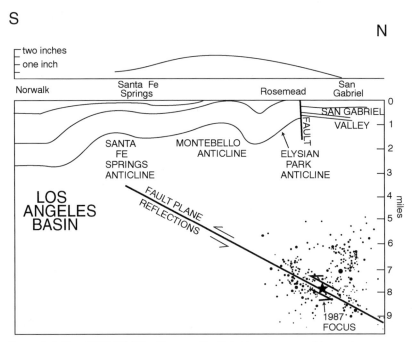

Figure 5-4. The 1987 Whittier Narrows Earthquake was caused by rupture on a blind-thrust fault. Although the fault cannot be observed at the surface or in oil wells, it is imaged by the fault-plane solution (Chapter 3) of the earthquake focus, the distribution of aftershocks, and direct observations on seismic profiles obtained by the petroleum industry in the search for oil and gas. The uplift pattern of the 1987 earthquake, as determined by Jian Lin of Woods Hole Oceanographic Institution and Ross Stein of the U.S. Geological Survey, showed a broad uplifted area over Montebello Anticline extending south to Santa Fe Springs Anticline. Maximum coseismic uplift was nearly two inches. Imaging of fault plane by John Shaw, Harvard University; and Peter Shearer, University of California at San Diego; geological interpretation by Gary J. Huftile, of Queensland University of Technology, and the author.

Chi, Taiwan, Earthquake of September 21, 1999, buildings close to the earthquake reverse fault on the hangingwall side underwent near-total destruction. This is a problem for the growing cities of the Transverse Ranges. People pay more to build their homes high in the hills, where there is less smog and more view. But if these view homes are in the hanging wall of a major reverse fault, they might be subject to greater damage than houses on the less-desirable lowlands of the footwall.

Ventura Basin and the Santa Barbara Channel

Earthquakes are not part of the culture of Ventura. The great earthquake of 1812 was too far back in time to have any meaning to the people who live there now. Ventura County is a prosperous place with a benign climate, and the major concern is avoiding the overdevelopment, traffic jams, and smog of Los Angeles, its neighbor looming across the Santa Monica Mountains. Citrus groves have not yet been displaced by housing subdivisions in the Santa Clara Valley, and the beaches are less crowded than they are farther south. I once testified to the Ventura County Board of Supervisors about active faults in a landfill east of Santa Paula. The supervisors listened to me politely and then voted to approve the landfill, faults or not. Earthquakes are a San Fernando Valley problem, a Los Angeles problem, but surely not a Ventura problem.

But north of the Ventura Basin, its center marked by the Santa Clara Valley, are two major north-dipping reverse faults—the San Cayetano Fault, mentioned above, with a slip rate of about one-quarter to one-third inch (6–9 mm) per year; and the Red Mountain Fault west of the Ventura River, with a slip rate officially estimated as lower, but which I believe to be in the same range as that of the San Cayetano (Figure 5-1). The east end of the San Cayetano Fault is north of Piru in the valley of Piru Creek, and the fault follows the base of the hills adjacent to Highway 126 to Fillmore, curves up Goodenough Road across Sespe Creek, crosses the south slopes of San Cayetano Mountain and Santa

Figure 5-5. San Cayetano Fault (upper left to lower right) in Silverthread Oil Field in Upper Ojai Valley. Rocks in hanging wall are older than Pliocene and Pleistocene rocks in the footwall. Photo by Robert Yeats.

Paula Peak past Thomas Aquinas College and the Upper Ojai Valley (Figure 5-5), and ends north of the Dennison Grade at the eastern entrance to the Ojai Valley. The northern edge of the Ojai Valley is not marked by an active fault, but south of the Ojai and Upper Ojai valleys, Sulphur Mountain rises up within the Ventura Basin on a blind deeper strand of the San Cayetano Fault that bridges the gap between the surface traces of the San Cayetano and Red Mountain faults. West of the Ventura River, the Red Mountain Fault sweeps around the north side of the Ventura Avenue Oil Field, reaches the coast at Rincon Point, and continues offshore south of Carpinteria, almost to Santa Barbara. Trench excavations on the San Cayetano Fault near Piru show that the most recent earthquake, which could have been larger than M 7, struck not long before the historical period, although no date is yet available.

South of the Santa Clara Valley rises Oak Ridge, uplifted along the south-dipping Oak Ridge Fault, with a slip rate less than one-quarter inch (4–5 mm) per year (Figure 5-3). The maximum displacement is probably at South Mountain, which towers over the city of Santa Paula. West of South Mountain, Oak Ridge decreases in elevation, and south of Saticoy, now a suburb of Ventura, Oak Ridge ends altogether. But the fault keeps going underground beneath housing developments south of the Santa Paula Freeway in east Ventura, largely as a left-lateral strike-slip fault that creates very little topography. The evidence for its activity consists of small uplifted pressure ridges of gravel called the Montalvo Mounds, with one east of Victoria Avenue south of the Ventura County Government Center, and another one farther west beneath the appropriately named Knoll Drive, now an industrial park. The pressure ridge near Victoria Avenue used to be a sizeable hill, but because it was made up of deformed gravel layers from the Santa Clara River, the gravel, a valuable resource, is being quarried away, and soon only flat ground will remain, ready for houses.

Satellite measurements from the Global Positioning System (Figure 5-2) show that the shortening across the Transverse Ranges, at a rate of a quarter inch (5–8 mm) per year, is concentrated on these two faults, the Oak Ridge and San Cayetano, together with the Red Mountain fault, which have been accumulating elastic strain for the next earthquake for more than two hundred years, with no earthquake releasing strain since the founding of the San Buenaventura Mission in 1782. It seems likely to me that one of these three fast-moving faults is likely to sustain an earthquake in the near future, but I can't be specific about how long the "near future" is likely to be, or which one of the faults will go first.

Another reason that Oak Ridge ends near Saticoy is that a deep strand of the Oak Ridge Fault follows a weak layer of rock nearly four miles deep beneath downtown Ventura and pushes up along the Ventura

Avenue Anticline to the north (Figure 3-9), site of a billion-barrel oil field. Displacement on the Oak Ridge Fault at Santa Paula took place at the same time as folding and uplift of the Ventura Avenue Anticline. Both are very young, geologically speaking, and the anticline is still being compressed. Oil wells were subjected to extremely high fluid pressures in the early days of oil exploration, evidence of tectonic squeezing of the anticline. The Ventura River eroded through the anticline as it was formed, creating the valley now followed by State Highway 33, the Ojai Freeway. The former bed of the Ventura River is warped over the crest of the anticline, as seen from the Serra Cross, in Grant Park north of Ventura City Hall. Along Foothill Boulevard and Poli Street in Ventura, a south-facing scarp called the Ventura Fault is found at the sharp kink between south-dipping layers of the anticline and flat-lying rocks of the Santa Clara Valley. Along the Rincon coast between Ventura and Carpinteria, the anticline heads out to sea, warping ancient beach deposits including the terrace followed by U.S. Highway 101. On the south side of the anticline, the beach deposits follow a delicate, stair-stepped pattern, evidence that they were raised by individual earthquakes uplifting the anticline. Each time an earthquake uplifted the anticline and the beach, storm waves cut a new beach cliff slightly lower than the older one (Stein and Yeats, 1989).

In the Santa Barbara Channel, the anticline is marked at the surface by oil wells on an artificial island near Rincon Point, and farther west, by offshore drilling platforms. Both the Oak Ridge and Red Mountain faults have been mapped by marine geophysical surveys. West of Santa Barbara, the blind continuation of the Red Mountain Fault is called the North Channel Slope Fault, and it can be followed all the way to Point Conception (Figure 4-7). GPS surveys between the Santa Ynez Range and the Northern Channel Islands show that the Santa Barbara Channel, like the Ventura Basin, is being squeezed together by north-south compression. One theory holds that the right-lateral strike-slip Hosgri Fault (discussed in Chapter 4) does not end at the western tip of the Santa Ynez Range but turns east and becomes a fold, part of the north-south shortening of the Transverse Ranges. An offshore earthquake of M 7 on November 4, 1927 west of Lompoc in western Santa Barbara County could have been generated on one of these structures. This earthquake was accompanied by a small tsunami that produced six-foot waves on the nearby coast and was recorded by tide gauges in Hawaii. Landslides triggered by this earthquake disrupted rail service on the Southern Pacific rail line south of Lompoc.

The cities of Santa Barbara and Carpinteria are crossed by a set of faults with the south side upthrown, producing hills south of Highway 101 on which the upscale Hope Ranch residential area is built and Mission Ridge in the northern part of Santa Barbara. These faults and related folds have deformed marine terraces along the coast and constitute a seismic hazard to the Santa Barbara metropolitan area. No historical surface rupture has been attributed to any of these faults, but the June 29, 1925 and August 13, 1978 earthquakes that damaged the city could have originated on one of these faults.

South of Oak Ridge, the Simi Fault (Figure 5-1) extends from Camarillo to Simi Valley across areas subject to heavy development pressure. At its west end, the fault forms pressure ridges—including Springville Dome, a nearly-circular uplift west of Camarillo, visible from Highway 101, on which the Spanish Hills development is built—and another ridge in downtown Camarillo on which the beautiful old Catholic church stands. North of town, the Simi Fault follows the south side of the Las Posas Hills, which are uplifted along the fault. Farther east, the Simi Fault is south of Moorpark, and it forms the northern edge of Simi Valley, both under development as Los Angeles suburbs. The slip rate is less than a millimeter per year based on data from the Camarillo Hills, and the fault is noteworthy mainly because of the rapid urbanization of the countryside through which it passes.

Metropolitan Los Angeles

Highway 126 continues past Piru into Los Angeles County and joins Interstate 5, which passes through the new suburbs of Valencia and Santa Clarita enroute to the San Fernando Valley. This populated lowland is crossed by the San Gabriel Fault, a former trace of the San Andreas Fault that accumulated forty miles of right-lateral offset before the San Andreas Fault shifted to its present location farther north, at the edge of the Mojave Desert, like a river abandoning an old channel (Figure 5-1). The San Gabriel Fault was thought to be inactive, but recent trench excavations show that it displaces Holocene deposits, although its slip rate is low.

To the south, the Santa Susana Mountains have been uplifted and driven southward on the Santa Susana Fault, the next north-dipping reverse fault east of the San Cayetano Fault. The Santa Susana Fault can be followed past San Fernando Pass, where Interstate 5 drops into the San Fernando Valley, and follows the range front of the San Gabriel Mountains along the northern edge of the San Fernando Valley north of Sylmar and Pacoima. On February 9, 1971, an earthquake of M 6.7 broke the surface on a previously unrecognized fault on the north side of the Mission Hills and at the southern margin of the San Gabriel foothills north of the Foothill Freeway. This earthquake was the wake-up call that showed that the reverse faults of the Los Angeles metropolitan area could generate large earthquakes.

I think the 1971 earthquake was on the Santa Susana Fault at depth, but at the surface the Santa Susana Fault splits into several north-dipping

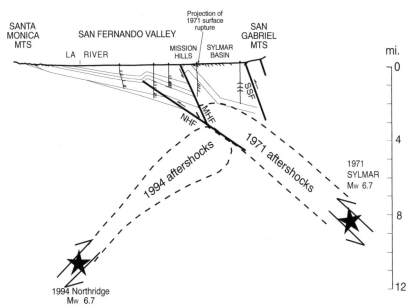

Figure 5-6. Cross section of the San Fernando Valley with faults that ruptured during the 1971 Sylmar Earthquake (north-dipping fault) and 1994 Northridge Earthquake (south-dipping fault). The 1994 earthquake was not accompanied by surface rupture, and the blind earthquake fault was not known prior to the earthquake. Compare with Figure 5-3 in the Ventura Basin. The 1994 Northridge Fault is the eastern continuation of the Oak Ridge Fault, and the north-dipping Santa Susana Fault (SSF) is the counterpart of the north-dipping San Cayetano Fault in Figure 5-3. Northridge Hills Fault (NHF) and Mission Hills Fault (MHF) are active but did not move in 1971 or 1994. Earthquake locations from Jim Mori, David Wald, and Rob Wesson of the U.S. Geological Survey; geological interpretation by Hiroyuki Tsutsumi, of Kyoto University, and the author. Lines with triangles at surface: oil well control. North is to right.

faults: a fault at the range front north of Sylmar that did not rupture; the next fault to the south that did rupture; and two more faults farther south—the Mission Hills Fault and Northridge Hills Fault—that did not rupture but might break in a future earthquake (Figure 5-6).

On January 17, 1994, another earthquake of the same magnitude ruptured a previously unknown reverse fault more than twelve miles beneath the flat-floored San Fernando Valley at Reseda and Northridge, trashing shopping malls, freeway interchanges, and the campus of California State University at Northridge. Earthquake aftershocks illuminated a south-dipping blind fault that terminated upward against the north-dipping Santa Susana Fault that had ruptured twenty-three years earlier (Figure 5-6). The south-dipping aftershock zone extended west beneath the Santa Susana Mountains, and it was soon recognized that it is the eastern continuation of the Oak Ridge Fault in the Ventura Basin to the northwest. The Oak Ridge Fault does not die out eastward like the San Cayetano Fault does, but it continues underground beneath the Santa Susana Fault to the San Fernando Valley. Like the blind thrust beneath the Coalinga Anticline in the San Joaquin Valley, this fault had a surface expression, too, because the Santa Susana Fault is folded into an anticline. The age of sediments involved in the folding allowed a slip rate to be determined on the Northridge Blind Thrust: less than one-tenth of an inch per year, in contrast with a rate three times higher on the exposed Oak Ridge Fault in the Ventura Basin. So the Northridge Earthquake ruptured that part of the Oak Ridge Fault with the slowest slip rate. The exposed part of the Oak Ridge fault with a faster slip rate is still waiting for its earthquake.

East of Interstate 405 (the San Diego Freeway), the Northridge Hills Fault and the Mission Hills Fault merge to form an active fault at the southwest margin of the Verdugo Mountains north of the Golden State Freeway in Glendale and Burbank. North of the Verdugo Mountains, the Santa Susana Fault merges with the Sierra Madre Fault at the San Gabriel range front at La Canada and Altadena. The Sierra Madre Fault contributes to the uplift of the San Gabriel Mountains and poses a major earthquake hazard to the San Gabriel Valley between Los Angeles and San Bernardino. The 1991 Sierra Madre Earthquake (M 6) ruptured a tear fault north of the Sierra Madre Fault. Farther east, the range-front fault is called the Cucamonga Fault, which joins the San Jacinto Fault south of Cajon Pass (Figure 4-14).

The central part of the Sierra Madre Fault appears to have a slower slip rate than the Santa Susana Fault to the west or the Cucamonga Fault to the east. A backhoe trench across the fault in Altadena (Figure 5-7) yielded alarming results: fault displacements in the trench show that the last two earthquakes were larger than M 7—possibly M 7.2 to 7.6. This means that the historical record in metropolitan Los Angeles, with no earthquakes larger than M 6.7, cannot be used by planners as an indicator of the largest earthquakes to be expected in greater Los Angeles.

The Ventura Basin and Santa Barbara Channel are characterized by reverse faults, but the Los Angeles Basin has more variety: left-lateral and right-lateral strike-slip faults as well as reverse faults. The right-lateral faults include the Whittier, Newport-Inglewood, and Palos Verdes faults, described in the preceding chapter. Left-lateral faults include the Santa Monica Fault and the Hollywood Fault at the southern edge of the Santa Monica Mountains; the Raymond Fault, which marks the northwestern end of the San Gabriel Valley south of the Verdugo Mountains; and the San Jose Fault at the northern end of the Puente Hills south of West Covina. Slip rates on these faults are low, and

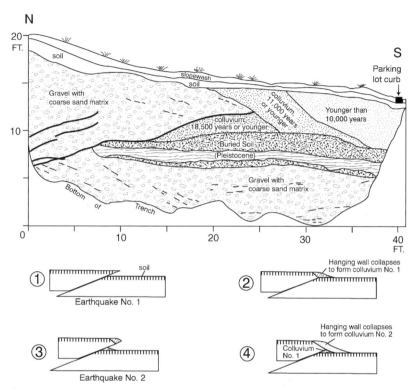

Figure 5-7. Backhoe trench excavation across the Sierra Madre Fault in Loma Alta Park east of Lincoln Boulevard in Altadena. Pleistocene gravel deposits were thrust over a buried soil zone, shedding deposits of colluvium down the fault scarp. A more recent earthquake on the same fault, probably during the past ten thousand years, overrode the colluvium from the first earthquake and produced a second zone of colluvium. Modified from the original trench log by Charles Rubin, Central Washington University; Scott Lindvall of William Lettis and Associates; and Tom Rockwell of San Diego State University and Earth Consultants International.

earthquake recurrence intervals, where known, are thousands of years. Most faults are so extensively urbanized that few places are available for paleoseismology trenches, and as a result, information on slip rates is scarce. The Raymond Fault accounted for an earthquake on December 3, 1988 of M 4.9 that caused damage in Pasadena, and the San Jose Fault was the source of earthquakes near Upland in the San Gabriel Valley on June 26, 1988 (M 4.6) and February 28, 1990 (M 5.2).

The Santa Monica Fault extends offshore west of Santa Monica and Pacific Palisades and skims the coastline farther west where it is known as the Malibu Coast Fault. Left-lateral stream offsets north of Point Dume and west of Malibu confirm that this is a left lateral strike-slip fault. Farther west, both Santa Cruz Island and Santa Rosa Island are bisected by left-lateral faults.

Reverse faults in Los Angeles are largely blind thrusts, with lower slip rates than reverse faults in the Ventura Basin. The faults give rise to anticlines, with the best known the Elysian Park Anticline north of downtown Los Angeles. Some scientists give the name "Elysian Park Blind Thrust" to a fault extending west beneath the Santa Monica Mountains and east beneath the Puente Hills, based on their analysis of the October 1, 1987 Whittier Narrows Earthquake of M 5.9. This leads to concerns about a huge blind-thrust earthquake that would dominate the earthquake-hazard estimate for Los Angeles. My belief is that the blind-reverse faults underlying the Santa Monica Mountains, Elysian Park Anticline, and Puente Hills are separate structures that would generate earthquakes smaller than M 7. However, the separate structures at the surface could merge at depths of ten miles where earthquakes nucleate, so the large-earthquake scenario could be correct. Scientists at the Southern California Earthquake Center (SCEC) have developed a *cascade model*, in which one earthquake triggers another, and another, and another, each on separate surface faults. Such earthquake behavior has been documented elsewhere in the world.

Blind-reverse faults tend to uplift the ground and be expressed at the surface as hills, and the Elysian Hills and Monterey Park Hills are a byproduct of uplift on the Elysian Park Anticline. The Montebello Hills were uplifted during the 1987 Whittier Narrows Earthquake by about an inch-and-a-half (4 cm) (Figure 5-4). South of the Puente Hills in Fullerton, the Coyote Hills and Coyote Anticline are the surface expression of a blind-reverse fault. This fault has not yet produced a large earthquake during the time of recordkeeping, although the 1929 Whittier Earthquake, one of the first to be studied by Charles Richter and Harry Wood in their new Seismological Lab at Pasadena, might have ruptured a tear fault west of the Coyote Hills.

One group of scientists has proposed a low-angle thrust fault called the Compton-Los Alamitos Thrust that would underlie most of the Los Angeles Basin. Even though the slip rate on this proposed fault— less than one-tenth of an inch per year—is low, the area of potential rupture is so large that it would be considered one of the most dangerous faults in California based on the number of people and the value of real estate impacted by an earthquake on this fault. Paleoseismic investigations have shown that the fault predates sediments as old as one hundred thousand years, so in a legal sense, the fault is not active. Other scientists doubt the very existence of this fault. It is another example of the problems scientists face when they cannot see the fault directly but must infer its presence based on indirect evidence.

The Las Cienegas blind fault in downtown Los Angeles has a very low slip rate based on shallow core holes drilled at the Rancho La Brea tar pits at Hancock Park on the upthrown side of the fault and another core hole drilled on the downthrown side.

Summary

It's clear that metropolitan Los Angeles, including the Los Angeles Basin, San Gabriel Valley, and San Fernando Valley, is laced with active faults. Most of these faults have very low slip rates, and limited paleoseismic evidence shows that the recurrence interval of earthquakes on individual faults is measured in thousands of years, in comparison with hundreds of years on the San Andreas Fault System. The reason these faults are so important to us is that earthquakes on them would affect millions of people in Los Angeles. An earthquake of M 5.9 at Whittier Narrows in 1987 killed three people and caused more than $350 million in damage, and the 1994 Northridge Earthquake of M 6.7 was one of the worst natural disasters in the history of the United States. Yet paleoseismological evidence from the Altadena trench tells us that Los Angeles could suffer even larger earthquakes—as large as M 7.6, which would be an overwhelming catastrophe.

An earthquake on any given fault in metropolitan Los Angeles is unlikely in our lifetime and even in the next thousand years. But a damaging earthquake with M greater than 6 on *some* fault beneath Los Angeles is likely. Los Angeles was struck by major earthquakes in 1933, 1971, 1987, and 1994, and the future is likely to see earthquakes at about the same frequency. So it's important that Los Angeles be prepared for a local earthquake somewhere in the metropolitan area, even though we can't say which fault will break.

The situation in the Ventura Basin is a little different. Slip rates on the Oak Ridge, San Cayetano, and Santa Susana faults—and probably the Red Mountain Fault as well—are higher, and earthquake recurrence intervals might be a thousand years or less. The cities of the Santa Clara Valley are smaller, so fewer people are at risk. However, the rapid spread of population from Los Angeles is increasing the population density to that of the San Fernando Valley. And here, too, the next earthquake could be larger than M 7.

Several faults underlie metropolitan Santa Barbara, and even though their slip rates are low, they must be considered a major hazard because of the number of people at risk. Santa Barbara suffered major damage from an earthquake of M 6.8 in 1925 and additional damage from a smaller earthquake in 1978, whereas the lower Santa Clara Valley, bordered by reverse faults with higher slip rates, has yet to experience a major earthquake in the past 220 years. In addition, there are big active structures offshore, farther south.

Which brings us back to where we started, the earthquake of December 21, 1812. This earthquake was accompanied by a wave from the sea, a tsunami, so its epicenter was in the Santa Barbara Channel. It could have been much larger than the 1925 or 1978 earthquakes, and it could have been as large as M 7, the size of the 1927 Lompoc Earthquake. Geologists disagree on the role and even the orientation of offshore faults in the Santa Barbara Channel, with one group suggesting that the entire Santa Barbara Channel is underlain by a huge blind thrust, and other groups assigning a larger role to the offshore Oak Ridge, Red Mountain, and North Channel Slope faults.

Suggestions for Further Reading

Sieh, K., and S. LeVay. 1998. *The Earth in Turmoil*. New York: W.H. Freeman and Company. 324p. Chapter 6 discusses the hazards of urban faults in Los Angeles.

Stein, R.S., and R.S. Yeats. 1989. Hidden earthquakes. *Scientific American*, v. 260, pp. 48–57. Blind-reverse faults and their surface expression as folds.

Southern California Earthquake Center. 1995. *Putting Down Roots in Earthquake Country*. A focus on hazards in urban southern California, with maps locating the faults and showing the probability of future earthquakes. Written for the lay person.

U.S. Geological Survey. 1996. *USGS Response to an Urban Earthquake: Northridge '94*. U.S. Geological Survey Open-File Report 96-263. 78p. Written for the lay person.

Ziony, J.J., editor. 1985. *Evaluating Earthquake Hazards in the Los Angeles Region —An Earth Science Perspective*. U.S. Geol. Survey Professional Paper 1760. 516p.

❧ 6 ❧
Shakes in the Backcountry: Decades of Violence, Millennia of Silence

"Everybody stopped for a minute. Then they started playing again. Not too long after it hit, [the slot machine area] got even busier than before."

> Candy McCain, Las Vegas tourist at The Mirage after the M 7.1 Hector Mine Earthquake that struck the Mojave Desert in the early morning hours of October 16, 1999, quoted in *Time* for October 25, 1999.

"It warn't no common shock, you bet! Not one of your wavy kind,
But licket-y-split and rattle-ty-bang, just which way it had a mind.
Houses throwed down? You'd best believe! There warn't a 'dobe wall
Nor yet a stone one, more'n one foot high, that didn't have to fall;
It throwed the bottoms clean from under, and crumbled the walls to dust,
And them as was sleepin' twixt 'dobe walls was them as fared the wust.
Anyone killed? Why where you bin, that you ain't heerd the news?
How women and young'uns and men lay dead in ones and threes and
*   twos?*
You see, 'twas two o'clock at night, and them as received their call
Never knowed what struck 'em, or if they did they hadn't no time to
*   squall!*
How many was dead? Well twenty-five, as near as we could count;
But some of the wounded and sick and maimed would likely swell that
*   amount.*
I only know that I'm here today, lookin' over this desolate sand,
And I only hope He'll deal kindly with them as is gone to the unknown
*   land."*

> W.H. Creighton in the Inyo *Independent* (1872).

Introduction:
The 1872 Owens Valley Earthquake of M 7.7

State Highway 14 slices across the Mojave Desert, joins U.S. 395 west of China Lake, and follows Owens Valley in the shadow of the Sierra Nevada (Figure 6-1). The Sierra is a barren desert range at its southern end, but from Lone Pine northward it rises to lofty, snow-clad summits between Mt. Whitney and Yosemite. Highway 395 is the route taken by Angelenos to ski at Mammoth, more than three hundred miles away, its economy so oriented to the

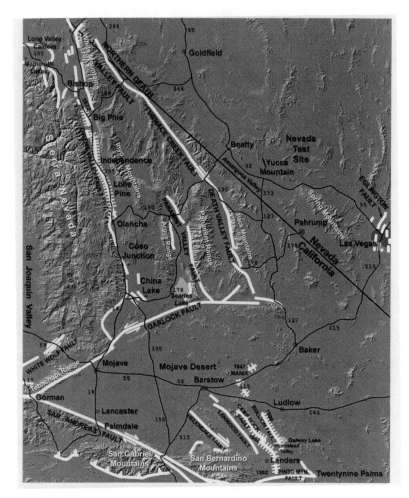

Figure 6-1. Computer-generated topographic map of eastern California and parts of Nevada, including the Mojave Desert, the Sierra Nevada and the ranges to the east, and metropolitan Las Vegas. Railroad track pattern across faults show surface rupture accompanying the 1872 Owens Valley Earthquake, 1947 Manix Earthquake, 1992 Landers Earthquake, and 1999 Hector Mine Earthquake. Also shown are the Long Valley Caldera (upper left corner) and the proposed Yucca Mountain Nuclear Waste Repository in Nevada.

Southland that it's generally considered part of southern California, even though it's due east of San Francisco. This economic tie is reinforced by the Los Angeles Aqueduct, which brings water from the High Sierra down Owens Valley to thirsty Los Angeles, draining the water from Owens Lake in the process—a fact that has never pleased the equally thirsty but outnumbered residents of Owens Valley.

The drive between Lone Pine and Bishop is spectacular. Owens Valley is a graben, a downdropped fault block between normal faults that have uplifted the Sierra on the west and the Inyo and White Mountains on the east. Little noticed is the Owens Valley Fault in the center of the valley, characterized by strike slip, like the San Andreas.

In 1872 the Owens Valley was untamed desert backcountry. The Sierra had recently been crossed by the Central Pacific Railroad, and in a few years the Southern Pacific would span the Mojave to link Los Angeles to the east coast. But the Modoc Indian rebellion was still a year in the future. Lone Pine, Independence, Big Pine, and Bishop Creek (now Bishop) were windswept settlements of adobe, stone, and brick, inhabited by a few prospectors and farmers attracted by water from the Owens River, which in 1872 was still theirs to use.

About 2:30 A.M. on March 26, the Owens Valley was wrenched by one of the three largest earthquakes to strike California in historic times. Lone Pine and Independence suffered intensities of X, and most of the adobe and many of the brick buildings collapsed, killing twenty-seven people in Lone Pine alone—one-tenth of its population. The Inyo County Courthouse, a two-story brick building at Independence, telescoped into a single story. The earthquake stopped clocks and woke people up from Red Bluff to San Diego, and from San Francisco to Elko, Nevada. John Muir, camped in Yosemite Valley, witnessed a gigantic rock fall at Eagle Rock shaken down by the earthquake (Chapter 9).

The first geologist on the scene was Josiah D. Whitney, for whom Mt. Whitney is named, but Whitney did not recognize the surface fault. In August 1883, more than eleven years after the earthquake, G.K. Gilbert of the newly established USGS described the fault rupture that accompanied the earthquake at Lone Pine, reporting both right-lateral strike-slip and vertical displacement. This experience would profoundly influence Gilbert in his analysis of normal faults in Utah and later in his study of the San Francisco Earthquake of 1906.

Later workers (see Beanland and Clark, 1994) mapped the 1872 rupture of the Owens Valley Fault for sixty miles from Owens Lake to Big Pine (Figures 6-2 and 6-3). The maximum right-lateral offset was more than thirty feet at Lone Pine, and displacements as much as twenty feet were common. So the earthquake was not much smaller than the largest earthquakes on the San Andreas Fault in 1857 and 1906. It resembled the San Andreas earthquakes both in sense of slip (right-lateral) and the amount of fault displacement due to the earthquake.

But the Owens Valley Fault differs in one important respect: its slip rate. It is less than one-tenth of an inch (1–2 mm) per year according to geological evidence, although GPS results suggest that it might be as high as one-fourth inch per year. The San Andreas Fault, in contrast,

Figure 6-2. Owens Valley Fault in the Poverty Hills, six miles south of Big Pine. Fault extends from upper left to right center of photo, cutting across two volcanic cinder cones. Straight-line pattern of fault is typical of strike-slip faults. This fault ruptured in the 1872 Owens Valley Earthquake. Photo from U.S. Geological Survey.

has a slip rate of more than an inch per year. Earthquakes on the San Andreas Fault recur every few hundred years, whereas the recurrence interval on the Owens Valley Fault is three to five thousand years.

Should the residents of Owens Valley and the engineers for the Los Angeles aqueduct relax, then, since the Owens Valley Fault is not likely to rupture for thousands of years in the future? Unfortunately not, because the valley is a graben, and the normal faults flanking the valley did not rupture in 1872. The Sierra Nevada on the west and the Inyo and White Mountains on the east have shaken their way skyward during hundreds of thousands of years by uplift along these earthquake faults. Their slip rates are less than a millimeter per year, and locally less than a tenth of a millimeter per year. Some of their displacement is by strike slip, and some is purely by normal faulting.

The Sierra Nevada, Owens Valley, and the Inyo and White Mountains, along with the rest of the interior of California and adjacent Nevada, are part of the Basin and Range Province, the diffuse boundary between the Pacific and North America plates. Part of the plate motion is taken up by faults within this broad region. The Basin and Range is capable of large earthquakes, such as the Owens Valley Earthquake of M 7.7 and an earthquake of M 7.6 in Pleasant Valley in northern Nevada, on October 3, 1915. But slip rates are, in most cases, low, and return times for earthquakes are measured in thousands and even tens of thousands of years. Offsetting the hazard is that most of the region is thinly populated, with the significant exceptions of metropolitan Las Vegas and Reno-Carson City, Nevada. The M 7.1 Hector Mine Earthquake of October 16, 1999 would have been a major catastrophe

Figure 6-3. Owens Valley Fault crossing an alluvial fan near Lone Pine. The fault is highlighted by a narrow, light band on the alluvial fan due to the photo being taken in the morning. The dark, curving line is an aqueduct carrying Owens Valley water to Los Angeles. Photo from U.S. Geological Survey.

if it had ruptured a fault near Reno or Las Vegas. It rattled the gaming tables in Las Vegas and derailed a train east of Barstow, but it caused no loss of life. Property damage was small because the earthquake struck an unpopulated area—a Marine Corps training center in the middle of the Mojave Desert.

The Owens Valley Earthquake illustrates the theme of this chapter: earthquake violence on a fault system for a short period of time, then thousands of years of inactivity on that fault system. Faults abound in the Basin and Range, and geologists have shown that some of them, at least, are capable of large earthquakes. The earthquake potential of most of the others is unknown. This is not a critical problem in the uninhabited part of the region, but in large cities such as Las Vegas and Reno, or even in small towns such as Alturas, Barstow, Bishop, Lancaster, Mojave, and Susanville, recognition of the earthquake potential of these silent faults could be a matter of survival.

Mammoth Lakes and the Long Valley Caldera

The 1872 rupture scarp ends north of Big Pine, but the normal faults at the base of the Sierra continue northward toward Bishop (Figure 6-1). There, U.S. 395 turns due west, then northwest over Sherwin Grade past Toms Place and Crowley Lake to a stunning Sierra view of Mt. Ritter, Mt. Banner, and the Minarets, a backdrop for the pine-clad tourist resort of Mammoth Lakes.

Many people who have lived in California have an area in the Sierra that is special to them, and this is mine. I climbed the mountains named for geologists (Dana, Lyell, McClure), and I met Norman Clyde (for whom the Clyde Minaret is named) on the shore of a lake high above the June Lake Loop. I introduced my two oldest sons to the High Sierra wilderness from the trails that strike out from Mammoth Lakes. I listened while a friend grieved the loss of his wife as we fished in Cascade Valley and then toiled up a high, trailless pass and descended to civilization at Convict Lake, our souls cleansed by the high-country experience. Most of the few modest skills I have as a skier were learned at Mammoth, and when I was shivering after a day on the slopes I warmed up at Hot Creek.

Geology created the beauty of the Mammoth Lakes region, but it exacted a price. The ski area is on the flanks of a sleeping volcano, and Hot Creek is warmed by geothermal energy from a magma reservoir far below. The entire region from Crowley Lake through Mammoth Lakes to the Devils Postpile road is part of a giant volcanic caldera, seventeen miles across from east to west.

Calderas are the most violent expressions of a restless Earth. Sixty-eight hundred years ago, Mount Mazama blew vast quantities of volcanic ash into the atmosphere, sagging back into the Cascades to form Crater Lake, Oregon, one of Earth's most spectacular calderas. Thirty-five hundred years ago, a great volcano erupted in the Aegean Sea, profoundly altering the fledgling civilizations in the eastern Mediterranean region and leaving the lovely caldera of Santorini Island as its sunken remnant. Both of these were small change compared to what happened at Mammoth and Bishop 760,000 years ago.

At that time, in the Pleistocene Epoch, a volcano exploded in a paroxysmal eruption, spewing 150 cubic miles of molten rock onto the Earth's surface or into the air—ten times the volume of the Mazama eruption that created Crater Lake and hundreds of times larger than the 1980 eruption of Mount St. Helens. Great avalanches of hot rock swept down the flanks of this volcano, obliterating everything in their path and burying the site of the future town of Bishop under thousands of feet of ash. A massive eruption column climbed many tens of thousands of feet into the sky and was caught in the jet stream, leaving a thick deposit of ash—called the Bishop Tuff—as far away as Nebraska and Texas. So much magma was vented to the surface that the volcano sank into the Earth's crust, creating an oval-shaped lowland known as the Long Valley Caldera (Figure 6-1).

This great caldera has not produced a major eruption in one hundred thousand years, but volcanic activity has continued. Mammoth Mountain itself formed long after the eruption of the Bishop Tuff. North of Mammoth, between Deadman Summit and Lee Vining on the east side of U.S. 395, the Inyo Craters were formed only six hundred years ago. And Paoha Island in the center of Mono Lake last erupted shortly before the arrival of American gold miners in the nineteenth century.

A pool of molten rock is still there beneath the surface of Long Valley Caldera, so that the caldera is still alive. For the past 150 years, the Long Valley Caldera has had one of the highest rates of seismicity at the magnitude 5 to 6 level in California. And in the past few decades, stirrings of the magma beneath the surface have been expressed as earthquakes and swelling of the surface of the caldera, casting a shadow on the future of this beautiful region.

On October 4, 1978, a M 5.8 earthquake shook Wheeler Crest, halfway between Mammoth Lakes and Bishop. A forty-foot geyser of hot water erupted for a day or two at Hot Creek, closing the pool. During the two-day period between May 25 and 27, 1980—one week after the climactic eruption of Mount St. Helens—the Mammoth Lakes area was struck by a swarm of earthquakes, four of them at M 6. One of these earthquakes triggered a huge landslide of rock, snow, and ice that roared down McGee Creek, less than ten miles southeast of Mammoth Lakes. Ground cracking was detected on the Hilton Creek Fault east of Mammoth Lakes, although it was later determined that this fault was not the source of the earthquakes.

At the same time, the floor of the Long Valley Caldera rose as much as ten inches in a single year, suggesting that the magma reservoir was becoming more active, causing the ground to swell like an angry abscess. A similar, although larger, bulging had preceded the May 18, 1980 eruption of Mount St. Helens. Much of the swelling was taking place along the south side of the caldera, near U.S. 395—the only access road to Mammoth Lakes. Should an eruption take place at this access road, the people of Mammoth Lakes, together with tourists and skiers, would be trapped.

Finally, after another two years of monitoring the progress of the puffing up of the caldera floor and recording thousands of additional earthquakes, the USGS and the Governor's Office released a Notice of Potential Volcanic Hazards, enraging the business community of Mammoth Lakes because it was issued just before Memorial Day, one of the biggest tourist weekends of the year. Most of the people who lived there were unaware of *any* active volcano in their part of the world. That story has already been told in Part I, and is described in greater detail by Nance (1988), Sieh and LeVay (1998), and Hill (1998). Dave Hill's story is particularly poignant because he was one of the USGS scientists trying to figure out how to inform the residents of Mammoth Lakes of the hazard without unduly alarming them.

In 1983, Mammoth and its only access road were rattled by a swarm of earthquakes, including two of M 5.3. By this time, townspeople could feel for themselves the ominous signs of activity reported by the USGS, and they were more cooperative than they had been the year before. A dirt road from Mammoth Lakes to U.S. 395 was plowed out in January 1983 and paved the following summer as an escape route ("Mammoth Lakes Scenic Loop"), although Mike Jenks, the chairman of the Mono County Board of Supervisors who had ordered its construction, later lost his seat in a recall election.

Another swarm of earthquakes struck in July 1984, and then seismicity dropped to a low level, although the caldera floor continued to rise. A new swarm of earthquakes started up in May 1989, and a year later up to three hundred earthquakes per day were being recorded in the southern part of the caldera. In addition, a sudden die-off of trees at several places near Mammoth Lakes was attributed to the emission of carbon dioxide gas from the magma reservoir. High levels of carbon dioxide were found in the soil and close to the ground, enough to kill trees.

At this writing, the seismic activity and the swelling of the caldera floor continue, but there has been no eruption. The caldera floor is now two-and-a-half feet higher than it was in 1979. The USGS, the Office of Emergency Services, Mono County, and the town of Mammoth Lakes have created an alert system to notify the residents of an emergency. The alerts consist of color-coded geometric shapes reminiscent of the degree of difficulty of a Mammoth ski run: a green circle for "no immediate risk," a yellow square for "watch," an orange diamond for "warning," and a red triangle for "eruption in progress."

But there is no full agreement on what Mammoth Lakes should expect. Is the swelling of the caldera floor just part of the normal slow development of a caldera, or is it the overture to a catastrophe? Should USGS scientists continue to inform people of the data they receive, even though they are not sure what it means for those who live and work at Mammoth? These questions are being pondered by the USGS and the Office of Emergency Services.

The Eastern California Shear Zone

The Mojave Desert is a high, arid plateau between the San Gabriel and San Bernardino mountains on the south and the Tehachapi Mountains on the north. From space, the Mojave is a giant, brown triangle (Figure 6-1), tapering westward to Interstate 5 near the community of Lebec, not far from Fort Tejon and the 1857 break on the San Andreas Fault.

The triangle owes its appearance to the plateau's boundary faults— the San Andreas Fault on the south and the Garlock Fault on the north. The center of the Mojave consists of low desert ranges, dry lake beds, a few dark volcanic cinder cones, and broad valleys—a contrast to the high ranges to the north and south. A set of northwest-trending faults crossing the region doesn't appear particularly active, even though they show some evidence of Holocene displacement. The subdued topography suggests to the geologist that this is not earthquake country.

But on April 10, 1947, an earthquake of magnitude 6.2 rattled the Manix rail station along the Mojave River east of Barstow (located on Figure 6-1). Although the earthquake was felt as far away as Los Angeles, damage was limited to rail facilities, ranch buildings, and gasoline stations on nearby U.S. Highway 91, now Interstate 15. The east-northeast-trending Manix Fault showed evidence of two to three inches of left-lateral strike slip; cracks in the ground were observed for about a mile. Oddly, the aftershocks followed a north-northwest trend, almost at right angles to the surface rupture on the Manix Fault.

Smaller earthquakes followed: the 1965 Calico Earthquake of M 5.2, the 1975 Galway Lake Earthquake of M 5.2, and the 1979 Homestead Valley Earthquake of M 5.6. These earthquakes were not large, and all were in thinly settled country between Barstow and Twentynine Palms.

Strangely, these earthquakes were all in a straight line trending south-southeast, parallel to the zone of aftershocks of the Manix Earthquake. It was as though they were all on a deeply buried fault with that orientation, which did not fit the surface geology of faults trending mainly southeast. However, just as for the Manix Earthquake, the orientation of the fault ruptures based on seismograms was consistent with the south-southeast trend, not the southeast trend. The seismograms showed that they were all right-lateral strike-slip faults, like the San Andreas Fault, but with a more southerly orientation.

In addition to lining up along a south-southeast trend, each earthquake was south of the last one, ominously migrating southward toward the southern edge of the Mojave and a small, unsuspecting, isolated desert community called Landers. It could be compared with ripping the buttons off a shirt, with Homestead Valley the last button and Landers the next button to rip.

Things then quieted down for the next ten years, although on July 8, 1986, a M 6 earthquake struck the San Andreas Fault north of Palm Springs, far to the south of the Homestead Valley Earthquake and about twelve miles west of the projected south-southeast trend (Figure 4-14).

But finally someone noticed the lineup of earthquakes. Amos Nur of Stanford University pointed out this strange trend as part of the Eastern California Shear Zone. Nur reasoned that maybe this was a new fault zone taking up strike slip east of the San Andreas Fault—a fault zone so new that the ruptures had not yet coalesced into a single zone that geologists could map at the surface. The trend was more southerly than the San Andreas, just as it was more southerly than the geologically mapped faults of the Mojave, but oddly enough the trend was almost exactly parallel to that of the Owens Valley rupture of 1872.

But the Mojave remained seismically quiet, and Nur's paper received little attention from other scientists and none at all from most people in California, who were hardly aware of any of the Mojave Desert earthquakes in the first place.

On April 22, 1992, a magnitude 4.6 earthquake struck east of Palm Springs, only five miles away from the San Andreas Fault and the epicenter of the 1986 earthquake. Except for the 1986 earthquake, this section of the San Andreas had not ruptured for more than three hundred years. The USGS issued a Hazard Level C alert, notifying the public that this small earthquake could be a foreshock to a much larger earthquake on the San Andreas Fault to the west.

It was a foreshock, but not for the San Andreas. Two-and-a-half hours later, the Joshua Tree Earthquake of M 6.1—the largest Mojave earthquake since Manix in 1947—struck in the same region. The hazard alert was raised by the USGS to Level B, indicating a five- to twenty-five-percent chance of a still-larger earthquake on the San Andreas Fault in the next three days. No earthquake struck, and the alert was canceled.

But seismologists observed that the aftershocks of the Joshua Tree Earthquake did not die out as quickly as an ordinary earthquake should. In addition, Amos Nur quickly pointed out that the Joshua Tree Earthquake fell on the same north-northwest-south-southeast trending line as the earlier earthquakes. The seismograph record of the mainshock also indicated a north-northwest trending fault. The only difference was that the earthquake had skipped over Landers and struck a region much closer to the San Andreas Fault. Landers appeared to be the only button on the shirt left unripped, although none of the residents of Landers had a clue that they were in a seismic gap. Furthermore, the scientists couldn't agree on what was going on. A seismic gap on a fault that couldn't be mapped at the surface? Foreshocks of a great San Andreas earthquake? Some seismologists were beginning to have sleepless nights.

Figure 6-4. Surface rupture of the Johnson Valley Fault during the June 28, 1992 Landers Earthquake. Church parking lot stripes are offset right laterally. Photo taken from a helicopter the day of the earthquake by Charles M. Rubin, Central Washington University.

On June 11, 1992, several small earthquakes were recorded north of the town of Joshua Tree. Seventeen days later, another group of earthquakes, the largest one M 3.0, was recorded a few miles to the west, between Yucca Valley and Landers, lined up in the gap between the Homestead Valley and Joshua Tree earthquakes.

Four-and-a-half hours later, in the early morning hours of June 28, the Landers earthquake ripped the last button on the shirt with an earthquake of magnitude 7.3—the largest earthquake in historical times in the Mojave Desert and the largest earthquake to strike anywhere in southern California since the Kern County Earthquake of 1952, forty years before. A child was crushed by a rock fireplace collapsing, two people died of heart attacks, and more than four hundred were injured.

Kerry Sieh was shaken awake at his home at Lake Arrowhead in the San Bernardino Mountains, and soon after daylight he was in a helicopter looking for surface rupture. It was spectacular: more than forty-three miles long, with right-lateral displacement of roads and off-road vehicle tracks (Figure 6-4) as large as twenty feet at Galway Lake Road north of Landers. The rupture had raced northward, jumping from one fault to another, ripping through the sites of the Homestead Valley and Galway Lake earthquakes (Figure 6-5).

But there was more. Three hours after the Landers mainshock, a second earthquake of M 6.2 struck near Big Bear Lake, about twenty miles west of Landers. Because this earthquake struck a more populated area than did Landers, it was more destructive. The cost of the two earthquakes was nearly $100 million. Seventy-seven homes and ten businesses were destroyed, and 4,446 homes and 166 businesses were damaged. Roads and bridges in San Bernardino and Los Angeles counties were damaged, and in Riverside County the damage was estimated at $950,000, mostly in the city of San Jacinto. One can only imagine the carnage if the earthquake had struck closer to Los Angeles.

The Big Bear Earthquake was west of the Eastern California Shear Zone, and on a left-lateral fault that trends northeast. Despite the great amount of damage, there was no surface rupture, nor was there a surface fault that could be related to the mainshock rupture.

Curiously, the Landers Earthquake triggered an increase in earthquake activity over much of the western United States, as far away as Yellowstone Park, Wyoming, more than six hundred miles away. The largest triggered earthquake was a M 5.6 event at Little Skull Mountain near the Nevada Test Site northwest of Las Vegas—the largest earthquake in that area since 1868. Seismicity was triggered in areas of geothermal activity, including the Geysers geothermal field north of San Francisco and areas east of the Sierra Nevada between Coso Junction and Lake Tahoe, but other triggered earthquakes at Cedar City, Utah, and Pasadena, California, were unrelated to geothermal activity. Before

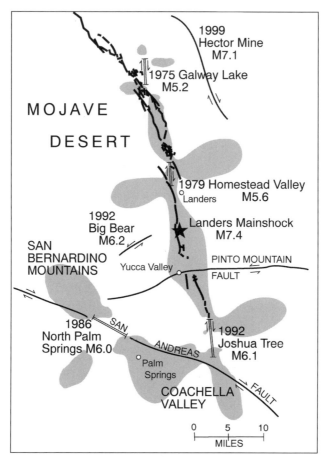

*Figure 6-5. Map of the surface ruptures accompanying the 1992 Landers
Earthquake of M 7.3; mainshock located by star. Locations of earlier
earthquakes are shown by double lines; these include the 1975 Galway Lake,
1979 Homestead Valley, 1986 North Palm Springs, and 1992 Joshua Tree
earthquakes. Dark bands show the areas where these earlier earthquakes
increased stress; these areas include nearly all of the rupture zone of the 1992
Landers Earthquake. Immediately after the earthquake, stress was abruptly
increased in the Big Bear area of the San Bernardino Mountains, which
experienced an earthquake of M 6.2 three hours after the Landers Earthquake.
Both the earlier earthquake and the 1992 earthquakes have increased stress on
the San Andreas Fault to the south, which has not experienced an earthquake in
more than three hundred years. However, the 1999 Hector Mine Earthquake
struck an area that was not predicted to have increased stress as a result of
these earthquakes although newer models disagree. Modified from an
illustration by Ross Stein, U.S. Geological Survey; Geoffrey C.P. King, Institute de
Physique du Globe de Paris; and Jian Lin, Woods Hole Oceanographic Institution.*

Landers, most seismologists did not believe an earthquake could trigger other earthquakes hundreds of miles away, but Landers made them believers. The reason for the triggered seismicity is still unclear.

In any case, the Landers Earthquake did show that an earthquake could be triggered by an earthquake on a nearby fault, although the triggered earthquake can take years to happen. The Joshua Tree Earthquake followed the Homestead Valley Earthquake by thirteen years (Figure 6-5). Landers led Ross Stein and his USGS colleagues to develop a theory of earthquake triggering that documented the buttons-off-the-shirt behavior of the Eastern California Shear Zone between Manix Lake and Landers (see Chapter 8). This theory has been applied to several earthquakes, including the Northridge Earthquake of 1994 and the recent Izmit, Turkey, Earthquake of 1999.

According to this theory, future earthquakes are more likely on unruptured parts of the Eastern California Shear Zone in the direction of Barstow and on the San Andreas Fault immediately south of the Joshua Tree Earthquake. This theory also predicted that strain would build up at right angles to the Eastern California Shear Zone, thereby explaining the Big Bear Earthquake on a left-lateral fault southwest of Landers (Figure 6-5).

Seven years later, on October 16, 1999, a M 7.1 earthquake was accompanied by surface rupture in the Marine Corps Training Center between Twentynine Palms and Barstow. It was named the Hector Mine Earthquake because there was no populated place that was close enough

Figure 6-6. Aerial view of 1999 Hector Mine surface rupture on Bullion Fault (dark band extending from lower left to upper right of photo). Note the tank track for scale. Photo by Chris Walls, Earth Consultants International.

to supply a name. The earthquake ruptured the Bullion Fault and the previously unknown Lavic Lake Fault about twelve miles southeast of the Pisgah Fault, with right-lateral surface rupture averaging ten feet and locally as high as seventeen feet (Figure 6-6). Unlike Big Bear, the area of the Hector Mine Earthquake was not expected to have an earthquake. The area should have had its stress reduced by the Landers Earthquake, although more recent studies show that stress may have increased. Even though the earthquake was northeast of the lineup of events marking the Eastern California Shear Zone, the trend of the rupture based on seismograms and on surface geology of the Bullion Fault and Lavic Lake Fault was the same: north-northwest.

Strong shaking derailed a train that happened to be traveling west toward Barstow at the time of the mainshock, caused minor damage to buildings along Interstate 40 and between Ludlow and Amboy, and temporarily diverted gamblers in Las Vegas, as pointed out at the beginning of the chapter.

Since World War II, the earthquake activity in the Mojave Desert has been greater than along any part of the San Andreas Fault, but the long-term slip rates on individual faults in the Mojave, including the Eastern California Shear Zone, are less than one-tenth as fast. However, GPS results suggest that the entire Eastern California Shear Zone might presently have a strike slip rate of one-half inch per year.

Earthquakes on the San Andreas Fault repeat every few hundred years, but on any given fault in the Mojave Desert the recurrence interval is measured in thousands of years. The slow slip rate is consistent with the subdued topography of the Mojave Desert; to a geologist used to time spans of thousands of years, the Mojave just doesn't look like a place that has lots of earthquakes.

The common explanation is that the earthquakes, starting with Manix in 1947, are part of an *earthquake cluster*. Paleoseismology has revealed evidence for prehistoric earthquakes in the past 1,000 years, but prior to that the Eastern California Shear Zone apparently was seismically quiet for several thousand years. It is the same story as the 1872 Owens Valley Earthquake; the recurrence interval is long, but the short historical record happened to coincide with big earthquakes.

Has the earthquake cluster finished? Can't tell. Another earthquake could strike north-northwest of Landers in the direction of Barstow. A more ominous possibility is a very large earthquake on the San Andreas Fault near San Bernardino, unruptured for more than three hundred years, where stress has increased because of the Landers and Hector Mine earthquakes.

Is the twentieth century unusual in its earthquake activity? Maybe it is for the Mojave Desert, but how about faults elsewhere in the California outback that have not suffered earthquakes in historical time?

Perhaps we should be more worried about these faults, even those with slow slip rates, that have not ruptured in the past 150 years or so, the time of recordkeeping in the Intermountain West. We first turn to another region with low population, and then we consider the earthquake hazards to metropolitan Reno and Las Vegas, outside California but tied to it economically as well as tectonically and seismically.

Central Nevada Seismic Zone

The Mojave Desert is bounded on the north by the Garlock Fault, discussed in a subsequent section. North of the Garlock Fault, the Basin and Range Province includes most of Nevada and part of southeast Oregon, southern Idaho, and western Utah. A journey along U.S. Highway 50 through Nevada and western Utah crosses the heart of the Basin and Range Province, an austere landscape of north-trending desert ranges alternating with broad valleys and salt flats. Most of the ranges are bounded by normal faults; some are strike slip, and a few have been the sources of historical earthquakes. If you had been traveling on Highway 50 between Austin and Fallon on December 16, 1954, you would have been stopped north of Fairview Peak by a surface rupture across the highway accompanying a large-magnitude earthquake.

The region between Winnemucca in northern Nevada and Tonopah in southern Nevada is typical of the Basin and Range, except in one important respect: large historical earthquakes (Figure 6-7). The earthquakes began on September 3, 1903, with a M 6 earthquake beneath the Wonder Mining District at the edge of the Clan Alpine Range north of Highway 50 and east of Fallon. This was followed on October 3, 1915 by the Pleasant Valley Earthquake south of Winnemucca with a magnitude of 7.6, the largest earthquake ever recorded in the Basin and Range Province. The western front of the Tobin Range was ruptured, and the fresh fault scarp six to fifteen feet high is still spectacularly preserved east of the Pershing County road through Pleasant Valley, south of Winnemucca. Despite the large size of the earthquake, the area was so thinly populated that damage was minimal.

On December 21, 1932, a M 7.2 earthquake, largely strike slip, struck the back country south of Highway 50 east of Gabbs and Mina, and just over a year later, on January 30, 1934, an earthquake of M 6.3 shook the Excelsior Mountains in Mineral County southeast of Hawthorne. Twenty years passed, and then an area east of Fallon became, for a short time, the earthquake center of the world.

The earthquakes began at the east edge of Carson Sink on the west side of the Stillwater Range with a shock of M 6.3 on July 6, 1954, followed by another earthquake of M 7 on August 24.

Nearly four months passed, then on December 16 an earthquake of M 7.2 struck the Fairview Peak region, raising fault scarps on Highway 50. (A sign on Highway 50 directs you south on a gravel road to the "earthquake fault" that was part of the Fairview Peak rupture. This site shows evidence of both strike slip and normal slip.) Four minutes later, another earthquake of M 7.1 hit the east side of the Stillwater Range at the edge of Dixie Valley, producing another set of fresh fault scarps that are still visible at the foot of the range west of the road north from Highway 50 to the Dixie Valley geothermal field.

Because of this remarkable earthquake sequence, this region is called the Central Nevada Seismic Zone. Bob Wallace pointed out that not all of this zone has ruptured (Figure 6-7). Part of the Stillwater Range front at the north end of Dixie Valley between the 1915 rupture to the north and the 1954 rupture to the south remains unbroken. Wallace called this area the Stillwater Seismic Gap, an area of increasing probability for a future quake. But when the aftershocks of the December, 1954 earthquakes had died away, the Central Nevada Seismic Zone calmed down seismically and has been quiet ever since. The Stillwater Seismic Gap remains unfilled by an earthquake.

Does the Central Nevada Seismic Zone have geological characteristics that set it apart from other parts of the Basin and Range? Trench excavations showed that the previous earthquake on the 1915 rupture occurred in the early Holocene, almost ten thousand years ago, and the previous earthquake in Dixie Valley was late Pleistocene! The earthquakes of the Central Nevada Seismic Zone, like those of the Eastern California Shear Zone, have return times of many thousands of years. They just happened to coincide with the time of recordkeeping, not much longer than 150 years in this part of Nevada. The Central Nevada Seismic Zone is not significantly different from other parts of the western Basin and Range that have not been visited by large historical earthquakes.

Both the Eastern California Shear Zone and the Central Nevada Seismic Zone have been the locations of *earthquake clusters*. They experienced a period of intense earthquake activity on faults with low slip rates and long recurrence intervals. One might refer to the behavior of such earthquake clusters as a few decades of violence and thousands of years of boredom! However, only the historical earthquakes are clustered: paleoseismic evidence from trenches shows that prehistoric earthquakes in both the Eastern California Shear Zone and the Central Nevada Seismic Zone were not clustered.

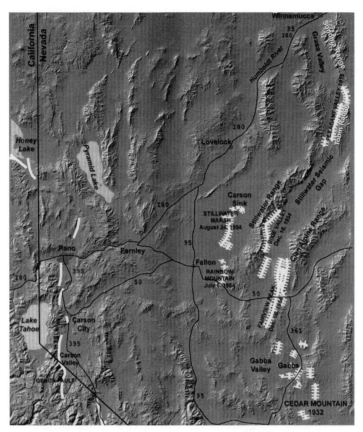

Figure 6-7. Computer-generated topographic map of northwestern Nevada and adjacent parts of California showing surface ruptures accompanying earthquakes in the Central Nevada Seismic Zone in 1915, 1932, and 1954. Reno and Carson City metropolitan areas are shown, along with a major fault west of those cities.

What about the rest of the Basin and Range? On December 14, 1950, an earthquake of M 5.6 was accompanied by surface rupture on a range front in the Honey Lake Valley in Lassen County, California, northwest of Reno. And on September 20, 1993, two earthquakes—the largest one M 6.0—struck Klamath Falls, Oregon, just north of the California line, killing two people and causing more than $7.5 million in damage. Other range fronts have ruptured in the Holocene, even though they have been seismically quiet in historic times. Perhaps these quiescent faults should be given more attention than the ones that have ruptured already. For example, the Klamath Falls earthquakes ruptured the normal fault forming the unpopulated western boundary of the Upper Klamath Lake graben; the more prominent eastern boundary fault, which extends through downtown Klamath Falls, remained still and thereby avoided (or delayed) a catastrophe.

Such faults are a major concern in the two largest population centers in the western Basin and Range, both in Nevada: Reno-Carson City with a population of nearly one-half million, and Las Vegas, with more than 1.2 million people. Between these cities lies the proposed national site for high-level nuclear wastes: Yucca Mountain.

Reno-Carson City, Las Vegas, and Yucca Mountain Nuclear Waste Repository

Nevada is the fastest-growing state in the Union, and most of its growth is taking place in its two largest cities, Reno and Las Vegas. The Reno area got its start as a mining camp, with the discovery and development of the Comstock silver deposits in the last half of the nineteenth century. Las Vegas was an arid railroad town between Los Angeles and Salt Lake City until Colorado River water impounded by Hoover Dam made its growth possible. Both cities turned to gambling, which led to skyrocketing growth, much of which is now fueled by tourism. Both are in earthquake country.

Several earthquakes struck the western Nevada region, including Reno, in the nineteenth century during the Comstock days, including an earthquake of M 7 on March 15, 1860 near Pyramid Lake, twenty-five miles northeast of Reno; and an earthquake of M 6.7 on December 26, 1869, in the Virginia Range fifteen miles east of Reno. Since then, seven earthquakes equal to or larger than magnitude 6 have struck the region. On September 12, 1994, an earthquake of M 5.9 struck at Double Spring Flat, twenty miles south of Carson City near the California state line. On the average, an earthquake of M 6 or larger strikes this part of western Nevada every few decades. Most result in some damage, but to date no one has been killed.

But Reno is in the Basin and Range Province, with geology like that of the Central Nevada Seismic Zone. The Carson Range and Peavine Mountain rise to the west of the basin in which Reno and Carson City lie, and the Virginia Range rises to the east. Many fault scarps cut the basin deposits near Reno, and some are found within the city itself.

The Carson Range Fault runs along the eastern foot of the Carson Range (Figure 6-7). Near the village of Genoa, south of Carson City, a quarry has removed the hanging wall deposits and exposed the face of this spectacular normal fault. Geologists with the Nevada Bureau of Mines and Geology estimate that major earthquakes, with magnitudes of 7.2 to 7.5, rupture this fault every few thousand years. The last one struck about 550 years ago, and the one before that 2,000 to 2,200 years ago. The estimated slip rate on this fault is one-tenth of an inch (2–3 mm) per year, faster than most Basin and Range faults.

dePolo et al. (1996) prepared a planning scenario for a hypothetical earthquake of M 7.1 on the Carson Range Fault. The effects of ground rupture, strong shaking, liquefaction, and landsliding on the metropolitan region were estimated, with specific attention to critical facilities such as schools, hospitals, and fire stations (see Chapter 13).

Las Vegas has more than twice the population of Reno-Carson City, yet the earthquake hazard is poorly understood in comparison to Reno. To the north, a zone of high seismicity extends east-west across Nye and Lincoln Counties, but Clark County, where Las Vegas is situated, has much lower seismicity. Like Reno, it is part of the Basin and Range Province, with Las Vegas Valley a graben bounded by the Spring Mountains on the west and by Frenchman Mountain on the east.

In addition, there are big fault scarps within and around the city, some of which are close to the Las Vegas Strip. The largest of these faults is the Eglington Fault north of town, with a scarp as high as seventy-five feet (Figure 6-1). Faults within Las Vegas are downdropped to the east, whereas a fault at the base of Frenchman Mountain east of town is downdropped to the west.

These faults cause environmental problems to urban development in Las Vegas. They develop fissures, which have destroyed houses built on top of them. But these fissures are probably not related to earthquakes. They are more likely caused by withdrawal of groundwater from Las Vegas Valley due to the overpumping of water wells, so that the ground subsides differentially across the faults. The fissuring problem has been known for half a century, and early workers thought that the fault scarps were entirely due to differential settlement accompanying groundwater withdrawal. But recent opinion has shifted to the view that these faults formed at least in part by earthquakes, although none has produced fault rupture in the short recorded history of Las Vegas. Some geologists think that the Eglington Fault could have a slip rate as high as a millimeter per year. The groundwater withdrawal problem has complicated the efforts to work out the slip rate and characterize the earthquake potential for these local faults.

Perhaps the larger hazard comes from across the state line, from strike slip on the Death Valley-Furnace Creek Fault Zone, with its closest point less than ninety miles from Las Vegas (Figure 6-1). The slip rate on these faults could be as high as a third of an inch (8 mm) per year— eight times the fastest rate estimated on the Eglington Fault, and faster than most faults in the Basin and Range Province. This fault zone has been studied mainly at its southern end, in Death Valley, but it extends north to the east side of the White Mountains, so that the fault is long enough to generate an earthquake greater than M 7.

Las Vegas is more likely to be damaged by an earthquake on the distant Death Valley-Furnace Creek Fault Zone because of its high slip rate than by an earthquake on a local fault. This view might be colored by the absence of any large local historical earthquakes, in contrast to Reno. But the Death Valley-Furnace Creek Fault Zone, with its higher long-term slip rate, has also been silent in recorded history.

So it is that Las Vegas and Reno, gambling centers of the West, are enmeshed in the greatest gamble of all: will they be struck by a major earthquake in the near future, and what should they do about it?

U.S. Highway 95 leaves the glitter of Las Vegas and traverses some of the most desolate terrain in the United States on the way to Beatty, Goldfield, and Tonopah. The desert ranges east of the highway would not be part of this story except for a series of decisions made in 1951, when many feared we were on the brink of World War III with the Soviet Union.

The Soviets detonated a nuclear bomb in 1949, and the following January, President Truman authorized a program to develop a hydrogen bomb. South Korea was invaded in June 1950, and in 1951, Julius and Ethel Rosenberg were convicted of nuclear espionage, leading to their execution in 1952. Nuclear weapons testing had been conducted by the Americans in the Marshall Islands in the western Pacific, but the site was too far from the United States to be reached conveniently and the military was worried about security. Could a site be found in the continental United States?

Although several sites were considered, the barren wasteland north of Las Vegas was favored over Dugway Proving Grounds, Utah or Alamogordo, New Mexico for several reasons. First, the area was virtually uninhabited, and second, a prevailing east wind would blow fallout away from the populated regions of California and Nevada. In addition, the government already owned it; it was the Las Vegas-Tonopah Bombing and Gunnery Range. On December 18, 1950, as Chinese forces were driving the Americans southward on the Korean peninsula, President Truman authorized the use of the Nevada facility for nuclear testing. On the following January 27, the first nuclear bomb was detonated at the Nevada Test Site.

The story of the atmospheric and underground nuclear test program and the effects of its fallout on residents downwind has been told elsewhere (Ball, 1986; Fradkin, 1989) and will not be repeated here. The Nevada Test Site is now under a moratorium for nuclear testing, and the stage is set for this desert region to serve a new role as an underground repository for high-level nuclear wastes.

A National Academy of Sciences report in the mid-1950s identified the need to find an underground site to dispose of spent nuclear fuel and other waste products. In 1976, Vincent McKelvey, Director of the

USGS, proposed to the Energy Research and Development Administration, the predecessor of the Department of Energy, that the Nevada Test Site be considered for disposal of high-level nuclear wastes. McKelvey cited the remoteness of the area in addition to its long history in testing nuclear weapons and its favorable geological site conditions. The Nuclear Waste Policy Act of 1982 provided for the investigation of three sites, including the Hanford Nuclear Reservation in Washington State (Yeats, 1998) and Yucca Mountain.

In 1987, Congress limited investigations to a single site, Yucca Mountain, at the west boundary of the Nevada Test Site (located on Figure 6-1), for further development as the nation's first underground repository for high-level nuclear wastes. More than ninety percent of the nuclear wastes to be stored at Yucca Mountain will be spent fuel from nuclear power plants; most nuclear wastes from the military are sent to the Waste Isolation Pilot Plant in New Mexico (Ewing, 1999). Since 1987, detailed studies costing $3 billion have been carried out with the plan to submit a license application to the Nuclear Regulatory Commission in 2001 or 2002 and to begin storing wastes at Yucca Mountain in 2010 (Hanks et al., 1999).

In contrast to site selection for nuclear testing, the studies at Yucca Mountain have been extremely thorough. It is a *critical facility*; that is, it must be constructed to such a high standard that even remote scenarios, such as a volcanic eruption or a large earthquake, must be considered. Following a recommendation from the National Research Council in 1995, Yucca Mountain is being evaluated for potential hazards spanning the next million years! This is long enough that it allows for climate change accompanying a future glaciation, and time for faults with very low slip rates to rupture, perhaps more than once.

Yucca Mountain lies within a zone of low to moderate seismicity crossing southern Nevada, and therefore a careful search has been made for faults with a potential for earthquakes. The Little Skull Mountain Earthquake of M 5.6 in 1992, triggered by the Landers Earthquake, highlighted the need for reinforcing the facility against even larger earthquakes. Eighty-eight faults with known or suspected Quaternary activity were identified within sixty miles of Yucca Mountain, and ten were identified within ten miles of the facility. Slip rates on these faults are only a fraction of a millimeter per year. Expected maximum magnitudes are in the low- to mid-6 range. The rationale is that even though an earthquake that might rupture the site is very unlikely, both the surface facility for handling wastes and the underground repository must be designed for such an event because of the catastrophic consequences of failure of the repository and escape of nuclear materials into the groundwater system or the atmosphere. The earthquake time frame for the licensing application is 10,000 years.

Do the detailed studies at Yucca Mountain provide an absolute guarantee against failure of the repository at some future time? This question has been asked by Nevada political leaders who are uncomfortable about their state being used as the nation's nuclear dumping ground. Hanks et al. (1999) point out that no ironclad guarantee is possible for Yucca Mountain nor for any other site on Earth. However, 70,000 metric tons of high-level nuclear waste, now in temporary storage at sites around the United States, must go somewhere—outer space, burial in polar ice sheets or on the deep-ocean floor, or to Yucca Mountain—or they must remain where they are (Hanks et al., 1999). These include fifty-four million gallons of radioactive wastes now being stored in 177 underground tanks at Hanford, Washington. The purpose of the Yucca Mountain evaluation is to reduce the danger to a minimum, but it cannot be eliminated completely. A project that considers hazards a million years into the future must be considered the ultimate in critical-facility planning.

Garlock Fault and the 1952 Kern County Earthquake

The Garlock Fault could have been discussed in the San Andreas chapter, for it is very much a part of that system. It is the second-longest strike-slip fault in California, more than one hundred fifty miles long; only the San Andreas is longer (Figure 6-1). Rupture of the entire Garlock would result in a single earthquake as large as M 7.8, close to the largest earthquakes expected on the San Andreas Fault. More likely, only part of the fault would rupture in a single earthquake, with a magnitude between M 6.6 and M 7.7.

Just as the Big Bear Earthquake on a left-lateral fault is paired to the Landers Earthquake on a right-lateral fault, the Garlock left-lateral fault is closely related to the right-lateral San Andreas Fault. The Garlock curves northeast away from the San Andreas along the southern margins of the Tehachapi and El Paso Mountains (Figure 6-1), across U.S Highway 395 south of Ridgecrest, heading into the China Lake Naval Weapons Center and Fort Irwin, where its strike is east-west. The fault ends north of the Avawatz Mountains and west of Highway 127, the highway between Baker and Death Valley. Here it intersects the right-lateral Death Valley Fault.

Evidence from offset stream channels and shoreline features of the dry lake bed of Searles Lake, east of China Lake and Ridgecrest, shows that the Garlock Fault has a slip rate higher than most of the desert faults east of the San Andreas system: one-fourth to one-third of an inch (6–8 mm) per year, with earthquakes recurring in intervals of less than a thousand years. This slip rate is much faster than that on faults of the Eastern California Shear Zone: one-half to one millimeter per year. Only the Death Valley-Furnace Creek Fault Zone, which joins the Garlock on the east, has a comparable slip rate, although this is not well documented.

Although the Garlock Fault is one of the most prominent in California, historical earthquake activity has concentrated on a less-obvious fault parallel to it and twenty miles to the northwest, on the opposite side of the Tehachapi Mountains. At 4:52 A.M. on July 21, 1952, an earthquake of M 7.5 struck this area, with its epicenter beneath Wheeler Ridge, in the San Joaquin Valley west of Highway 99 (now Interstate 5) south of Bakersfield. This was the largest earthquake to strike California since the 1906 San Francisco Earthquake. The zone of aftershocks trended northeast, and an irregular zone of surface rupture twenty miles long appeared on the White Wolf Fault (Figure 6-1). Twelve people lost their lives, and damage amounted to about $50 million, including $10 million in the Los Angeles metropolitan area. Eleven of the deaths occurred at Tehachapi, on the road between Bakersfield and Mojave, with the main cause poor building construction. Bakersfield, the largest city close to the epicenter, received damage both from the mainshock and from an aftershock of M 5.8 on August 22.

The White Wolf Fault underwent both reverse slip and left-lateral slip, and the earthquake was accompanied by uplift of the Tehachapi Mountains to the southeast. The slip rate on the fault is estimated at about a quarter inch (3–9 mm) per year, and the recurrence interval for earthquakes the size of the 1952 shock is estimated at one hundred seventy to four hundred fifty years, with considerable uncertainty due to the lack of paleoseismic evidence of earlier ruptures.

The 1952 earthquake lies within a zone of moderate seismicity, higher than seismicity associated with the Garlock Fault. This seismic zone extends from the southern San Joaquin Valley across the southern Sierra Nevada. Another earthquake of M 6.3 occurred in this zone at Walker Pass in the southern Sierra on March 15, 1946. Aside from the White Wolf Fault, the seismic zone does not appear to correspond to any zones of faulting beneath the southern Sierra.

The 1975 Oroville Earthquake: Can Earthquakes Be Caused by People?

Earthquakes would appear to be a natural hazard not caused or influenced by humans. But maybe not. The August 1, 1975 earthquake of M 5.7 at Oroville, in the Sierra foothills north of Sacramento, was probably induced by human activity.

The Oroville Earthquake struck an area with low seismicity. The Foothills Fault System was well known to geologists, but it was not known to be active. The earthquake was preceded by foreshocks starting on June 28. The foreshock sequence died down during July, but on August 1, twenty-one foreshocks, the largest one M 4.7, struck the area. The mainshock was accompanied by about two miles of surface cracks with maximum displacements a fraction of an inch on the Cleveland Hill Fault, part of the Foothills Fault System (Figure 4-2). Aftershocks showed that the fault dips westward and is a normal fault.

The northernmost surface faulting was about three miles south of Lake Oroville, raising the possibility that the earthquake might have been caused by filling the reservoir behind a dam 600 feet high. The 1967 Koyna, India earthquake of M 6.5, which resulted in hundreds of deaths, had been attributed to reservoir filling, as had another large earthquake in China. Some earthquakes struck almost immediately after the reservoir was filled, whereas others, including Koyna, struck several years later.

At the time it was thought that the cause of the Oroville Earthquake might have been the weight of the water in the reservoir, but a more widely accepted explanation now is that filling the reservoir increases the pore-water pressure in the underlying rocks, which makes it more likely that the rock will fail.

Nearly eight years elapsed between the time that Lake Oroville first began to fill and the earthquake. The reservoir had been as high as it was at the time of the earthquake eight times without an earthquake, and the water level had been increased to its highest level a few months before the 1975 earthquake. The earthquake, aftershocks, and surface rupture were all south of Lake Oroville, and there was no appreciable earthquake activity beneath the lake itself. However, the Cleveland Hill Fault was traced northward beneath the reservoir, and it is possible that water entered the fault zone beneath the reservoir, weakening the fault, which failed at a point south of the lake.

The Oroville Earthquake placed a bump in the road for the Feather River Project to build large dams to carry water from the Sierra Nevada southward to water-deficient cities in southern California. In 1979, a thin-arch dam near Auburn was cancelled after ten years of planning and the expenditure of more than $200 million. The Foothills Fault Zone was shown to pass beneath the foundation of the dam, and the U.S. Bureau of Reclamation concluded that a fault rupture accompanying an earthquake could cause the dam to fail.

There are other examples of increased seismicity related to filling a reservoir behind a dam. Lake Mead was impounded behind Hoover Dam, accompanied by an increase in earthquake activity. In Ventura County, the filling of Lake Casitas behind the Casitas Dam was accompanied by small earthquakes on the Red Mountain Fault, which extends at depth beneath the reservoir.

Summary

The interior regions of California and Nevada contain many faults whose earthquake potential is poorly known. Two clusters of earthquakes struck the region in the twentieth century: the Central Nevada Seismic Zone and earthquakes on the Eastern California Shear Zone. Each of these earthquake clusters released more earthquake energy than the San Andreas Fault did since the 1906 earthquake, yet the long-term slip rates on the source faults are only a small fraction of slip rates on the San Andreas Fault. Fortunately, most of the area is thinly populated, and an earthquake in most of the region would not be catastrophic.

The Reno-Carson City and Las Vegas metropolitan areas are large enough that an earthquake near one of those cities could be a great disaster, and a better assessment of the hazard is necessary. This is underway in both metropolitan areas, with studies in Reno more advanced than those in Las Vegas because of the difficulty in distinguishing between displacement caused by earthquakes and displacements caused by groundwater withdrawal in Las Vegas.

Is the hazard the same throughout the Basin and Range? GPS surveys from the Sierra Nevada to the Colorado Plateau show that the Sierra Nevada is moving northwest with respect to Colorado at a rate of one-half inch (12 mm) per year, with the motion accommodated along normal faults like those in Dixie Valley and strike-slip faults like those in Owens Valley and Death Valley. Even though there are active faults throughout the Basin and Range, more than half of this motion takes place in the western part between the Sierra Nevada and the Central Nevada Seismic Zone, a region that includes Reno and Carson City. A subsidiary zone of extension is found at the eastern edge of the Basin and Range near Salt Lake City. South of Reno, motion is concentrated on faults between Owens Valley and the California-Nevada border, and still farther south, right-lateral strike slip across the Eastern California Shear Zone is about one-half inch per year. This broad zone has been the site of most of the large historical earthquakes in the Basin and Range, but only a few of the faults in the zone have ruptured historically.

But with slip rates of a fraction of an inch per year and recurrence intervals measured in thousands of years, it seems unlikely that the past history of earthquakes will lead to an accurate forecast of the next one, unless monitoring of short-term signals is more successful in forecasting than it has been in the past. So the main defense is in zoning for land use and in upgrading building codes.

The Mammoth Lakes region poses a different problem: living on top of a volcanic caldera that is rising and producing damaging earthquakes from time to time. The Earth gives signals at Mammoth— bulging of the caldera floor for more than twenty years, swarms of earthquakes, and carbon dioxide gas killing trees in the forest—but the USGS is unable as yet to give a reliable warning that an earthquake or a catastrophic eruption is about to take place. An uneasy truce exists between the residents of Mammoth Lakes and the scientists dedicated to protect them against a natural disaster. One would hope that USGS volcanologists and seismologists become as acceptable as the TV meteorologist, whose forecasts also sometimes miss the mark.

Oroville is perhaps the most intriguing earthquake to strike the interior of California. Although the idea that the filling of Lake Oroville behind a high dam actually caused the earthquake is still controversial, the possibility is likely enough that Oroville has greatly impacted damsite engineering and led to cancellation of at least one major dam in the Sierra foothills. But just as we are aware that humans have an effect on the ozone layer and global warming, we now are aware that humans might have an effect on some earthquakes as well. Could we use this to our advantage, triggering small earthquakes on a fault before the strain builds up enough for a big one? Should we worry about other high dams around the world, even though it's been years since they were built? These are questions to ponder for the future.

Suggestions for Further Reading

de Polo, C.M., editor. 1998. Proceedings of a conference on seismic hazards in the Las Vegas region. Nevada Bureau of Mines and Geology Open File Report 98-6. 107p.

de Polo, C.M., et al. 1996. Planning scenario for a major earthquake in western Nevada. Nevada Bureau of Mines and Geology Special Publication 20. 128p.

de Polo, D.M., and C.M. de Polo. 1999. Earthquakes in Nevada 1852-1998. Nevada Bureau of Mines and Geology Map 119.

Hanks, T.C., I.J. Winograd, R.E. Anderson, T.E. Reilly, and E.P. Weeks. 1999. Yucca Mountain as a radioactive waste repository. U.S. Geol. Survey Circular 1184. 19p.

Hill, D.P. 1998. Science, geologic hazards, and the public in a large, restless caldera. Seismological Research Letters, v. 69, pp. 400–404.

Nevada Bureau of Mines and Geology. 2000. *Living with Earthquakes in Nevada*: Special Pub. 27, 36p.

Sieh, K., and S. LeVay. 1998. *The Earth in Turmoil*. New York: W.H. Freeman. Chapter 7, pp. 141–158 on Mammoth Lakes; chapter 8, pp. 159–179 on Basin and Range Province.

ᗡ 7 ᗡ
Cascadia

"Then there were lightning flashes, rumblings, and peals of thunder, and a great earthquake. It was such a violent earthquake that there has never been one like it since the human race began on Earth."

Book of Revelation 16:18

"Earthquake said, 'Well, I shall tear up the Earth.' Thunder said, 'That's why I say we will be companions, because I shall go over the whole world and scare them . . .' So [Thunder] began to run, and leaped on trees and broke them down. Earthquake stayed still to listen to his running. Then he said to him, 'Now you listen: I shall begin to run.' He shook the ground. He tore it and broke it in pieces . . . All the trees shook; some fell."

Yurok legend told by Tskerkr of Espeu, recorded by A.L. Kroeber

Introduction

Del Norte and Humboldt counties, in the northwestern corner of California, are as unlike the rest of the state as they are similar to western Oregon and Washington to the north. The region survives on an economy of logging and tourism, but it's also the abode of environmentalists, survivalists, refugees from urban California, and longtime residents who would just as soon be left alone. Great stands of timber, partly logged away, shade a misty rainforest with patches of damp farmland fronting on roaring rivers that give way to the thundering surf of a violent coastline.

The geological boundary between the Pacific Northwest and the rest of California is at Cape Mendocino within Humboldt County, south of Eureka (Figure 7-1), reached by a twisting road over the rugged Wildcat Grade to a wind-whipped coastline that was uplifted during an earthquake in 1992. This road curves into the valley of the Mattole River past the small settlements of Petrolia and Honeydew, rejoining U.S. 101 at Humboldt Redwoods State Park north of Weott. Petrolia is the "official" location of the famed Triple Junction discussed in the San Andreas chapter of this book, where the Pacific, North America, and Gorda plates meet (Figures 2-4 and 2-6).

Cape Mendocino gives its name to a great undersea fault, the Mendocino Fracture Zone (Figure 2-4), that extends westward across the Pacific Ocean floor for more than twenty-five hundred miles. About one hundred sixty miles from Cape Mendocino, the Fracture Zone is joined on the north by a seafloor spreading center, the Gorda Ridge. Oceanic crust of the Gorda Plate moves away from the Gorda Ridge to the base of the continental slope off northern California, where it drives northeastward beneath California at the Cascadia Subduction Zone at a rate of nearly one-and-a-half inches (35 mm) per year.

This region resembles Oregon and Washington in many ways, but it differs in one important respect: its seismicity. The communities facing the Cascadia Subduction Zone from Vancouver, B.C. to Eureka all await a cataclysmic earthquake along the plate boundary, but during the waiting period, the Cascadia region north of California has had relatively few earthquakes. Not so northern California, which has seismicity far greater than the rest of the Northwest—greater than any other section of California: one-fourth the state's total.

Earthquakes in the rest of California are found only in continental crust, but Cascadia earthquakes occur in three very different settings:

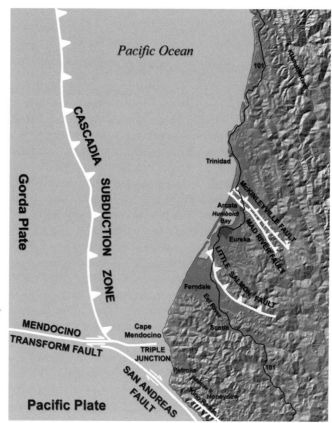

Figure 7-1. Computer-generated topographic map of California north coast showing the Triple Junction, the San Andreas Fault, the Mendocino Transform Fault, the Cascadia Subduction Zone, and the most active thrust faults onshore.

the Cascadia subduction zone, the downgoing Gorda Plate, and the North America crust (Figure 2-5). The earthquakes do not separate easily into these three settings. The 1992 Cape Mendocino Earthquake on the Cascadia Subduction Zone had numerous aftershocks in the Gorda Plate, and reverse faults in North America crust north and south of Eureka are an expression of distributed deformation on the onshore extension of the Cascadia Subduction Zone. Most of the historical seismicity is within the Gorda Plate and on the Mendocino Fracture Zone. Except for the 1992 earthquake and some of its aftershocks, the subduction zone separating the two plates is strangely silent.

The Cascadia Subduction Zone: The Big One

The Quietest Subduction Zone on the Pacific Rim

The 700-mile-long Cascadia Subduction Zone is at the base of the continental slope where oceanic crust of the Juan de Fuca and Gorda Plates drives northeastward beneath the edge of North America at a rate of one-and-a-half to two inches per year. Such great masses of rock grinding past each other should result in the release of tremendous amounts of strain energy as earthquakes, and in most of the world's subduction zones, it does. Ninety percent of the seismic energy released worldwide takes place at subduction zones in earthquakes that sometimes exceed M 9.

But not Cascadia, at least not in recorded history. Unlike most of the other subduction zones, Cascadia has not suffered a great earthquake in the two centuries since written records have been kept. Seismographs monitoring the region show so few microearthquakes that it was first thought that the seismographs were not sensitive enough to detect microearthquakes on the subduction zone. The seismic networks run by the USGS, the University of California at Berkeley, and the University of Washington were upgraded. A new source of seismic data was provided by the U.S. Navy, which has arrays of hydrophones on the ocean floor to monitor the noise made by the engines of Soviet submarines. These hydrophone arrays record sound transmitted through the water (*T-phase waves*), including engine noise, whale calls, and earthquakes. The release of the hydrophone data to the National Oceanic and Atmospheric Administration at Newport, Oregon, resulted in more detailed information about seismicity of the ocean floor. But even at these more sensitive listening levels, the Cascadia Subduction Zone is as seismically silent as Kansas.

In the early days of plate tectonics, it was assumed that subduction in the Pacific Northwest took place quietly, and that the oceanic crust somehow eased beneath the major cities of the Northwest without building up strain that would be released by earthquakes. Another view held that subduction had stopped at Cascadia in the past few thousand years. This idea was abandoned when it was learned that continental crust adjacent to the subduction zone is being slowly deformed, just as it is near the San Andreas Fault.

The Case for Great Earthquakes

In 1980, Jim Savage and his colleagues at the USGS began repeated measurements of survey benchmarks around Seattle, Olympic National Park, and the Hanford Nuclear Reservation in Washington State. Their conclusion: the crust beneath these networks is being slowly deformed in a way that is best explained by elastic strain building up in the crust. At about the same time, John Adams, a young New Zealand geologist transplanted to the Geological Survey of Canada, began comparing leveling surveys of highways done by the National Geodetic Survey (the old U.S. Coast and Geodetic Survey) over a period of several decades. Comparing the latest survey with earlier surveys showed Adams that the Coast Range of Oregon and Washington was tilting eastward toward the Willamette Valley and Puget Sound. Again, these results could be best explained by elastic strain buildup in the crust as the oceanic Juan de Fuca Plate drove eastward against the continent.

In 1984, Tom Heaton and Hiroo Kanamori of Caltech compared Cascadia with other subduction zones around the world, including Chile and Alaska, which had experienced earthquakes greater than M 9 in 1960 and 1964, respectively. They found that for some subduction zones in the western Pacific, very old, dense oceanic crust does descend beneath the volcanic arc, with only some of the strain released as earthquakes. But even these subduction zones have earthquakes greater than M 7, and the instrumental seismicity is high. At Cascadia, the subducting crust is relatively young, which means that it's still cooling from being formed by sea floor spreading. This makes the crust more buoyant and harder to subduct. (The comparison I use is that of trying to stuff an air mattress beneath a floating raft.) Heaton and Kanamori found that Cascadia resembles the subduction zones off Alaska and southern Chile, which are capable of earthquakes greater than M 9. Even though these subduction zones have produced great earthquakes in this century, at present they are quiet, like Cascadia.

Could it be that the lack of seismic activity at Cascadia is an indication that this subduction zone is *completely locked*? After all, earthquakes record the release of seismic energy, whereas the geodetic results record the buildup of strain. Maybe the time during which records have been kept—about two hundred years—is too short for us to conclude that Cascadia is not prone to great earthquakes. These speculations, relatively convincing in hindsight, were not enough to convince residents of the Pacific Northwest that they live in earthquake country. Something more tangible was needed.

Figure 7-2a. Tree roots from a spruce forest submerged abruptly seventeen hundred years ago in Niawiakum Estuary at Willapa Bay, Washington, exposed at very low tide. The tree roots match the forest ecosystem in the distance and document an abrupt subsidence of about ten feet. The 300-year subsidence event is represented by a soil zone halfway up the cut bank and is better seen in the following illustration. Photo by Robert Yeats.

Figure 7-2b. In this close-up view of the Niawiakum exposure, the 300-year soil is marked by the shovel blade. Note the exposed tree root at the right edge of the photo. A marsh similar to the one at the top of the picture was overwhelmed by the ocean, and gray clay with fossils was deposited on top. Photo by Brian Atwater, U.S. Geological Survey.

Two years after Heaton and Kanamori published their findings, Brian Atwater of the USGS was paddling a kayak up the Niawiakum Estuary at Willapa Bay in southwestern Washington. He was there to examine soft sediment along the banks of the estuary, which he could do only at very low tide. This young sediment, only a few hundred years old, might contain evidence that would support or refute the idea that Cascadia releases tectonic strain by great earthquakes.

There Atwater made an astonishing discovery. Just beneath the marsh grass is gray clay containing microscopic marine fossils—evidence that it had once been deposited beneath the surface of the sea. Below the

Figure 7-3. Dead forest of western red cedar sticking up through a brackish-water tidal marsh at Copalis River on the Washington coast. The forest was killed during rapid subsidence accompanying a Cascadia Subduction Zone earthquake. Tree rings from the dead trees provide evidence that they died sometime after the end of the A.D. 1699 growing season and before the beginning of the A.D. 1700 growing season. This age is consistent with the age based on a Japanese tsunami, discussed below. The forest in the background is above the highest tides. Photo by Brian Atwater, U.S. Geological Survey.

gray clay is a soil and peat layer from an older marsh, together with dead spruce stumps from an ancient forest. These stumps had been covered by the marine gray clay, in which the present marsh grass has grown (Figures 7-2 and 7-3). Why are the fossil forest and fossil marsh overlain by clay with marine fossils? Atwater concluded that the old marsh flat and the coastal spruce forest could have suddenly dropped down to be covered by the marine waters of Willapa Bay—not gradually, but instantly! What could have caused this?

Atwater described his discovery to George Plafker, also of the USGS. Plafker told him that the same thing had happened after the great earthquakes in southern Chile in 1960 and the Gulf of Alaska in 1964. Coastal areas had subsided and had been permanently inundated by the sea (shown for the Gulf of Alaska in Figure 7-4). Atwater made the comparison and thought the unthinkable. The marshes and coastal forests of the Pacific Northwest had been downdropped during a great prehistoric earthquake.

After Atwater's discovery, scientists found the same thing in estuaries from Port Alberni, on Vancouver Island, to Humboldt Bay in northern California: ancient marsh deposits, sometimes with tree stumps, abruptly overlain by marine or freshwater gray clay. At some places, the buried marsh is overlain by a thin layer of sand that appears to have been derived from the sea. This sand could have been deposited by a great tsunami caused by an earthquake (Figure 7-5). At most localities, the uppermost buried marsh is underlain by another gray

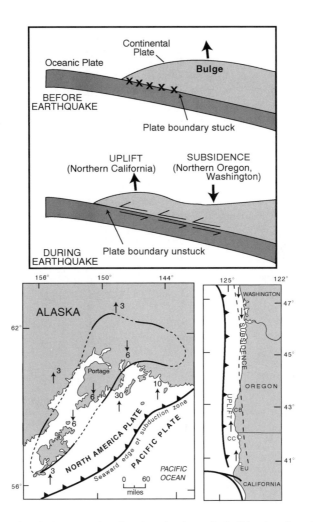

Figure 7-4 (Top). Cross section showing elastic-strain buildup in edge of continental plate before earthquake, then sudden release (elastic rebound) during earthquake, causing part to go up and part to go down. From central Oregon northward, the coast goes down during an earthquake, but in northern California, which is closer to the subduction zone, the coast goes up. Modified from Brian Atwater, U.S. Geological Survey. (Lower left). Map of part of southern Alaska, locating crust that went down (arrows pointing down) in the great 1964 earthquake (M_w 9.2) and crust that went up (arrows pointing up). Numbers show subsidence or uplift in feet. Modified from George Plafker, U.S. Geological Survey. (Lower right) Uplift and subsidence expected from a Cascadia Subduction Zone earthquake based on locations of subsided marshes and uplifted wave-cut platforms. The northern California coast would experience uplift. EU, Eureka; CB, Cape Blanco; CC, Crescent City.

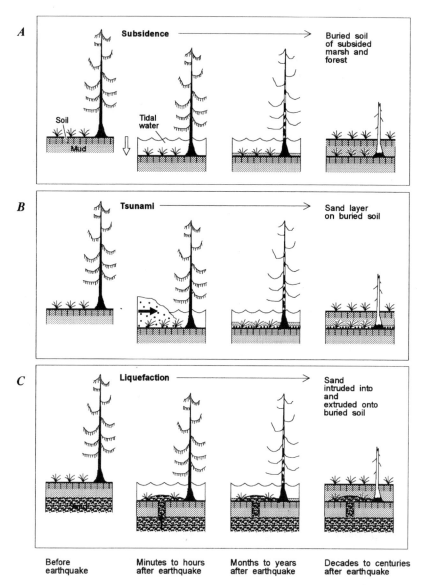

Figure 7-5. Coastal features used as evidence for great subduction-zone earthquakes: (a) Sudden subsidence of coastal forest, killing trees and depositing tidal sediment containing marine fossils directly on the forest litter. (b) Subsidence accompanied by a tsunami (seismic sea wave, see Chapter 10), depositing a layer of sand on top of the forest deposits. (c) Buried sand can be liquefied during an earthquake (see chapter 9), erupting onto surface; this is relatively uncommon in the Cascadia buried marshes. Image courtesy of Brian Atwater, U.S. Geological Survey.

clay, then another marsh, and another gray clay, and another marsh . . . up to seven at one locality. In all cases, radiocarbon dates showed that the most recent marsh burial took place about three hundred years ago.

At Humboldt Bay, the work was taken up by Gary Carver of Humboldt State University in Arcata. As a graduate student at the University of Nevada, Carver had already gained experience in active fault research, working on the 1872 Owens Valley Earthquake rupture, and he was also familiar with the downdropped forests on Kodiak Island in the Gulf of Alaska. To study the sediments beneath the Humboldt Bay marsh grass at Mad River Slough, west of Arcata, Carver had to drive a corer into the mud, but when he did he found the same thing Atwater had found: buried marsh deposits overlain by deep bay mud. At Mad River Slough, there are five of these buried marsh deposits.

After Atwater's discovery, geologists from Japan, England, and New Zealand, including specialists in the ecology of marshes and estuaries, critically scrutinized the evidence to look for defects in Atwater's earthquake hypothesis and to search for another, less apocalyptic, explanation. For some of the marsh deposits, the evidence is ambiguous. These could have formed after gigantic Pacific storms (which could be catastrophic in their own right!), breaching of a barrier sand bar, or changes in the configuration of the estuary itself. But an earthquake origin seemed most logical to explain the abrupt contact between marsh and overlying marine clay, although some experts disagreed about a few of the buried marsh soils. For example, the buried marshes at Mad River Slough are due to local thrust faulting and downwarping of a syncline in Humboldt Bay, even though the youngest marsh is 300 years old—the same age as the subduction-related buried marshes farther north. But all agreed that the burial of marshes that took place 300 and 1,700 years ago in southwest Washington was caused by sudden submergence of the coast during great Cascadia earthquakes. The average difference in age of successive marsh and forest burials was found to be five hundred years, although the age difference for some was as small as 150 years and for others as large as 1,000 years.

Recently, Chris Goldfinger of Oregon State University and Hans Nelson of Texas A&M University have found sand deposits on the Juan de Fuca Plate shaken loose by Cascadia earthquakes. These sand deposits repeat every 500 years or so, the same recurrence time as that based on buried marshes, but with a paleoseismic record longer than 10,000 years.

Magnitude 8 or Magnitude 9?

Although scientists became convinced that Cascadia has the potential for great earthquakes, a new controversy arose about whether the earthquake would have a moment magnitude of 8 or 9. Would the earthquake rupture the entire subduction zone from Vancouver Island to Cape Mendocino, or would there be a series of earthquakes—one in northern California, one or two in Oregon, and others in Washington and Vancouver Island? Even though all the radiocarbon dates point to an earthquake about three hundred years ago, radiocarbon dating is not precise enough to show that all the subsidence events were simultaneous. They could be separated by several decades and still give the same radiocarbon age.

Tree-ring dating can get closer than radiocarbon dating. Gordon Jacoby of Columbia University and Dave Yamaguchi of the University of Washington compared the pattern of growth rings of trees killed in several estuaries in southwest Washington. Variations in the growth pattern of trees allowed these scientists to conclude that trees in four of these estuaries were inundated sometime between the end of the growing season in 1699 and the beginning of spring growth in 1700. However, these dates are available only from several sites in southwestern Washington and they have not been confirmed elsewhere in Cascadia, which would strengthen the case for a M 9 earthquake three hundred years ago.

Gary Carver refers to this controversy as an *instant of catastrophe* (M 9) or a *decade of terror* (several M 8 earthquakes).

This might sound like arguing about the difference between getting run over by a Volkswagen or by an eighteen-wheeler, but the differences are important. A magnitude 9 earthquake would impact all of western Washington and Oregon, southwestern British Columbia, and north coastal California at the same time, so that emergency-response teams would have to come from central and southern California and from inland cities in other states. Intense shaking from a magnitude 9 earthquake would last two to four minutes; a magnitude 8 event would have strong shaking for about half that time. A building might survive strong shaking lasting a minute but not twice or three times as long. For comparison, the strong shaking accompanying the Kobe and Northridge earthquakes lasted less than thirty seconds.

The earthquake would trigger landslides in the coastal mountains and even on the submerged continental slope, where they could cause tsunamis. For even a M 8 event, large sand bars—such as the one enclosing Arcata Bay with the coastal communities of Fairhaven, Samoa, and Manila—could become unstable and liquefy. The uninhabited sand bar at Big Lagoon north of Trinidad and Patricks Point State Park did liquefy after an earthquake in 1980. Seismic sea waves, or tsunamis, could be as high as thirty to forty feet with a M 9 earthquake, but less than half that with a M 8. Aftershocks would continue for years, some with magnitudes greater than 7—large earthquakes in their own right.

Because a magnitude 9 earthquake would devastate such a large area, it would have severe effects on the economy of the Northwest and of California as far south as the San Francisco Bay Area. The rest of California could come to the aid of its stricken northwest counties, but could local government continue to serve its people? Could insurance companies, with their coverage extending throughout the western states, pay their claims? These possible outcomes show that the debate over M 8 or M 9 is not just an academic discussion. It affects the entire economy and how we prepare for earthquakes.

Finally, a Date from a Tsunami in Japan

The difficulty in figuring out the maximum size of a Cascadia earthquake is the lack of local historical records at the time the last great subduction-zone earthquake struck the Pacific Northwest. But there is one last chance. Suppose the earthquake generated a tsunami that was recorded somewhere else around the Pacific Rim where people *were* keeping records. This leads us to Japan, where written records have been kept for more than thirteen hundred years.

In May 1960, an earthquake of moment magnitude 9.5, the greatest earthquake of the twentieth century, shook the coast of southern Chile. This earthquake generated a large tsunami that traveled northwestward across the Pacific Ocean and struck Japan twenty-two hours later, causing 140 deaths and great amounts of damage (Figure 7-6). Cascadia is closer to Japan than Chile, and if a magnitude 9 earthquake ruptured the Cascadia Subduction Zone, the resulting tsunami should have been recorded in Japan. The height of the tsunami wave could give evidence about whether the earthquake was a magnitude 9 or only 8.

The southwestern part of Japan, closer to the ancient civilization of China, developed first, and the first local subduction-zone earthquake to strike that region was recorded in A.D. 684. Records of earthquakes, tsunamis (*tsunami* is a Japanese word derived from the characters for "harbor wave"), and volcanic eruptions were kept at temples and villages, principally in southwestern Japan, until A.D. 1192, when the government was moved to the fishing village of Kamakura on Tokyo Bay, leaving the emperor in isolated splendor far to the west, in Kyoto. In A.D. 1603, the Tokugawa rulers moved the administrative capital farther north to Edo, another small outpost which would become the modern capital of Tokyo. By this time, the entire Pacific coast of Honshu, which faces Cascadia, had been settled, and written records were being kept throughout Japan.

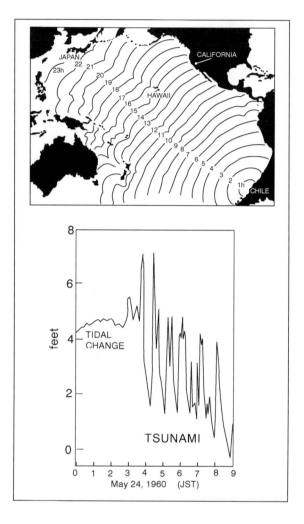

*Figure 7-6. (Top)
Wave fronts of
tsunami
accompanying the
great 1960 Chilean
Earthquake (M_w 9.5)
in hours, as tsunami
crossed Pacific
Ocean. (Bottom)
Tide-gauge record of
1960 tsunami
recorded at Miyako,
Japan, in hours.
From Kenji Satake,
Geological Survey of
Japan.*

    At the time, the Japanese did not necessarily make a connection
between earthquakes and tsunamis, but compilation of ancient records
by Japanese scientists and historians in recent years shows that most
of the tsunamis recorded from the earliest times were related to the
great subduction-zone earthquakes that frequently struck the Japanese
Home Islands. But a few tsunamis did *not* accompany a local earthquake.
Japanese investigators were able to correlate most of these "mystery"
tsunamis to subduction-zone earthquakes in South America, where local
records were kept. Earthquakes in Peru in A.D. 1586 and 1687, before
the Cascadia earthquake, and in Chile in A.D. 1730 and 1751, after the
event, produced tsunamis that were recorded in Japan.

But Kenji Satake of the Geological Survey of Japan, found records for one tsunami that could not be correlated to a local Japanese earthquake and had no apparent source in other subduction zones around the Pacific where records were kept, including South and Central America and the Kamchatka Peninsula off Siberia. On January 27 and 28, 1700, this tsunami produced waves as high as nine feet that were recorded at six different coastal sites on the main island of Honshu from the far north, near Hokkaido, to the Kii Peninsula south of Kyoto. Houses were damaged, and rice paddies and storehouses were flooded. The distribution of recording sites along most of the Pacific coast of Honshu ruled out a local source of the tsunami, such as a submarine landslide or a volcanic eruption.

At an earthquake conference at Marshall, California in September 1994, Satake was having lunch with Alan Nelson of the USGS. Nelson had been worrying about whether buried marshes at Coos Bay, Oregon had been downdropped by earthquakes. He explained to Satake that subsided marshes along the Northwest coast from British Columbia to California had all been radiocarbon dated at about three hundred years ago. These radiocarbon dates could not be pinned down any closer than a few decades around A.D. 1700 (the tree-ring dating had not yet been done). Could the Japanese tsunami of that year have been the result of a great Cascadia earthquake?

First, Satake and his Japanese coworkers had to exclude all other subduction zones around the Pacific Rim that, like Cascadia, were not settled by people keeping records in A.D. 1700—for example, Alaska and the Aleutian Islands. But the great 1964 Alaska Earthquake of M 9.2, the second-largest earthquake of the twentieth century, had generated only a very small tsunami in Japan—although it generated a destructive tsunami in the Pacific Northwest, including Crescent City, California (Chapter 10). This was due to the orientation of the Aleutian Subduction Zone, parallel to Japan rather than perpendicular to it, so that the largest tsunamis were propelled to the south and southeast, away from Japan. The Kamchatka-Kurile Islands Subduction Zone was another possibility, but explorers and traders were there as early as the 1680s, and again, the orientation of the subduction zone was parallel to Japan. By process of elimination, this left Cascadia.

Could the tsunami have been caused by a local typhoon? The records for the day of the tsunami show that central Japan had sunny or cloudy weather and was not visited by a storm. Even if weather records were unreliable, a monster typhoon would not have affected all the recording stations at the same time. Also, most typhoons strike Japan during the summer months and would have been most unusual in January.

Satake knew how fast tsunamis traveled in the open ocean. By backtracking the Japanese tsunami across the Pacific to the Cascadia

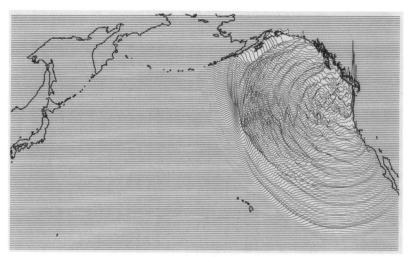

Figure 7-7. Computer model of the tsunami resulting from a great earthquake on the Cascadia Subduction Zone on January 26, A.D. 1700. The tsunami has already reached southern Alaska and the first wave is approaching the Hawaiian Islands. Japan is at far left. Note how far individual waves are separated from one another, and how high the waves are due west of Cascadia, in the direction of tsunami wave propagation, compared to wave heights off southern California, at lower right. From Kenji Satake, Geological Survey of Japan.

coastline, he calculated that if the earthquake generating the tsunami had come from Cascadia, it would have occurred about 9 P.M. on January 26, 1700. Satake's computer model of a Cascadia tsunami on its way to Japan is shown as Figure 7-7.

Native Americans Were Making Observations, After All

Could there be confirmation in the oral traditions of Native Americans living along the coast at that time? Garry Rogers of the Pacific Geoscience Centre in Sidney, B.C., found in the provincial archives in Victoria a report that an earthquake had struck Pachena Bay on the west coast of Vancouver Island during a winter night. It was discovered the following morning that the village at the head of the bay had disappeared. This is consistent with Satake's calculated time of the earthquake based on the Japanese tsunami. Traditions of the Chinook included references to ground shaking. The Makah, Tillamook, and Coos tribes have stories of the inundation of coastal settlements by "tidal waves" or tsunamis.

Gary Carver's wife, Deborah Carver, has collected stories recorded early in the twentieth century from Wiyot, Yurok, Tolowa, and Chetco tribal members living on the coast of northern California and southern Oregon. Many stories tell of strong shaking from a great earthquake along at least two hundred miles of coastline, followed by many aftershocks, liquefaction of sediments, subsidence of coastal regions, and tsunamis that lasted for several hours. Six of these stories said that the earthquake struck at night. The earthquake and tsunami destroyed many villages and drowned many people living there.

A Tolowa legend recorded by P.E. Goddard is presented at the beginning of Chapter 10. This legend tells the story of an earthquake followed by rising water from the sea at the same time that all the streams were overflowing. It's a gripping tale of a tsunami following a local earthquake. As for timing, the streams would most likely be overflowing during the winter. Gary Carver, Deborah's husband, studied uplifted sand deposits at Clam Beach, near the mouth of the Mad River, and found that the uplift occurred after the leaves had fallen and before new growth appeared on the trees; that is, probably during the winter.

M 8 or M 9? Where Do We Stand?

Satake developed computer models calculating the size of the tsunami generated from earthquakes of different moment magnitude. His computer model (Fig. 7-7) suggested that the nine-foot waves recorded in Japan must be produced by an earthquake of M 9; a tsunami from an earthquake of M 8 in Cascadia would produce a much smaller tsunami, probably too small to be recorded in Japan at that time. In addition, the tsunami record in Japan provides evidence for only one Cascadia earthquake (an "instant of catastrophe") and not a series of smaller earthquakes over several years (a "decade of terror"), because none of them would have been large enough to be recorded in Japan.

Participants in a scientific conference held at Seaside, Oregon in June 2000 were asked their opinions on M 9 vs. M 8 for the 1700 earthquake. The vote was overwhelming for an earthquake of M 9. However, this doesn't mean that all the earlier earthquakes recorded in the marsh deposits were M 9 as well. Atwater found that some of the paleoseismic sites at Willapa Bay recorded drowning of a coastal forest, whereas others recorded drowning of marsh grasses—evidence of less subsidence. If marsh grasses rather than forests were drowned, would this indicate a smaller earthquake, closer to M 8? In addition, the interval between earthquakes is variable, just as it is along the San Andreas Fault. Most of the forest drownings came a long time after the preceding earthquake, suggesting that if strain is allowed to accumulate for a longer time, a larger earthquake will result. This seems like a great idea except that the 1960 Chilean earthquake, the largest of the twentieth century, was preceded by great earthquakes in 1835 and 1837—less than one hundred thirty years earlier.

So even though scientists agree that the 1700 earthquake was M 9, earlier ones—and by inference, the next one, which is the main reason we are concerned about this—could be smaller. This is particularly true for that part of the subduction zone off the coast of northern California.

The subduction zone in northern California is different from the rest of Cascadia. Off Oregon and Washington, it lies at the base of the continental slope, but in northern California, as it approaches the Mendocino Escarpment, it turns toward the southeast and angles up the continental slope, headed for the Triple Junction beneath the village of Petrolia (Figure 7-1).

The southern end of the subduction zone ruptured during the April 25, 1992 Cape Mendocino Earthquake of M 7.1, the only part of the subduction zone to have broken in an earthquake during the seismograph era. This earthquake caused $64 million in damage; 202 buildings were destroyed and 356 people were injured, although nobody was killed. Damage was limited because the high-intensity zones of VII-IX covered only the small towns east of Cape Mendocino and not the larger cities of Eureka and Arcata which were farther away.

The mainshock, a zone of shallow aftershocks, and GPS observations before and after the earthquake suggest that the earthquake produced ten to sixteen feet of slip on an east-dipping fault plane with the mainshock at about six miles depth. There was no surface rupture onshore, although a fifteen-mile section of coastline was uplifted one to five feet, killing off a tidepool community of barnacles, mussels, sea urchins, and coralline algae (Figure 7-8). Several kinds of evidence,

Figure 7-8. Rocky platform on beach uplifted by the 1992 Cape Mendocino Earthquake on the Cascadia Subduction Zone, covered with bleached algae and shellfish killed by uplift. In northern California, where the subduction zone is close to the coast, coseismic deformation is by uplift, whereas in Oregon and Washington, coseismic deformation is by subsidence. Gary Carver included for scale. Photo by T. Dunklin, Humboldt State University.

including older marine terraces uplifted by prehistoric earthquakes and a comparison of slip in 1992 with the long-term convergence rate between the Gorda and North America Plates, give a recurrence interval for 1992-type earthquakes of a few hundred years, perhaps as low as one hundred fifty to two hundred years. However, the prehistoric Holocene terraces were uplifted in a longer section of beach than the 1992 uplift, suggesting that the older earthquakes were larger.

This recurrence interval is about half as long as the recurrence interval of Cascadia earthquakes in Oregon and Washington based on buried marshes, and the M 7.1 earthquake is small compared to the M 8 or M 9 earthquake that is awaited by the rest of Cascadia. Should this part of the subduction zone expect earthquakes in the M 7.0 to 7.5 range rather than the monster event Satake envisioned in A.D 1700? For insight, we return to southwest Japan, where part of the Nankai Subduction Zone comes ashore at the Izu Peninsula, just as the Cascadia Subduction Zone heads for the coast at Cape Mendocino. A long historical record in Japan shows that large earthquakes occur on the land part of the Nankai Subduction Zone at Izu Peninsula at intervals of seventy to eighty years, whereas the more typical part of the subduction zone is struck by earthquakes of M 8 or larger every one hundred to one hundred fifty years. Some of the Izu earthquakes were M 6.5 to M 7.1, and in addition, some of the large M 8 events ruptured across the peninsula as well as along the subduction zone at the base of the continental slope. This could explain the short recurrence interval near Cape Mendocino as well as the absence of the three hundred-year buried marsh at some sites in Humboldt Bay. Some of the Mendocino earthquakes would be local, like the 1992 event, and some would rupture the entire subduction zone, like the 1700 event. However, at the moment, this is just a guess.

M 8 or M 9? The last one was M 9, but the next one could be smaller. This means that we should plan for an earthquake of M 9 while hoping that it will be smaller. Even at M 8, a Cascadia Subduction Zone earthquake would be larger than any recorded on the San Andreas Fault. And no one believes that the San Andreas Fault or any other fault in California could generate an earthquake of M 9.

Earthquakes in the Gorda Plate

Commotion in the Ocean

The Juan de Fuca Plate is entirely oceanic, with thin crust made up of basalt. No part of it is above sea level. The crust is nowhere more than a few tens of millions of years old, meaning that it is still hot from being formed at a spreading center, which makes it weak and buoyant. At its northern and southern ends, where the spreading center is closest to the base of the continent and the descending crust is youngest and weakest, the oceanic plate is being actively deformed internally— deformation that is marked by high seismicity. These seismically active parts of the Juan de Fuca Plate are commonly referred to as separate plates, the Explorer Plate off Vancouver Island and the Gorda Plate off northern California. The Juan de Fuca Plate between its northern and southern ends has few earthquakes, indicating that internal deformation is less important there.

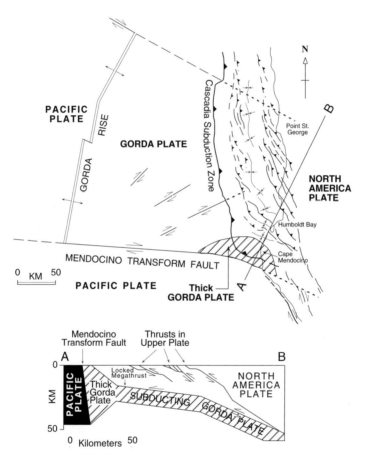

Figure 7-9. The Cascadia Subduction Zone approaches the coastline in northern California, where active folds and thrust faults were studied by Gary Carver and his associates. The subduction zone ends at the Mendocino Transform Fault, which turns southeast to become the San Andreas Fault. The Gorda Plate is internally deformed along the Cascadia Subduction Zone and Mendocino Transform Fault. Gorda Rise = spreading center. 10 km = 6.2 miles. Based on a drawing and cross section by Gary Carver, Humboldt State University.

The Gorda Plate is completely oceanic, with no parts of it above sea level, so that we are not able to measure its displacement rates directly using GPS but instead must rely on geophysical evidence. All permanent seismic stations are onshore, resulting in considerable inaccuracy in locating earthquakes on the plate. However, the use of T-phase waves from the U.S. Navy's hydrophone detection system has allowed scientists of the National Oceanic and Atmospheric Administration in Newport, Oregon, to improve greatly the accuracy and sensitivity for measuring smaller earthquakes far from the coast.

Mapping of the distribution of earthquakes shows that the seafloor spreading center generates low-level seismicity related to the movement of molten rock that rises to the surface and forms new oceanic crust. These earthquakes are mostly too small to be detected by ordinary seismographs onshore.

The Gorda Plate is cut by large strike-slip faults that rupture frequently to cause earthquakes (Figure 7-9). The Gorda Plate west of Arcata sustained an earthquake of M 7.3–7.6 on January 31, 1922 that was felt in Oregon, Nevada, and as far south as San Jose. Another earthquake of M 6.9–7.4 on November 8, 1980 thirty miles west of Trinidad destroyed a bridge, liquefied the sand bar at Big Lagoon, and caused $1.75 million in damages and six injuries. In 1991, the Gorda Plate was shaken by an earthquake of M 6.9 on July 12, another one of M 6.3 on August 16, and the largest one of M 7.1 on August 17, three hours after a crustal earthquake at Honeydew. On April 26, 1992, one day after the M 7.1 Cape Mendocino Earthquake on the Cascadia Subduction Zone, two aftershocks of M 6.0 and M 6.5 struck the Gorda Plate twelve and eight miles offshore. One of these aftershocks trashed the commercial district of the small town of Scotia. These were the largest of hundreds of aftershocks of this earthquake in the Gorda Plate, complicating the problem of whether the Cape Mendocino Earthquake was mainly a subduction-zone earthquake or a Gorda Plate earthquake. Except for the 1980 earthquake and the two Cape Mendocino Earthquake aftershocks, these Gorda Plate earthquakes were far enough offshore that intensities on the coast did not exceed V or VI.

The Gorda Plate has accounted for more damaging historical earthquakes in northern California than any other source, including the Cascadia Subduction Zone and the North America Plate. However, it could not produce earthquakes in the M 8 to 9 range, such as those expected on the Cascadia Subduction Zone.

The Mendocino and Blanco Transform Faults: Oceanic Cousins of the San Andreas

In Chapter 2, we considered two types of plate boundaries: *ocean ridges* or *spreading centers,* where new oceanic lithosphere is created as plates move away from each other; and *subduction zones,* where oceanic crust is recycled back into the interior of the Earth as plates move toward each other. The Gorda Ridge is a spreading center, and the Cascadia Subduction Zone occurs at the convergence of two plates. We also considered a third type of plate boundary where plates neither converge nor diverge but instead move past each other without creating or destroying lithosphere. Such a boundary is called a *transform fault* because it transfers plate motion between two spreading centers, or between two subduction zones. It involves the entire lithosphere and not just the Earth's upper crust.

The San Andreas Fault is a transform fault in which continental rocks of the North America Plate move past continental rocks of the Pacific Plate. The transform nature of the San Andreas Fault can be seen in Figure 4-16, which shows the Brawley Seismic Zone, a spreading center, separating the San Andreas and Imperial transform faults. Transform faults in the Pacific Northwest, on the other hand, are found on the deep ocean floor, where they form linear topographic features called *fracture zones.* The Blanco Fracture Zone separates the Gorda and Juan de Fuca Ridges; and the Mendocino Fracture Zone and its continental counterpart, the San Andreas Fault, separate the Gorda Ridge and spreading centers in the Gulf of California. The grinding of one oceanic plate past another along these fracture zones results in many earthquakes, some of which are felt every year in northern California and southern Oregon.

At first glance, the Blanco Fracture Zone resembles a left-lateral strike-slip fault because of the apparent left offset of the Juan de Fuca and Gorda ridges (Figure 2-6). But this apparent left offset would be left slip only if the two ridges had once been a continuous ridge that was later separated along the Blanco Fracture Zone. This is not the case. Remember that the Juan de Fuca and Gorda plates are moving away from the Pacific Plate at these spreading centers. Imagine yourself standing on the Pacific Plate looking northward across the Blanco Fracture Zone to another person standing on the Juan de Fuca Plate. The person on the Juan de Fuca Plate would move from left to right with respect to your position on the Pacific Plate. This means that the transform fault marked by the Blanco Fracture Zone is a *right*-lateral—not a *left*-lateral—fault.

As another thought experiment, imagine two jigsaw puzzle pieces that lock together by a tab that projects from one piece into the other. Now pull the pieces slowly apart. They are difficult to separate because the sides of the tab resist being pulled apart. In the same way, the Pacific and Juan de Fuca plates are being pulled apart, with magma welling up in the spreading centers as the plates are separated. Along the Blanco Fracture Zone, the crustal plates push past each other, generating friction and producing earthquakes. These earthquakes could be as large as M 7, or even somewhat larger, but probably not 8. The crust is too warm and therefore too weak to generate such large earthquakes. Accordingly, despite the high instrumental seismicity on the Blanco Fracture Zone, including many earthquakes felt onshore, the Blanco does not constitute a major hazard to communities along the coast, in part because the earthquakes are many miles offshore, and in part because these offshore earthquakes are not large enough.

At Cape Mendocino, the San Andreas Transform Fault turns west and becomes oceanic, like the Blanco: the Mendocino Transform Fault and Fracture Zone (Figure 2-4). Earthquakes on the Mendocino Transform Fault are frequent. The first major recorded earthquake, of M 6.5–7.3, struck close to Cape Mendocino on January 22, 1923, resulting in intensities of VIII and damage to buildings in Petrolia. Other earthquakes include three earthquakes of M 6.0–6.6 in 1941, and other earthquakes with magnitudes greater than 6 in 1954, 1960, and 1984. The 1984 earthquake of M 6.6, 155 miles west of the coast, was felt from Oregon to San Francisco, but intensities onshore did not exceed V because of its great distance from shore. On September 1, 1994, an earthquake of M 6.9 struck the Mendocino Transform Fault eighty-five miles offshore, the largest earthquake to strike the United States that year—larger even than the Northridge Earthquake of the preceding January. Because it was so far offshore, it did no damage, but it was felt from southern Oregon to Marin County, California.

Mendocino earthquakes could be larger than M 7, like those on the Blanco. But Mendocino and Blanco earthquakes are not likely to be as large as those on the continental San Andreas Fault, which could be as large as M 8. Because they are offshore, they are unlikely to result in great damage except where the Mendocino Fracture Zone is close to shore. The oceanic transform faults cause many earthquakes, but they are the weaker relatives to the San Andreas Transform Fault.

Slab Earthquakes

Although the Cascadia Subduction Zone is seismically quiet for the moment, earthquakes within the downgoing oceanic plate are frequent and have caused damage, particularly in the Puget Sound region of Washington. These *slab earthquakes* are much deeper than crustal earthquakes, with depths as great as fifty and sixty miles. The greater depth can be explained in two ways. First, the depth of earthquakes is controlled by the temperature of the rock in which they occur, and the downgoing oceanic plate is colder than the lower crust of the North America Plate. Second, the descending plate includes peridotite from the upper mantle, and this rock remains brittle at higher temperatures than basalt. It isn't clear why slab earthquakes have been recorded only at the northern and southern ends of Cascadia; they haven't been recorded beneath most of western Oregon.

The slab earthquakes beneath Puget Sound are part of an earthquake cluster, with earthquakes in 1909, 1939, 1946, 1949, and 1965. The largest were the Olympia Earthquake of M 7.1 in 1949 and the Seattle Earthquake of M 6.5 in 1965. These are described elsewhere (Yeats, 1998) and only the highlights are summarized here.

Because the earthquake mainshocks were deeper than thirty miles, they did not generate intensities as high as crustal earthquakes of the same magnitude. Only the Olympia Earthquake had intensities as high as VIII; the others were no higher than VII. But the area of highest intensity was unusually large for both earthquakes compared to a crustal earthquake, a reflection of the greater distance earthquake waves had to travel upward from the source to the Earth's surface. Also in contrast to crustal earthquakes, the slab earthquakes lacked a significant number of aftershocks: there was a big shake, and that was about it.

What about the Gorda Plate? An earthquake of M 6.75 or larger on November 23, 1873, on the thinly settled Oregon-California border might have been a slab earthquake. After this earthquake, cracks in the ground appeared on the trail between Crescent City and Gasquet in the Smith River Valley, and all the chimneys were knocked down. The highest intensity recorded was VIII, in a limited area in the northwestern corner of California, but intensities of V were felt over a broad area from Red Bluff in the south to McMinnville, Oregon, in the northern Willamette Valley south of Portland. Newspaper accounts did not report any aftershocks.

Northern California has a large number of earthquakes deeper than twenty miles (Figure 2-5), similar to western Washington and Vancouver Island, but unlike Oregon and the rest of California, which have only shallow earthquakes. These earthquakes lie within the descending Gorda Plate and can be traced as far east as Redding and Mt. Shasta. By analogy with the Puget Sound cluster of earthquakes, the thinly populated Klamath Mountains west of Interstate 5 could produce an earthquake as large as the 1949 Olympia Earthquake of M 7.1, but probably not much larger than that.

Crustal Earthquakes

The three sources of northern California earthquakes—the subduction zone, Gorda Plate, and the crust—are so interconnected that it's difficult to isolate faults and earthquakes that are limited to North America

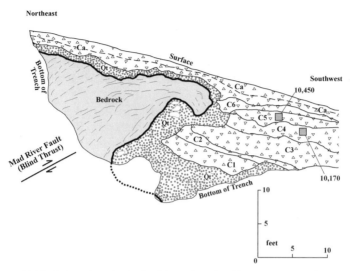

Figure 7-10. Paleoseismological evidence in a backhoe excavation for earthquakes on the Mad River Thrust Fault at McKinleyville. Bedrock was thrust over sediments radiocarbon dated at ten thousand years. The marine terrace platform (heavy solid line) was folded, indicating that the Mad River Fault is blind at this locality. (1 m = just over 3 ft 3 in.) From Gary Carver, Humboldt State University.

continental crust. Underwater investigations off Washington and Oregon show that the Cascadia Subduction Zone is not a single fault but a broad zone of deformation marked by folds and thrust faults. This zone is called an *accretionary wedge*, because it's formed of sediment from the incoming Juan de Fuca and Gorda plates that is scraped off and added to the edge of North America, like snow on the blade of a snowplow. Where the subduction zone turns to the southeast near the Mendocino Fracture Zone, it isn't a single fault but a zone, fifty to sixty miles wide (Figure 7-9), of thrust faults and warped marine terraces in addition to the buried fault that ruptured in the 1992 Cape Mendocino Earthquake, which doesn't reach the surface—at least not onshore. Plate motion causes deformation within the continental crust of North America as well as within the offshore Gorda Plate.

Although many faults in this region may have some Holocene displacement, two zones are the most active: the Mad River Fault Zone between Trinidad and Arcata, which includes the Mad River, McKinleyville, Trinidad, Fickle Hill, and Blue Lake faults, and the Little Salmon Fault south of Eureka (Figure 7-1). These structures account for about a third of an inch of shortening per year, which is about twenty to twenty-five percent of the convergence rate between the Gorda and North America plates. Backhoe trench excavations across these fault zones (Figure 7-10) provide paleoseismologic evidence that the last two earthquakes on the McKinleyville Fault and Mad River Fault produced displacement of at least eight feet for each event—evidence that these earthquakes were greater than M 7. Trench excavations across the Little Salmon Fault reveal evidence for three earthquakes in the past seventeen hundred years, each with displacements of eight to ten feet. The last earthquake struck about three hundred years ago. The late Holocene slip rate on the Little Salmon Fault alone is one-fifth inch (3–7 mm) per year.

At Clam Beach, near the McKinleyville Fault, Gary Carver found an uplifted beach cliff and tidepool platform carved by waves from an ancient sea. The beach sand resting on this platform contains a driftwood log that is one thousand to twelve hundred years old, based on radiocarbon dating. Another beach sand deposit overlies the driftwood log. This sand was colonized by beach grass and a coastal forest. A dead tree in this forest, still rooted in soil on top of the beach deposit, is no more than three hundred years old. This tree and its soil are overlain by still another beach deposit, perhaps recording subsidence related to movement on the McKinleyville Fault at the time of the three hundred year-old Cascadia Subduction Zone Earthquake.

Between these two fault zones are Arcata Bay and Humboldt Bay, where subsided marshes have been found. At first, the marsh subsidence was thought to be related to rebound from a subduction-zone earthquake, as was the case for marshes in Oregon and Washington and in marshes downdropped during the 1964 Alaska Earthquake (Figure 7-4). But this area is so close to the subduction zone that the coast would have been uplifted during an earthquake, just as islands close to the Alaska subduction zone were uplifted in 1964 (Figure 7-4). The bay becomes downwarped due to crustal deformation, especially slip on the Little Salmon Fault. Because the age of the drowned marsh is three hundred years, like the age of the youngest subsided marshes in Oregon and Washington, the crustal deformation must have occurred at the same time as the subduction-zone earthquake.

Uplifted marine terraces cut by storm waves provide additional evidence of crustal deformation. If there were no crustal deformation, the older, uplifted marine terraces would be completely level, like the present marine platform. But the older terraces are tilted and warped, as seen by viewing the coast north from Patricks Point. This shows that the Earth's crust in this region is on the move, up and down, through folding and faulting, producing earthquakes in the process.

An earthquake of M 5.9–6.4 on June 6, 1932 near Arcata produced intensity as high as VIII, resulting in one death and considerable damage in Eureka. On December 21, 1954, an earthquake of M 6.5–6.6 struck twelve miles east of Arcata in the vicinity of the McKinleyville Fault

Zone, causing one death and $3.1 million in damage. And on August 17, 1991, a M 6.2 earthquake struck at seven miles depth beneath the community of Honeydew on the Mattole River. The official estimate of damage in this relatively unpopulated region was $50,000, but this estimate is probably low. Intensities of VII and VIII were encountered, as they were in the two earlier crustal earthquakes.

It's clear that for their size, the crustal earthquakes were the most damaging. They struck at shallow depth close to population centers, whereas most of the Gorda Plate earthquakes were offshore, some so far offshore that no damage was done onshore.

Summary

Cascadia, the region between the Cascade Range and the Pacific coast, is the most seismically active region in California. During the period of recordkeeping, the region has experienced more than eighty earthquakes with magnitude greater than 5.5 or intensity greater than VI, not including damage from the 1906 San Francisco Earthquake on the San Andreas Fault to the south. At least sixty of these historical earthquakes resulted in damage.

Furthermore, the subduction-zone earthquakes that struck this region in the recent geological past were larger than any anticipated in the rest of California, including the San Andreas Fault. The January 26, 1700 earthquake on the Cascadia Subduction Zone was probably M 9.

The California portion of the Cascadia Subduction Zone is less well understood than it is farther north, in large part because it moves up the slope toward the coast at Cape Mendocino. As a result, the coast is uplifted in California during subduction-zone earthquakes, not downdropped as is the case farther north. The buried marsh deposits in Humboldt Bay are probably related to the Mad River Fault Zone and Little Salmon Fault. These faults rupture continental crust, but in a real sense, they are part of the broad Cascadia Subduction Zone, even though they are on land rather than at the base of the continent. The slip on these faults three hundred years ago is consistent with an earthquake of M 7 to 7.5, not M 8 or 9. Were these fault ruptures part of the great January 26, 1700 Earthquake, or did they precede, or follow, that event as part of a cluster?

One reason for the high seismicity is the deformation of the Gorda Plate, caught in the crunch between the Pacific Plate and North America Plate so that it actively deforms by strike-slip faulting. Some of this internal faulting is accompanied by earthquakes greater than M 7. When these earthquakes strike close to the coast, they cause destruction. Gorda Plate earthquakes can occur underneath the continent to depths of fifty miles or more, with deep earthquake activity recorded as far east as Interstate 5. These subcontinental earthquakes are called slab earthquakes; the earthquake in Del Norte County on the Oregon border in 1873 might have been a slab earthquake.

Other earthquakes occur on the Mendocino Fracture Zone, a transform fault that is the oceanic extension of the San Andreas Fault; and the Blanco Fracture Zone between the Juan de Fuca Ridge and the Gorda Ridge. These transform faults account for many earthquakes, just as the San Andreas Fault does, but these earthquakes are less of a hazard because they are offshore and their anticipated magnitudes are smaller than a "Big One" on the San Andreas Fault.

If there is a positive side to the dubious distinction Cascadia has as the earthquake center of California, it is that many of the earthquakes are offshore, and most people in the region live in wood-frame houses, which are more likely to survive an earthquake than masonry. The area is relatively thinly populated, but a major earthquake has not yet struck close to the major cities of Eureka, Arcata, or Crescent City during the times that records have been kept. An earthquake with magnitude greater than 7 on the Little Salmon Fault or the Mad River Fault Zone would cause much greater havoc than the Cape Mendocino Earthquake of 1992, which was far from any cities.

This region, like the rest of Cascadia, awaits the apocalyptic Cascadia Subduction Zone Earthquake of magnitude 8 to 9, with a little more uncertainty about whether the California part of the subduction zone will rupture with the rest of the zone, or thrust faults at the surface north and south of Eureka will rupture instead of (or in addition to) the subduction zone. The Cape Mendocino Earthquake apparently did rupture a small part of the subduction zone close to the Triple Junction. Will other subduction-zone earthquakes rupture larger parts of the plate boundary, but still not the entire plate boundary? Answers to these questions are not yet at hand.

Suggestions for Further Reading

Dengler, L., and K. Moley. 1999. Living on shaky ground: How to survive earthquakes & tsunamis on the North Coast. Humboldt Earthquake Education Center, Humboldt State University. 3rd edition, 24p. A simple guide to protection against earthquakes and tsunamis. Free. Web site: http://sorrel.humboldt.edu/~geodept/earthquakes/eqk_info.html

Gore, R., and J. Richardson. 1998. Cascadia: Living on Fire. *National Geographic*, v. 193, no. 5, pp. 6—37.

Hyndman, R.D. 1995. Great earthquakes of the Pacific Northwest. *Scientific American*, v. 273, no. 6, pp. 50–57.

Yeats, R.S. 1998. *Living with Earthquakes in the Pacific Northwest*. Corvallis: Oregon State University Press. 309p.

⤳ 8 ⤳
Memories of the Future:
The Uncertain Art of
Earthquake Forecasting

"What's past is prologue."

William Shakespeare, *The Tempest,* Act II

"Since my first attachment to seismology, I have had a horror of predictions and of predictors. Journalists and the general public rush to any suggestion of earthquake prediction like hogs toward a full trough."

Charles Richter,
Bulletin of the Seismological Society of America, 1977

A Mix of Science and Astrology

Predicting the future does not sit well with most earthquake scientists, including Charles Richter, quoted above. Yet the first question an earthquake scientist is asked is, "When's the next one?" Great contributions have been made toward alleviating hazards from earthquakes, but society insists that we also work toward prediction, no matter how elusive that goal may be.

Experts are asked to predict many things, not just earthquakes. How will the stock market perform? Will next year be a good crop year? Will peace be achieved in the Middle East? The answers to any of these questions, including the chance of an earthquake near you in the near future, depend on complex bits of information. For each question, experts are asked to predict outcomes, and they often disagree. Mathematicians tell me that predicting earthquakes and predicting the behavior of the stock market have a lot in common, even though one is based on physical processes in the Earth and the other is not.

But earthquake prediction carries with it a whiff of sorcery and black magic, of ladies with long, dangling earrings in dark tents, reading the palm of your hand. Geologists and seismologists involved in earthquake prediction research find themselves sharing the media spotlight with trendy astrologers, some with business cards, armed with maps and star charts. Thurston Clarke interviewed Jerry Hurley, a high school math teacher in Fortuna, California, who gets migraine headaches and a feeling of dread before an earthquake. His symptoms are worst when he faces in the direction of the impending earthquake. Hurley is a member of MENSA, the organization for people with high IQ, and he would just as soon somebody else had this supposed "talent." He and other "earthquake sensitives" report their findings to Christopher Dodge of the Science Policy Research Division of the Library of Congress, who keeps track of them as part of his hobby, "Project Migraine."

Some people claim that their predictions have been ignored by those in authority, especially the USGS, which has the legal responsibility to advise the President of the United States on earthquake predictions. They go directly to the media, and the media see a big story. In 1990, a self-styled climatologist named Iben Browning forecast a disastrous earthquake on December 3, 1990 in the small town of New Madrid, Missouri. The forecast was picked up by the media, even after a panel of experts—the National Earthquake Prediction Evaluation Council (NEPEC)—had thoroughly reviewed Browning's prediction and had concluded that it had no scientific basis (Spence et al., 1993). By rejecting Browning's claim, the nay-saying NEPEC scientists inadvertently built up the story. Browning, who held a Ph.D. in zoology from the University of Texas, had based his prediction on a supposed 179-year tidal cycle that would reach its culmination on December 3, exactly 179 years after a series of earthquakes with magnitudes close to 8 had struck the region. His prediction had been made in a business newsletter that he published with his daughter and in lectures to business groups around the country. Needless to say, he sold lots of newsletters.

Despite the rejection of his prediction by the seismological establishment, Browning got plenty of attention, including an interview on *Good Morning America*. As the time for the predicted earthquake approached, more than thirty television and radio vans with reporting crews descended on New Madrid. School was let out and the annual Christmas parade was canceled. Earthquake T-shirts sold well, and the Sandywood Baptist Church in Sikeston, Missouri announced an Earthquake Survival Revival.

The date of the earthquake came and went. Nothing happened. The reporters and TV crews packed up and went home, leaving the residents of New Madrid to pick up the pieces of their lives. Browning instantly changed from earthquake expert to earthquake quack and became a broken man. He died a few months later.

The USGS once funded a project to evaluate strange behavior of animals before earthquakes to check out the possibility that some animals can sense a premonitory change not measured by existing instruments. The project found no correlation between animal behavior and earthquakes. The study was aborted for fear that it might earn Senator William Proxmire's Golden Fleece Award for the month's most ridiculous government waste of taxpayers' money.

Earthquake Prediction by Scientists

Most of the so-called predictors, even those who have been interviewed on national television, will claim that an earthquake prediction is successful if an earthquake of *any* magnitude occurs in the region. Let's say that I predict an earthquake for the San Francisco Bay Area in the first two weeks of June of this year. An earthquake occurs, but it is of M 3, not "large" by anyone's definition. Enough M 3 earthquakes occur randomly in this part of California that a person predicting an earthquake of unspecified magnitude in the area is likely to be correct. Or say that someone predicts that an earthquake of M 6 or larger will occur somewhere in the world in June of this year. Again, it's quite likely that some place will experience an earthquake of that size around that time. Unless damage is done, this earthquake might not make the newspapers or the evening news, except that the predictor would point to it as a successful prediction ignored by the scientific establishment.

To issue a legitimate prediction, a scientist—or anyone else, for that matter—must provide an approximate *location, time,* and *magnitude,* and the prediction must be made in such a way that its legitimacy can be checked. The prediction could be placed in a sealed envelope entrusted to a respected individual or group, which would avoid frightening the public in case the prediction was wrong. But for a prediction to be of value to society it *must* be made public, and until prediction becomes routine (if it ever does), one must consider the negative impact on the public of a prediction that fails.

Prediction was one of the major goals of the federal earthquake program when it was established in 1977 (see Part I), and at one time it looked as if that goal might be achieved sooner than expected. In the early 1970s, a team of seismologists at Columbia University suggested that the speed of earthquake waves passing through the Earth's crust beneath the site of a future earthquake would first decrease, then return to normal speed just before the earthquake. The changes in speed of earthquake waves had been reported before small earthquakes in the Adirondacks of New York State and in Soviet Central Asia.

In 1973, Jim Whitcomb, a seismologist at Caltech, reported that seismic waves had slowed down, then speeded up just before the 1971 Sylmar Earthquake in the San Fernando Valley. Two years later, he observed the same thing happening near the aftershock zone of the Sylmar Earthquake: a slowdown of earthquake waves, presumably to be followed by a return to normal speed and another earthquake. Other seismologists disagreed. Nonetheless, Whitcomb issued a "forecast"— not his term, for he characterized it as "a test of a hypothesis." If the changes in the speed of earthquake waves were significant, then there should be another earthquake of magnitude 5.5 to 6.5 in an area adjacent to the Sylmar shock in the next twelve months.

My students and I happened to be doing field work on the Santa Susana Fault just west of the San Fernando Valley during this twelve-month period. Each night when the coyotes started to howl at our campsite near the fault we would sit bolt upright in our sleeping bags and wonder whether we were about to have an earthquake.

Whitcomb became an overnight celebrity and appeared in *People* magazine. An irate Los Angeles city councilman threatened to sue both Whitcomb and Caltech. In the meantime, the predicted timespan for the earthquake expired quietly. Meanwhile, other scientists tested the Columbia University theory and found a relatively poor correlation between the variation in speed of earthquake waves in the crust and future earthquakes. (Maybe Whitcomb was right in location but off on the time and magnitude. The Northridge Earthquake struck the San Fernando Valley twenty-three years after the Sylmar event. Its magnitude was 6.7, larger than expected.)

At about the same time as the San Fernando "test of a hypothesis," a prediction was made by Brian Brady, a geophysicist with the U.S. Bureau of Mines specializing in mine safety (Olson, 1989). Between 1974 and 1976, Brady published a series of papers in a respected international scientific journal, *Pure and Applied Geophysics,* in which he argued that characteristics of rock failure leading to wall collapses in underground mines are also applicable to earthquakes. Brady's papers combined rock physics and mathematical models to provide what he claimed to be an earthquake "clock" that would predict the precise time, place, and magnitude of a forthcoming earthquake. Brady observed that earthquakes in 1974 and 1975 near Lima, Peru had occurred in a region where no earthquakes had occurred for a long time, and he forecast a much larger earthquake off the coast of central Peru. Brady's work was supported by William Spence, a geophysicist with the USGS.

His prediction received little attention at first, but gradually it became public—first in Peru, where the impact to Lima, a city of five million people, would be enormous; later in the United States, where various federal agencies grappled with the responsibility of endorsing or denying a prediction that had very little support among mainstream earthquake scientists. The prediction received major media attention when Brady announced that the expected magnitude would be greater than 9, and the preferred date for the event was June 28, 1981. The Peruvian government asked the American government to evaluate the prediction that had been made by one of its own scientists. In response to Peru's request, a NEPEC meeting was convened in January, 1981 to evaluate Brady's prediction and to make a recommendation to the director of the USGS on how to advise the Peruvians. The panel of experts considered the Brady and Spence prediction and rejected it.

Did the NEPEC report end the controversy? Not at all, and Brady himself was unconvinced that his prediction had no scientific merit. Charles Osgood of *CBS News* interviewed Brady shortly after the January NEPEC meeting, but the interview was not broadcast until June 1981— close to the predicted time of the earthquake. Officials of the Office of Foreign Disaster Assistance took up Brady's cause, and the press labeled the NEPEC meeting a "trial and execution" (Olson, 1989) and described the NEPEC panel as a partisan group that would rather destroy the career of a dedicated scientist than endorse his earthquake prediction.

John Filson, an official with the USGS, made a point of being in Lima on the appointed day to reassure the Peruvian public. No earthquake arrived to keep Brady's appointment with Lima, Peru— and no earthquake has arrived to this day.

Forecasting Instead of Prediction

A more sophisticated but more modest forecast was made by the USGS for the San Andreas Fault at Parkfield, California, a backcountry village in the Central Coast Ranges (discussed in Chapter 4). Before proceeding, we must distinguish between the term *prediction*, such as that made by Brady for Peru, in which it is proposed that an earthquake of a specified magnitude will strike a specific region in a restricted time window (hours, days, or weeks), and the term *forecast*, in which a specific area is identified as having a higher statistical chance of an earthquake in a time window measured in months or years. Viewed in this way, Parkfield was a forecast, not a prediction.

Parkfield had been struck by earthquakes of M 5.5 to 6.5 in 1901, 1922, 1934, and 1966, and newspaper reports suggested earlier earthquakes in the vicinity in 1857 and 1881. These earthquakes came with surprising regularity every twenty-two years—give or take a couple of years—except for 1934, which struck ten years early. The 1966 earthquake arrived not twenty-two but thirty-two years later, resuming the schedule followed by the 1922 and earlier earthquakes. Seismograms indicated that the last three earthquake epicenters were in nearly the same spot. Furthermore, foreshocks prior to the 1966 event were similar in pattern to foreshocks recorded before the 1934 earthquake.

Scientists of the USGS viewed Parkfield as a golden opportunity to "capture" the next earthquake with a sophisticated, state-of-the-art array of instruments. These instruments were installed to detect very small earthquakes, changes in crustal strain, changes of water level in nearby monitored wells, and changes in the Earth's magnetic and electrical fields. The strategy was that detection of these subtle changes in the Earth's crust might lead to a short-term prediction and aid in forecasting larger earthquakes in more heavily populated regions.

At the urging of the California Office of Emergency Services, the USGS took an additional step by issuing an earthquake forecast for Parkfield. In 1984, it was proposed that there was a ninety-five percent chance—or probability—that an earthquake of a magnitude similar to the earlier ones would strike Parkfield sometime in the period 1987 to 1993. A system of alerts was established whereby civil authorities would be notified in advance of an earthquake. Parkfield became a natural laboratory test site where a forecast false alarm would not have the social impact of a forecast in, say, San Francisco or Los Angeles.

The year 1988, the twenty-second anniversary of the 1966 shock, came and went with no earthquake. Five years passed and still there was no earthquake. By January 1993, when the earthquake still had not occurred, the forecast was rated by most people as a failure.

One scientist compared the forecast to a man waiting for a bus that is due at noon. Noon comes and goes, then ten minutes past noon, then twenty past. No bus. The man looks down the street and figures that the bus will arrive any minute. The longer he waits, the more likely the bus will show up. In earthquake forecasting, this is called a *time-predictable model*—the earthquake should follow a schedule, like the bus.

But there is another view: the longer the man waits, the *less* likely the bus will arrive. Why? The bus has had an accident, or a bridge collapsed somewhere on the bus route. The "accident" for Parkfield might have been an earthquake of M 6.7 in 1983, east of Parkfield, away from the San Andreas Fault near the oil-field town of Coalinga in the San Joaquin Valley. The Coalinga Earthquake might have redistributed the stresses building up on the San Andreas Fault to disrupt the twenty-two-year earthquake schedule at Parkfield.

Another idea of the 1970s was the *seismic gap theory*, designed for subduction zones around the Pacific Rim but also applicable to the San Andreas Fault. According to theories of plate tectonics, about the same amount of slip should occur over thousands of years along all parts of a subduction zone like the Aleutians or Central America (or central Peru, for that matter, leading Brady toward his prediction). Most of the slip on these subduction zones should be released as great earthquakes. But some segments of each subduction zone have been seismically quiet a lot longer than adjacent segments, indicating that those segments that have gone the longest without an earthquake are the most likely to be struck by a future earthquake. This is a variation of the time-predictable model of waiting for the bus. The longer you wait, the more likely the bus will show up.

The San Andreas Fault ruptured in earthquakes in 1812, 1857, and 1906, and smaller earthquakes at Parkfield more frequently than that. But the southeasternmost section of the fault from San Bernardino to the Imperial Valley has not ruptured in the 230 years people have been keeping records. Paleoseismological evidence shows that the last earthquake struck around 1680, meaning that this section has gone more than three hundred years without a major earthquake. Is this reach of the fault the most likely location of the next San Andreas earthquake? How good is the seismic gap theory in forecasting?

Yan Kagan and Dave Jackson, geophysicists at UCLA, compared the statistical prediction in 1979 of where earthquakes should fill seismic gaps in subduction zones with the actual experience in the following ten years. If the seismic gap theory worked, then the earthquakes of the 1980s should neatly fill the earthquake-free gaps in subduction zones identified in the 1970s. But the statistical correlation between seismic gaps and earthquakes of the next decade was found to be poor. Some seismic gaps had been filled, but earthquakes also struck where they were not expected. Some seismic gaps remain unfilled to this day, including the San Andreas Fault southeast of San Bernardino.

Nonetheless, most scientists still believe in the underlying validity of the seismic gap hypothesis, although the model used in the 1979 seismic gap forecast was overly simplistic.

The Japanese had been intrigued by the possibility of predicting earthquakes even before a federal earthquake-research program was established in the United States. However, in contrast to the broad-based program initiated in the U.S., the Japanese focused on prediction, with their major efforts targeting the Tokai area along the Nankai Subduction Zone southwest of Tokyo. Like the San Andreas Fault at Parkfield, the Nankai Subduction Zone appeared to rupture periodically, with M 8 earthquakes in 1707 and 1854, and a pair of earthquakes in 1944 and 1946. But the Tokai area, at the east end of the Nankai Subduction Zone, did not rupture in the 1944 earthquake, although it had ruptured in the previous two earthquakes. Like Parkfield, the Tokai Seismic Gap was heavily instrumented by the Japanese in search of short-term precursors to an earthquake. Unlike Parkfield, Tokai is a heavily populated area, and the benefits to society of a successful earthquake warning there would be very great.

According to some leading Japanese seismologists, there are enough geologic differences between the Tokai segment of the Nankai Subduction Zone and the rest of the zone that ruptured in 1944 and 1946 to explain the absence of an earthquake at Tokai in the 1940s. The biggest criticism was that the Japanese were putting too many of their eggs in the prediction basket, concentrating their research on the Tokai prediction experiment at the expense of a broader-based study throughout the country. The folly of this decision became apparent in January 1995, when the Kobe Earthquake ruptured a relatively minor strike-slip fault far away from Tokai. The Kobe fault had been identified

Cartoon illustrating American and Japanese forecasting strategies, from Scholz (1997). Cartoonist: Morika Tsujimura.

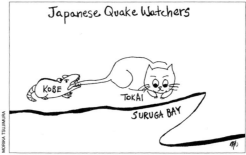

by Japanese scientists as one of twelve "precautionary faults" in a late stage of their seismic cycle, but no official action had been taken.

After the Kobe Earthquake, the massive Japanese prediction program was subjected to an intensive critical review. In 1997, the Japanese concluded at a meeting that their prediction experiment was not working—but they elected to continue supporting it anyway, at a reduced level. Similarly, research dollars are still being invested at Parkfield, but the experiment has gone back to its original goal: an attempt to "capture" an earthquake in this well-studied natural laboratory and to record it with the network of instruments set up in the mid-1980s, and upgraded since then. Indeed, Parkfield has already taught us a lot about the earthquake process, even though it has yet to "capture" its earthquake.

Have the Chinese Found the Way to Predict Earthquakes?

Should we write off the possibility of predicting earthquakes as simply wishful thinking? Before we do so, we must look carefully at earthquake predictions in China, a nation wracked by earthquakes repeatedly throughout its long history. More than eight hundred thousand people lost their lives in an earthquake in north-central China in 1556, and another one hundred eighty thousand died in an earthquake in 1920.

During the Zhou Dynasty in the first millennium B.C., the Chinese came to believe that heaven gives wise and virtuous leaders a mandate to rule, and removes this mandate if the leaders are evil or corrupt. This became incorporated into the Taoist view that heaven expresses its disapproval of bad rule through natural disasters such as floods, plagues, or earthquakes.

In March 1966, the Xingtai Earthquake of M 7.2 struck the densely populated North China Plain 200 miles southwest of the capital city of Beijing, causing more than eight thousand deaths (Ma et al., 1990). It might have been a concern about the mandate from heaven that led Premier Zhou Enlai to make the following statement:

"There have been numerous records of earthquake disasters preserved in ancient China, but the experiences are insufficient. It is hoped that you can summarize such experiences and will be able to solve this problem during this generation."

This call for action may be compared to President Kennedy's call to put a man on the Moon by the end of the 1960s. Zhou had been impressed by the earthquake-foreshock stories told by survivors of the Xingtai event, including a M 6.8 event fourteen days before the mainshock, fluctuations in groundwater levels, and strange behavior of animals. He urged a prediction program "applying both indigenous and modern methods and relying on the broad masses of the people." In addition to developing technical expertise in earthquake science, China would also involve thousands of peasants who would monitor water wells and observe animal behavior. Zhou did not trust the existing scientific establishment, including the Academia Sinica and the universities, and in 1970 he created an independent government agency, the State Seismological Bureau (SSB).

Following an earthquake east of Beijing in the Gulf of Bohai in 1969, it was suggested that earthquakes after the Xingtai Earthquake were migrating northeast toward the Gulf of Bohai and Manchuria. Seismicity increased, the Earth's magnetic field underwent fluctuations, and the ground south of the city of Haicheng in southern Manchuria rose at an unusually high rate. This led to a long-range forecast that an earthquake of moderate magnitude might strike the region in the next two years. Monitoring was intensified, earthquake information was distributed, and thousands of amateur observation posts were established to measure various phenomena. On December 22, 1974, a swarm of more than one hundred earthquakes—the largest one M 4.8—struck the area of the Qinwo Reservoir near the city of Liaoyang. At a national meeting held in January 1975, an earthquake of M 6 was forecast somewhere within a broad region of southern Manchuria.

As January passed into February, anomalous activity became concentrated near the city of Haicheng. Early on February 4, more than five hundred small earthquakes were recorded at Haicheng. This led the government of Liaoning Province to issue a short-term earthquake alert. The people of Haicheng and nearby towns were told to move outdoors on the unusually warm night of February 4. The large number of foreshocks made this order easy to enforce. Not only did the people move outside into temporary shelters, they also moved their animals and vehicles outside as well. So when the M 7.3 earthquake arrived at 7:36 P.M., casualties were greatly reduced, even though in parts of the city more than ninety percent of the houses collapsed. Despite a population in the epicentral area of several million people, only about a thousand people died. Without the warning, most people would have been indoors and losses of life would have been many times larger. China had issued the world's first successful earthquake prediction.

However, in the following year, despite the intense monitoring that had preceded the Haicheng Earthquake, the industrial city of Tangshan, 220 miles southwest of Haicheng, was struck without warning by an earthquake of M 7.6. The Chinese gave an official estimate of about two hundred fifty thousand people killed, but the U.S. estimate was closer to six hundred fifty thousand. Unlike Haicheng, there were no foreshocks. And there was no general warning.

What about the mandate from heaven? The Tangshan Earthquake struck on July 28, 1976. The preceding March had seen major demonstrations in Tiananmen Square by people laying wreaths to the recently deceased pragmatist Zhou Enlai and giving speeches critical of the Gang of Four, radicals who had ousted the pragmatists, including Deng Xiaoping, who would subsequently return from disgrace and lead the country. These demonstrations were brutally put down by the military (as they would be again in 1989), and Deng was exiled. The Gang of Four had the upper hand. But after the Tangshan Earthquake, Chairman Mao Zedong died and was succeeded by Hua Guofeng. The Gang of Four, including Mao's wife, opposed Hua, but Hua had them all arrested on October 6. Deng Xiaoping returned to power in 1977. One could say that the mandate from heaven had been carried out!

Was the Haicheng prediction a fluke? In August 1976, shortly after the Tangshan disaster, the Songpan Earthquake of M 7.2 was successfully predicted by the local State Seismological Bureau. And in May 1995, a large earthquake struck where it was predicted in southwestern China. Both predictions led to a great reduction of casualties. As at Haicheng, both earthquakes were preceded by foreshocks.

Why have the Chinese succeeded where the rest of the world has failed? For one thing, Premier Zhou's call for action led to a national commitment to earthquake research unmatched by any other country. Earthquake studies are concentrated in the China Seismological Bureau

(CSB—the new name for the SSB), with a central facility in Beijing and offices in every province. The CSB employs thousands of workers, and seismic networks cover the entire country. Earthquake preparedness and precursor monitoring are carried out at all levels of government, and in keeping with Chairman Mao's view that progress rests with "the broad masses of the people," many of the measurements are made by "volunteers," including schoolchildren.

Perhaps most of the apparent Chinese success is luck. All of the successful forecasts included many foreshocks, and at Haicheng the foreshocks were so insistent that it would have taken a major government effort for the people *not* to take action. No major earthquake in recent history in the United States or Japan is known to have been preceded by enough foreshocks to lead to a short-term prediction useful to society. Also, despite the few successful predictions in China, many predictions have been false alarms, and the Chinese have not been forthright in publicizing their failures. Their false alarms are more than would have been acceptable in a Western country.

A Strange Experience in Greece

On a pleasant Saturday morning in May 1995, the townspeople of Kozáni and Grevena in northwestern Greece were rattled by a series of small earthquakes that caused people to rush out of their houses. While everyone was outside enjoying the spring weather, an earthquake of M 6.6 struck, causing more than $500 million in damage, but no one was killed. Just as at Haicheng, the foreshocks alarmed people and they went outside. The saving of lives was not due to any official warning; people simply did what they thought would save their lives.

No official warning? Into the breach stepped Panayiotis Varotsos, a solid-state physicist from the University of Athens. For more than fifteen years, Varotsos and his colleagues Kessar Alexopoulos and Konstantine Nomicos have been making earthquake predictions based on electrical signals they have measured in the Earth using a technique called VAN, after the last names of its originators. Varotsos claimed that his group had predicted an earthquake in this part of Greece some days or weeks before the Kozáni-Grevena Earthquake, and after the earthquake he took credit for a successful prediction. In fact, Varotsos had sent faxes a month earlier to scientific institutes abroad pointing out signals indicating that an earthquake would occur in this area. But the actual epicenter was well to the north of either of two predicted locations, and the predicted magnitude was variously about 5 or between 5 and 6, depending on location. The uncertainties of his magnitude predictions amounted to a factor of 1,000 in energy release.

The VAN prediction methodology has evolved greatly over the past sixteen years and the proponents claim to be able to predict earthquakes of magnitude greater than M 5 one or two months in advance, including a devastating earthquake near Athens in 1999. As a result, Varotsos' group in Athens received for a time about forty percent of Greece's earthquake-related research funds—all without review by his scientific colleagues. His method has been widely publicized in Japan, where the press has implied that if the VAN method had been used the Kobe Earthquake would have been predicted. Although several leading scientists believe that the VAN method is measuring something significant, the predictions are not specific as to time, location, and magnitude. However, VAN has received a lot of publicity in newspapers and magazines, on television, and even in Japanese comic books.

The discussion on prediction concludes with two quotations from eminent seismologists separated by more than fifty years.

In 1946, the Jesuit seismologist James Macelwane wrote in the *Bulletin of the Seismological Society of America*: "The problem of earthquake forecasting [he used the word *forecasting* as scientists now use *prediction*] has been under intensive investigation in California and elsewhere for some forty years, and we seem to be no nearer a solution of the problem than we were in the beginning. In fact the outlook is much less hopeful."

In 1997, Robert Geller of Tokyo University wrote in *Astronomy & Geophysics,* the Journal of the Royal Astronomical Society: "The idea that the Earth telegraphs its punches, i.e., that large earthquakes are preceded by observable and identifiable precursors—isn't backed up by the facts."

Reducing Our Expectations: Forecasts Rather than Predictions

Our lack of success in predicting earthquakes has caused earthquake program managers, even in Japan, to cut back on prediction research and focus on earthquake engineering, the effects of earthquakes, and the faults that are the sources of earthquakes. Yet in a more limited way we can say something about the future; indeed we must, because land-use planning, building codes, and insurance underwriting depend on it. We do this by adopting the strategy of weather forecasting— twenty percent chance of rain tonight, forty percent tomorrow.

Earthquake forecasting, a more modest approach than earthquake prediction, is more relevant to public policy and our own expectations about what we can tell about future earthquakes. The difference between a prediction and a forecast has already been stated: a prediction specifies time, place, and magnitude of a future earthquake, whereas a forecast gives the statistical chances of an earthquake.

Two types of forecasts are used: *deterministic* and *probabilistic*. A deterministic forecast estimates the largest earthquake that is likely on a particular fault or in a given region. A probabilistic forecast deals with the likelihood of an earthquake of a given size striking a particular fault or region within a future time interval of interest to society.

An analogy may be made with hurricanes. The National Weather Service can forecast the likelihood of southern Florida being struck by a hurricane as large as Hurricane Andrew in the next five years; this is probabilistic. It can also give you the odds of a particular locality in the hurricane-prone Caribbean being hit by a Category 5 hurricane: once in sixteen hundred years. This is also probabilistic. It could also forecast how large a hurricane might be: two hundred mile-per-hour winds near the eye of the storm, for example. This is deterministic.

The Deterministic Method

No historical earthquake in metropolitan Los Angeles has exceeded M 6.7, the size of the Northridge Earthquake of 1994. Yet paleoseismic evidence from backhoe excavations in the San Gabriel Valley (Figure 5-7) suggests that prehistoric earthquakes in that area have been as large as M 7.2 to M 7.6. So urban planners must consider the possibility of future earthquakes as large as M 7.6. This is essentially a deterministic recommendation. What *has* happened *can* happen. We try to define the *maximum credible earthquake*, or MCE, for a given area.

How do we do this? In Chapter 3, it was pointed out that the moment magnitude (M_w) of an earthquake could be estimated from the area (length times depth) of the fault that ruptures and the amount of slip on that fault. The length of a potential earthquake rupture on a fault can be estimated even if the fault has not ruptured in historic time. The slip per earthquake can often be worked out from paleoseismic excavations along a fault scarp. These values can be compared with hundreds of earthquakes around the world that relate M_w to fault length and slip per earthquake.

For example, we know the length of the Cascadia Subduction Zone from northern California to Vancouver Island, and based on slip estimated from other subduction zones worldwide and on our own paleoseismic estimates of the greatest amount of subsidence of coastal marshes during an earthquake, we can estimate a maximum moment magnitude, assuming that the entire subduction zone ruptures in a single earthquake. If this happened, the subduction zone would rupture in an earthquake as large as magnitude 9. Most scientists believe that the last earthquake on the Cascadia Subduction Zone on January 26, 1700 was of magnitude 9. However, many scientists believe that earlier earthquakes might have ruptured only part of the subduction zone with a maximum magnitude of only 8.2 to 8.4 (see discussion in

Chapter 7), implying that the next earthquake could be M 8.2 to 8.4 rather than M 9. While the debate on maximum earthquake size continues, we go with the larger number—particularly for critical facilities such as power plants and dams.

Some probability is built into a deterministic assessment. A nuclear power plant should be designed for a maximum credible earthquake even if the recurrence time for it is measured in tens of thousands of years. The result of an earthquake-induced failure of the core reactor would be catastrophic, even if the chance of this happening is very small. Yet there is a limit. The possibility that California might be struck by a comet or asteroid, producing a version of nuclear winter and mass extinction of organisms, including ourselves, is real but is so remote— measured in tens of millions of years—that we do not incorporate it into our preparedness planning.

In the Los Angeles metropolitan area, two deterministic estimates are possible: a magnitude 7.6 earthquake on a local fault, based on paleoseismic evidence, and a magnitude 8 earthquake on the more-distant San Andreas Fault. Because the local earthquake would strike within the city rather than farther away on the San Andreas Fault, a separate deterministic estimate is necessary. The smaller but closer earthquake could be more destructive of life and property.

Probabilistic Forecasting

Introduction

We turn now to *probabilistic forecasting* of earthquakes. Examples of probability are: (1) the chance of your winning the lottery, (2) the chance of your being struck in a head-on collision on the freeway, or (3) the chance your house will be destroyed by fire. Even though you don't know whether you will win the lottery or your house will burn down, the probability or likelihood of these outcomes is sufficiently well known for the general population that lotteries and insurance companies can show a profit (see Chapter 11).

In probabilistic forecasting, we use geodesy, geology, seismicity, and paleoseismology to work out the likelihood of a large earthquake in a given region or on a particular fault at some time in the future. A time frame of thirty to fifty years is commonly selected because that length of time is likely to be within the attention span of political leaders and the general public. Besides, most home mortgages are for thirty years. A one-year time frame would yield a probability too low to get the attention of the state legislature, whereas a one-hundred-year time frame—longer than most life spans—might not be taken seriously, even though the probability would be much higher.

The Gutenbert-Richter Relationship

In 1954, Beno Gutenberg and Charles Richter of Caltech studied the instrumental seismicity of different regions around the world and observed a systematic relationship between earthquake magnitude and earthquake recurrence. Earthquakes of a given magnitude are about ten times more frequent than those of the next higher magnitude (Figure 8-1). The departure of the curve from a straight line at low magnitudes is explained by the inability of seismographs to measure very small earthquakes. These small events would be detected only when they are close to a seismograph; others that are farther away would be missed. So Gutenberg and Richter figured that if seismographs could measure all the events, the smaller ones would fall on the same straight line as the larger ones that are sure to be detected, no matter where they occur in the region of interest.

This is known as the *Gutenberg-Richter (G-R) relationship* for a given area. Clarence Allen and his colleagues at Caltech showed that thirty years of earthquakes in southern California and adjacent northern Baja

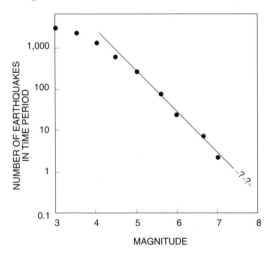

Figure 8-1. Illustration of the Gutenberg-Richter (G-R) relationship for thirty years of seismicity data for the Imperial Valley of southern California. Shown are the number of earthquakes of a given magnitude for the time period. Note that both scales are logarithmic; that is, each unit is ten times larger than the preceding one, as earlier discussed for magnitude. For this reason, the straight line might be somewhat misleading. The drop-off in seismicity for lower magnitudes is generally related to the sensitivity of the seismic network; it does not record all the smaller events. Projecting the straight line downward, G-R predicts 0.4 earthquakes of M 8 in the thirty-year time period, or one M 8 earthquake every seventy-five years. This prediction is questionable, as is the timing of still larger earthquakes. From C.R. Allen, Caltech, in Yeats et al., 1997.

California seemed to predict the recurrence of larger events within the region, up to a point. But for smaller regions of California and for individual faults, the Gutenberg-Richter relationship did not hold up well.

A flaw in the assumptions built into the relationship (or rather, a misuse of the relationship, unintended by Gutenberg and Richter) is that the line would continue to be straight for earthquakes larger than those already measured. For example, if the Gutenberg-Richter curve predicted one M 7 earthquake in a hundred years for the region, this would imply one M 8 per thousand years, one M 9 per ten thousand years, and one M 10 per hundred thousand years. Clearly this cannot be so, because no earthquake larger than M 9.5 is known to have occurred. The rocks of the crust are unlikely to be strong enough to release enough elastic strain energy to result in such a large earthquake.

Clarence Allen has pointed out that if a single fault ruptured all the way around the Earth—an impossible assumption—the magnitude would be only 10.6. So the Gutenberg-Richter relationship, used (or misused) in this way, fails us where we need it the most—in forecasting the frequency of large earthquakes that are most devastating to society.

The Gutenberg-Richter relationship contains another questionable assumption: the more earthquakes recorded on seismographs, the greater the chance of much larger earthquakes in the future. Suppose your region had more earthquakes of magnitudes below 7 than the curve shown in Figure 8-1. This would imply a larger number of big earthquakes and a greater hazard. At first, this seems logical. If you feel small earthquakes from time to time, you would worry more about bigger ones.

Yet the instrumental seismicity of the San Andreas Fault leads to exactly the opposite conclusion. Those parts of the San Andreas Fault that ruptured in great earthquakes in 1857 and 1906 are seismically very quiet today. This is illustrated in Figure 8-2, a seismicity map of central California, with the San Francisco Bay Area in its northwest corner. The San Andreas Fault extends from the upper left to the lower right corner of this map. Those parts of the San Andreas Fault that release moderate-size earthquakes frequently, like Parkfield and the area northwest of Parkfield, stand out on the seismicity map. The fault is unlikely to store enough strain energy to release an earthquake as large as magnitude 7. However, the fault in the northwest corner of the map (part of the 1906 rupture) has relatively low instrumental seismicity, and the fault in the southeast corner (part of the 1857 rupture) is marked by no earthquakes at all (see also Frontispiece). The segments of the fault with the lowest instrumental seismicity have the potential for the largest earthquakes, close to M 8.

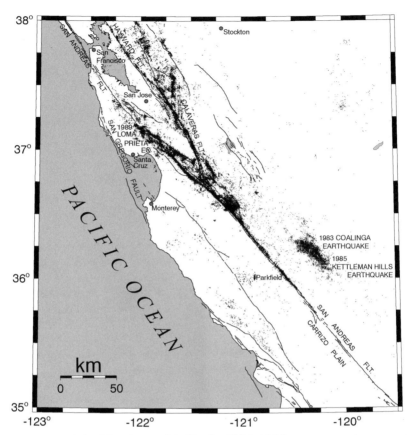

Figure 8-2. Seismicity of central California, 1980–1986, to compare the seismicity of that part of the San Andreas Fault that ruptured in 1857 (southeast, or lower right corner), which does not image the fault at all, to the seismicity of that part of the San Andreas Fault that ruptures frequently, as at Parkfield, or creeps accompanied by very small earthquakes, which images the fault very well. That part of the fault in the northwest, or upper left corner of the map ruptured in 1906, but is not well imaged by microearthquakes. From David Oppenheimer, U.S. Geological Survey.

The Cascadia Subduction Zone north of California has essentially zero instrumental seismicity. Yet evidence summarized in Chapter 7, in particular a Cascadia tsunami recorded in Japan, leads to the conclusion that Cascadia ruptured in an earthquake of magnitude 9 on January 26, 1700.

The flaw in the extrapolation of the Gutenberg-Richter curve to higher magnitudes is that seismicity, which measures the release of stored elastic strain energy, depends on the strength of the crust being studied. The San Andreas Fault at Parkfield would have many small earthquakes because the crust could not store enough strain to release a large one. A strong fault like the San Andreas Fault north of San Francisco would release few or no earthquakes until strain had built up enough to rupture the crust in a very large earthquake, such as the earthquake of April 18, 1906.

Characteristic Earthquakes

Paleoseismicity leads to still another criticism of the Gutenberg-Richter relationship. Dave Schwartz and Kevin Coppersmith, then of Woodward-Clyde Consultants in San Francisco, were able to identify individual earthquakes in backhoe trench excavations of active faults in Utah and California based on fault offsets of sedimentary layers in the trenches. They found that fault offsets tend to be about the same for different earthquakes in the same backhoe trench, suggesting that the earthquakes producing the fault offsets tend to be about the same size. This led them to the concept of *characteristic earthquakes*: a given segment of fault tends to produce the same size earthquake each time it ruptures. This would allow us to dig backhoe trenches across a suspect fault, determine the slip on the last earthquake rupture (but preferably on more than one rupture event), and forecast the size of the next

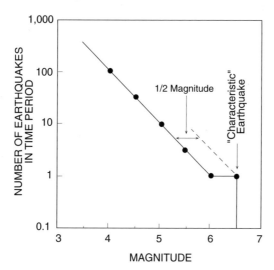

Figure 8-3. Comparison of the Gutenberg-Richter (G-R) relationship with the characteristic earthquake model, derived from geological studies that suggest that the largest earthquake for a particular segment of a fault will be a similar size, event after event. When earthquake recurrence intervals are taken into consideration, G-R underpredicts the size of the characteristic earthquake and does not allow for extrapolation to higher magnitudes. From Kevin Coppersmith and Robert Youngs, Geomatrix Consultants, San Francisco.

earthquake. When compared with the Gutenberg-Richter curve for the same fault, which is based on instrumental seismicity, the characteristic earthquake, when combined with its recurrence interval, tends to be different than the curve would predict (Figure 8-3). Furthermore, the Gutenberg-Richter curve cannot be used to extrapolate to earthquake sizes larger than the characteristic earthquake. The characteristic earthquake is as big as it ever gets on that particular fault.

These two examples suggest that the link between the Gutenberg-Richter relationship for small and moderate-size earthquakes and for large earthquakes is not strong. The period of seismographic observation is only a century, and historical records are complete for California for less than two centuries. Thousands of years might be required for a stronger relationship.

Uncertainty: How to Quantify what We Don't Know
Before considering a probabilistic analysis for the San Francisco Bay Area in northern California, we introduce the idea of *uncertainty*. There is virtually no uncertainty in predicting the times of high and low tides, solar or lunar eclipses, or even the return period of Halley's Comet. These events are based on well-understood orbits of the Moon, Sun, and other celestial bodies. However, the recurrence interval of earthquakes is controlled by many variables, as we learned at Parkfield. The strength of the fault may change from earthquake to earthquake.

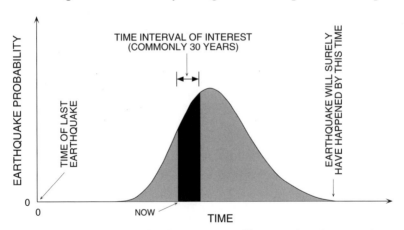

Figure 8-4. The probability for the recurrence of large earthquakes on a given fault or in a given region. Time increases from left to right, and the higher the curve, the greater the likelihood of an earthquake. The previous earthquake happened at time 0. The dark band is the time of interest for the probability calculation, commonly thirty years. The left side of the dark band is today. According to this probability, the earthquake will surely have happened by the time the probability curve returns to zero at the right side of the curve.

Other earthquakes may alter the buildup of strain on the fault, as the 1983 Coalinga Earthquake might have done for the forecasted Parkfield Earthquake that did not strike in 1988. Why does one tree in a forest fall today but its neighbor of the same age and same growth environment take another hundred years to fall? That is the kind of uncertainty we face with earthquake forecasting.

How do we handle this uncertainty? Figure 8-4 shows a *probability curve* for the recurrence of the next earthquake in a given area or along a given fault. Time in years advances from left to right, starting at zero at the time of the previous earthquake. The chance of an earthquake at a particular time since the last earthquake increases upward at first. The curve is at its highest at that time we think the earthquake is most likely to happen, and then the curve slopes down to the right. We feel confident that the earthquake will have occurred by the time the curve drops to near zero on the right side.

The graph in Figure 8-4 has a darker band, which represents the time frame of interest in our probability forecast. The left side of the dark band is today, and the right side is the end of our time frame, commonly thirty years from now. There is a certain likelihood that the earthquake will occur during the time frame we have selected.

This is similar to weather forecasting, except we are talking about a thirty-year forecast rather than a five-day forecast. If the meteorologist on the six-o'clock news says there is a seventy percent chance of rain tomorrow, this also means that there is a thirty percent chance that it will *not* rain tomorrow. If it doesn't rain, the weather forecaster isn't "wrong"; it's just that we experienced the less likely outcome.

Imagine turning on your TV and getting a thirty-year earthquake forecast: The TV seismologist says, "There is a seventy percent chance of an earthquake of magnitude 6.7 or larger in our region in the next thirty years." If you live in the San Francisco Bay area, you actually received this forecast in October 1999, covering a thirty-year period starting at January 2000. This forecast might not affect your vacation plans, but it could affect building codes and insurance rates. It also means that there is a thirty-percent chance that the San Francisco Bay area will *not* have an earthquake of M 6.7 or larger in the next thirty years. More about that forecast later.

How do we draw our probability curve? We consider all that we know: frequency of earthquakes based on historical records and geologic evidence, the long-term slip rate at which a fault moves, and so on. A panel of experts is convened to debate the various lines of evidence and arrive at a consensus about probabilities. The debate is often heated and agreement might not be reached in some cases. We aren't even sure that the curve in Figure 8-4 is the best way to forecast an earthquake. The process might be more irregular, even chaotic.

Our probability curve has the shape that it does because we know something about when the next earthquake will occur, based on previous earthquake history, fault slip rates, and so on. But suppose we knew nothing about when the next earthquake would occur; that is to say, our data set has no "memory" of the last earthquake to guide us. The earthquake would be just as likely to strike one year as the next. This is the same probability that controls your chance of flipping a coin and having it turn up heads: fifty percent. You could then flip the coin and get heads the next five times, but the sixth time, the probability of getting heads would be the same as when you started: fifty percent.

However, our probability curve is shaped like a bell; it "remembers" that there has been an earthquake on the same fault or in the same region previously. We know that another earthquake will occur, but we are unsure about the displacement per event or the long-term slip rate, and nature builds in an additional uncertainty. The broadness of this curve builds in all these uncertainties.

Viewed probabilistically, the Parkfield forecast was not really a failure; the next earthquake is somewhere on the right side of the curve. We're sure there *will* be another Parkfield earthquake, but we don't know when the right side of the curve will drop down to near zero. Time 0 is 1966, the year of the most recent Parkfield earthquake. The left side of the dark band is today. Prior to 1988, when the next Parkfield earthquake was expected, the high point on the probability curve would have been in 1988. The time represented by the curve above zero would be the longest recurrence interval known for Parkfield, which was thirty-two years (between the 1934 and 1966 events). That time is long past; the historical sample of earthquake recurrences at Parkfield, although more complete than for most faults, was not long enough. But some seismologists expect the earthquake very soon, based on a new probability estimate taking into account the delay caused by the nearby Coalinga Earthquake of 1983. (Perhaps it will have happened by the time you read this.)

How about the next earthquake to rupture the entire Cascadia Subduction Zone? Time 0 is 1700 A.D., when the last earthquake occurred. The left edge of the dark band is today. Let's take the width of the dark band as thirty years, as before. We are still to the left of the high point in the probability curve. Our average recurrence interval based on paleoseismology is five hundred years, and it has been only three hundred years since the most recent earthquake. What should be the time when the curve is at zero again? Not five hundred years after 1700, because paleoseismology shows that there is a great variability in the recurrence interval. The earthquake could strike tomorrow, or it could occur one thousand years after 1700, or 2700 A.D.

Earthquakes Triggered by Other Earthquakes: Do Faults Talk to Each Other?

A probability curve for the San Andreas Fault or the Cascadia Subduction Zone treats these faults as individual structures, influenced by neither adjacent faults nor other earthquakes. A probability forecast for the San Francisco Bay Area in 1988 considered each fault separately.

But the Landers Earthquake in the Eastern California Shear Zone appears to have been triggered by the earlier Homestead Valley and Joshua Tree Earthquakes (Figure 6-5). The Landers Earthquake also triggered earthquakes hundreds of miles away, including an earthquake within the Nevada Test Site. The North Anatolian Fault, a San Andreas-like fault in Turkey, had a series of earthquakes starting in 1939 and then continuing westward during the next sixty years, like falling dominos, culminating in a pair of earthquakes in 1999 at Izmit and Düzce that killed tens of thousands of people (LeVay, 1999).

Ross Stein and his colleagues Ruth Harris and Bob Simpson at the USGS figure that an earthquake on a fault increases stress on some adjacent faults and decreases stress on others. An earthquake temporarily increases the probability of an earthquake on nearby faults because of this increased stress. For example, the Landers and Hector Mine Earthquakes might have advanced the time of the next great earthquake on the southern San Andreas Fault by about fourteen years. This segment of the fault has a relatively high probability anyway since it experienced its most recent earthquake around 1680, but the nearby Eastern California Shear Zone earthquakes have increased the probability even further.

In the same way, a great earthquake can reduce the probability of an earthquake on nearby faults. In the San Francisco Bay Area, the seventy-five-year period before the 1906 earthquake was unusually active, with at least fourteen earthquakes with magnitude greater than 6 on the San Andreas and East Bay faults. Two of these earthquakes were greater than M 6.8. But in the next seventy-five years after 1906, this same area experienced only one earthquake greater than M 6. It appears that the great 1906 earthquake cast a stress shadow over the entire Bay Area, reducing the number of earthquakes that would have been expected based only on slip rate and the time of the most recent earthquake on individual faults. But the 1989 Loma Prieta Earthquake might mean that this quiet period is at an end.

However, just to keep us humble, the 1999 Hector Mine Earthquake struck an area of the Mojave Desert that at the time was believed to be in the stress shadow of the 1992 Landers Earthquake. As in so many other areas of earthquake forecasting, nature turns out to be more complicated than our prediction models. Faults might indeed talk to each other, but we don't understand their language very well.

Forecasting the 1989 Loma Prieta Earthquake: Close but no Cigar

Harry Reid of Johns Hopkins University started this forecast in 1910. Repeated surveys of benchmarks on both sides of the San Andreas Fault before the great San Francisco Earthquake of 1906 had shown that the crust deformed elastically before the earthquake, and the elastic strain was released during the earthquake. Reid figured that all he had to do was to continue measuring the deformation of survey benchmarks, and when the elastic deformation had reached the stage that the next earthquake would release the same amount of strain as in 1906, the next earthquake would be close at hand.

In 1981, Bill Ellsworth of the USGS built on some ideas developed in Japan and the Soviet Union that considered patterns of instrumental seismicity as clues to an earthquake cycle (Harris, 1998). A great earthquake (in this case, the 1906 San Francisco Earthquake) was followed by a quiet period, then by an increase in the number of small earthquakes leading to the next big one. Ellsworth and his coworkers concluded that the San Andreas Fault south of San Francisco was not yet ready for another Big One. However, after seventy years of quiet after the 1906 earthquake, signs pointed to earthquakes of M 6 to M 7 during the next seventy years, similar to those experienced in the nineteenth century.

Most forecasts of the 1980s relied on past earthquake history and fault slip rates, and much attention was given to the observation that the southern end of the 1906 rupture, north of the mission village of San Juan Bautista, had moved only two to three feet—much less than in San Francisco or farther north. In 1982, Allan Lindh of the USGS wrote that an earthquake of greater than magnitude 6 could occur at any time on this section of the fault. His predicted site of the future rupture corresponded closely to the actual 1989 rupture, but his magnitude estimate was too low. In 1984, Lynn Sykes and Steve Nishenko of Columbia University published a probability forecast for the San Andreas, San Jacinto, and Imperial faults.

In 1985, at a summit meeting in Geneva, General Secretary Mikhail Gorbachev handed President Ronald Reagan a calculation by a team of Soviet scientists that forecasted a *time of increased probability* (TIP) of large earthquakes in a region including central and most of southern California and parts of Nevada. This forecast was based on a sophisticated computer analysis of patterns of seismicity worldwide. In 1988, the head of the Soviet team, V.I. Keilis-Borok, was invited to a meeting of the National Earthquake Prediction Evaluation Council (NEPEC) to present a modified version of his TIP forecast. He extended the time window of the forecast from the end of 1988 to mid-1992 and restricted the area of the forecast to a more limited area of central and southern California, an area and time window that included the site and date of the future Loma Prieta Earthquake.

Several additional forecasts were presented by scientists of the USGS, including one that indicated that an earthquake on the Loma Prieta segment of the San Andreas Fault was unlikely. These, like earlier forecasts, were based on past earthquake history, geodetic changes, and patterns of seismicity, but none could be rigorously tested.

In early 1988, building on the work of Sykes and Nishenko, the Working Group on California Earthquake Probabilities (WGCEP) published a probability estimate of earthquakes on the San Andreas Fault System for the thirty-year period 1988—2018, based on past fault history and slip rate. This estimate was based primarily on the slip rate and earthquake history of individual faults, not on interaction among different faults in the region. The 1988 estimate stated that the thirty-year probability of a large earthquake on the Southern Santa Cruz Mountains (Loma Prieta) Segment of the San Andreas Fault was one in five, with considerable disagreement among working-group members because of uncertainty about fault slip on this segment. They forecast the likelihood of a somewhat smaller earthquake (M 6.5 to M 7) as about one in three, although they considered this forecast to be relatively unreliable. Still, this was the highest probability of a large earthquake on any segment of the San Andreas Fault except for the Parkfield segment, which was due for an earthquake that same year (an earthquake that has yet to arrive).

Then on June 27, 1988, a M 5 earthquake rattled the Lake Elsman-Lexington Reservoir area near Los Gatos, twenty miles northwest of San Juan Bautista and a few miles north of the northern end of the Northern Santa Cruz Mountains segment described by WGCEP as having a relatively high probability for an earthquake. Allan Lindh of USGS told Jim Davis of the California Division of Mines and Geology that this was the largest earthquake on this segment of the fault since 1906, raising the possibility that the Lake Elsman Earthquake could be a foreshock. All agreed that the earthquake signaled a higher probability of a larger earthquake, but it was unclear how much the WGCEP probability had been increased by this event. On June 28, the Office of Emergency Services issued a short-term earthquake advisory to local governments in Santa Clara, Santa Cruz, San Benito, and Monterey counties—the first such earthquake advisory for the San Francisco Bay Area in its history. This short-term advisory expired on July 5.

On August 8, 1989, another M 5 earthquake shook the Lake Elsman area, and another short-term earthquake advisory was issued by the Office of Emergency Services. This advisory expired five days later. Two months after the advisory was called off, the M 6.9 Loma Prieta Earthquake struck the Southern Santa Cruz Mountains, including the area of the Lake Elsman earthquakes.

So was the Loma Prieta Earthquake forecasted? The mainshock was deeper than expected, and the rupture had a large component of reverse slip, also unexpected, raising the possibility that it was on a fault other than the San Andreas. Some of the forecasts were close, and as Harry Reid had predicted eighty years before, much of the strain that had accumulated since 1906 was released. Still, the disagreements and uncertainties were large enough that none of the forecasters was confident enough to raise the alarm. It was a learning experience.

The 1990 Probability Forecast

The Working Group on California Earthquake Probabilities went back to the drawing boards and issued a new probability estimate in 1990, one year after the Loma Prieta Earthquake. Like the earlier estimate, this one was based on fault slip rate and earthquake history. Unlike the earlier estimate, this one gave a small amount of weight to fault interaction. The Southern Santa Cruz Mountains segment of the San Andreas Fault, which ruptured in 1989, was assigned a low probability of an earthquake of M greater than 7 in the next thirty years. The North Coast Segment of the San Andreas Fault also was given a low probability, even though at the time of the forecast it had been eighty-four years since the great 1906 earthquake on that segment. The mean recurrence interval on this segment is two to three centuries, and it is still fairly early in its cycle. On the other hand, probabilities on the Rodgers Creek Fault and the northern East Bay segment of the Hayward Fault, including the cities of Berkeley and Oakland, were raised to almost thirty percent in the next thirty years.

The 1999 Bay Area Forecast

The new ideas of earthquake triggering and stress shadows from the 1906 earthquake, together with much new information about the paleoseismic history of Bay Area faults, led to the formation of a new working group of experts from the USGS, the California Division of Mines and Geology, university scientists, and consultants. The group considered all the major faults of the Bay Area, as well as a "floating earthquake" on a fault the group hadn't identified. A summary of fault slip and paleoseismic data was published by the USGS in 1996. The new estimate was released on October 14, 1999 on the USGS web site and as a USGS Fact Sheet to be followed by a Circular.

The new report raises the probability of an earthquake with magnitude greater than M 6.7 in the Bay Area in the next thirty years to seventy percent (Figure 8-5). Earthquake probability on the Rodgers Creek Fault and the northern end of the Hayward Fault was given as thirty-two percent; the probability is somewhat lower on the northern San Andreas Fault, the rest of the Hayward Fault, and the Calaveras

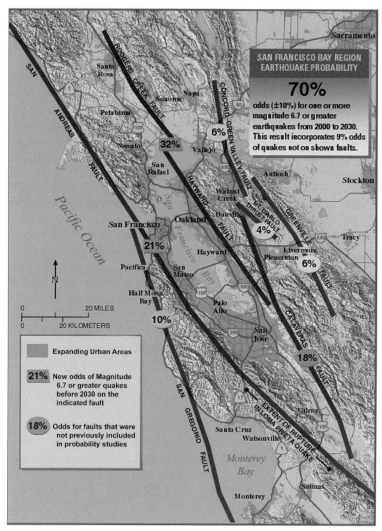

Figure 8-5. Thirty-year probabilities of an earthquake of M 6.7 or larger in the San Francisco Bay Area for the period 2000–2030, issued in October 1999. The probability that one of the Bay Area faults will produce an earthquake this large or larger is seventy percent, or about two chances out of three. The probability that any given fault will produce this size earthquake in that time period is given on each of the faults. For example, the Hayward-Rodgers Creek Fault has a thirty-two-percent chance of rupturing; the San Andreas Fault has a twenty-one-percent chance; and the Concord-Green Valley Fault only six percent. This forecast is revised as new information becomes available. From USGS Circular 1189.

Fault. A two-out-of-three chance of a large earthquake is a sobering thought for residents of the Bay Area.

Is this the last word? Clearly, it isn't. A new project called the Bay Area Paleoseismic Experiment (BAPEX), involving government, academic, and industry scientists, is underway to learn more about the paleoseismic history and slip rates on the key faults. It won't be long before another report updates this one. However, it's unlikely to change significantly the probability estimates in this report.

Similar estimates are underway in southern California, led by the Southern California Earthquake Center (SCEC), a consortium of government, academic, and industry scientists funded in large part by the National Science Foundation and the USGS. The slip rates and paleoseismic histories of southern California faults were published by Peterson and Wesnousky (1994), and a preliminary estimate of earthquake probabilities was published in 1995 by the Working Group on California Earthquake Probabilities. A map showing these probabilities in terms of the expected amount of strong shaking is given in the circular *Putting Down Roots in Earthquake Country,* available free on request from SCEC. (Probability of strong shaking is discussed further in the following chapter.) The report gives an eighty- to ninety-percent chance of an earthquake of M 7 or greater in the southern California region—a higher probability than for the Bay Area, but the area investigated is much larger and includes regions of low population.

But this still is not the final word. The preliminary report considered that the historical seismicity in California for the past two hundred years was unusually low, but a more recent analysis by Ross Stein and Thomas Hanks of the USGS indicates that the historical seismicity is about the same as that forecast for the next thirty years. A final estimate of earthquake probabilities will be presented probably in 2002, when SCEC completes its assignment as a National Science Foundation Science and Technology Center. This report will summarize the results of an intensive paleoseismic study of the southern San Andreas Fault as well as faults of metropolitan Los Angeles.

"Predicting" an Earthquake after It Happens
Seismic shock waves travel through the Earth's crust much more slowly than electrical signals. A large earthquake on the San Andreas Fault, for example, would set off seismographs close to the fault, which could send signals that could trigger the shutdown of critical facilities in cities such as Los Angeles before the shock wave arrived. Major gas mains could be shut off, schoolchildren could start a duck-cover-and-hold drill (see Chapter 16), heavy machinery could be shut down, and hospitals could take precautions in operating rooms. Automatic shutdown systems have been in use since the 1970s to stop high-speed

trains in Japan. Congress has charged the USGS with the job of submitting a plan to implement a real-time alert system (discussed further in Chapter 14). A real-time system is practical only for a distant earthquake, such as a warning to Los Angeles for a large earthquake on the San Andreas Fault. The system must be fail-safe; that is, it must be activated only by a large earthquake rather than by strong shaking from a local earthquake. The social and financial consequences of a false alarm could be enormous. The estimated cost for implementing such a system over five years in the San Francisco Bay Area is $53 million.

Additional information on the proposed Advanced National Seismic System, within which this system would operate, is available from Benz et al. (2000), USGS (1999), and http://geohazard.cr.usgs.gov/pubs/circ

What Lies Ahead

In New Zealand, Vere-Jones et al. (1998) proposed that we combine our probabilistic forecasting based on slip rates and estimated return times of earthquakes with the search for earthquake precursors. Geller (1997) has discounted the possibility that earthquakes telegraph their punches, and up to now the Americans and Japanese have failed to find a "silver bullet" precursor that gives us a warning reliable enough that society can benefit. Yet precursors, notably earthquake foreshocks, gave advance warning of the 1975 Haicheng, China Earthquake.

Possible precursors now under investigation include patterns in seismicity (such as foreshocks, but in other instances a cessation of small earthquakes), changes in the fluid level of water wells, rapid changes in crustal deformation as measured by permanent GPS stations, anomalous electrical and magnetic signals from the Earth, faults being stressed by adjacent faults that recently ruptured in an earthquake, and even the effects of Earth tides. For this method to be successful, massive amounts of information must be analyzed by high-speed computers so that real-time data can be compared quickly with other data sets where the outcome was known. A single precursor might not raise an alarm, but several at the same time might lead to an alert. The mistake made by previous scientific predictors, including the Chinese, was to put too much dependence on a single precursor and an unrealistic view of how reliable that precursor would be in predicting time, location, and magnitude of a forthcoming earthquake.

In the future, we could see earthquake warning maps, published periodically in newspapers and on TV, that point out an increased risk beyond that based on earthquake history, analogous to maps showing weather conditions favorable to tornadoes or hurricanes. The TV seismologist or earthquake geologist could become as familiar in major California cities as the TV meteorologist.

Here's a hypothetical example, arbitrarily set in December 2009. Seismographers observe an increased level of seismicity in Riverside County between Riverside and Indio, combined with increases in water level of three water wells being observed near Indio. In addition, permanent GPS stations show that the San Jacinto Mountains southwest of Palm Springs and the Cottonwood Mountains east of Indio are moving away from each other at a rate ten percent higher than observed in the preceding five years. This information is given to the Office of Emergency Services, the Seismic Safety Commission, and the general public as part of a three-month status report that also includes the long-term probability forecast for faults in southeastern California. This status report, including a map of the area, is published in major newspapers and included in TV news broadcasts. Twenty temporary seismographs are set up in the area of increased seismicity.

Scientists are concerned because this area includes that portion of the San Andreas Fault that has not ruptured since around 1680. This segment of the San Andreas Fault was listed as having a relatively high probability of a large earthquake in the SCEC forecast published in 1995 and the final SCEC report published in 2002.

In January 2010, new measurements of crustal deformation based on a network of GPS stations in the target area show increased movement indicating that the Coachella Valley is increasing its length east-west and becoming constricted north-south at a rate twice that observed for the preceding twenty years. At the end of January, the seismicity shows a sudden decrease. The USGS notifies the Office of Emergency Services, which issues a long-term alert after a meeting with the Governor and the Federal Emergency Management Agency. At the request of county boards of supervisors and city councils in the area, emergency managers in Riverside County and adjacent areas conduct earthquake-response drills, and drills in schools are increased to one per week. Fire engines are parked outside fire stations for the duration of the alert. Strong-motion sensors are placed in several additional buildings in Riverside, Palm Springs, Indio, and San Bernardino. Automatic gas shutoffs are installed in major trunk gas lines in the area, and hospitals test their emergency power generators in case of a loss of electrical power. Residents are urged to bolt heavy furniture to the walls, to purchase earthquake kits, and to make sure that they have a wrench next to their gas shutoff valve. The Red Cross offers several workshops on earthquake preparedness in the target area; these workshops are well attended. Water-well monitoring is increased, involving employees of local water districts.

I stop the scenario here. If a M 7.8 earthquake struck the San Andreas Fault during this period, clearly the public would be much better prepared than if no warning had been issued, but there would be no panic, no fleeing for the exits. If no earthquake followed, the social impact would not be great, although many local residents would surely be grousing about how the earthquake guys couldn't get it right. Earthquake insurance actuaries would be alarmed, and companies might raise insurance premiums as policies came due. But the insurance effects would be no greater than after long-term hurricane forecasts.

Although we do not have a statewide system in place, the USGS maintains an alert system at Parkfield on the San Andreas Fault and at Mammoth Lakes in the eastern Sierra, where volcanic hazard is present in addition to earthquake hazard. Unusual phenomena at either of these places are evaluated and reported to the public. Patterns of seismicity are monitored routinely by the USGS and networks run by University of California at Berkeley and Caltech. The monitoring system for metropolitan Los Angeles and the San Francisco Bay Area is becoming sophisticated enough that anomalous patterns of seismicity or other phenomena would be noticed by scientists and pointed out to the public by way of the Governor's Office of Emergency Services. Indeed, the Lake Elsman earthquakes of 1988 and 1989 were reported to the Office of Emergency Services, and alerts were issued.

Who can order an evacuation or declare an emergency? Not the USGS, and not the California Division of Mines and Geology. These organizations advise the Governor through the Office of Emergency Services, and only the Governor (or the President of the United States) can make those decisions.

Dangerous Faults to Watch
As a conclusion to this chapter and the four that precede it, I present my own list of faults that I think are likely to produce an earthquake in the near future. Except for Parkfield, none of these faults has sustained a large, damaging earthquake in the historical period starting with the Spanish missions. Unlike the Bay Area and SCEC reports, this "forecast" is one person's opinion, although it is strongly influenced by working-group reports for the two large metropolitan areas.

I limit myself to those faults that have a slip rate high enough that recurrence intervals are measured in hundreds rather than thousands of years. The uncertainty in forecasting the next earthquake on a fault with a recurrence interval of several thousand years is so large that the next earthquake cannot be forecast in time scales of decades without some fairly obvious short-term precursors. So here goes.

1. **The Rodgers Creek Fault-Northern Hayward Fault in the Bay Area.** The Bay Area Working Group gives this fault one chance in three of generating an earthquake of M 6.7 or larger in the next thirty years. The last earthquake on this part of the fault system struck more than three hundred years ago, and it has a slip rate close to one-third inch

(7–11 millimeters) per year. The chance for an earthquake on a Bay Area fault is more than two out of three. Future forecasts are unlikely to change these odds significantly for the Rodgers Creek-Northern Hayward Fault System.

2. **The Southern San Andreas Fault between Cajon Pass and Indio.** The Coachella Valley Segment of the San Andreas Fault between San Gorgonio Pass and Indio is the only locked section of the plate-boundary fault that has not produced a historical earthquake. The most recent prehistoric earthquake struck about 1680. The slip rate on the Coachella Segment and the adjacent San Bernardino Segment is about an inch per year. The recurrence interval based on the past four earthquakes is 220 years, yet it's been 320 years since the most recent earthquake. The San Bernardino Segment last ruptured in 1812. The recurrence interval based on the past six earthquakes at Wrightwood on this segment is 133 years, and it has been 188 years since the 1812 earthquake. The Landers and Hector Mine earthquakes have added stress to the San Andreas Fault, thereby shortening the time to the next earthquake. This part of the San Andreas is clearly overdue!

3. **Parkfield on the San Andreas Fault.** The Parkfield forecast for an earthquake in 1988 turned out to be a dud, but that may have been because the dampening effect of the 1983 M 6.7 Coalinga Earthquake was not taken into consideration. Recent calculations suggest that the Coalinga Earthquake reduced the likelihood of a M 5.8 Parkfield earthquake by as much as forty percent for fifteen years. Strain is building up to the 1983 level, and a Parkfield earthquake is expected by some scientists in the next few years.

4. **Santa Susana, San Cayetano, Oak Ridge, and Red Mountain faults, Ventura Region.** All but the Red Mountain Fault are known to have slip rates of about a quarter inch per year. The north side of the Ventura Basin is closing on the south side at about one-third inch per year, and the faults are locked. None of these faults has ruptured in the past 230 years. I doubt that this region will go much longer without an earthquake on one of these four faults, especially since their counterparts in the San Fernando Valley ruptured in 1971 and 1994. The SCEC report assigns a sixty-percent probability of strong ground motion in the Ventura and San Bernardino regions combined.

Why Do We Bother with all This?

By now you're probably unimpressed with probabilistic earthquake forecasting techniques. Although probability estimates for faults with high slip rates such as the San Andreas Fault are improving, it's unlikely that we'll be able to improve probability estimates for faults with low slip rates such as the Owens Valley or Newport-Inglewood faults, unless we're more successful with short-term precursors. Yet we continue in our attempts, because insurance underwriters need this kind of statistical information to establish risks and premium rates. Furthermore, government agencies need to know whether the long-term chances of an earthquake are high enough to require stricter building codes, thereby increasing the cost of construction. This chapter began with a discussion of earthquake *prediction* in terms of yes or no, but probabilistic *forecasting* allows us to quantify the "maybes" and to say something about the uncertainties. Much depends on how useful to society the forecasts are for the Bay Area and southern California, especially the most recent forecast of a seventy-percent chance for an earthquake of M 6.7 or larger in the Bay Area in the next thirty years. To put it another way, will the earthquakes arrive on schedule or will they be delayed, as the 1988 Parkfield earthquake was; or will they strike in an unexpected place?

Why are we not farther along in scientifically reliable earthquake forecasting? The answer might lie in our appraisal in Chapter 2 of the structural integrity of the Earth's crust—not very strong, not up to code. Some scientists believe that the Earth's crust is in a state of critical failure—almost but not quite ready to break. In this view, the Earth is not like a strong, well-constructed building that one can predict with reasonable certainty won't collapse. The crust is more like a row of old tenement shacks, poorly built in the first place with shoddy workmanship and materials, and now affected by rot and old age. These shacks will undoubtedly collapse some day, but which one will fall down first? Will the next shack collapse tomorrow or ten years from now? This is the dilemma of the earthquake forecaster.

But society and our own scientific curiosity demand that we try.

Suggestions for Further Reading

Lomnitz, C. 1994. *Fundamentals of Earthquake Prediction*. New York: John Wiley & Sons. 326p.

Olson, R.S. 1989. *The Politics of Earthquake Prediction*. Princeton, N.J.: Princeton University Press. 187p.

Southern California Earthquake Center. 1995. Putting Down Roots in Earthquake Country. 29p.

Working Group on California Earthquake Probabilities. 1999. Earthquake probabilities in the San Francisco Bay Region: 2000 to 2030—a summary of findings. USGS Circular 1189 and http://quake.usgs.gov/study/wg99/of99-517/index.html

⤙ Part III ⤚
Shaky Ground and Big Waves

U p to this point, we have discussed *earthquake sources*: where earthquakes are likely to strike, how large they might be, and how often they might be expected. From the preceding chapter, you might well conclude that we are not very far along in our ability to forecast the time when an earthquake might occur, although we have devised some fairly elaborate statistical procedures to describe what we do and don't know (probabilistic forecasting).

It's also important to describe the geologic setting *at the Earth's surface*, in particular the response of the ground to an earthquake. Most of us are less concerned about the strength of the earthquake itself than we are about its effects where we are at the time, or where we live, own property, or work. That is to say, earthquake *intensity* is more important to us than earthquake *magnitude*. Like politics, all earthquakes are local.

I am continually amazed at the apparently random damage of a major earthquake. After the 1994 Northridge Earthquake, I visited the Fashion Square Mall at Northridge, in which several major stores and a large parking garage were demolished. Nearby, other shopping malls were hardly damaged at all. A new parking structure at California State University at Northridge was so badly damaged that it had to be taken down, yet directly across the street from it were small, single-family homes that suffered only minimal damage. Interstate 10, the major east-west artery between Santa Monica and downtown Los Angeles, on the south side of the Santa Monica Mountains and far from the epicenter, suffered severe damage, including the collapse of a major interchange. But condominiums and houses perched high in the Santa Monica Mountains, closer to the epicenter, were not severely damaged. Why?

In recent years, we have come to recognize certain geologic settings where buildings are likely to suffer much more earthquake damage than in other places. Under the provisions of the Seismic Hazard Mapping Act, the Division of Mines and Geology has prepared maps of cities in the Los Angeles and San Francisco Bay metropolitan areas that show the susceptibility for ground failure during an earthquake. Although no two earthquakes will produce the same damage pattern in a given region, certain sites can be recognized as hazardous in advance of decisions to develop them.

Some of the greatest losses of life and property come not directly from the shaking but from the dislodging of great masses of earth as landslides and rockfalls. These are not the normal mudslides that plague California during a severe winter storm. In some cases, they are much larger volumes of rock and soil that would not move even during very heavy rainfall. For example, a M 7.9 earthquake on the subduction zone off the coast of Peru on May 31, 1970, caused a slab of rock and ice hundreds of feet across to break off a near-vertical cliff high on Mt. Huascarán, the highest mountain in Peru. The mass of rock and ice fell several thousand feet, disintegrated, slid across a glacier, then overtopped low ridges below the glacier and became airborne. After falling back to the ground, the rock mass swept down the valley of the Shacsha River, entraining the water of the river as it did so. This flow of mixed debris and water reached speeds of 120 miles per hour. Seven miles from its source, this rapidly moving mass split into two streams of debris, one of which overtopped a ridge and buried the town of Yungay. The other mass of mud, rock, and ice swept through and obliterated the city of Ranrahirca. Nearly twenty-five thousand people lost their lives in this single landslide. Most of the residents of these overwhelmed cities died instantly, without warning. The entire time from first collapse high on Huascarán to destruction of these cities was less than four minutes.

But landslide danger is not limited to steep slopes. Nearly flat areas underlain by clean, water-saturated sand might fail by liquefaction of the buried sand layer, which bursts to the surface as fountains and causes the ground to subside. The liquefied layer might cause the ground to move like a gigantic snowboard, snapping utility lines. During the Northridge Earthquake, a mass of land along Balboa Boulevard slid along a very gentle slope, rupturing a buried water line and a gas line. Escaping gas led to a fire that destroyed many homes in the vicinity. Television newscasts showed the odd combination of flames leaping above Balboa Boulevard combined with torrents of water.

People living on the coast face another hazard: gigantic ocean waves, or *tsunamis*. Tsunamis have produced catastrophic losses of life numbering in the tens of thousands. The earthquake generating a deadly tsunami can be thousands of miles away, across the ocean. Crescent City, California had its own deadly tsunami on Easter weekend of 1964, after a great earthquake in southern Alaska.

One of the main reasons the danger is increasing is that we are building in increasingly unstable and dangerous areas. The demand for housing has caused urban development to expand onto river floodplains, steep hillslopes, unstable beach cliffs, and sand bars such as Coronado and Silver Strand on the west side of San Diego. These environments pose hazards other than earthquakes. High winter storm waves batter beach cities, and accompanying landslides and debris flows surge down soggy hillsides. The costly homes in the hills above Malibu, some owned by celebrities, serve as an example of living on the edge, under threat from mudslides, brush fires, and storm waves along the Pacific Coast Highway. They have yet to experience their earthquake on the active Malibu Coast Fault at the base of the cliffs.

California now has legislation that requires inspection of building sites with respect to earthquake hazards and geologic stability. (See Chapter 15 for a definition and discussion of grading ordinances.) These ordinances are a response to the enormous pressure from developers and their customers to build on sites that have spectacular views but are geologically flawed.

It is possible to assess the geologic hazards to construction and, in most cases, to "engineer" around them, although strengthening a building site against earthquakes increases the cost of development. The person considering building on a particular site (or moving to an already-built house on such a site) must weigh the risk of an unlikely but potentially catastrophic earthquake against the possibility that the house could remain safe for a lifetime. In the two chapters that follow, I consider these hazards and conclude that, indeed, we know quite a lot about predicting *how* a particular site will respond, even though we cannot say *when* an earthquake will strike. We know enough, in fact, that California law now requires that a buyer be made aware of geologic hazards before investing in a piece of property—a useful precaution to the new home buyer. Most local grading ordinances require inspection of building sites against possible geologic hazards, including earthquake hazards, in addition to inspection of the building itself. I will return to such ordinances in Chapter 15.

∽ 9 ∽
Solid Rock and Bowls of Jello

"Anyone who hears my words and puts them into practice is like the wise man who built his house on rock. When the rainy season set in, the torrents came and the winds blew and buffeted his house. It did not collapse; it had been solidly set on rock. Anyone who hears my words but does not put them into practice is like the foolish man who built his house on sandy ground. The rains fell, the torrents came, the winds blew and lashed against his house. It collapsed under all this and was completely ruined."

Book of Matthew 7:24-27

Introduction

We live in earthquake country, but we don't want to leave the West Coast. Fortunately, we know how to improve our chances for survival simply by making intelligent choices about where we live or work and how we build. The technology is at hand to evaluate the geologic setting of a building site with respect to earthquake hazard.

Three different earthquake problems are associated with surface sites: (1) amplification of seismic waves by soft surficial deposits; (2) liquefaction of near-surface sediments; and (3) failure of hillslopes by landslides, rockfalls, and debris flows.

1. Amplification of Seismic Waves by Soft Surficial Deposits

It is a short stroll from Fort Mason, west of Ghirardelli Square and Fisherman's Wharf in San Francisco, to the fashionable townhouses of the upscale Marina District, yet the intensity of shaking of these two areas during the earthquake of October 17, 1989 was dramatically different. The Marina District experienced intensities as high as IX— higher than at the epicenter itself, more than sixty miles away (Figure 3-15). Fort Mason and Fisherman's Wharf had intensities of only VII.

On April 18, 1906, Fort Mason was under the command of Captain M.L. Walker of the U.S. Army Corps of Engineers. The great San Francisco Earthquake had shaken Captain Walker awake, but he had then gone back to bed, thinking that the earthquake was "no more than a mild shaker." Brigadier General Frederick Funston, on Sansome Street in the maelstrom of collapsed buildings and towering fires, sent

Captain Walker an urgent summons to muster his company of troops. The captain had to be roused a second time.

Why was Fort Mason spared the worst of both earthquakes? Fort Mason is built on bedrock, and the Marina District that was damaged in 1989 is built on soft sediment. The geologic foundation material made all the difference.

The Marina District was built on fine sand from San Francisco Bay that was hydraulically emplaced after the 1906 earthquake, together with rubble from buildings destroyed by that earthquake. This material was pushed together to make a building site for an international exposition in 1915 that said to the world, "San Francisco is back!" Yes, San Francisco was back, all right, but the sand and rubble contained a time bomb: the foundation was too poorly consolidated to hold up well during the next earthquake. In October 1989, the bomb went off.

Figure 9-1 shows seismograms of an October 21 aftershock of magnitude 4.6 recorded at Fort Mason (MAS), established on bedrock; and two sites in the Marina District, one (PUC) on dune sand from an ancient beach and the other (LMS) on the artificial fill emplaced after the 1906 earthquake. Notice that the seismic waves were much stronger at PUC and LMS than at MAS—an indication of more violent seismic shaking, leading to more damage. Engineers call a station like MAS a *rock site*, and stations like PUC and LMS *soil sites*.

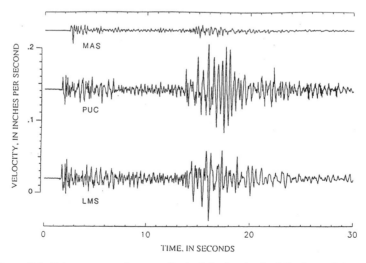

Figure 9-1. Seismograms of a magnitude 4.6 aftershock of the Loma Prieta Earthquake on October 21, 1989 at three temporary stations at the northern end of San Francisco Peninsula, showing amplification of ground motion in two soil sites in the Marina District (PUC, LMS) compared to a bedrock site at Fort Mason (MAS). From U.S. Geological Survey.

An analogy is commonly made between these two types of site and a bowl of jello on a table, an experiment that can be done at home. Stack two or three children's blocks on top of one another on the table top, then stack some more blocks on top of the jello. Then jolt the table sideways. The blocks on the jello will fall over, whereas the blocks directly on the table top might remain standing. The shaking of the blocks on the table illustrates the effect of a seismic wave passing through bedrock. When the shaking reaches the bowl of jello, however, the waves are amplified so that the top of the jello jiggles and causes the blocks to topple. In a similar fashion, the soft foundation materials at a soil site will amplify the seismic waves, which results in much more vigorous shaking than would be expected at a rock site.

A tragic illustration of this was provided by the magnitude 7.9 Mexico City Earthquake of 1985. Actually, the epicenter of the earthquake was in the Pacific Ocean on a subduction zone, hundreds of miles from Mexico City. It's sometimes called the Mexico City Earthquake because of the terrible losses suffered by that city. More than fifteen million people live in Mexico City, many in substandard housing—one reason why so many lives were lost. But more important is the geologic foundation: Mexico City is built on the former bed of Lake Texcoco. The clay, silt, and sand of this ancient lake, in part saturated with water, greatly amplified the seismic waves traveling through the crust from the subduction zone. More than five hundred buildings fell down and more than eight thousand people were killed. The floor of Lake Texcoco truly acted like the bowl of jello resting on the table top that is the Earth's crust beneath the lake deposits.

The Mexico City Earthquake provides a lesson for the major cities of California. Part of the foundation of these cities is soft sediment: sand, Bay mud, and artificial fill around the shore of San Francisco Bay; soft, alluvial deposits of the Los Angeles, San Gabriel, and Santa Ana rivers in the Los Angeles Basin; sand and mud around the edges of San Diego Bay. These soft sediments would amplify the seismic waves and cause more damage than those parts of the cities built on bedrock. Fortunately, building standards in California are higher than those in Mexico City, so we would not expect as many buildings to collapse as in Mexico City. In addition, geotechnical experience with many earthquakes around the world allows an estimate of the effects of near-surface geology on seismic waves from various earthquake sources. In other words, this is a problem we can do something about.

A property of a seismic wave that is used for determining the hazard to buildings is *peak horizontal acceleration*, expressed in *percentage of gravity* (percent g). Acceleration is the rate of increase in speed of an object. If you step off a cliff and fall through space, your speed accelerates from zero at a rate of thirty-two feet (9.8 meters) per second every second, due to the gravitational attraction of the Earth. We call this an acceleration of 1 g. When an earthquake has a vertical acceleration greater than 1 g, stones or clods of earth are thrown into the air, as first observed during a great earthquake in India in 1897. During the 1971 Sylmar Earthquake in the San Fernando Valley, vertical accelerations greater than 1 g were recorded, causing a fire truck with its brakes set to be tossed about the Lopez Canyon Fire Station, leaving tire marks on the garage door frame three feet above the floor.

Horizontal accelerations can be measured as well. A car accelerating at a rate of 1 g would travel 100 yards—the length of a football field—from a stationary position in slightly more than four seconds. As we will see later, horizontal accelerations are particularly critical. Many older buildings constructed without consideration for earthquakes are designed to withstand vertical loads, such as the weight of the building itself, but are not designed to survive forces coming from side to side, which commonly happens during an earthquake. A higher peak acceleration, horizontal or vertical, results in a higher earthquake intensity at a given site.

Other properties of strong ground motion that relate to damage are *velocity*—how fast a building shakes back and forth during an earthquake—and *displacement*—how far the seismic wave moves from side to side. In general, the higher the acceleration, the higher the velocity and displacement. However, it does not follow that the higher the magnitude of the earthquake, the higher the acceleration. Some of the highest accelerations ever recorded have occurred during earthquakes of magnitude less than 7. The Yountville Earthquake of September 3, 2000, had a magnitude of only M 5.2, yet it resulted in accelerations up to 0.5 g.

Acceleration is measured by a special type of seismograph called a *strong-motion accelerometer*. These instruments solve the problem that an ordinary, continuous-recording seismograph might go offscale during a strong earthquake. The strong-motion instrument does not record continuously but is triggered to start recording when the first earthquake wave arrives, and it stops recording when the waves diminish to a low level. Strong-motion instruments are equipped with batteries because the electric power may go off during a strong earthquake.

Accelerometers record the acceleration in percent g. Measurements of acceleration and velocity are of particular use to structural engineers, who use the recordings to determine how buildings vibrate during an earthquake. Several instruments may be placed in a single tall building, in the basement and on upper floors, showing very different responses to shaking of different levels of the building. Strong-motion accelerometers normally are installed in major structures in California such as dams or tall buildings. The installation cost is very small compared to the cost of the building, and the information revealed during an earthquake is invaluable in future engineering design. These instruments and the data they provide are part of the Strong Motion Instrumentation Program (SMIP) in the California Division of Mines and Geology.

Another consideration is the *period* of the earthquake waves that are potentially damaging. Period is the length of time it takes one wave length (Figure 3-12) to pass a given point. We have already encountered *frequency*, the number of wave lengths to pass a point in a second. The period is equal to 1 divided by the frequency. As I pointed out in Chapter 3, earthquakes, like symphony orchestras, produce waves of short period and high frequency (piccolos and violins) and long period and low frequency (tubas and bass violins).

Since the 1994 Northridge Earthquake, engineers and seismologists have tried to predict the effects of various types of earthquakes on accelerations and velocities in urban areas. The information they use to construct their models includes the slip on the assumed earthquake fault and the near-surface geology. Boreholes are drilled to measure the density (weight per given volume) of the various sedimentary layers they encountered as well as the speed of sound waves passing through the sediments. Soft sediment such as sand or clay are low in density, whereas bedrock such as basalt or granite has a high density.

As earthquake waves pass from bedrock to soft sediment, they slow down and increase in amplitude (wave height). The increase in amplitude causes greater acceleration of the ground at a particular site, which leads to more intensive shaking. For these reasons, the thickness and density of the soft sediment layers directly beneath the surface are critical to the calculation of shaking and potential damage.

At the Cedar Hill Nursery, atop a narrow hill fifty feet high in Tarzana, a maximum acceleration of 1.78 g—at least twice the acceleration at sites at the base of the hill—was recorded during the Northridge Earthquake. The shape of the hill focused the seismic waves and caused accelerations that were higher than would have been expected otherwise (about 0.7 g). The same site also recorded unusually high accelerations in the 1987 Whittier Narrows Earthquake. This phenomenon is not understood well enough to use in land-use planning; other local hilltops apparently did not have such high accelerations. However, after the 1971 Sylmar Earthquake, shattered soil was found on ridge tops in the foothills of the San Gabriel Mountains—evidence of acceleration high enough to break up the soil into loose clods.

Another factor important in strong ground motion is the *attenuation* of seismic waves as they leave the earthquake focus and reach a particular locality of concern. Attenuation is affected by the strength and rigidity of the crust through which the seismic wave must pass. Imagine putting your ear against the cut surface of a long log that is struck on the other end by a hammer. If the log is made of sound wood, the vibration of the log caused by the hammer might be enough to hurt your ear. The attenuation of the wave in the log is low. However, if the log is made of rotten wood, you might hear a dull "thunk," indicating that the attenuation is high. In the crust, high attenuation means that the strength of the earthquake wave falls off fairly rapidly with distance from the focus.

In this discussion, we have been concerned about the effect on earthquake shaking of the topography and of the sediments at or near the surface of the ground. In addition, the *path* traveled by an earthquake wave from the source to the surface can have a dramatic effect on shaking. Kim Olsen and Ralph Archuleta of the University of California at Santa Barbara constructed elaborate computer models of the effects of a M 7.75 earthquake on the San Andreas Fault on shaking in the Los Angeles Basin, thirty to forty miles away. The Los Angeles Basin is filled to depths of four to six miles with sedimentary rocks that have a much lower density than crustal rocks beneath the basin or in the adjacent mountain ranges. Olsen and Archuleta showed that their simulated earthquake would generate surface waves that would slow down and increase dramatically in amplitude as they entered the thick sedimentary rocks of the Los Angeles Basin. In addition, the seismic waves would echo off the base and the steep sides of the Los Angeles Basin, so that strong shaking would last much longer than it would at the source of the earthquake. The Los Angeles Basin is Nature's example of a fine concert hall: it has great acoustics!

This behavior, related to the path the earthquake wave takes from the source to the site, could be considered a very large-scale example of the bowl of jello. In soft soil sites, surface waves are amplified, but in the Los Angeles Basin, the shaking is related to the path of the earthquake wave through the sedimentary basin—analogous to the focusing of light through a lens. The concentration of damage in the 1994 Northridge Earthquake in an east-west zone south of the Santa Monica Mountains has been attributed to a lens-like focusing of seismic waves upward through sedimentary deposits in the northwestern Los Angeles Basin—something like using a magnifying glass to focus the rays of the sun on a dead leaf, setting it on fire. The maximum peak horizontal acceleration in this area was 0.2 to 0.4 g. However, the damage zone followed the course of Ballona Creek, which, prior to 1825, was the channel of the Los Angeles River, which had deposited soft sediments subject to strong shaking.

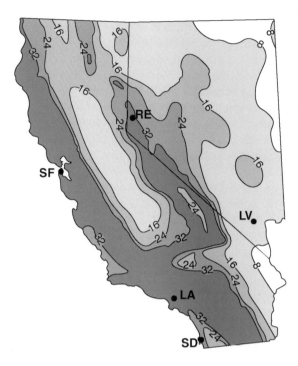

Figure 9-2. Map of California and Nevada with contours showing a ten-percent probability that a given maximum (peak) acceleration will be equaled or exceeded in the next fifty years. Numbers are in percent gravity. The highest numbers, greater than thirty-two-percent gravity, follow the San Andreas Fault and related faults in the Coast Ranges, Transverse Ranges, and Peninsular Ranges; the Cascadia Subduction Zone on the north coast; the Garlock and Death Valley Faults; and faults along the eastern front of the Sierra Nevada, extending north to Reno (RE). Lowest accelerations, less than sixteen-percent gravity, are found in the Great Valley and along the Colorado River in eastern California and most of eastern and northern Nevada. Other city symbols: LA, Los Angeles; LV, Las Vegas; SD, San Diego; SF, San Francisco. From U.S. Geological Survey.

The Northridge Earthquake was the result of rupture on a blind reverse fault. Study of the damage caused by that earthquake revealed that structures on the hanging wall of the reverse fault underwent higher strong-ground motion than those on the footwall. Laboratory modeling experiments by Jim Brune at the University of Nevada at Reno show much more violent motions in the hanging wall. The 1999 Chi-Chi Earthquake in Taiwan was the result of rupture of a reverse fault in a highly urbanized area; there, too, damage was much more severe in the hanging wall of the fault.

The USGS has produced a probabilistic map of the United States showing the maximum horizontal accelerations of rock sites expected over the next fifty years, based on our current understanding of active faults. This map is revised as new information becomes available. Only rock sites are considered; the map does not take into account the increased shaking due to soft soils or to the effect of a thick sedimentary basin. The map estimates the peak, or maximum, horizontal acceleration in percent g that has a ten-percent chance of being exceeded in the next fifty years. Acceleration, rather than magnitude or intensity, is calculated because this is the property that structural engineers need in revising building construction standards.

The acceleration map for California and Nevada is shown as Figure 9-2. The highest accelerations forecast for California are greater than 0.32 g. The area with the highest accelerations includes the San Andreas Fault and other strike-slip faults of the Peninsular Ranges southeast of Los Angeles and the San Francisco Bay Area east of the San Andreas Fault. It also includes the Garlock Fault and the faults along the California-Nevada border between Death Valley and Reno. It also extends along the north coast because that region is closest to the Cascadia Subduction Zone. A band of high accelerations between sixteen- and thirty-two-percent g extends into west-central Nevada (Central Nevada Seismic Zone) and into northeastern California and south-central Oregon in the vicinity of Klamath Falls. Relatively low accelerations are expected in the California Great Valley north of the 1952 Kern County Earthquake, and the lowest accelerations are expected along the Colorado River south of Needles.

2. Liquefaction: When the Earth Turns to Soup

Soft, unconsolidated sand deposits saturated with water can, under certain conditions, change from a solid to a liquid when shaken. You can observe this property in wet beach sand. Just tap-tap-tap your foot on the saturated sand at the water's edge. The sand will first start to bubble and eject a mixture of sand and water. Then the saturated sand from which the bubbles are emanating will flow downslope toward the sea.

Liquefaction is defined as "the act or process transforming any substance into a liquid." If you have the misfortune of building a house on liquefiable sediment, and an earthquake strikes, your house might sink into the ground at a crazy angle as the sediment liquefies and turns into quicksand. Liquefaction is especially common in clean, loose sand, or gravelly sand saturated with water. Most sand layers with liquefaction potential are Holocene in age (less than ten thousand years old) and are unconsolidated.

Sands that are subject to liquefaction are almost always buried to depths of less than thirty feet. At greater depths, the burial pressure is high enough to prevent liquefaction from taking place, unless the shaking is extremely strong. When earthquake waves shake the sand, the pressure of the waves deforms and compresses the sand for an instant, raising the water pressure in the pore spaces between sand grains, thereby turning the sand-water mixture into a liquid. This temporary overpressuring (*cyclic shear stress* or *cyclic loading*) is repeated as long as strong shaking takes place. Such sand is generally overlain by a more cohesive material such as clay, soil, or pavement, which serves to confine the compressed water in the sand. If the sediment layer is on a slight slope, it will move downslope *en masse*; this is called a *lateral spread*. A lateral spread can move down a slope as low as 0.2 percent, which would hardly appear as a slope at all.

Perhaps the most spectacular expressions of liquefaction occur when watery sand vents to the surface through a clay cap, where it can spout up in the air like a fountain or geyser for minutes to hours after the mainshock, leaving a low crater or mound (*sand boil*) after the fountain has died down (Figures 9-3, 9-4). Excavation of sand boils by a backhoe or bulldozer reveals a vertical filling of sand within the clay cap, called a *sand dike*. The sand dike marks the place where sand at depth has vented to the surface. Geologists can use sand dikes in sediments as evidence for prehistoric earthquakes.

The liquefaction susceptibility of sand can be determined by standard geotechnical engineering tests such as the Standard Penetration Test. During this test, a sampling tube is driven into the ground by dropping a 140-lb weight from a height of thirty inches (okay, it isn't rocket science, but it works because every foundation engineer does it exactly the same way). The penetration resistance is the number of blows (number of times the weight is dropped) it takes to drive the sampler one foot into the soil. A low penetration resistance would be fewer than ten blows per foot; a high resistance would be greater than thirty blows per foot. Liquefiable sands have a very low penetration resistance; it's very easy to drive the sampling tube into the sand.

Much of the severe damage in the Marina District of San Francisco during the 1989 earthquake was due to liquefaction of the artificial fill that had been emplaced after the 1906 earthquake. Sand boils erupted into townhouse basements, streets, yards, and parks. Lateral

Figure 9-3. Sand boil caused by liquefaction accompanying the Imperial Valley Earthquake of October 15, 1979. Photo credit: University of Colorado.

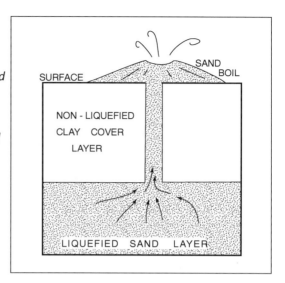

Figure 9-4. Vertical cross section through a sand boil, showing the liquefied sand layer, the overlying nonliquefiable clay cap, and the sand dike transmitting the liquefied sand to the surface, forming a sand boil or sand volcano. Modified from Steve Obermeier, U.S. Geological Survey.

displacement of the ground surface broke underground utility lines, leaving about a thousand homes without gas or water. The broken gas lines caused large fires to break out.

Liquefaction of beach deposits during the same earthquake severely damaged the San Jose State University Marine Laboratory at Moss Landing (Figure 9-5).

Strong ground motion in the floodplain of Ballona Creek in Los Angeles south of the Santa Monica Mountains was accompanied by liquefaction of the floodplain sediments, destroying homes and breaking water pipes. Similarly, the floodplain of the Los Angeles River in Sherman Oaks, which experienced horizontal accelerations as high as 0.6 g, underwent severe liquefaction, breaking water pipes and sewer lines and destroying more than one hundred thirty buildings near

Figure 9-5. Tilted buildings at San Jose State University Marine Laboratory at Moss Landing, due to liquefaction of beach deposits during the October 1989 Loma Prieta Earthquake. Photo by G.W. Wilson, U.S. Geological Survey.

Ventura Boulevard. The worst damage was close to the edge of the floodplain, suggesting that there had been a greater degree of focusing of seismic waves there than in the center of the floodplain.

Liquefaction during the Good Friday Earthquake of 1964 in Alaska destroyed part of the new Turnagain Heights subdivision of Anchorage, situated on a thirty-foot bluff overlooking Cook Inlet. Earthquake waves liquefied a layer of sand and clay, causing part of the subdivision to break up and slide toward the bay. Homes, patios, streets, and trees tilted at crazy angles, and gaping chasms opened, swallowing up and burying alive two small children. One house slid more than twelve hundred feet toward the sea, destroying itself as it did so (Figure 9-6). The instability of the water-saturated layer within the Bootlegger Cove Clay, had been pointed out in a report by the USGS in 1959, five years before the earthquake, but this information apparently had no influence on development plans for Turnagain Heights.

Liquefaction can be triggered by earthquake accelerations as low as 0.1g. It has been observed with earthquakes with magnitudes as low as 5, and it becomes relatively common with larger magnitudes. Liquefaction is more extensive with a longer duration of shaking, which is itself related to moment magnitude: very large earthquakes can have strong shaking lasting for more than a minute.

The California Division of Mines and Geology is mapping zones with liquefaction potential throughout the urban areas of the state,

Figure 9-6. Destruction of part of Turnagain Heights subdivision of the City of Anchorage, Alaska, by liquefaction of a sand layer in the Bootlegger Cove Clay, accompanying the Good Friday 1964 Earthquake in the Gulf of Alaska. The ground and the houses were disrupted; note the tilted trees. Photo by George Plafker, U.S. Geological Survey.

concentrating at first on the San Francisco and Los Angeles urban areas. The City of San Diego has developed and adopted regulations against liquefaction hazard as part of its building code. Urban hazard mapping by the Oregon State Department of Geology and Mineral Industries describes strong ground motion hazard separate from liquefaction and lateral spreading hazard, whereas the California Division of Mines and Geology focuses on liquefaction and lateral spreading. The Oregon maps show that, in general, the areas subject to liquefaction are also subject to strong ground motion, so perhaps it's unnecessary to map these separately. An example of lateral spreading during the Loma Prieta Earthquake is shown in Figure 9-7.

The potential for liquefaction can be reduced by various foundation engineering techniques to strengthen the soil. These techniques include driving deep piles or piers through the liquefiable layer, emplacing concrete grout through weak layers, or even replacing liquefiable sediments with earth materials not subject to liquefaction. Sloping areas with a potential for lateral spread can be buttressed in the downslope direction. Such solutions are expensive, but they were shown to work during the Loma Prieta Earthquake. The Marina District suffered greatly from liquefaction, but sites that had received foundation engineering treatment, including Treasure Island, Emeryville, Richmond, Union City, and South San Francisco, had little or no damage to the ground or to structures built on them.

Figure 9-7. Lateral spread on Hazel Dell Road, Santa Cruz County, near the San Andreas Fault, accompanying the October 1989 Loma Prieta Earthquake. Photo by Michael Rymer, U.S. Geological Survey.

3. Landslides Generated by Earthquakes

Liquefaction tends to be most pronounced in low, flat areas underlain by Holocene deposits. But in earthquake country, it might not help to escape to the hills. Most of the thousands of landslides generated during a major earthquake are small, but some are very large, as described previously in the 1970 earthquake in Peru.

On July 10, 1958, an earthquake of M 7.9 on the Fairweather Fault, Alaska, triggered a landslide on the side of a mountain overlooking Lituya Bay, in Glacier Bay National Park. A great mass of soil and rock swept down the mountainside into the bay, crossed the bay, and had enough momentum to ride up the opposite side to a height of 900 feet, denuding the forest cover as it did so. The slide created a huge water wave 100 feet high that swept seaward, carrying three fishing boats over the sand spit at the mouth of the bay into the ocean. An earthquake of M 7.6 on August 18, 1959, in Montana, just north of Yellowstone National Park, triggered a landslide that swept down a mountainside and through a campground, burying a number of campers together with their tents and vehicles. The landslide crossed the Madison River and continued up the other side of the valley, damming the river and creating a new lake.

Earthquakes less than M 5.5 generate dozens of landslides, and earthquakes greater than M 8 generate thousands. The Northridge Earthquake triggered more than eleven thousand landslides, mostly in the Santa Susana Mountains and north of the Santa Clara River.

Some of the most common landslide types are rockfalls and rockslides. Although rockfalls can have a nonseismic origin, Bob Schuster of the USGS found that large rockfalls damming lakes on the eastern Olympic Peninsula of Washington State were most likely formed during a large earthquake nearly a thousand years ago. No rockfalls as large as these are known from this area in historic time, which included earthquakes as large as M 7.1 as well as many severe winter storms.

Anyone who has hiked in the mountains has observed that many rocky talus slopes appear to be quite precarious, and seismic shaking can set these slopes in motion. John Muir, who experienced the 1872 Owens Valley earthquake (M 7.7) in Yosemite Valley, described it best:

> At half-past two o'clock of a moonlit morning in March, I was awakened by a tremendous earthquake, and though I had never before enjoyed a storm of this sort, the strange thrilling motion could not be mistaken, and I ran out of my cabin, both glad and frightened, shouting, "A noble earthquake! A noble earthquake!" feeling sure I was going to learn something. The shocks were so violent and varied, and succeeding one another so closely, that I had to balance myself carefully in walking as if on the deck of a ship among waves, and it seemed impossible that the

high cliffs of the Valley could escape being shattered. In particular, I feared that the sheer-fronted Sentinel Rock, towering above my cabin, would be shaken down, and I took shelter back of a large yellow pine, hoping that it might protect me from at least the smaller outbounding boulders. For a minute or two the shocks became more and more violent—flashing horizontal thrusts mixed with a few twists and battering, explosive, upheaving jolts,—as if Nature were wrecking her Yosemite temple, and getting ready to build a still better one.

I was now convinced before a single boulder had fallen that earthquakes were the talus-makers and positive proof soon came. It was a calm moonlight night, and no sound was heard for the first minute or so, save low, muffled, underground, bubbling rumblings, and the whispering and rustling of the agitated trees, as if Nature were holding her breath. Then, suddenly, out of the strange silence and strange motion there came a tremendous roar. The Eagle Rock on the south wall, about a half a mile up the Valley, gave way and I saw it falling in thousands of the great boulders I had so long been studying, pouring to the Valley floor in a free curve luminous from friction, making a terribly sublime spectacle—an arc of glowing, passionate fire, fifteen hundred feet span, as true in form and as serene in beauty as a rainbow in the midst of the stupendous, roaring rock-storm. The sound was so tremendously deep and broad and earnest, the whole earth like a living creature seemed to have at last found a voice and to be calling to her sister planets. In trying to tell something of the size of this awful sound it seems to me that if all the thunder of all the storms I had ever heard were condensed into one roar it would not equal this rock-roar at the birth of a mountain talus.

The great landslides of Peru, Madison River, and Lituya Bay were rock avalanches, generally triggered by rockfalls at the time of the earthquake. Nearly all rockfalls are small, although locally damaging or deadly, and many have nonseismic origins. However, great rock avalanches seem to be unique to earthquakes, or earthquakes combined with volcanism, as in the huge avalanche in Washington State that crashed into Spirit Lake and blocked the Toutle River during the Mt. St. Helens eruption of May 18, 1980. That avalanche was triggered by an earthquake of M 5.2, but both the avalanche and the earthquake might have been an effect of the eruption, which blew out the north side of the mountain.

Submarine landslides are an increasingly recognized phenomenon, principally because of the availability of side-scan sonar and new methods to map the topography of the sea floor. On November 8, 1980, an earthquake of M 7 west of Trinidad in Humboldt County triggered a submarine landslide more than fifteen miles across. The slide occurred on a featureless surface that had been receiving sediments from the Klamath River. After the earthquake, fishers reported fresh

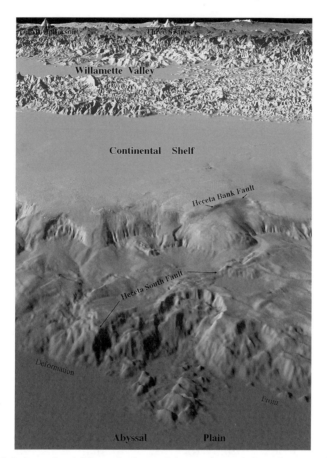

Figure 9-8. Large landslide at the base of the continental slope (bottom of image) west of Florence, Oregon. Slide is five miles across. Debris has slid across the deformation front onto the Juan de Fuca abyssal plain. The active Heceta South Fault marks part of the northern side of the slide. Image created by Chris Goldfinger of Oregon State University from SeaBeam bathymetric maps of the National Oceanic and Atmospheric Administration and digitized land topographic maps from the U.S. Geological Survey.

scarps on the ocean floor. The continental slope off southern Oregon is largely composed of huge landslides, including the one off Florence, Oregon illustrated in Figure 9-8. Chris Goldfinger of Oregon State University has mapped a landslide at the base of the continental slope off central Washington in which individual mountain-size blocks rode down onto the abyssal plain, leaving skid marks on the sea floor in their wake. These landslides were so large that it seems likely they generated huge sea waves, or tsunamis, as similar landslides have done in Hawaii and Alaska. Other landslides have been mapped west of Big Sur, south of Santa Barbara, and west of Los Angeles and San Diego.

The Coast and Peninsular Ranges bear the scars of thousands of landslides that have been mapped by geologists. It cannot be proven that these landslides have an earthquake origin, but certainly many of them do. Some of the smaller ones are slides or flows of soil material, which tend to be tongue- or teardrop-shaped and to travel down gullies and steep canyons. Many of these form during a wet winter and are unrelated to earthquakes, but David Keefer and Randy Jibson of the USGS summarize geotechnical evidence that suggests that some slides would not have been generated by wet weather during winter storms alone but would require seismic shaking to be triggered.

The thousands of landslides in the mountains northwest of the epicenter of the Northridge Earthquake blocked roads, but otherwise did not cause much structural damage, because at the time, the hillsides had not yet been developed. However, Los Angeles is expanding into these hills, and a comparable earthquake a few years from now will produce much higher losses from landslides, including loss of life. A sign of the future could be the fate of homes in the foothills of the Santa Monica Mountains in Sherman Oaks, Tarzana, and Woodland Hills after the Northridge Earthquake. These homes were built on flat pads in which bedrock was cut out of the hillside and redeposited as fill to form a flat site large enough for a house. The fills underwent horizontal deformation and settlement, with the appearance of ground cracks up to several inches across. Damage to these homes often was $50,000 to $100,000 per lot. Engineering geologists and geotechnical engineers are developing better grading practices to alleviate this problem in future earthquakes, but even when this is done, thousands of California homes will still be at risk.

Spectacular damage to buildings occurred in the Santa Cruz Mountains as a result of the 1989 Loma Prieta Earthquake. Landslides are frequent in this region due to winter storms, but the area was unusually dry at the time of the earthquake. In Santa Cruz County, more than a hundred residences were damaged or destroyed. State Highway 17 between Santa Cruz and Los Gatos, which normally carries sixty thousand vehicles per day, was closed for thirty-three days by a rock slide that cost $1.8 million to repair (Figure 9-9). Lawson (1908) reported that the 1906 earthquake also triggered many landslides in the Santa Cruz Mountains, including one that traveled a half mile, plowed through a grove of redwood trees, and wrecked a shingle mill.

The 1989 earthquake also caused major damage to coastal bluffs. Steep coasts closest to the epicenter experienced horizontal accelerations as high as 0.64 g and intensities of VIII. Rock falls were common. A person was killed in the collapse of a coastal bluff at Bonny Doon

Figure 9-9. Aerial view of landslide blocking northbound lanes of Highway 17 in the Santa Cruz Mountains. Landslide was triggered by the October 1989 Loma Prieta Earthquake. Photo by Thomas Holzer, U.S. Geological Survey.

Figure 9-10. Dust cloud caused by ground shaking and landsliding in hills adjacent to the San Fernando Valley following an aftershock of the 1994 Northridge Earthquake. Dust clouds carried fungal spores of valley fever (coccidioidomycosis) onto urban areas, causing more than sixty illnesses and three deaths. Photo by Kerry Sieh, Caltech, at 11 A.M., on January 18, 1994.

Beach near Davenport. Landslides blocked roads and destroyed homes along the sea cliffs from Aptos to Davenport.

Landslides are not strictly an earthquake phenomenon; they are caused by winter storms as well. In evaluating a site for its landslide potential, Scott Burns of Portland State University uses a three-strike rule. Strike 1 is unstable soil, strike 2 is a steep slope, and strike 3 may be either an earthquake or a heavy winter rainstorm that saturates the ground. By careful selection of building sites, strikes 1 and 2 can be avoided, so that neither rainfall nor earthquake will cause a landslide.

Much of the loss of life related to an earthquake is caused by landslides. In some cases, the slide mass moves slowly enough that people can get out of its way, but in rockfalls and rock avalanches, such as the large slides in Alaska, Peru, and Montana discussed in a previous section, the motion of the rock and soil mass is so quick that people are overwhelmed before they can move out of its path.

Earthquakes commonly cause dust clouds as the rock falls and landslides break up and disintegrate. Dust clouds rose from the Santa Susana Mountains during the mainshock and several aftershocks of the 1994 Northridge Earthquake Figure 9-10). The clouds, bearing fungal spores, drifted over the city of Simi Valley, causing an outbreak of valley fever (*coccidioidomycosis*) that resulted in three deaths.

4. Earthquake Hazard Maps of Metropolitan Areas

In 1990, following major liquefaction and landsliding losses as a result of the Loma Prieta Earthquake, the California legislature passed the Seismic Hazard Mapping Act, which requires the California Division of Mines and Geology (CDMG) to identify and map the state's most prominent earthquake hazards from landsliding and liquefaction. This Act adds to earlier legislation (the Alquist-Priolo Act) in which CDMG is required to map zones of surface faulting. The focus for the Seismic Hazard Zone maps is the Los Angeles and San Francisco Bay metropolitan regions, but eventually maps will cover all urban areas in the state. For the latest information on map availability, consult the CDMG home page at http://www.conserv.ca.gov/

The maps show areas where geotechnical site investigations are required before a development and construction permit can be issued. These investigations must show that a site can be made suitable for building construction. In addition, property owners must advise prospective buyers that the property, even if undeveloped, lies within a seismic hazard zone. The mapping program is supported by building-permit fees, supplemented in the Los Angeles metropolitan area by a grant from the Federal Emergency Management Agency and the California Office of Emergency Services.

Suggestions for Further Reading

Keller, E.A. 1988. *Environmental Geology*, Fifth Edition. Columbus, Ohio: Merrill Publishing Co. 540p.

Kramer, S.L. 1996. *Geotechnical Earthquake Engineering*. Englewood Cliffs, N.J.: Prentice-Hall.

McCalpin, J.P., ed., *Paleoseismology*. San Diego: Academic Press. Pp. 331–438.

↜ 10 ↜
Tsunami!

"If the earth shakes east and west the sea will rise up . . . The earth did truly shake from the west and everything on the earth fell down . . . [A brother and sister] ran on up the hill and the water nearly overtook them . . . The water was also coming up the mountain from the east because all the streams were overflowing . . . After ten days the young man went down to look about and when he returned, he told his sister that all kinds of creatures both large and small were lying on the ground where they had been left by the sea. 'Let us go down' his sister said . . . But when they came there, there was nothing, even the house was gone. There was nothing but sand. They could not even distinguish the places where they used to live."

From a Tolowa legend recorded by P.E. Goddard in the early 1900s, apparently describing a tsunami on the north coast of California

1. The Easter Weekend Tsunami of 1964

The warning about a cataclysmic earthquake on the Cascadia Subduction Zone has a mythical cast to it, as if the Earth could not in fact shudder and gyrate in the way scientists have stated it would. But this doomsday scenario is based on an actual subduction-zone earthquake that wracked southern Alaska without warning on Good Friday, March 27, 1964. Alaska is not a heavily populated state, of course, and it had even fewer people in 1964 than it does now. So the human toll was less than that of, say, the Kobe Earthquake in Japan, which was more than a hundred times smaller. But the area of destruction was enormous, stretching for great distances, devastating the city of Anchorage and small towns hundreds of miles away.

The instantaneous effects on the landscape were of a scale seen only once before in this century, in southern Chile in May 1960. Parts of Montague Island in the Gulf of Alaska rose more than thirty feet into the air. Farther away from the subduction zone, a region five hundred miles long and almost a hundred miles across, extending from Kodiak Island to the Kenai Peninsula and Anchorage and the mountains beyond (Figure 7-4), sank as much as eight feet, so that sea water drowned coastal marshes and forests permanently, just as the last great Cascadia Earthquake had drowned the coastline from central Oregon to Vancouver Island three hundred years ago. The sudden change in elevation of the land had its equivalent on the sea floor, causing fifty thousand square miles of ocean floor to be abruptly heaved up or dropped down. This produced an effect entirely separate from the earthquake waves that radiated outward through the crust to lay waste the communities of southern Alaska. The depression and elevation of the sea floor generated an unseen wave in the sea itself that rushed out in all directions. Fifteen minutes after the first subduction-zone rupture had permanently dropped the coastline, a monstrous ocean wave twenty to thirty feet high roared up Resurrection Bay toward the burning city of Seward, carrying ahead of it flaming wreckage, including a diesel locomotive that rode the wave like a surfboard. Residents living near the Seward Airport climbed onto their roofs as the first wave smashed through the trees into their houses, carrying some of them away. Then came a second wave, as strong as the first.

But Seward was ablaze because it had already been hit by a different kind of sea wave, striking less than sixty seconds after the beginning of the earthquake, when the ground was still shaking violently. A section of waterfront slid piecemeal into Resurrection Bay. This landslide triggered three waves up to thirty feet high that reverberated throughout the upper part of Resurrection Bay until the first tectonic tsunami wave arrived fourteen minutes later. Thirteen people died.

Similar scenes were played out in Cordova and Valdez. The entire waterfront of Valdez slid into the harbor, and the submarine landslide generated monster waves over one hundred sixty feet high, taking thirty lives. Valdez ultimately would be relocated to safer ground.

These were the waves that headed to the nearby Alaskan shore. But other waves rolled silently southward into the Pacific Ocean at hundreds of miles per hour (Figure 10-1). A ship on the high seas might encounter these long-period waves, and its crew would not be aware of them. There would just be an imperceptible lifting of the hull as the waves passed underneath. But when a wave entered the shallows, it slowed down and gained in height until it towered above the shoreline in its path. The movement of the sea floor that had triggered the tsunami had a directivity to it, preferentially southeast rather than south toward Hawaii or southwest toward Japan. The Alaska Tsunami was like a torpedo fired directly at the coast of Vancouver Island, Washington, Oregon, and the north coast of California.

An hour and twenty-six minutes later, the Pacific Tsunami Warning Center at Ewa Beach, Hawaii, west of Honolulu, issued a tsunami advisory indicating that a sea wave could have been generated by the earthquake. None had yet been confirmed, despite the damage to towns along the Alaska coastline, mainly because communications between Alaska and Hawaii had been lost. The main concern in Honolulu was for a tsunami in Hawaii, similar to previous destructive tsunamis in 1946, 1952, 1957, and 1960. The warning center gave an expected arrival time of the tsunami in Hawaii.

Figure 10-1. Computer simulation of tsunami following 1964 Good Friday Earthquake in the Gulf of Alaska. Top image shows waves one hour after the earthquake; successive images show waves at two, three, and four hours after the earthquake. Japan at left; west coast of United States on right; Hawaii at bottom center of lower image. Tsunami has reached Vancouver Island in third image and is

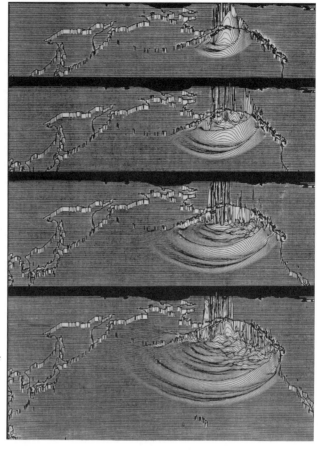

about to strike Crescent City, California in bottom image. Note that waves approaching Japan are much smaller than those approaching the United States; also note how waves turn toward the coast as they slow down. From Kenji Satake, Geological Survey of Japan.

Fifty-three minutes after the tsunami advisory was issued, a report from Kodiak Island, Alaska, told of seismic sea waves ten to twelve feet above normal. Thirty-five minutes later, a second report was received from Kodiak, and based on those two reports the Pacific Tsunami Warning Center upgraded its tsunami advisory to a tsunami warning. At almost the same moment, nearly three hours after the earthquake, the tsunami made landfall on Vancouver Island.

First to be struck was Hot Springs Cove, an Indian village near the northern tip of the island, where eighteen houses were damaged. Then the wave passed down the west coast of the island, deeply indented with fjords carved out by glaciers during the Pleistocene. The fjords concentrated the force of the tsunami like air scoops, with the effect that towns at the landward end felt the worst effects of the waves. The tsunami swung left past Cape Scott into Quatsino Sound and bore down on Port Alice, ripping away boat ramps and seaplane moorings, flooding buildings, floating twelve houses off their foundations, and tumbling thousands of feet of logs along the waterfront like jackstraws.

Farther south, the wave turned inland past Ucluelet into Barclay Sound, thundering past Bamfield Lighthouse and a group of fifty startled teenagers on Pachena Beach. The lighthouse raised the alarm, which gave ten minutes' notice to the twenty-five thousand residents of Port Alberni, at the head of the fjord nearly two-thirds of the way across Vancouver Island. Larry Reynolds, eighteen, raced from his house on high ground to watch after the first wave had hit. As the second wave surged into the street, Reynolds could hear people screaming and could see men running in front of the wave as it crashed into the town. He watched as two large, two-story houses were lifted from their foundations; they floated serenely out into the Somass River, where they broke up and sank. A row of six tourist cabins along the river bank bowed gracefully as they rose up simultaneously, but then they came down separately as the wave passed. The Japanese freighter *Meishusan Maru* broke away from its moorings and rode the wave like a giant surfboard, landing on the mudflats. The captain and crew, perhaps wise in the ways of tsunamis, simply waited for the next wave, which refloated the ship, and they were able to regain the harbor.

Southward the wave rolled past Vancouver Island, and it was recorded by the tide gauge at Neah Bay. Logs were scattered in Quilcene Bay near Hood Canal. But the main tsunami continued on past Cape Flattery and the wild, uninhabited coastline of Olympic National Park. Incredibly, no lives had been lost on Vancouver Island nor on the Washington side of the Straits of Juan de Fuca.

By this time, warnings of the oncoming tsunami were being broadcast throughout the Pacific Northwest. Hearing the warning was Mrs. C.M. Shaw, whose daughter and son-in-law were spending the weekend at Kalaloch Resort in Olympic National Park with their eleven-year-old daughter, Patty, along with another couple, Mr. and Mrs. Charles W. Elicker, and the Elickers' eleven-year-old son, Drew. Mrs. Shaw phoned the resort, and an employee found Elicker. Horror-struck, Elicker raced for the beach, where the two children had been given permission to camp for the night. Elicker routed them from their sleeping bags, and Drew raced for a forty-foot embankment of clay with a sparse cover of salmonberry. But Patty wanted to collect her pup tent and sleeping bag. Elicker realized that there was no time. In the moonlight, he could see the great wave rumbling toward them, a churning wall of water jumbled with logs and driftwood. He grabbed Patty's hand and they raced toward the embankment and safety.

But Elicker was losing the race with the tsunami. Gripping Patty's hand, he scrambled up the embankment, grasping at brush, and finally managed to cling to a spindly tree as the wave drenched them up to hip level. As the wave retreated, Elicker climbed higher, where another wave hit them at leg level. But they were safe. The next day, they found Patty's pup tent and sleeping bag a half mile down the beach.

On came the wave down the coast, refracting to the east and heading for shore at a low, oblique angle. It struck the Quinault Indian Reservation, routing four Tacoma men from their tent on the beach at Taholah, south of Pt. Grenville. On went the wave to the tiny community of Copalis Beach, where the firehouse siren in the shopping area began to wail its alarm. Leonard Hurlbert dashed out of the Surf and Sand Restaurant, where his wife worked in the kitchen, to race home and check on their sleeping children. He was driving close to fifty miles an hour when he reached the bridge across the Copalis River. A few seconds earlier and he would have made it. But he reached the bridge at the same time as a wall of water from the sea. The bridge began to buck and heave, and over it went, casting Hurlbert, still in his car, into the river. Trapped underwater, he forced open the door on the driver's side against the pressure of the water. But as he was escaping, he found his leg pinned between the top of the door and the roof of the car. With the desperate force of a man who knew he would drown, Hurlbert somehow freed his leg and hurled himself toward air, severely damaging the ligaments in his left arm as he did so.

A half mile north of Copalis Beach, Mr. and Mrs. David Mansfield and their children Robert, twenty, Linda, fourteen, and David, seven, were camped on the beach in their trailer. They had been up until eleven o'clock, walking on the beach in the moonlight. Shortly after they turned out the light their trailer began to rock, and as they looked outside their window they saw their car floating away. The trailer began to roll, with the Mansfields still inside, and they suddenly found themselves tumbling outside the trailer, under water. They swam toward land, but as they tried to reach a place where they could stand, they were battered by a huge log that threatened to crush them. Linda was drifting away, but Robert grabbed her and finally, miraculously, they all reached firm ground. The force of the waves had torn off most of their clothes; all Mrs. Mansfield had on was a T-shirt when they wandered into a tavern looking for help.

And still the giant waves rolled relentlessly south, past four Renton boys driven from their tent at Long Beach, past Cape Disappointment to the Oregon coast, where the tsunami turned deadly. At Seaside, the waves pushed the Necanicum River back up its bed, overflowing and drowning out a trailer park. Mary Eva Deis, fifty, died of a heart attack when the waves struck her house. Farther south at Cannon Beach, a wharf was swept away, carrying several small boats out to sea, and several houses were ripped from their foundations.

At Beverly Beach, north of Newport, Monte McKenzie, a Boeing engineer from Seattle, his wife Rita, and their four children—Louis, eight, Bobby, seven, Ricky, six, and Tammy, three—had come to spend the Easter weekend camping. On Friday, they were following a trail along the coast when they found a driftwood shelter. What an experience to camp directly on the beach on such a beautiful spring weekend! They got permission from the caretaker of Beverly Beach State Park to camp there and settled in for the night, when a small wave caught them in the shelter. They had time to grab the kids, and they were running for the beach cliff when the first of the great waves struck. Rita was a senior Red Cross lifesaver and had taught all her children to swim. She gripped two of them by the hands, but great, shifting logs knocked her unconscious. Monte was thrown against the cliff, where he climbed up and vainly tried to flag down cars on Highway 101. He ran to the caretaker's house, and police were called, but it was too late. Rita was found on the beach four hundred yards away from their campsite, battered but alive. But the kids were gone. They found Ricky's body, but the other three were never recovered.

The tsunami swept down the Oregon coast, tearing out docks at Gold Beach and smashing small boats at the mouth of the Rogue River, and on into California. Crescent City lay in its path.

The California Disaster Office issued a bulletin at 11:08 P.M. to emergency response officials and the California Highway Patrol in all coastal counties that a tsunami was possible. This bulletin was received at the Del Norte County Sheriff's headquarters, and by 11:20, the civil defense director and the sheriff had arrived at headquarters. At 11:50, the California Civil Defense Office estimated the arrival time of the tsunami at midnight. By the time a second bulletin had arrived at 11:50, sheriff's deputies had been sent to low-lying areas to warn people of a possible sea wave. However, they did not order an evacuation.

The first wave arrived on schedule at 11:59 P.M., after the warning had been repeated by both radio stations. But the first wave was fairly small, reaching across the beach only to Front Street and doing little damage other than depositing some debris. Civil Defense authorities had received a report from Neah Bay, Washington, that the tsunami had done no damage there. People began to relax. The next wave at 12:40 A.M. on March 28 was larger, but still not too bad. The sea waves were behaving like tsunamis that had hit Crescent City in 1946, 1952, 1957, and 1960: flooding some low-lying areas and that was about it. The worst appeared to be over, and some people headed for their homes or to the waterfront to survey the damage to their businesses and begin to clean up. The sheriff's office still had not issued a general alarm.

Then at 1:20 A.M. came the third wave, a giant wall of water fifteen feet high that breached a jetty, smashed into the fishing fleet at Citizens Dock at Elk Creek, and roared across Highway 101 south of town. Jack McKellar and Ray Thompson had gone down to the harbor earlier to check on Thompson's boat, the *Ea*. As they loosened the moorings, the wave spun the *Ea* around like a top, and the boat shot out of the harbor into the open sea. The two men were carried so far from shore that they were spared the worst effects of the tsunami.

The wave caved in the west wall of the Long Branch Tavern at Elk Creek, terrifying the patrons when the lights went out. People jumped up on the bar and juke box, with scarcely any headroom for breathing. Everyone climbed up onto the roof, and Gary Clawson and Mack McGuire swam out to get a boat. When they returned, seven people, including Clawson and his parents, got into a rowboat. The water was smooth, and they headed across Elk Creek toward Front Street. They were only a few boat lengths away from the stream bank when the drawdown began, pulling the boat sideways toward the Elk Creek bridge. Bruce Garden lunged and grabbed the bridge, which kept him from going under. The other six were slammed against a steel grating on the far side of the bridge, choked with debris. Clawson, a strong swimmer, came up for air, and as the water receded he tried to revive the others. But the other five passengers drowned in the darkness.

The fourth wave at 1:45 A.M., largest of all, crested at nearly twenty-one feet. Peggy Sullivan, six months pregnant, saw the waves from the front door of her room at Van's Motel. She told her son Gary, nine, to dress, and threw a quilt around her twenty-three-month-old daughter Yevonne. As they stepped outside with Yevonne's bottle, a wall of water came toward them, carrying houses like matchboxes. Gary was carried off in one direction and Sullivan and the baby in the other: Sullivan's shoes and the baby's quilt were torn away at the same time. She was swept down the driveway and became jammed against a sports car, driftwood piled at her back, but still held onto Yevonne and her bottle. Gary was swept into the back of a garage, where he was rescued by a stranger. Severely injured, Sullivan was taken to the hospital. Although she and her two children survived, she lost her unborn child.

The third wave swept into downtown Crescent City, tearing out a twenty-five-ton tetrapod used in the construction of the seawall. Stores along Front Street crumbled. At first, boats were washed four blocks inland, then they and the wreckage of buildings were carried out to sea by the suction as the water retreated (Figures 10-2 and 10-3). The Texaco oil tank farm burst into flames and the tanks exploded, causing fires that burned out of control for more than ten hours.

Wally Griffin described the scene from the sheriff's office when the lights went out: "There was a continuous crashing and crunching sound as the buildings gave way and splintered into rubble, and there were flashes from high powered electrical lines shorting out that resembled an electrical storm approaching from the east, except some of the flashes were blue. Added to the display were two explosions that could have been mistaken for thunder without the normal rolling sound."

A big log crashed through the walls of the post office, and, as reported by Griffin, "when the water receded, it sucked the letters out like a vacuum cleaner." The letters were later found festooning the parking lot and nearby hedges. Adolph Arrigoni, seventy, drowned in his house on B Street, and James Park, sixty, drowned when the wave floated his trailer off its foundation.

Peggy Coons, curator of the Battery Point Lighthouse on an island west of the Crescent City Jetty, had gotten up before midnight to go to the bathroom when she noticed in the moonlight that all the rocks around the island on which the lighthouse stood had disappeared. She and her husband dressed and went outside, where they saw a huge,

Figure 10-2. Aerial view of Crescent City, California, after the tsunami accompanying the 1964 Good Friday Earthquake in southern Alaska. Harbor is toward the viewer. Photo courtesy of Lori Dengler, Humboldt State University.

Figure 10-3. Damage from the 1964 tsunami in Crescent City, California. Photo courtesy of Washington Division of Geology and Earth Resources.

debris-choked wave, high above the outer breakwater, bearing down on the town. Then the water roared back past them at high speed, leaving the beach strewn with debris. The second wave passed them, and they saw lights blinking out along the shoreline. Again the water drained back past them to the sea.

The third wave started fires in the town, and sparks flew. When the water drained out this time, three-quarters of a mile from the normal shoreline, it revealed the sea bottom, a "mystic labyrinth of caves, canyons, basins and pits, undreamed of in even the wildest fantasy" (Peggy Coons in Griffin, 1984).

In the distance, Coons could see a massive, black wall of water, with boiling and seething whitecaps glistening in the moonlight. A Coast Guard cutter and several smaller boats two miles offshore appeared to be riding high above the wall. The water struck with great force and split around the island, picking up driftwood logs as it struck the mainland. They saw bundles of lumber at Dutton's Lumber Yard fly into the air as other bundles sailed away. There was a great roar, and buildings, cars, boats, and lumber were moving and shifting. Then the return wave came past them, carrying a slurry of mattresses, beds, furniture, television sets, and clothing. Coons saw more waves, but they were smaller. The damage had been done.

The waves destroyed twenty-nine blocks and left one hundred fifty businesses a total loss. Eleven people had died. Governor Edmund G. Brown asked the president to declare Crescent City a disaster area.

And still the tsunami sped south, trapping Stuart Harrington and Donald McClure, two Air Force sergeants eel fishing at the mouth of the Klamath River. A wall of water, choked with driftwood, picked them up and carried them a half mile up the river. They scrambled through the driftwood to the surface, and McClure helped Harrington climb up on a larger log that appeared to offer protection. They heard a response to their cries for help. Then the water and floating logs began to rush back toward the sea, and both men slipped into the water to swim for shore. McClure had helped Harrington remove his jacket and shirt to make it easier for him to swim. Harrington swam through the maelstrom to the shore, below the boat docks, where he found to his horror that McClure, who had saved his life, had not made it.

The tsunami continued south of Cape Mendocino, causing havoc on the Mendocino coast. The wave was still three feet high near the Golden Gate Bridge. At Sausalito, the mooring cables of the sixty-six-year-old ferryboat *Berkeley* snapped, causing the ferry to list and damage the pier. Altogether, the damage to boats in San Francisco Bay amounted to nearly a million dollars. A ship ran aground at Gaviota, boats were damaged farther east at Santa Barbara, and Los Angeles suffered $200,000 in losses. Damage was reported in San Diego, and ten-foot waves struck Catalina Island off the southern California coast. An alarm was raised on the west coast of Mexico, but the tsunami, finally, was spent. Tide gauges recorded the tsunami all around the Pacific Ocean; it was recorded in Peru nearly ten hours after the fourth wave struck Crescent City and nearly sixteen hours after the earthquake.

What was learned? First, except for the tsunami at Seward and Valdez, Alaska, the loss of life was entirely preventable, because there was plenty of time to evacuate low-lying coastal areas even as far north as Vancouver Island. The first two waves at Crescent City were no larger than previous tsunamis, convincing local authorities that the worst was over and no evacuation order was necessary. For warnings to be heeded, people had to have their radios or television sets on; a siren would have been more effective, combined with emergency-service personnel noisily alerting people to the danger.

A quarter-century would pass before Kenji Satake would develop computer models showing the directivity effects of tsunamis, the pointed gun of the Alaska Earthquake aimed directly at the west coast of North America. And there were many low-lying coastal areas that were *not* hard hit, indicating that the wave was strongly controlled by the bottom topography of the sea floor that channeled and accentuated the tsunami as it headed for shore.

2. Other Tsunamis in California

Although the 1964 tsunami was the most devastating in California since the establishment of the missions, it was not the only one. Native American folklore mentions a tsunami accompanying a great earthquake—probably the January 26, 1700 earthquake, as noted in the beginning of this chapter. The earthquake of December 21, 1812, probably in the Santa Barbara Channel, caused a tsunami that did considerable damage in Santa Barbara, as reported in Chapter 5.

Starting with the 1812 earthquake, California has had fourteen tsunamis with wave heights exceeding three feet. Six were destructive. The Aleutian Subduction Zone Earthquake of 1946 is best known for what it did to Hawaii, but damage was reported in California, where wave heights up to ten feet were witnessed between Cape Mendocino and San Francisco. One person was killed at Santa Cruz, railroad tracks were flooded at Port Hueneme, homes were flooded at Half Moon Bay, and damage was reported from Drakes Bay and San Pedro. The 1960 Chilean Earthquake, largest of the twentieth century, mainly damaged other areas around the Pacific, but in California, five-foot waves caused one death and damage of up to $1 million in the Los Angeles and San Diego areas. Seven-foot waves produced more than $50,000 in losses at Crescent City, which would experience the disastrous 1964 tsunami less than four years later.

3. Some Facts about Tsunamis

First, a tsunami is *not* a tidal wave. Tides are affected by the attraction between the Moon and Earth, and tsunamis are completely unrelated. If a tsunami arrived at the same time as a high tide, as it did at Crescent City, its effects would be worse than if it arrived at low tide, because the wave could travel farther onto the land. Another term is *seismic sea wave*. This is correct for most tsunamis, but not all, for tsunamis can be generated by submarine volcanic eruptions or submarine landslides. The cataclysmic eruption in 1883 of Krakatau, a volcanic island in Indonesia, was followed by a sudden collapse of the central volcano and an inrush of water, generating a tsunami that, together with the eruption, killed more than thirty-six thousand people.

We use the Japanese word *tsunami*, from the Japanese characters for *harbor wave*, in light of the fact that a tsunami increases in height as it enters a harbor, as it did at Port Alberni and Crescent City.

In the Alaska Earthquake of 1964, a section of sea floor more than four hundred miles long and one hundred miles across suddenly arched upward, forcing the overlying water upward and outward as if the sea floor were a giant paddle (Figures 7-4 and 10-4). Although this happened almost instantaneously, it was not the *speed* of the uplift but the sheer *volume* of water displaced that produced the powerful tsunami. A tsunami generated by a sudden change in the deep ocean floor is a wave that extends from the sea surface to the bottom, miles below. The wave travels at great speed, five hundred miles an hour or faster, depending on the depth of water.

The wave travels fastest through the deep ocean and slows down as it approaches the land, as can be observed in the computer simulation in Figure 10-1. The waves traveling down the coast are slower than those in the open sea, so that the wave front makes a sweeping turn to the left and attacks the coast almost head on.

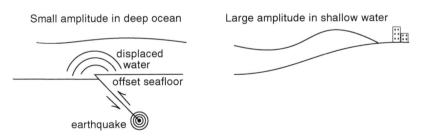

Figure 10-4. (Left) Formation of a tsunami by sudden offset of the sea floor. Wave has a low amplitude as it travels in the deep sea. (Right) Wave amplitude grows as tsunami enters shallow water and approaches the land.

Tectonic tsunamis have very long wave periods. (Figure 3-12 illustrates wave amplitude and wavelength; the period is the length of time it takes a full wavelength to pass a point.) An ordinary ocean wave breaking on the beach has a period of five to fifteen seconds, but a tsunami generated by a subduction-zone earthquake has wave periods ranging from seven minutes to nearly an hour, depending on the origin of the tsunami. It was the long periods of twenty-five to forty minutes that caused so much havoc at Crescent City and elsewhere. The wave rushes onshore and then it recedes, causing more chaos, including the deaths of the people in the rowboat at the Elk Creek bridge in Crescent City. Observers assume that the tsunami differs from an ordinary ocean wave in size only: if the next wave does not arrive in the next few minutes, they assume that the danger is past. They return to the shore, out of curiosity or a desire to help in rescue or cleanup operations. Then, perhaps as much as an hour later, another giant wave strikes. The loss of life from the follow-up wave, which might be bigger than the first one, is commonly larger than that from the initial wave.

A tsunami has almost no expression on the ocean surface. (Here Figure 10-1 is misleading, because it gives the impression that great wave heights are found in the deep ocean as well as along coastlines.) The height of a tsunami on the open ocean is typically only a few feet—less than the normal surface waves. Ships at sea cannot give warning, because people on board cannot detect the passage of the tsunami. During a deadly tsunami that struck Hilo, Hawaii in 1946, the crew of a freighter anchored offshore was surprised to see huge waves breaking over buildings and trees onshore (Figure 10-5), because they were not strongly affected by the wave passing under their ship.

As a tsunami enters shallow water, it slows down but does not lose energy. It converts to a gigantic surface wave (Figures 10-4 and 10-5). The way in which the tsunami approaches the shore is of critical importance in tsunami hazard analysis. It depends on the direction and energy of the approaching tsunami, of course, but it is also influenced by the configuration of the sea floor. Hilo Harbor in Hawaii is particularly susceptible to tsunamis because the adjacent sea floor is shaped like a scoop, concentrating the energy of the wave into a smaller area. In a similar fashion, the Vancouver Island fjords funneled the wave energy of the 1964 tsunami like the nozzle of a fire hose, smashing against the communities at the heads of the fjords. Crescent City has a similar problem. Because the tsunami is controlled by water depth, even in deep water the configuration of offshore banks and submarine canyons influences the size of a tsunami. Topographic maps of the sea floor, called *bathymetric maps*, are available for the west coast of the United States from the National Oceanic and Atmospheric Administration (NOAA). These bathymetric maps are important in

Figure 10-5. Tsunami in 1946 striking the beachfront area at the Puumaile Tuberculosis Hospital east of Hilo on the Island of Hawaii, twenty-four hundred miles from the earthquake source in the Aleutian Islands to the north. Waves here were more than twenty feet high, topping the breakwater and causing flooding at the hospital. Photo by Mrs. Harry A. Simms, Sr., courtesy of the National Oceanic and Atmospheric Administration.

determining which sections of a coastline are most susceptible to tsunamis.

In the 1964 earthquake, the sea floor was suddenly pushed upward and outward to the southeast, so that the first evidence of the tsunami in the Pacific Northwest was the great wave that crashed on the beach and entered the harbors. But at Seward, Alaska, on the north side of the uplift, the force of the earthquake propagated *away* from the town. People at Seward saw a huge wave approaching them, but as they looked at the remains of the small-boat harbor they observed that it had been magically drained of water. This was part of the tsunami, too, but the sea had rushed away from land rather than toward it, immediately followed by the first wave to drive into the port and town.

Seward, and Cook Inlet behind it to the northwest, abruptly subsided during the earthquake, just as the coastal marshes of central Oregon, Washington, and Vancouver Island had subsided during the great Cascadia Earthquake of A.D. 1700, and previous earthquakes as well. If the next Cascadia earthquake behaves like the illustration in Figure 7-4, then the first evidence of the accompanying tsunami in northern Oregon or Washington might be a sudden outrushing of water, followed by a great wave. Coastal areas would see exposed parts of the sea floor that people living there had never before seen exposed, even at the lowest tides. There would be a great temptation to go to the beach to see this phenomenon—which could be fatal because there would not be enough time to get back to high ground before the first wave struck.

Computer modeling of a Cascadia Subduction Zone tsunami predicts a different outcome for northern California because the coastline is much closer to the subduction zone than it is farther north (Figure 2-6). The northern California coast would be suddenly uplifted, whereas the coast farther north would suddenly subside (Figure 7-4). The first evidence of the tsunami might be a wave rushing *toward* the coast rather than a sudden draining of coastal waters.

4. Tsunami Sounds

Most observers of a great tsunami are so horrified that they remember only what they saw rather than what they heard. However, Jerry Eaton, a seismologist with the USGS, was at a bridge across the Wailuku River in Hilo, Hawaii, on the night of May 22, 1960, as a tsunami from a monster earthquake in Chile approached the city. Eaton heard "an ominous noise, a faint rumble like a distant train, that came from the darkness far out in Hilo Bay. Two minutes later, . . . the noise became deafening" (Atwater et al., 1999). Carol Brown, sixteen, heard "a low rumbling noise that soon became louder and was accompanied by sounds of crashing and crunching" (Atwater et al., 1999).

5. Tsunami Warning Systems

The tsunami at Crescent City struck more than four hours after the earthquake. Loss of communication with Alaska delayed the issuance of a tsunami advisory for nearly an hour-and-a-half after the earthquake, and the advisory was not upgraded to a warning until two hours and twenty minutes after the earthquake—about the time the first wave was striking the north end of Vancouver Island.

The warning system in place at that time—the Pacific Tsunami Warning Center—was established in Hawaii after a disastrous tsunami in Hawaii in 1946 caused by an earthquake on the Aleutian Subduction Zone of Alaska. The Hawaii center was not designed to warn against tsunamis like the one produced by the 1964 Alaska Good Friday Earthquake, so a second warning center was set up—the West Coast/Alaska Tsunami Warning Center in Palmer, Alaska. Both are operated by NOAA. The Alaska center initially was organized to warn against tsunamis only in Alaska, but now it's responsible for alerting Alaska, British Columbia, Washington, Oregon, and California about all earthquakes around the Pacific that might produce a tsunami.

Seismographs and tide gauges around the Pacific Rim report immediately to Ewa Beach, Hawaii and Palmer, Alaska, and tsunami arrival times are estimated for shorelines around the Pacific. The Deep-ocean Assessment and Reporting of Tsunamis (DART) Project has developed pressure gauges to be emplaced on the deep ocean floor, permitting tracking of tsunamis in the deep sea in real time, which has never before been possible. NOAA has three of these DART deep-sea tsunami detectors, two off the Aleutian Islands and one west of the Cascadia Subduction Zone. By the end of 2001, NOAA plans to have additional pressure gauges off the Aleutian Islands and Cascadia and an additional detector on the equator. In addition, the seismic networks in southern Alaska, western Washington and Oregon, and northern California have been upgraded.

When a subduction-zone earthquake of moment magnitude 7.5 or larger strikes anywhere around the Pacific Ocean (magnitude 7.0 or larger on the Aleutian Subduction Zone), the tsunami warning centers swing into action. After the epicenter of the earthquake has been located (commonly within a few minutes) and the earthquake is confirmed as shallow, rupturing the subduction zone, the travel time of a potential tsunami is estimated and stations near the epicenter are alerted. A *tsunami warning* is issued to all communities within three hours of the first wave. For communities three to six hours away from the first wave, a *tsunami watch* is established. For coastal regions that are still farther away, an *advisory bulletin* is issued and is updated as more information becomes available, such as confirmation of a tsunami by observers, tide gauges, or deep-sea pressure gauges. For the West Coast, the tsunami warning would come from Palmer, Alaska. As the tsunami advances, its progress is monitored and the warning is updated with new projected arrival times of waves and possible wave heights. This gives time for local authorities to order evacuation of low-lying areas. If a tsunami warning is issued for Hawaii, evacuation of low-lying areas is mandatory, but in California the decision to evacuate is made by local authorities.

Computer modeling of tsunamis gives more confidence to the warnings, although modeling is not yet used by the tsunami warning centers in issuing warnings or alerts. This might change, because models can take into account the strong directivity of tsunamis. It's important to learn not only the location of the epicenter and the magnitude of an earthquake, but also the direction of motion of the ocean floor, which can be determined by studying the wave forms of seismograms of the mainshock recorded at many seismograph stations. Armed with such information, the warning of the 1964 Alaska tsunami could have been more strongly directed to the west coast of North America and less toward Japan, which recorded the tsunami but suffered no damage.

A tsunami wave was once compared to the waves in a pond radiating out from a pebble that is thrown into it, with the pebble representing the earthquake. The directivity of a tsunami leads to a better analogy. It's more like rolling a log into the water; waves in front of the log are much higher than the waves at the ends.

Tsunami warning systems worked well for two distant tsunamis that traveled great distances: the tsunamis of 1952 and 1957. But they were of limited value in saving lives from the 1960 Chile tsunami that traveled from Chile to Japan, and the 1964 Alaska tsunami that did damage as far away as southern California. Furthermore, more than seventy-five percent of the tsunami warnings were false alarms.

What about warnings to coastal areas when the earthquake occurs on a fault that is just offshore? Tsunami warnings were of no use to towns in southern Alaska struck by the 1964 tsunami. How about an earthquake on the Cascadia Subduction Zone or on a reverse fault in the Santa Barbara Channel? There is little time—perhaps less than ten or fifteen minutes—before the first wave reaches the coast. A tsunami struck Okushiri Island off the northwest coast of Japan only two to three minutes after a large offshore earthquake, killing schoolchildren on the beach.

The best advice now for regions subjected to subduction-zone earthquakes, including the north coast of California, is to get to high ground immediately when the shaking from a great earthquake stops long enough to allow one to move. Get to high ground immediately. There will be no tsunami warning.

A problem that may or may not be important in California is that some earthquakes generate tsunamis that are unusually large for the amount of shaking they cause. This can happen for two reasons. Some earthquakes are characterized by wave motion that is so slow that little shaking damage occurs, even though the earthquake magnitude is large. A *slow earthquake* in Nicaragua on September 2, 1992 produced a tsunami that killed hundreds of coastal villagers, even though the amount of shaking was deceptively small. If a slow earthquake struck coastal California, people might not take the tsunami potential of the earthquake seriously until it was too late.

The second reason is that an earthquake can trigger a submarine landslide. On July 17, 1998, more than twenty-two hundred villagers along a fifteen-mile stretch of the north coast of Papua New Guinea lost their lives in a tsunami that was generated by an earthquake of M 7.1. The earthquake apparently caused a submarine landslide, and the earthquake and landslide together produced a tsunami with wave heights of thirty to forty-five feet. The tsunami arrived about twenty minutes after the earthquake. In contrast to the long periods of tsunamis from a distant source, the Papua New Guinea tsunami had wave periods of one to five minutes.

In the 1964 Alaska Earthquake, Seward and Valdez were hit by tsunamis from two different sources. The first one was triggered by submarine landslides immediately offshore, extending onshore and causing collapse of the waterfronts of both towns. In some areas, waves began to strike less than sixty seconds after the beginning of the earthquake, while strong shaking was still going on. The landslide-generated tsunamis generated the largest waves, more than one hundred sixty feet high at Valdez, with waves echoing off the sides of the narrow bays leading into the towns for ten to fifteen minutes. Then, about fifteen minutes after the beginning of the earthquake, the tectonic tsunami arrived, generated by the sudden change in depth of the sea floor in Prince William Sound. The tsunamis were worse because both towns are at the heads of narrow fjords.

The 1992 Cape Mendocino Earthquake generated a small tsunami that arrived at Eureka twenty minutes after the earthquake and at Crescent City forty-seven minutes after the quake. Waves continued to arrive for about ten hours, with the strongest waves eighteen inches high at Crescent City almost four hours after the earthquake.

As was shown in the 1964 tsunami, a warning system needs more than notification by radio. A siren system would wake people up if the tsunami struck at night, as it did in 1964. The siren at Copalis Beach, Washington probably saved lives there. However, a siren might be knocked out by a local earthquake. Crescent City now has a siren, but it will be activated for distant tsunamis only. If a siren system is proposed for your community, make sure that funds are provided to maintain and test it. The county emergency manager (see Chapter 15) is a logical person to be responsible for a siren system.

6. Tsunami Hazard Maps

Following the 1992 Cape Mendocino Earthquake, the California Governor's Office of Emergency Services and the Federal Emergency Management Agency (FEMA) funded a study of the effects of an earthquake of M 8.4 on the Cascadia Subduction Zone for the 150-mile distance between Cape Mendocino and Cape Blanco, Oregon. This was published by the Division of Mines and Geology as Toppozada et al. (1995). As part of this scenario, NOAA produced tsunami inundation studies of the Crescent City and Humboldt Bay areas (Figure 10-6). In the scenario, the tsunami arrived just minutes after the earthquake, which meant that there was not enough time to order an evacuation. Waves were higher than thirty feet. The Samoa Peninsula was inundated, as was the village of King Salmon, which faces the opening of Humboldt Bay. Earthquake damage to road approaches would prevent immediate aid from reaching the Samoa Peninsula. A possible refuge for residents would be a ridge of wooded dunes just west of Manila, two miles north of Samoa and four miles north of Fairhaven. At Crescent City, the scenario tsunami runup was higher than the 1964 tsunami, with severe damage expected in the developed area along the shoreline south of Front and M Streets.

In October 1994, Senator Mark Hatfield of Oregon asked for a report on preparedness against tsunamis, especially a tsunami generated on the Cascadia Subduction Zone. A year later, the Senate requested a plan for implementation with a budget. This led to the establishment in December 1996 of the National Tsunami Hazard Mitigation Program for the five Pacific Coast states, under the direction of NOAA. This program, with a budget of about $2 million per year, supports tsunami inundation modeling in states bordering the Pacific Ocean, tsunami mitigation activities, upgrading seismic networks, and deep-ocean pressure gauges. As part of this program, the Center for Tsunami Inundation Mapping Efforts (TIME) was established in Newport, Oregon. Tsunami inundation maps are constructed using computer models of the earthquake source as well as the configuration of the continental slope and shelf and coastal bays, harbors, and estuaries. The tsunami maps show where tsunamis are likely to be focused, such as they were at Hilo, Hawaii and Crescent City, California.

During the first year of the program, all of the mapping funds went to Oregon and Washington. In 1995, Oregon enacted legislation that

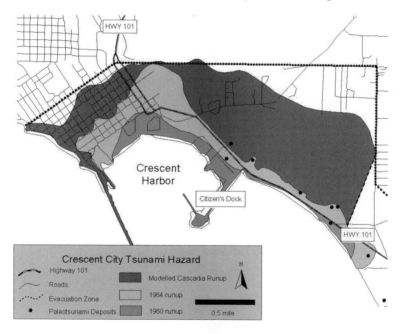

Figure 10-6. Map of Crescent City showing inundation from tsunamis in 1960 and 1964 and expected inundation from a tsunami accompanying a magnitude 8.5 earthquake on the Cascadia Subduction Zone. Suggested evacuation routes are shown. Modified from Toppozada et al. (1995) by Lori Dengler, Humboldt State University.

limits construction of new essential facilities and special-occupancy structures in tsunami flooding zones. Directed by this new law, the Department of Geology and Mineral Industries (DOGAMI) prepared a series of tsunami hazard maps at a scale of one inch to 2,000 feet of the entire Oregon coast (available as Open-File Reports O-95-09 through O-95-66 and explained in O-95-67, which also contains an index map of the individual tsunami warning maps).

DOGAMI also designed a tsunami warning logo to be posted on Oregon beaches. This logo (Figure 10-7) now has been adopted by all the other Pacific Coast states, including California.

Inundation modeling is underway for four additional regions in California. Preliminary maps have been completed for San Francisco to San Mateo County, Santa Barbara County, the Santa Monica-Long Beach area, and the Carlsbad-San Diego coastline. Costas Synolakis of the University of Southern California, who is doing the studies, has found that modeling California tsunamis south of the Cascadia Subduction Zone is more complicated than it is farther north. There is a much longer coastline and a much larger population at risk. The quality of submarine topographic data is patchy. The source of the largest locally generated tsunamis in southern California might be submarine landslides, although reverse-fault sources in the Santa Barbara Channel are also being evaluated.

Even though California laws dealing with surface fault rupture, liquefaction, and landsliding are the strongest in the United States, California has no tsunami hazard laws comparable to those in Oregon. One reason is that too little is known about the tsunami hazard, particularly from submarine landslides and from offshore faults in southern California. On the other hand, management of the California coastal zone has a high priority and tsunamis can be one of the hazards that need to be addressed, along with severe winter storms and oil spills.

What warning should be given to coastal residents in case of an earthquake? On the Oregon and Washington coast, strong shaking is likely to mean an earthquake on the subduction zone, and residents are advised to evacuate to higher ground without waiting for a tsunami

Figure 10-7. Tsunami warning logo designed by the Oregon Department of Geology and Mineral Industries and adopted by all Pacific Coast states.

warning. But California, including Humboldt and Del Norte counties adjacent to the Cascadia Subduction Zone, has many crustal earthquakes that do not generate tsunamis. The city of Santa Cruz underwent strong shaking during the 1989 Loma Prieta Earthquake, and Santa Monica was damaged by the 1994 Northridge Earthquake. Should the residents evacuate without official notice in earthquakes like those? Probably not. Even the 1906 San Francisco Earthquake, which had its epicenter offshore west of the Golden Gate, did not generate a tsunami large enough to warrant evacuation.

7. California Tsunami Hazard Programs

In 1992, the California Seismic Safety Commission issued a publication on tsunami hazards in California. This was followed by the planning scenario for an earthquake on the Cascadia Subduction Zone accompanied by a tsunami, published by the Division of Mines and Geology (Toppozada et al., 1995). The Governor's Office of Emergency Services (OES), with support from FEMA and NOAA, has taken the lead in tsunami hazard mitigation in California and in developing educational materials, tsunami warning signs, and detailed studies of coastal areas to determine evacuation routes. In 1996, OES sponsored an exercise to deal with strong shaking and a tsunami in Mendocino, Humboldt, and Del Norte counties. In that same year, OES issued a free pamphlet describing how to survive a tsunami.

In 1997, prior to beginning NOAA's tsunami inundation modeling program, OES held tsunami hazard mitigation workshops for emergency managers from coastal counties. In the following year, a state tsunami working group was established, and in 1999, guidelines for addressing tsunami hazards were given to coastal emergency managers. In 2000, regional workshops were held in Eureka, Oakland, Santa Barbara, Los Angeles, and San Diego, including a special workshop on tsunamis generated by submarine landslides in southern California.

On the north coast, the Humboldt Earthquake Education Center is largely the brainchild of Lori Dengler in the Department of Geology at Humboldt State University at Arcata. And the Redwood Coast Tsunami Work Group meets bimonthly to coordinate tsunami planning among local, state, and federal agencies, including Redwood National Park.

8. Paleoseismic Evidence for Tsunamis

Did giant tsunamis occur on the Cascadia Subduction Zone in the past? Paleoseismic evidence indicates that they did. The buried peat deposits of Willapa Bay, Washington are directly overlain by a thin layer of laminated sand that shows evidence of originating from the sea. Sand thickness and grain size diminish away from the sea (Figure 10-8). In

Figure 10-8. Exposure at low tide of sediments below the modern tidal marsh at Willapa Bay, southwest Washington. The shovel blade is at the top of the dark soil layer marking a former marsh that subsided abruptly in A.D. 1700 during the last Cascadia Subduction Zone earthquake. The strongly layered sediments just above the soil layer are sands deposited by a tsunami that immediately followed the subsidence. Photo by Brian Atwater, U.S. Geological Survey.

southern Oregon, some of the coastal lakes that have formed behind sand bars show evidence of giant waves sweeping across the sand bars. In northern California, Gary Carver found that a prehistoric tsunami at the mouth of Redwood Creek reached wave heights of sixty feet. Waves as high as thirty-three feet struck the Crescent City area in the prehistoric past, and along the coast near Humboldt Bay, wave heights were fifteen to thirty feet. So it is likely that the next Cascadia Subduction Zone earthquake will be accompanied by a tsunami.

9. What's the Tsunami Hazard in California?

The danger of a tsunami from a distant source is reasonably well understood, based on the experiences of the 1960 Chile and 1964 Alaska tsunamis that did damage in California. Estuaries and bays are especially at risk, including Crescent City, Humboldt Bay, San Pedro, and San Diego. Warning systems now in place should provide adequate notice of this kind of tsunami, especially if the warnings from the NOAA warning centers are supplemented by local evacuation orders with sirens for people not watching TV or listening to a radio.

Response to a tsunami with a local source is not as well understood or agreed upon. North of Cape Mendocino, local offshore reverse faults (Figure 7-9) could undergo seismic displacements as large as those documented for the Little Salmon Fault onshore (Figure 7-1) based on paleoseismology. South of Cape Mendocino, offshore active faults are largely strike slip, on which displacement would not be expected to generate a tsunami. The epicenter of the 1906 San Francisco Earthquake was offshore, but that earthquake was not accompanied by a tsunami. An exception is the set of reverse faults in the Santa Barbara Channel, including the North Channel Slope Fault, Oak Ridge Fault, and Red Mountain Fault. The tsunami potential from submarine landslides might be much larger than that from reverse faults. The 1812 tsunami at Santa Barbara could have been caused by an earthquake-triggered landslide in the Santa Barbara Channel.

For locally generated tsunamis, there is no time for a tsunami warning. If the earthquake lasts twenty seconds or longer, one should evacuate for higher ground as soon as strong shaking stops, or to the upper stories of a building if higher ground is more than a few minutes away (Governor's Office of Emergency Services, 1996).

Because this book is written for Californians, a few of whom are into extreme sports, be advised that tsunamis are NOT surfable. The wave does not curl. It generally comes ashore as a rapidly rising surge of turbulent water choked with debris, including large logs. Even if a surfer managed to avoid being bashed to death by the maelstrom of debris, he or she could never "catch" the wave.

Suggestions for Further Reading

Atwater, B.F., V.M. Cisternas, J. Bourgeois, W.C. Dudley, J.W. Hadley, and P.H. Stauffer, compilers. 1999. Surviving a Tsunami—Lessons Learned from Chile, Hawaii, and Japan. U.S. Geol. Survey Circular 1187. 18p.

Bernard, E.N., et al. 1991. *Tsunami Hazard: A Practical Guide for Tsunami Hazard Reduction.* Dordrecht, The Netherlands: Kluwer Academic Publishers.

Dudley, W.C., and M. Lee. 1988. *Tsunami!* Honolulu: University of Hawaii Press.

Governor's Office of Emergency Services. 1996. Tsunami! How to survive the hazard on California's coast. Free pamphlet available from OES.

Humboldt Earthquake Education Center. 1999. Living on shaky ground: How to survive earthquakes and tsunamis on the north coast.

Nance, J.J. 1988. *On Shaky Ground.* New York: William Morrow & Co. 416p. Description of the 1964 tsunami in Alaska.

Toppozada, T., G. Borchardt, W. Haydon, M. Peterson, R. Olson, H. Lagorio, and T. Anvik. 1995. Planning scenario in Humboldt and Del Norte counties, California, for a great earthquake on the Cascadia Subduction Zone. California Division of Mines and Geology, Special Publ. 115. 157p.

ᔕ Part IV ᔕ
Prevention and Countermeasures

I t's one thing to be convinced that earthquakes are a threat. We face dangers from ground shaking, landslides, liquefaction, tsunamis, and surface rupture. But what can we do about it?

The chapters that follow describe the human response to earthquakes at all scales, from the federal government to the individual. Should we purchase earthquake insurance? If so, it might be useful to learn about the problem from an insurance company's point of view, which means we need to learn about risk. The cost of your insurance may be influenced by the actions you take as a homeowner or renter to make your house more secure against earthquakes. These actions can also save your life or prevent serious injury during an earthquake. How about the safety of the building where you work, or the bridge you must cross on the way to work, or the dam upstream from your home?

The government is involved at all levels—federal, state, and local. Much of the research on earthquakes and on earthquake engineering is funded in the United States by the federal government, and we turn to the federal government for help in a disaster. The California state government is involved in a major way in earthquake hazard reduction, spurred on by the havoc earthquakes have raised in the past. Building codes and grading ordinances, where they are in effect, give us some security that the structure we live or work in will not collapse during an earthquake, or that the ground on which that structure is built will remain stable during an earthquake. But even though California has enacted the most advanced legislation in the world regulating building sites against geological hazards, builders and developers sometimes resist such laws because they increase their cost of doing business.

Finally, what should each of us do to plan against an earthquake?

⌒ 11 ⌒
Earthquake Insurance:
Betting Against Earthquakes

"What would happen if someone discovered how to predict earthquakes? No more earthquake insurance."

Richard J. Roth, Jr., California Department of Insurance, 1997

"We can't predict the future—we can only protect it."

California Earthquake Authority

1. Some Philosophical Issues

S hould you buy earthquake insurance for your house? For your business? Before addressing these questions directly, let's take a look at insurance in general and then at the particular problems in insuring against earthquakes.

You own a house, and you don't want to lose it in a fire, a flood, or an earthquake. You might take chances on the little things in life, but not your home; there's too much at stake. Fortunately, you are contacted by a company that offers to take the risk for you—at a price. The company is gambling that it can assume the risk of the loss of your house, and the houses of a lot of other people, and the price it gets for doing so will allow it to make money. The company is not offering you charity, but a business deal in which it expects to earn a profit. This doesn't bother you if the insurance is affordable, because you figure that the price you have paid is worth not having to worry about losing your home.

The company that takes on the risk is an *insurance company*, and the price you have paid is called the *premium*. The danger you are insuring against—fire, hurricane, or earthquake—is called a *peril*. An earthquake is often referred to in other contexts as a *hazard*, but the insurance industry defines "hazard" as something that makes your danger worse, like failing to reinforce your house against an earthquake, or allowing dense brush to grow against your house so that it is more vulnerable to summer brush fires. You can do something about the hazard, but you can't do much about the peril.

The company sells you fire insurance or automobile insurance, betting that your house won't burn down or you won't wreck your car so that the company can keep your premium and make money. The company wins its bet when your house doesn't burn down and you

261

don't wreck your car. You read about house fires almost every day in the newspaper, and thousands of people die in traffic accidents, but enough people pay fire and auto insurance premiums that the insurance company can cover its losses and still make money.

The insurance company wants to charge you a premium low enough to get your business, but high enough that it can make money after paying off its claims. It can do this because it calculates approximately how many house fires and auto accidents it is likely to have to pay off during the premium period. The larger the number of contracts it writes, the more likely the actual results will follow the predicted results based on an infinite number of contracts—a statistical relationship known as the *Law of Large Numbers*.

But suppose that an evil spirit casts a spell on automobile drivers so that instead of the usual number of auto accidents, there are hundreds of times more. Or an army of arsonists goes around setting houses on fire. The claims on the insurance company would be many times more costly than the number the company had figured on when it calculated premiums, and it would lose money. It could even go broke.

In a way, this is what an insurance company faces in a large urban earthquake, and indeed in any natural catastrophe, such as Hurricane Andrew. The difference is that the insurance company is dealing not with claims from a large number of individual automobile accidents or house fires, but from a single gigantic "accident"—an earthquake or a hurricane. The losses from the 1994 Northridge Earthquake were $20 billion, and those caused by the Kobe Earthquake may have been as high as $200 billion.

A large, destructive earthquake is an extremely rare event in any given place, and most of the time the insurance company collects your earthquake-insurance premium and makes money. But when an earthquake finally strikes a big city, the losses could be so great as to bankrupt the company. If earthquake scientists could finally get it right and make accurate probabilistic forecasts of when, where, and how large an earthquake will be (see Chapter 8), then the company could charge a premium high enough to keep it from bankruptcy, even from a rare catastrophic event. But unlike the situation with fire and auto insurance, the insurance industry lacks enough reliable information on catastrophic events to estimate its possible losses, and therefore to set a realistic premium. The losses from an earthquake might be so high that the premiums necessary to stay in business would be prohibitively expensive, discouraging homeowners from buying earthquake insurance at all.

Consider the earthquake losses from the great San Francisco Earthquake of 1906. (The dollar figures are small, but so was the size of the insurance industry at that time.) The Fireman's Fund Insurance

Company found that it was unable to meet its loss liabilities of $11,500,000, and it closed down to be reformed as a new company, paying off claims with 56.5 percent cash and 50 percent stock in the new company. Four American and two British companies, including Lloyds of London, paid their liabilities in full, but forty-three American and sixteen foreign companies did not, spending months and years in legal battles to avoid paying off their claims. Four German companies immediately stopped doing business in North America to avoid paying anything. Another offered to pay only a fraction of its losses.

The insurance industry had underestimated its potential losses in a catastrophic earthquake. The premium was not *cost-based*.

This is why the controversy about whether the next Cascadia earthquake will be a magnitude 8 or 9 is being followed with nervous fascination by the insurance industry. Insurance companies have no problem with a Landers Earthquake, not even with several Landers Earthquakes. It might even handle a magnitude 7.9 earthquake on the thinly populated central San Andreas Fault between Parkfield and Cajon Pass. But a magnitude 7.6 in the middle of Los Angeles gives insurance underwriters fits. Can the insurance industry survive a magnitude 7.6 in Los Angeles (rather than the magnitude 6.7 earthquakes it sustained in 1971 and 1994) and still stay in business and meet its obligations? Can it survive two urban earthquakes back to back?

2. A Brief Primer on Insurance

Insurance is our social and economic way of spreading the losses of a few across the greater population. We are pretty sure our house won't burn down, but we buy fire insurance for the peace of mind that comes from knowing that on the odd chance that it *does* burn down, our investment would be protected. Our insurance premium is our contribution to setting things right for those few people whose houses do burn down, since the house that burns down could be our own.

Insurance is a business, but it's also a product. There is a consumer's market, insurance has value, and the product has a price—called the premium. But insurance differs from other products in that its cost to the company is determined *only after it is sold*. For this reason, the company tries hard to estimate in advance what that cost is likely to be.

For an insurance company to stay in business, it must be able to (1) predict its potential losses, (2) calculate a price for premiums that will compensate for its losses and leave a profit, (3) collect the premium, and (4) pay off its claims as required in the insurance contract. The company has an executive department that determines overall corporate direction (including the basic decision about whether or not the company wants to be in the earthquake insurance business at all), a department that sends out your statement, a department that settles your claim, and a department that worries about risk so that the price of the premium fits the risk exposure of the company. This last process, called *rating*, is done by an *actuary*. To determine a rating for earthquake insurance for your house, the actuary may take into account the quality of construction, its proximity to known active faults, and the ground conditions. *Underwriting* is the determination of whether to insure you at all. The underwriter uses the rates established by the actuary and accepts the risk by establishing the premium. For example, if you are an alcoholic and have had several moving automobile violations, including accidents that were your fault, the underwriter might refuse you automobile insurance at any price. If a decision is made to insure you, the underwriter would establish the premium and deductible appropriate to the company's risk exposure.

An insurance company has *reserves*, money for the payment of claims that have already been presented but have not been settled, probably because the repair work has not yet been completed or the claim is in litigation. Reserves are not available for future losses; these losses show as a liability on the company's books. A *policyholder surplus*, or *net worth capital*, or *retained earnings* are funds that represent the value of the company after all its liabilities (claims) have been settled. This is the money available to pay for future losses.

It turns out that the insurance company, too, wants to hedge its bets against the future by transferring part of its risk to someone else. To meet this need, there are insurance companies that insure other companies—a process called *reinsurance*. Let's say that the original company insures a multimillion-dollar structure but wants to spread the risk. So it finds another company to share that risk, and that company—a reinsurance company—then receives part of the premium. It might well be the reinsurance industry that is most interested in the results of scientists and engineers in earthquake probability forecasting and in assessing ground response to earthquake shaking.

Some say that even the reinsurance industry would be unable to pay all claims arising from a catastrophic M 7.9 earthquake on the San Andreas Fault in an urban area such as San Francisco Bay or San Bernardino, and only the federal government, with its large cash reserves, can serve as the reinsurer of last resort. I return to this question later in the chapter.

We start with that which insurance does best: insure against noncatastrophic losses such as auto accidents, fires, and death. These are called *insurable risks*. The loss must be *definite*, *accidental*, *large*, *calculable*, and *affordable*. Enough policies need to be written so that the Law of Large Numbers kicks in. The *principle of indemnity* (which excludes life insurance, of course) is to return the insured person or business to the condition that existed prior to the loss. This means replacing or repairing the property or paying out its value as established in the insurance contract. The contract might include both *direct coverage*, replacing the property that was damaged or destroyed, and *indirect coverage*, taking care of the loss of income in a business or loss of use of the property. Protection against liability might be included. The contract commonly contains a *deductible clause*, which states that the insurance company will pay only those losses exceeding an agreed-upon amount. The higher the deductible, the lower the premium. This reduces the risk exposure for the company and reduces the number of small claims submitted.

The underwriter has calculated the exposure risk using the Law of Large Numbers. A lot of historical information about fire and auto accident losses is available, so the risk exposure is calculable; that is, the underwriter can recommend premium levels and types of coverage with considerable confidence that the company will be able to offer affordable coverage and still make a profit. The underwriter also looks for favorable factors that might reduce the risk. For fire insurance, a metal roof and vinyl siding would present less risk than a shake roof and wood siding. Auto insurance might include discounts for nondrinkers or for students with a grade-point average of B or better. The underwriter also looks for general trends, like the effect of the elimination of the fifty-five mile-per-hour speed limit on auto accident risk (increasing risk exposure), or of laws requiring seat belts and child restraints in automobiles (reducing risk exposure).

3. Catastrophe Insurance

Insurance against natural catastrophes is much more complex and much less understood, and a large company might employ engineers, geologists, and seismologists to help it calculate the odds. The insurance market in California changed drastically after the 1989 Loma Prieta Earthquake and the 1994 Northridge Earthquake. If a magnitude 9 earthquake struck the Cascadia Subduction Zone, the devastation would spread across a large geographic area, including many cities and towns. As a result, an insurance company would have a large number of insured customers suffering losses in a single incident, thereby defeating the Law of Large Numbers. Potential insurance losses after a major earthquake determine *insurance capacity*.

Insurance capacity is in part controlled by the fact that all the insurance companies in a region can write only so much insurance, controlled by their financial ability to pay the claims. (This is not the same as *insurance surplus*, which is simply assets minus liabilities.) Part of the role of the executive department of an insurance company is to decide how to distribute its surplus among different kinds of losses.

For example, an insurance company might be so concerned about the uncertainties in writing earthquake insurance that it is only willing to risk, say, ten percent of its surplus—which then defines its capacity for earthquake insurance. It could sustain losses in a major urban earthquake but risk a small enough percentage of its total coverage that it would not go out of business.

In making its decision about capacity, the company estimates its *probable maximum loss (PML) exposure* to earthquakes, meaning the highest loss it is likely to sustain. If the company finds that its estimated PML is too high, it reduces its capacity for earthquake insurance in favor of noncatastrophic insurance, thereby reducing its PML exposure. The company might decide to get out of the earthquake insurance business altogether. Insurance capacity was reduced after the losses following the 1994 Northridge Earthquake; there was too much uncertainty in figuring out the risk.

After a major earthquake, the capacity becomes reduced at the same time the demand increases for earthquake insurance. This creates a seller's market for the underwriter, who can set conditions more favorable to the company. These conditions might include the stability of the building site, the proximity to active faults, and the structural upgrading of the building to survive higher earthquake accelerations. If you are a building owner, your attention to these problems can have an economic payoff in lower earthquake insurance rates, just as a good driving record can lower your automobile insurance premium.

Just as health insurers prefer to insure healthy people, earthquake insurers prefer properties that are most likely to survive an earthquake. Your premium will be higher (or you might be uninsurable) if your house is next to the San Andreas Fault. If your building is constructed on soft sediment of the Los Angeles River or on beach deposits along the coast, which might liquefy or fail by landsliding, your premium might be higher than if you had built on a solid rock foundation. Unfortunately for the insurance company, people living next to the San Andreas Fault or on unstable sediments in an earthquake-prone region such as the San Francisco Bay Area are more likely to buy earthquake insurance than people living in, say, Sacramento or Fresno, not known for their earthquakes. This is called *adverse selection*.

The result is that the risk of earthquake damage is not spread over a large enough group of people. This makes earthquake insurance more expensive for everybody and causes people either to refuse to buy earthquake insurance or drop their existing coverage.

Maps of the Los Angeles and San Francisco Bay metropolitan areas showing regions susceptible to liquefaction and landsliding related to earthquakes were designed to highlight those areas where the danger from earthquakes might be much greater than other areas. It's possible to superimpose on such maps an overlay of the building types classified by their vulnerability to earthquakes.

An insurance company asked to insure a large building in one of these areas could use these maps to set the premium, but Proposition 103, passed by voters in 1988, requires all insurance companies to get their rates approved by the Department of Insurance. Once a rate for a particular class of risk has been filed with and approved by the Department of Insurance, the insurance company may not deviate from this rate. The company would have to request a deviation from the approved rate based on new information contained in a hazard map.

Insurance underwriters are very much aware that the principal damage in an earthquake is to buildings that predate the upgrading of building codes. They know that buildings constructed under higher standards are more likely to ride out the earthquake with minimum damage. Therefore, your premium might be lower (or your building might be insurable) if it's constructed or retrofitted under the most modern building codes, thereby reducing the risk to the company as well as to yourself.

From an insurance standpoint, building codes are a set of minimum standards, and these standards are designed for *life safety* rather than *property safety*. The building code works if everybody gets out of the building alive, even if the building itself is a total loss. If your structure has been engineered to standards much higher than those required by the code, so that not only the people inside but also the property itself survives, your insurance premium could be significantly lower. You would need to determine whether the reduced premium more than offsets the increased construction costs or the retrofit costs necessary to ensure that your building rides out the earthquake.

The insurance company can reduce its PML exposure by establishing a high deductible. A common practice is to express the deductible as a percentage of the value of the covered property at the time of loss. For example, your house is insured for $200,000 and your deductible is fifteen percent of the value of the house at the time of loss. An earthquake strikes, and damage is estimated at $50,000. Fifteen percent of $200,000 is $30,000, so the insurance company pays you $20,000, the difference between the deductible and the estimated damage.

Now we get into some gray areas. First, liability insurance. Suppose the owner of the building where you work or rent your apartment has been told that the building is not up to earthquake code but chooses not to retrofit. An earthquake destroys the building, and you are severely injured. Do you have a negligence claim against the building owner that his liability insurance would be required to pay off?

Another gray area is government intervention. A major catastrophe such as the Northridge Earthquake brings immediate assistance from the Federal Emergency Management Agency (FEMA), including low-interest loans and direct assistance. The high profile of any great natural catastrophe—a hurricane as well as an earthquake—makes it likely that the President of the United States and the director of FEMA will show up on your doorstep. Billions of dollars of federal assistance will be forthcoming, although this is generally a one-shot deal—aid that is nonrecurring. However, major transportation systems and utilities—called *lifelines*—will be restored quickly. After the Northridge Earthquake, the highest priority was given by Caltrans to reopen the freeways, and Southern California Gas Company quickly repaired the ruptured gas trunk line on Balboa Boulevard.

The net effect of this aid is to compensate for the large losses in the affected region, although not necessarily the losses of insurance companies. This aid follows the insurance principle that losses are spread across a larger population—in this case, the citizens of the state of California and the United States. However, much of this aid focuses on *relief* rather than *recovery*.

4. Government Intervention

State governments have already intervened in the insurance business, thanks to the McCarran Ferguson Act of 1945. The California Insurance Commissioner must approve the rates charged by an insurance company within the state and must monitor the financial strength of a company and its ability to pay its claims. An *admitted* insurance company is licensed by the Insurance Commissioner to do business in California. *Nonadmitted* companies not licensed by the Insurance Commissioner are not members of the California Insurance Guarantee Association (CIGA) and can do business only through *surplus line brokers*. CIGA is supposed to help people settle claims against insurance companies that have gone broke, but CIGA would be of no help in settling claims against a nonadmitted company.

People naturally distrust insurance companies. We see their gleaming downtown office buildings at the same time our premiums are increasing, or we get the runaround when we submit a claim. A state department of insurance might respond to this distrust by developing an adversarial relationship with the insurance industry within the state. Or a state insurance commissioner might develop too cozy a relationship with the industry being regulated. The high cost of insurance has become a political issue in California—first, health insurance costs, and more recently, following Northridge, earthquake insurance costs.

This adversarial relationship can be a particular problem in insuring against catastrophes. The insurance industry has developed computer models to estimate its losses in a major catastrophe, models that suggest that premiums are not high enough, are not *cost based*. But these models are proprietary, meaning that an insurance company might not want to release the details of the model to the Insurance Commissioner and the public and lose its competitive advantage. Some state departments of insurance might not accept or trust these models, or they might regard them as biased in favor of the industry. However, this is not a problem for the California State Department of Insurance; the California Earthquake Authority, described below, uses computer models.

Government intervention could be taken to an extreme: the government could take over catastrophic insurance altogether, rather than merely regulating insurance at the state level. The United States government is already involved in flood insurance; a federal insurance program is administered by the Federal Insurance Administration, part of FEMA. There is also a federal crop insurance program. However, there is no federal program of earthquake insurance.

In 1987, a group of insurance-industry trade associations and some insurance companies organized a study group called the Earthquake Project to consider the effects of a great earthquake on the U.S. economy in general and the insurance industry in particular. This group, renamed the Natural Disaster Coalition after the multibillion-dollar losses from Hurricane Andrew, concluded that the probable maximum losses from a major disaster would far exceed the insurance industry's capacity to respond, and that a federal insurance partnership was necessary. The study group proposed legislation to establish a primary federal earthquake insurance program for residences and a reinsurance program for commercial properties. However, the proposal was criticized as an insurance-industry bailout, and no action was taken. A revised proposal attracted more congressional support, but the potential federal liability in the event of a great disaster doomed this proposal as well. In 1996, the Natural Disaster Coalition proposed a more modest plan that would reduce federal involvement and establish a national commission to consider ways to reduce the costs of catastrophic insurance. This failed to win sufficient White House support for adoption, but it might be considered by a future Congress.

However, the federal government does respond to disasters, and it did so after Northridge. Disaster relief is sure to be provided, but recovery from the disaster is a political issue and is fraught with uncertainties. Grants might be available from the Federal Emergency Management Agency or the Department of Health and Human Services.

Another proposed solution is to allow insurance companies to accumulate tax-free reserves to be available to pay claims in the event of a catastrophe. Let's say that a disaster with losses of $100 million will occur once every ten years—far in excess of the premiums expected in the year the catastrophe struck. If the insurance industry collected and accumulated $10 million annually for ten years, then it could meet its claims in the year of the catastrophe. However, under present accounting regulations, the $10 million collected during a year in which no catastrophe occurs must be taxed as income. For this reason, the insurance company must pay off its $100 million losses with the $10 million in premiums that it collected that year plus income collected earlier on which it has already paid taxes. The proposal to accumulate tax-free reserves against a catastrophe has met with enough congressional resistance to prevent it from being passed into law.

Government has become involved in earthquake insurance in California, where the state has orchestrated the establishment of a privately financed earthquake authority, and New Zealand, where the government has gotten into the insurance business directly.

California

In California, earthquake insurance was offered even before the 1906 San Francisco Earthquake, with major problems paying claims from that disaster, as we have seen. But since then, earthquake insurance has been profitable for the insurance industry, up until the 1989 Loma Prieta Earthquake, followed by the 1994 Northridge Earthquake. For most of the period since the 1906 San Francisco Earthquake, claims and payments were far less than premiums, even including three large earthquakes (1971 Sylmar, 1983 Coalinga, 1987 Whittier Narrows), two of which struck densely populated areas. But the claims and payments rose dramatically from less than $3 million for the Sylmar Earthquake to about $1 billion for earthquake shaking damage after the Loma Prieta Earthquake. In 1989, as a result of the Loma Prieta Earthquake, claims and payments exceeded premiums for the first time since 1906.

But the 1994 Northridge Earthquake really broke the bank: about $15.3 billion, with more than $9 billion in insured losses to residential properties—far more than all the earthquake premiums for residences collected for decades. One insurance company severely underestimated its potential for losses from the Northridge Earthquake; it would have gone out of business except for a buyout from another carrier. If a similar size earthquake had struck a major urban area on the heels of the Northridge Earthquake, even some major companies would not have been able to cover their losses. Northridge losses were covered in part by the use of income from investments to pay claims.

Not all of the $15.3 billion paid out was earthquake insurance, which covers damage from shaking. About twenty percent of the loss was paid from other types of insurance, including insurance against fire, property damage and liability, commercial and private vehicle losses, loss of life, disability, medical payments, and so on.

These figures point out another trend in the earthquake insurance market: the sharp rise in insurance premiums and claims after California began to require in 1985 that a company offering homeowners' insurance must also offer earthquake insurance, although the homeowner was not required to buy it. Because the Northridge Earthquake broke the Law of Large Numbers, the insurance industry was faced with a problem larger than simply earthquake insurance—the much larger market for homeowners' insurance that had become legally linked to earthquake insurance.

After Northridge, insurance companies asked the Legislature to uncouple homeowners' insurance from earthquake insurance. The Legislature refused for the reason that it would have left millions of homeowners unable to buy earthquake insurance at an affordable price. In response, insurance companies representing ninety-three percent of the homeowners' insurance market severely restricted capacity for not only earthquake insurance but homeowners' insurance as well, with some companies getting out of the homeowners' insurance business altogether. Demand greatly outstripped supply, and homeowners' insurance premiums skyrocketed. In response to complaints about the high premiums, companies pointed to studies that suggested that future losses could exceed $100 billion, losses that would bankrupt many companies. Losses of $200 billion from the Kobe Earthquake of 1995 in Japan solidified that view, although only a small fraction of the Kobe Earthquake loss was covered by insurance. Insurance companies and homeowners took their concerns to the California legislature in Sacramento.

The Legislature then established a reduced-coverage catastrophic residential earthquake insurance that would cover the dwelling but would exclude detached structures. This "mini-policy" included a fifteen-percent deductible, $5,000 in contents coverage, and $1,500 in emergency living expenses. Despite strong public support, the mini-policy did not lure insurance companies back into the residential insurance market. By mid-1996, the lack of availability of residential insurance was threatening the vitality of the California housing market.

The result was the California Earthquake Authority (CEA), signed into law by Governor Pete Wilson in September 1996. In exchange for pledging $3.5 billion to cover claims after an earthquake, insurers transferred their earthquake risk to the CEA. The CEA then bought $2.5 billion in reinsurance—the largest single reinsurance purchase in history. Premium payments and additional lines of credit raised the amount available to pay claims to more than $7.2 billion, leading the CEA to claim that it can cover losses from at least two Northridge-type earthquakes. This was accomplished without the use of public funds.

Insurance companies representing more than seventy percent of the residential property insurance market agreed to participate by signing a Participating Carrier Agreement to write policies on all eligible categories in the CEA. Insurance premiums have more than doubled, and payouts are expected to be lower. One estimate for residential claims if the CEA had been in operation at the time of the Northridge Earthquake: $4 billion less than the amount actually paid out.

The CEA earthquake insurance is the "mini-earthquake policy" established in 1996. Structural damage to residences is covered, with a deductible of fifteen percent of the value rather than ten percent. The state requires a minimum coverage of $5,000 for personal property; this turns out to be the maximum coverage offered by CEA. Emergency living expenses up to $1,500 are provided—a token payment if you lost the use of your home for several weeks. Swimming pools, fences, driveways, outbuildings, and landscaping are not covered at all. Claims are processed by individual insurance companies and paid by the state. If the CEA ran out of money, policyholders would get only partial payment of claims, and there could be a surcharge of up to twenty percent on their policy if claims exceeded $6 billion.

Participation by insurance companies is voluntary, but insurers representing two-thirds of the market—including the three largest insurers, State Farm, Allstate, and Farmers—are committed to the CEA. But many smaller carriers have stayed out, in part because they cannot pick and choose among the eligible risks they would cover and risks they would not cover; it's all or nothing. Using mid-1998 figures, this means that the CEA will be able to pay out only about $7 billion instead of the $10.5 billion estimated with 100 percent participation. Some insurance actuaries believe that the premiums are still too low to protect against catastrophic losses; that is, CEA is still not cost based. The higher cost has been criticized by consumer advocates such as United Policyholders; it has driven many homeowners away from obtaining or renewing earthquake coverage. At present, no more than twenty-five percent of California homeowners have earthquake insurance. Even so, the CEA is now the largest provider of residential earthquake insurance in the world, with more than 900,000 policyholders and $163 billion in insured risk.

Under the CEA, insurance premiums vary from region to region; California is divided into nineteen separate rating territories. Much of the San Fernando Valley, which suffered two damaging earthquakes in less than twenty-five years, is paying forty percent more than most of the rest of the Los Angeles metropolitan area. But the city of Palmdale, in the Mojave Desert adjacent to that part of the San Andreas Fault that ruptured in 1857 in an earthquake of M 7.9, pays significantly lower rates than much of Los Angeles! San Francisco Bay Area residents are paying rates four-and-a-half times higher than residents of Eureka, on the northern California coast—an area that has experienced the greatest number of large earthquakes in California, and indeed, in the United States. The north coast was struck by a M 7.1 earthquake in 1992 and is at risk from an earthquake on the Cascadia Subduction Zone, yet the region has rates that are among California's lowest. Perhaps the lesson to be learned here is that if your area has recently had an earthquake, earthquake insurance will be very costly, but if not, earthquake insurance could be a bargain.

Put another way, the insurance industry is more sensitive to historical earthquakes and instrumental seismicity than it is to geological evidence for prehistoric earthquakes and slip rates on active faults.

Controversy over the great disparity in earthquake insurance rates from region to region has led to a review of the CEA's probabilistic hazard model by the California Division of Mines and Geology under contract to the State Department of Insurance. Revised models will undoubtedly make regional differences in earthquake insurance rates more realistic.

The age and type of home also affect rates. The owner of a $200,000 wood-frame house in Hollywood or Westwood in Los Angeles would pay $540 in earthquake insurance if the house was built in 1979 or later, $660 if the house was built between 1960 and 1978, and $700 if the house was built before 1960—a recognition of higher construction standards in recent years. The percent damage to homes from the Northridge Earthquake was thirty-five percent for buildings constructed before 1970 to twenty percent for houses that had just been completed at the time of the earthquake. But if the house was not of wood-frame construction, the premiums would be $960 in Hollywood.

The new insurance rates recognize the value of well-constructed houses in which earthquake risks have been taken into consideration. For information about earthquake insurance rates in your area, see the CEA Rate Calculator at http://date.insure.com/state/ca/home/cea/tool.cfm or call a toll-free number, 1-877-797-4300.

If you want to lower your rates by retrofitting, low-interest loans for retrofitting are available through the CEA.

Are there alternatives to the CEA mini-policy? Two new companies, GeoVera (www.geovera.com) and Pacific Select (www.pacificselect.com, http://quakeinsurance.net/homequote.com), offer stand-alone policies available without homeowners' or business coverage. You might be able to obtain separate homeowners and earthquake policies for less than the combined CEA policy, but the reason for this may be a more conservative selection of risks to be covered. If you live close to the San Andreas Fault or on a site subject to liquefaction or seismically triggered landslides as determined by the Seismic Hazard Mapping Act, these companies are likely to deny you earthquake coverage. It's possible to obtain earthquake coverage for non-CEA eligible risks through CEA participating companies, including State Farm, Liberty Mutual, USAA, and Armed Forces Insurance. These policies are backed by reinsurers, not the CEA. In addition, in June 1999, the CEA began to offer a lower deductible of ten percent, personal property coverage up to $100,000, and living expenses up to $15,000, but you should compare premiums offered by CEA and non-CEA companies. As in any other business decision, check out the financial rating of the insurance company before you buy a policy. A.M. Best is the standard insurance company rating system; consult www.ambest.com or the California Department of Insurance at www.insurance.ca.gov

The CEA claims that its rates, averaging $2.79 per $1,000 of coverage statewide, are competitive with the average rates of non-CEA insurers, $2.92 per $1,000 coverage. CEA rates vary based on assumed risk from $0.95 to $4.70 per $1,000 coverage. A better understanding of earthquake risk has led to two rate reductions; rates are now fifteen percent lower than they were when CEA went into operation in 1996.

One factor affecting rates was a decision by the Internal Revenue Service that the CEA is a nonprofit organization so that premiums can accumulate without being taxed as profit in the year they are collected. The IRS ruling is based on the CEA's commitment to earthquake mitigation programs benefiting all Californians, not just those with CEA policies. In September, 1999, the CEA began an earthquake mitigation program in eight Bay Area counties called State Assistance For Earthquake Retrofitting (SAFER), which includes low-cost inspections and assessments of older homes by structural engineers and low-interest loans to pay for seismic retrofits. The CEA worked with Oakland's KTVU Television to produce a public awareness program on the tenth anniversary of the Loma Prieta Earthquake.

The earthquake insurance business in California is changing rapidly. Check the web sites in this chapter for the latest information.

New Zealand

New Zealand, like California, is a land of great natural beauty in which the spectacular mountains and volcanoes are related to natural hazards, especially earthquakes and volcanic eruptions. Written records have been kept for less than 200 years, but during this period, New Zealand has suffered damaging earthquakes in 1848, 1855, 1888, 1929, and 1931. The country was thinly populated during most of the historical period, and losses, although locally severe, did not threaten the economy of the nation.

In June and August 1942, the capital city of Wellington and the nearby Wairarapa Valley were struck by earthquakes that severely damaged thousands of homes. It was the darkest period of World War II, with the war being waged in Pacific islands not far away to the north. Because of the war, there was little money for reconstruction after the earthquakes, and two years later, much of the rubble in the Wairarapa Valley had not even been cleared. Something had to be done.

In 1944, while the war still raged to the north, Parliament passed the Earthquake and War Damage Act, and in January 1945, the government began collecting a surcharge from all holders of fire insurance policies. The Earthquake and War Damage Commission was established to collect the premiums and accumulate a fund to pay out damage claims from war or earthquakes. Later, coverage against tsunamis, volcanic eruptions, and landslides was added.

In 1988, Parliament changed the commission from a government department with a state insurance commissioner to a corporation responsible for its own fund, and paying a fee for a government guarantee to cover its losses in case a great natural disaster exhausted the fund. In 1993, Parliament changed the name of the administering agency to the Earthquake Commission. Under the new law, the insurance automatically covers all residential properties that are insured against fire. It provides full replacement of a dwelling up to a value of $112,500 (in New Zealand dollars, including goods and services tax) and contents up to $22,500. Since 1996, only residential property has been covered, and every property is rated the same, regardless of ground conditions or proximity to an active fault.

The arrangement has worked well since 1944, in large part because New Zealand has not suffered a disastrous earthquake in an urban area since the commission was established. Earthquake premiums have continued to accumulate at a rate of about $150 million per year in those years when there are few claims, and as of December 1998 the fund had $3.3 billion to cover earthquake losses. The damages paid out as a result of the 1987 Edgecumbe Earthquake (M 6.6) were nearly $136 million, as compared to $2.4 million after the much larger 1968 Inangahua Earthquake (M 7.1) nearly twenty years earlier. (Most of the Edgecumbe damages were to commercial property, no longer covered; residential losses were $22 million in 1987 dollars.) The sharp increase in losses, even after earthquakes of moderate size in rural areas, indicates that the past will not be the key to the future, especially after a disastrous urban earthquake.

The entire $3.3 billion in the Earthquake Fund might cover less than one-third of losses from a M 7.5 earthquake in Wellington, where an active fault runs through the center of the city. The New Zealand government guarantees that it will cover all claims in excess of the fund in case of a major catastrophic earthquake. For this guarantee, the government buys reinsurance from international corporations, for which it charges the Earthquake Commission a reinsurance premium of $10 million per year. The domestic losses, including losses in productivity, would be offset in part by reinsurance money flowing into the country from overseas for reconstruction. Although the short-term losses would be immense, the net impact over a ten-year period would be largely minimized due to this inflow of overseas money. However, after the Earthquake Fund had been exhausted by a single large earthquake, the government would have to step in and cover even small claims until the commission had built up its assets once more.

Because the Earthquake Commission is responsible for its solvency in case of a great earthquake, and because all residences in the country are covered, it's good business for the commission to take an active role in disaster prevention, public preparedness, and earthquake research as a way to reduce potential losses.

5. What to Do if You Have an Earthquake Claim

United Policyholders, founded in 1991, is a nonprofit insurance consumer education organization with headquarters in San Francisco. It publishes a newsletter, *What's UP*, from which much of the information for this section was obtained.

The most important thing you can do is *before* the earthquake: *make an inventory*. List everything you own, room by room, showing the number of items, their description, age, and cost of replacement. Take photos. Keep all bills and receipts. Keep your inventory and supporting documents someplace other than your house, such as a safe deposit box. Jack Watts of State Farm Insurance Co. told me that "It is difficult to overstate the value of an inventory, photos and receipts. The adjuster is there to work with the claimant in establishing the claim, but it is so much easier when these documents have been kept updated and stored in a separate location from the residence."

After the earthquake, tell your agent that you have damage and are submitting a claim. Do this even if you are not sure you have an earthquake policy; some losses might still be covered. Review the fine print in your policy, especially the "Declarations" page with categories of coverage and dollar limits. Categories include *dwelling, contents, loss of use* (or additional living expenses), *other structures*, etc. Annual inflation factors increase your limits. You might need advice from an independent professional. If your policy and declarations page were destroyed in the earthquake, contact your insurance agent *in writing* for a duplicate copy.

Don't give a sworn statement, and don't sign over a final "Proof of Loss" form to your insurer until you are convinced that you understand your coverage, your rights, and the full extent of your claim. Don't be rushed into a quick settlement. Documenting a major loss requires comparing cost estimates from at least two or three reputable contractors, including the one you intend to hire for the actual repairs. Contractors might suggest various repair methods, and if your home or foundation is seriously damaged you should consult a structural engineer. Keep a diary and record the name and phone number of each person you talk to. It is better, of course, to have photos or receipts to claim destroyed property, but it's recognized that these might have been destroyed during the earthquake. After the earthquake, take photos and keep all receipts.

In rebuilding your home, you're entitled to "like kind and quality." If you have "guaranteed" or "extended" replacement cost coverage, you're entitled to the same style and quality home even if the replacement exceeds the amount of your policy.

For compensation of additional living expenses or loss of use, keep all receipts for meals, lodging, and purchases from the time of the earthquake until your house is rebuilt.

For additional information, contact United Policyholders at info@unitedpolicyholders.org

6. Summary Statement and Questions for the Future

Earthquake insurance is a high-stakes game involving insurance companies, policyholders, and in some cases, governments. Because earthquakes are so rare at a given location (in a human time frame, at least), consumers tend to underestimate the need for catastrophic coverage. In most states, the percentage of property owners with earthquake insurance is much lower than California's twenty-five percent.

The demand for earthquake insurance shoots up after a catastrophic earthquake at the same time the willingness and capacity of insurance companies to offer such insurance sharply decreases. Insurance is, after all, a business, and for the business to succeed it must make money.

Insurance companies might underestimate the premiums they should charge in a region like the Pacific Northwest, where a catastrophic earthquake has not occurred in nearly two hundred years of record keeping. But premiums might be priced too high to attract customers in places that have recently suffered major losses, such as the San Fernando Valley or the San Francisco Bay Area. Indeed, the entire state of California might be in this fix. The CEA offers a policy with reduced coverage and higher premiums, which causes many people to drop their earthquake insurance altogether. Yet many underwriters in the insurance industry are still not convinced that the reduced policy is cost based.

The quality of construction, particularly measures taken against earthquake shaking, will have an increasing impact on premium costs. The Institute of Building and Home Safety (IBHS), an association of insurance companies, has an Earthquake Peril Committee whose goal is the reduction of potential losses. This includes discouraging developers from building in areas at risk from earthquakes and other natural disasters. If a project is awarded an IBHS Seal of Approval, it might be eligible for hazard reduction benefits, including lower premiums.

The federal government still has not determined what its role should be. What should the general taxpayer be required to contribute? Should FEMA's efforts include not simply relief but recovery? Aid in reconstruction rather than low-interest loans? Should earthquake insurance be mandatory for properties in which the mortgage is federally guaranteed? Should it be subsidized by the government, particularly for low-income families who are most likely to live in seismically dangerous housing but cannot afford the premiums if they are truly cost based? The unattractiveness of the CEA mini-policy is causing many Californians to drop all earthquake coverage, which raises a new problem for the finance industry. Thousands of uninsured homeowners might simply walk away from their mortgages and declare bankruptcy if their uninsured homes are destroyed by an earthquake.

Problems such as these tend to be ignored by the public and by government except in the time immediately following an earthquake. There is a narrow time window (teachable moment) for the adoption of mitigation measures and the consideration of ways to deal with catastrophic losses, including earthquake insurance.

Suggestions for Further Reading

California Department of Conservation. 1990. Seismic Hazard Information Needs of the Insurance Industry, Local Government, and Property Owners of California. California Department of Conservation Special Publication 108.

Kunreuther, H., and R.J. Roth, Sr. 1998. *Paying the Price: The Status and Role of Insurance against Natural Disasters in the United States*. Washington, D.C.: Joseph Henry Press.

Palm, R., and J. Carroll. 1998. *Illusions of Safety: Cultural and Earthquake Hazard Response in California and Japan*. Boulder, CO, Westview Press.

Roth, R.J., Jr. 1997. Earthquake basics: Insurance: What are the principles of insuring natural disasters? Earthquake Engineering Research Institute publication.

⤺ 12 ⤻
Is Your Home Ready for an Earthquake?

". . . severe and appalling as this great convulsion of the earth unquestionably was, it is a settled conviction with all here that not a person would have been killed or hurt had their houses all been made of wood."

Editorial, Inyo *Independent*, 1872.

Introduction: How Safe is Safe Enough?

C hances are two out of three that you'll be at home when the next big earthquake strikes, and one out of three that you'll be in bed. So, your home's ability to withstand an earthquake affects not only your pocketbook but also your life and the lives of those who live with you. If you are an owner or even a renter, you can take steps to make your home safer against an earthquake.

But first you need to make some decisions. Sure, you want to be safe, but how much are you willing to spend to protect your home and family against an earthquake? Is it your goal that *you and those around you* walk away from your house without serious injury, or that your *house* survives the earthquake as well? This would be an easier decision if scientists could tell you when the next earthquake will strike. But they can't. You could be spending a lot of money protecting against an earthquake that might not strike during your lifetime.

This chapter reviews the steps you can take to protect your home, your valuables, and yourself from earthquake shaking, and it presents those steps in order of importance. The chapter does not consider damage to your house from liquefaction, landslides, surface rupture, subsidence, or tsunamis. It assumes that the ground on which your house is built will be shaken but not permanently deformed by the earthquake.

It is critical to keep your house from collapsing or from catching on fire, so those preventive steps are presented first. This is followed by discussion of other, less critical prevention measures. Then you can make the decision about how much protection is enough for you.

1. Some Fundamentals: Inertia, Loads, and Ductility

Imagine for a moment that your house is anchored to a flatcar on a moving train. Suddenly the train collides with another train and the flatcar stops abruptly. What happens to your house? If it's a wood-frame house, as most houses in California are, it probably would not collapse, although your brick chimney might topple over. If your house is made of brick or concrete block, unreinforced by steel rebar, then the entire house might collapse.

This analogy introduces an important concept. The jolt to your house during the train wreck is analogous to the shocks the house would receive during a large earthquake, except that the earthquake jolts would be more complicated. The motion might be sharply back and forth for tens of seconds, combined with ups and downs and sideways motions. The response of the house and its contents (including you) to these jolts follows the *principle of inertia*.

The principle of inertia says that a stationary object will remain stationary, or an object traveling at a certain speed in a certain direction will continue traveling at that speed and in that direction, unless acted on by some outside force. Because of inertia, your body is pulled to the right when you turn your car sharply left. Inertia is the reason seat belts are necessary. If your car hits a tree and you're not wearing a seat belt, your body's inertia keeps you moving forward at the same rate as the car before it hit the tree, propelling you through the windshield.

Stack some blocks on a towel on a table. Then suddenly pull the towel out from under the blocks and toward you. The blocks will fall *away* from you, as if they were being propelled by an opposing force. This force is called an *inertial force*. The inertia of the blocks tends to make them stay where they are, which means that they must fall away from you when you pull the towel toward you.

I saw a graphic illustration of inertia at the Los Angeles County Olive View Medical Center, which was destroyed by the Sylmar Earthquake in February 1971. Upper stories of the hospital seemed to weather the earthquake without damage. (In fact, glasses of water on bedside tables on the top floor weren't even spilled.) But the walls on the ground floor—which had much more open space and, therefore, was much weaker than the upper floors—were tilted in one direction. The ground beneath the hospital had moved suddenly in a horizontal direction, but the inertia of the hospital building caused it to appear to move in the opposite direction (Figure 13-11). The inertial forces were absorbed in the weaker ground floor. (For an illustration of inertial forces affecting a garage, see Figure 12-5.)

Engineers refer to the forces acting on a building as *loads*. The weight of the building itself is called a *dead load*. Other forces, such as the weight of the contents of the building—including people, snow on the roof, a Santa Ana wind roaring out of the desert, or earthquakes—are called *live loads*. The building must be designed to support its own weight, and this is standard practice. It also must be designed to support the weight of its contents, and this is also standard practice—although occasionally the news media report the collapse of a gymnasium roof due to a load of snow and ice.

Except for high winds and earthquakes, all the loads mentioned above are *vertical loads,* commonly accounted for in engineering design. But the wind load is a *horizontal load.* In designing buildings in a location subject to gale-force winds, horizontal wind loads are indeed taken into account. Earthquake loads are both vertical and horizontal. They are very complex, and in contrast to wind loads (except for tornadoes) they are applied suddenly, with high *acceleration.*

I have already discussed acceleration as a percentage of the attraction of the Earth due to its gravity, or *g.* During a space shuttle launch, astronauts are subjected to accelerations of several g as they rocket into space. A downhill ride on a roller coaster temporarily counteracts the Earth's gravity to produce zero g, and this accounts for the thrill (and sometimes queasy feeling) we experience. Acceleration during an earthquake is the Earth's answer to a roller-coaster ride. If the shaking is enough to throw objects into the air, the acceleration is said to be greater than one g. High accelerations, particularly high horizontal accelerations, can cause a lot of damage.

The dead weight of a building and its contents can be calculated fairly accurately and accounted for in engineering design. These loads are called *static loads;* they do not change with time. Wind loads and earthquake loads change suddenly and unpredictably; these are called *dynamic loads.* The engineer must design a structure to withstand dynamic loads that may be highly variable over a very short period of time, a much more difficult task than designing for static loads alone. Because the awareness of the potential for earthquake loads is only a few decades old, many older buildings have not been designed to stand up against the dynamic loads caused by earthquakes.

In Chapter 2, rocks of the crust were described as either *brittle* or *ductile.* Brittle crust fractures under the accumulated strain of the motion of tectonic plates and produces earthquakes. The underlying warm and pliable ductile crust deforms without earthquakes.

Structural engineers use these terms to refer to buildings. A building that is *ductile* is able to bend and sway during an earthquake without collapsing. In some cases, the building "bounces back" like a tree swaying in the wind, and it isn't permanently deformed. Deformation is *elastic,* as described earlier for balloons and boards. In other cases, the building deforms permanently but it still doesn't collapse, so that people inside can escape even though the building might be a total loss. Steel-frame buildings tend to be ductile. Wood-frame houses are also ductile. Fortunately, most of us live in wood-frame houses.

In contrast, a *brittle* structure is unable to deform during an earthquake without collapsing. Brittle buildings include those made of brick or concrete block joined together with mortar but not reinforced with steel rebar, or adobe buildings from California's pioneer days. In an earthquake, your wood-frame house might survive, but your chimney, made of brick not reinforced with rebar, might collapse. Your house is ductile, but your chimney is not.

The reinforcing techniques described below are for a house that has already been built; this is called a *retrofit*. These techniques are also applicable to new construction, in which case they are a lot less expensive. This is immediately apparent in shoring up the foundation: it's the difference between working comfortably on a foundation before the house is built on top if it and working in a confined crawl space.

2. Protecting Your Foundation

If you have a poured-concrete foundation, first check on its quality by hitting it with a hammer. If the hammer makes a dull thud rather than a sharp ping, or there are throughgoing cracks more than an eighth of an inch wide, or the concrete is crumbly, you'll need professional help.

Let's assume that the concrete is okay. The next job is to see whether your house is bolted to the foundation and is adequately braced. Otherwise, horizontal inertial forces could slide the foundation out from under the house, which happened to wood-frame houses in northern California during earthquakes in October 1989 and April 1992.

Some houses are built on a concrete slab, or floor. Others have a concrete foundation around the edge of the house. In these, a board called a *mudsill* is generally found between the house and its foundation. Older houses were not required to be bolted to the foundation through the mudsill. In 1974, the Uniform Building Code began to require that walls be anchored to foundations (Figure 12-1). The standard retrofit technique is to drill a hole through the mudsill and into the foundation with a rotary hammer or a right-angle drill, which can be rented, although you should purchase your own drill bit. Next, using a sledge

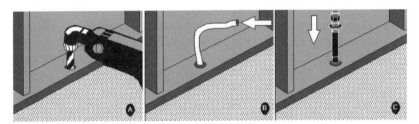

Figure 12-1. Bolt the cripple wall to the foundation through the mudsill, using a sill bolt. (A) Drill hole, using a right-angle drill. (B) Blow powder out of hole, using flexible tubing. (C) Hammer in sill bolt. Tighten nut to expand bolt. From U.S. Geological Survey.

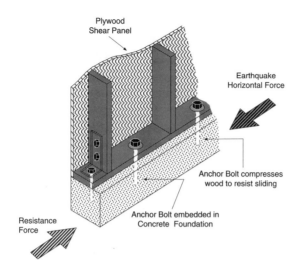

Plywood
Shear Panel

Earthquake
Horizontal Force

Anchor Bolt compresses
wood to resist sliding

Anchor Bolt embedded in
Concrete Foundation

Resistance
Force

Figure 12-2. Anchor cripple wall to foundation using sill bolts, and to mudsill by hold-down. Cripple wall is further strengthened by plywood shear panel. From Earthquake Engineering Research Institute.

hammer, drive a *sill bolt* (or *anchor bolt*)) into the hole you've just drilled, having first cleaned out the hole and made sure that it's deep enough to accommodate the sill bolt. The sill bolt has a washer on top and an expanding metal sleeve at the base that slides up, spreads, and wedges in the concrete. Bolt sizes range from one-half by seven inches to three-quarters by ten inches; a standard size is five-eighths by eight-and-one-half inches. The larger ones give more protection against lateral loads and are preferred if the house has more than one story. If the nut on top of the bolt won't tighten, or the bolt climbs out of the hole as you tighten it, the concrete might be decomposing. If so, you could set the bolt with epoxy cement, if allowed by local building codes.

In new construction, the sill bolt is set when the foundation is poured, a fairly simple operation.

The spacing of bolts, in both new construction and in retrofits, is at least one every six feet, and one within twelve inches of the end of any mudsill. Placing the bolts midway between the studs (the vertical members that support the walls) makes it easier to work on them.

The next step is stiffening the *cripple wall,* which is made of short studs and sits between the mudsill and the floor joists of the house itself (Figure 12-2). The cripple wall bounds the crawl space under the house where you're working. The problem here is that if these vertical studs are not braced, they can tilt over like a set of dominoes due to horizontal inertial forces, so that your house collapses on its crawl space and flops down on its foundation.

Since 1973, the Uniform Building Code has required bracing of cripple walls; the bracing requirements were increased in 1991. If your home was built before those critical dates, you might need to brace the cripple wall yourself. The recommended stiffening technique is to use one-half-inch plywood; five-eighths-inch if you use a nail gun (Figure 12-2). Treat the plywood with a preservative prior to installation to prevent rot. Ideally, you should sheathe the entire cripple wall in plywood, but at a minimum, install eight linear feet of plywood from each interior corner of the crawl space for one-story houses; sixteen feet for two-story houses. Anchor the plywood panels with eight-penny nails four inches apart around the edges of each panel and six inches apart on each interior stud. (The nailing pattern is important; one of the most memorable sounds of a house breaking up during an earthquake is the wrenching noise of nails being pulled from the walls.) Drill vent holes one inch in diameter to prevent moisture buildup.

Ideally, this plywood sheeting should be at least twice as long as it is tall. If it isn't, the sheeting should be reinforced with anchors and hold-downs (Figure 12-2). These anchors bolt into the foundation and into corner posts of the cripple walls, increasing the bracing. Another solution, particularly if the cripple wall is very short or if the floor joists of the house rest directly on the foundation, is quarter-inch structural steel bolted with expansion bolts into the foundation and into the floor joists.

If you're a do-it-yourselfer, you'll spend at least $600 for the materials. However, working in crawl spaces is messy and confined, and you might wish to employ a professional. This will cost you several times as much as doing the job yourself; a contractor might charge as much as twenty-five dollars per installed bolt. But reinforcing the cripple wall and foundation is the most important step you can take to save your house. For examples of cripple-wall failure, see Figures 12-3 and 12-4.

The California Earthquake Authority (CEA) offers a five percent discount on your earthquake insurance premium if you seismically retrofit your house. For most areas, this is a twenty-five- to fifty-dollar annual discount, which must be compared to an average retrofit cost of $2,000 if you contract it out. The CEA has been urged to increase its discount to encourage more people to retrofit their houses.

3. Soft-story Buildings

A common failure in California's recent earthquakes was the two- or three-car garage with living space overhead. Many condominiums have most of the first floor devoted to parking, with apartment space in the upper floors. The large amount of open space at the garage door means less bracing against horizontal forces than in standard walls, so these open areas are the first to fail in an earthquake (Figure 12-5). Similar problems arise, although on a smaller scale, with large picture windows, sliding-glass patio doors, or double doors.

Figure 12-3. This Victorian wood-frame house in Ferndale, California, was built on a post-and-pier foundation but was not bolted to its foundation, so it slid off during the 1992 Cape Mendocino Earthquake. The floor level of the house was at the same height as the front steps at left. The house moved to the right and down with respect to the steps. Note also the wooden skirting, formerly part of the outside wall, which is now flat on the ground. Photo courtesy of National Oceanic and Atmospheric Administration.

Figure 12-4. This house south of Petrolia, California shifted off its foundation during the 1992 Cape Mendocino Earthquake because it was not anchored to its foundation and its cripple wall was not reinforced. The house shifted to the right, as seen by the collapsed wooden skirting. The separation of the house and the small porch is an example of connection failure. Photo courtesy of National Oceanic and Atmospheric Administration.

Make sure that the wall around the garage door and the wall in the back of the garage, on the opposite side from the door, are sheathed with half-inch plywood, just as cripple walls are. Because of the limitations for bracing on the garage door itself, bracing the back wall, opposite from the door, will increase the overall resistance of the structure to earthquake ground motion sideways to the door.

Figure 12-5. Soft-story failure to three-car garage during 1971 Sylmar Earthquake. The large door opening resulted in inadequate shear resistance to horizontal ground motion. Photo by J. Dewey, U.S. Geological Survey.

Plywood sheathing should completely surround any large picture window or set of double doors. The sheathing should be at least as wide as the opening and extend from bottom to top of the opening. The interior wall is finished in drywall or plaster, so the best time to add sheathing is during initial construction or remodeling of your house.

4. Utility Lines

One of the greatest dangers in an earthquake is fire. Fire caused much of the loss of life and property in the 1906 San Francisco Earthquake and the 1995 Kobe Earthquake, and large fires destroyed property in the Marina District of San Francisco after the 1989 Loma Prieta Earthquake. The problem is natural gas.

If gas connections are rigid, they are likely to shear during an earthquake, releasing gas that needs only a spark to start a fire. Gas connections should be flexible. After an earthquake you must shut off the main gas supply to the house (Figure 12-6). Learn where the gas supply line is and ensure that the shut-off valve is not stuck in place by turning it one-eighth turn (one-quarter turn is the closed position). Your gas company will sell you an inexpensive wrench that should be kept permanently *near the valve*. Tell all members of the family where the wrench is and how to use it. In the event of a major earthquake, shutting off the gas is a top priority. You won't have time to rummage around a heavily damaged house looking for a wrench.

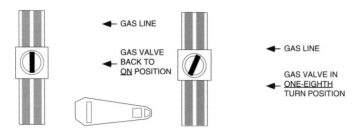

Figure 12-6. Shut-off valve for the main gas supply line to house. Top: valve is in "on" position. Bottom: Check to be sure valve is not frozen by turning it one-eighth turn. Specialized wrench available from gas company is also shown.

For $400 to $600, you can have an automatic shutoff valve installed on the gas line. This valve, located between the gas meter and the house, is actuated by earthquake shaking, which knocks a ball or cylinder off a perch inside the valve into a seat, thereby shutting off the gas. Consider an automatic shutoff valve if you are away from home a lot and are not likely to be around to shut off your gas after an earthquake. A disadvantage of the automatic shutoff valve is that you wouldn't be able to tell easily if you had a gas leak in your house after the valve had shut off the gas. If you're confident that you don't have a gas leak, you should know how to reset the valve yourself, because after a major earthquake weeks might go by before the gas company or a plumber could get to your house and reset the valve for you. Remember that when the valve is reset, you must immediately relight all the pilot lights in your appliances.

All gas lines and water pipes should be supported at least every four feet. Earthquake vibrations can be strongly exaggerated in unsupported pipe in your basement or crawl space. If pipes are not supported, strap them to floor joists or to walls.

If liquefaction occurs, underground utility lines might be severed, even if your house is anchored below the liquefying layer and doesn't fail. Underground gas lines failed due to liquefaction in the Marina District of San Francisco, triggering many fires.

A generator can supply emergency power, but this should be installed by a licensed contractor. The generator should be installed in a well-ventilated place outside the home or garage, and fuel should be stored according to fire regulations.

5. Strapping the Water Heater and Other Heavy Appliances and Furniture

Your water heater is the most unstable appliance in the house. It's heavy, being full of hot water, and it's tall, likely to topple over due to horizontal forces from an earthquake.

Strap the water heater in place, top and bottom, with strong nylon webbing or with plumber's tape (perforated metal tape). Anchor the tape to studs in the wall at both ends (Figure 12-7). Make a complete loop around the water heater before anchoring it to the studs. This precaution is very easy and inexpensive to do and will not reduce the effectiveness of the water heater at all.

If the water heater is right against the wall, brace it against the wall with two-by-fours so that it doesn't bang against the wall during an earthquake. If it's against a concrete wall, install heavy-duty eye screws on both sides of the water heater and run steel cable through the eye screws, again making a complete loop around the heater.

Built-in appliances such as dishwashers, stoves, and ovens might not be braced in place; they may only rest on a trim strip. One homeowner was quoted in *Sunset Magazine* after the October 1989 Loma Prieta Earthquake: "I assumed built-in appliances are fixed in place. NOT SO! Our built-in oven and overhead built-in microwave slid out." Make sure your appliances are securely braced (Figure 12-8). A gas stove might topple over, snapping the gas line and causing a fire. Secure the refrigerator to the wall. Babyproof refrigerator door locks are effective in preventing food in the refrigerator from spilling out on the floor.

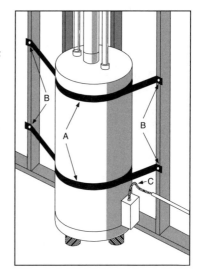

Figure 12-7. Strap water heater, top and bottom, with plumber's tape (A), which is attached to studs (B). If the water is heated by gas, the gas supply line (C) should be flexible. In this example, water heater rests against stud. If water heater is against drywall or plaster wall, brace it with a two-by-four so that it does not bang against the wall.

Figure 12-8. Damage to contents of the kitchen in a residence in Petrolia, California as a result of the 1992 Cape Mendocino Earthquake. Appliances shifted several inches away from the wall. All items were shaken off the shelves with considerable glassware breakage. Photo courtesy of National Oceanic and Atmospheric Administration.

Look around your house for tall, top-heavy furniture such as a china cabinet, tall chest of drawers, or wardrobe. These should be attached to studs in the wall to keep them from falling over. There are two concerns. One is the loss of heirloom china in your china cabinet. The other is the possibility of a heavy piece of furniture falling on you or on a small child. For either of these reasons alone, securing these large pieces of furniture to the wall is a good idea.

6. Safety Glass

A major problem in an earthquake is shattered glass windows, which might flex and essentially blow out, showering those within range with sharp glass fragments. An expensive option is to replace glass in large picture windows or sliding doors with tempered or laminated glass. A much cheaper alternative is safety film, which costs about three to four dollars per square foot, installed. This bonds the glass to a four-mil thick acrylic sheet; the adhesive strengthens the glass and holds it together if it breaks, like the safety glass in a car windshield. You can do this yourself, but it's difficult to prevent air bubbles from being trapped under the film, so consider having it installed professionally.

7. Cabinets

Kitchen cabinets will blow open during an earthquake, spewing their contents onto the kitchen floor. Magnetic catches often fail. However,

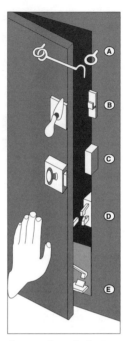

Figure 12-9. Safety latches for earthquakes. The simple hook and eye (A) is expensive and secure, but you might not remember to close it each time you use the cabinet because it takes an extra step to do so. Some latches (B, C) mount on the surface of the door; others (D) mount inside the door, hold the door firmly shut, and are opened by being pushed gently inward. A childproof latch (E) prevents the door from being opened more than an inch or two. It closes automatically, but is more trouble to open.

inexpensive babyproof catches will keep cabinet doors closed during an earthquake (Figure 12-9). Heavy, spring-loaded latches are advised, especially for cabinets containing valuable dishes.

If small children live in your house, you might already have babyproof catches, but they're probably only on cabinets near the floor, within a child's reach. For earthquake protection, the most important places for babyproof catches are the *highest* cabinets, particularly those containing heavy, breakable dishes or fragile glassware. Don't forget the medicine cabinet in the bathroom, where prescription medicine could fall on the floor and mix, producing a toxic combination.

Put layers of foam or paper between heirloom plates that are seldom used but are at great risk during an earthquake. Line your shelves with nonskid shelf padding, available at marine- and recreational-vehicle supply houses, because they are also useful to keep items on the shelf during a heavy sea or when your recreational vehicle is traveling down a bumpy road. In a similar vein, consider a rail around open shelves to keep items from falling off (Figure 12-10). Hold-fast putties are small balls that flatten and stick to the bottom of a large vase to keep it from toppling over; these putties will peel off and leave no residue. Lead weights in old socks can be placed in the bottom of vases or table lamps to keep them in place.

You won't take all these precautions. But a third of your life is spent in bed, so lie on your bed and look around for items that could fall on

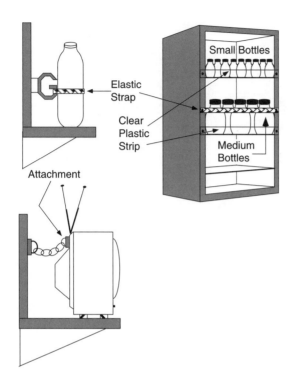

Figure 12-10. Securing items on open shelves: (Upper left) Attach counter-top items to wall with bungee cord. (Right) Secure small items with a vertical strip and larger items with a strip and bungee cord. (Lower left) Large items such as a TV set can be attached to wall with chain.

you during an earthquake. A heavy chest of drawers? A large wall mirror? A ceiling fan? A large headboard? Secure those items that might endanger your life. Then do the same for the beds where other members of your family sleep, particularly small children. (Maybe it's simpler to move the bed than to secure the furniture!)

Renters might be restricted by the landlord from fastening furniture to the wall. A discussion with the landlord might help, particularly if you are willing to patch the holes in the wall when you move.

8. Bricks, Stonework, and Other Time Bombs

If you live in an old, unreinforced brick house, you are in real danger, and none of the retrofit techniques mentioned above will do much good outside of a major costly reinforcing job. Fortunately, old brick houses in California are being phased out of the building inventory; most of us live in wood-frame houses.

But one part of your house is still likely to be unreinforced—your masonry chimney (Figure 12-11). Chimneys collapse by the hundreds during major California earthquakes. Most commonly, they snap at the roof line. A tall chimney is likely to be set in motion by the earthquake waves, resulting in collapse. The taller the chimney, the more likely it is to fall through the roof into your house. Some recent

Figure 12-11. Brick chimney on this house in Petrolia, California collapsed during the 1992 Cape Mendocino Earthquake. The fireplace inside the house was also shattered. Photo courtesy of National Oceanic and Atmospheric Administration.

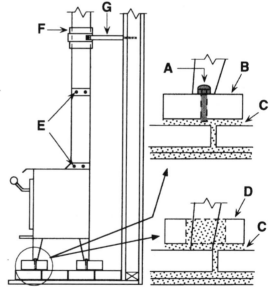

Figure 12-12. For a stove built on a brick hearth, anchor stove with three-eighths-inch diameter bolt (A) through one-half-inch hole to new brick (B). Grout brick to the existing hearth with one inch of new grout (C). Or build an eight-inch-square brick pad with grout pocket (D) at each leg. There should be at least one inch of grout around each leg; fill pocket completely with grout. Provide sheetmetal screws (E) at flue exit and between stovepipe sections. Provide a radiation shield with pipe clamp (F) braced to wall, using tension ties attached to wall stud with three-eighths-inch by three-inch lag screws. From Humboldt Earthquake Education Center, Humboldt State University.

building codes require internal and external bracing of chimneys to make them more likely to survive an earthquake.

Perhaps the rule of thumb is how much of a threat your chimney poses. If someone could be killed or severely injured by a falling chimney, take it down. Prefabricated metal chimneys can be attached to an existing brick firebox so that no brick projects above the roof line.

Inside, there's the mantel. In many houses, the mantel is field stone—very attractive, but very heavy if it fails, particularly if the mortar has been weakened by a chimney leak. Field stone and brick veneer on the outside of the house may pose a hazard as well. If you want a natural stone appearance, install the lightest-weight material you can.

Freestanding wood-burning stoves are popular in northern California. A study done by Humboldt State University found that more than half the wood-burning stoves in the area near the epicenter of the April 1992 M 7.1 Cape Mendocino Earthquake moved during the earthquake, and several fell over. Fire codes in some states leave stoves unsupported on all four sides, which might cause them to slide or turn over during an earthquake. If a stove tips over and separates from its stovepipe, cinders or sparks can easily cause a fire.

The following steps are recommended (Figure 12-12). (1) Anchor a stove resting on a brick hearth, attaching the legs of the stove to the hearth with bolts. Mobile-home-approved stoves have predrilled holes in the legs for anchoring to the floor framing. (2) For a stove resting on a concrete slab, anchor the stove directly to the concrete. (3) Anchor the stovepipe to the flue, and tie together each of the stovepipe segments.

In the Kobe Earthquake, thousands of people were killed in their beds in wood-frame houses because their roofs were of tile, which made the houses top-heavy and more subject to collapse. Clay tile roofs are the heaviest; composition or wood roofs are lighter. If you reroof your house, add plywood shear panels over the rafters. This is required in much new construction and might be required if you remodel. It strengthens the house.

9. Propane Tanks

Above-ground propane tanks can slide, bounce, or topple during an earthquake, causing a potential fire hazard from a gas leak. You can reduce the fire danger by doing the following (Figure 12-13): (1) Mount the tank on a concrete pad and bolt the four legs of the tank to the pad. (2) Install flexible hose connections between the tank, the supply

Figure 12-13. Propane tank. Mount tank on six-inch-thick concrete pad (A) using four half-inch diameter bolts (B) with three-inch minimum embedded into concrete. Provide a flexible hose connection (C) between tank and the rigid supply line. From Humboldt Earthquake Education Center, Humboldt State University.

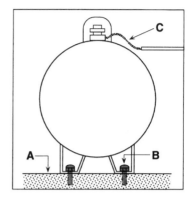

line, and the entrance to your house. (3) Clear the area around the tank of objects that could fall and rupture the tank or its gas supply line. (4) Keep a wrench tied near the shut-off valve, and make sure all family members know where it is and how to use it. For large tanks, such as those used commercially or on a farm, install a seismic shut-off valve.

10. Connections

One of my most instructive memories of the 1971 Sylmar Earthquake was a split-level house, where earthquake shaking accentuated the split between the garage with a bedroom over it and the rest of the house (Figure 12-14). A common sight is a porch that has been torn away, or

Figure 12-14. Split-level house in Crestview Tract, San Fernando Valley showing failure of the connection between the single story (right) and the two-car garage with bedrooms above during the 1971 Sylmar Earthquake. Note the difference in height between the front steps and the single story, indicating cripple-wall failure of the single story. Photo by Robert Yeats.

a fallen deck or balcony. These connections are the potential weak link in the chain that is your home. Make sure that everything is well connected to everything else so that your house behaves as a unit during shaking (see also Figure 12-4).

11. Mobile Homes and Manufactured Houses

Because these houses must be transported to their destination, they are more likely than an ordinary house to behave as a coherent structural unit during an earthquake. Manufactured houses are built on one or more steel I-beams that provide structural support in the direction of the I-beam. However, mobile homes and manufactured houses are commonly not bolted to a foundation, but instead rest on concrete blocks that are likely to collapse during even low horizontal accelerations (Figures 12-15, 12-16). This would cause the house to flop down onto its foundation, as illustrated earlier for cripple-wall failures. A mobile home is likely to undergo less structural damage than an ordinary house, but is more likely to suffer extensive damage to the contents of the house. The house could be prevented from sliding off its blocks during an earthquake by replacing the blocks with a cripple wall and securing it as described above for ordinary houses. This would make the house insurable against earthquakes.

A double-wide mobile home must be well connected at the join between the two halves (*marriage line*) so that the two halves do not fail at the join and move independently during strong shaking. Ridge

Figure 12-15. This manufactured home slipped off its supporting piers during an earthquake. This can be avoided by bolting the house to its foundation, as required for other houses in California. From Karl Steinbrugge Collection, Earthquake Engineering Research Center, University of California Berkeley.

Figure 12-16. Mobile home has slid off its supports during an earthquake. Photo courtesy of California Governor's Office of Emergency Services.

beams should be attached with half-inch carriage bolts spaced at a maximum of forty-eight inches at ninety degrees and three-eighths-inch lag screws, with washers, spaced every twenty-four inches at forty-five degrees maximum angle. Floor connections must use three-eighths-inch lag screws with washers installed diagonally at forty-five degrees or less, with spacing not exceeding thirty-two inches. Even so, it's likely that a double-wide manufactured home will fail at the marriage line if it slips off its concrete block foundation during an earthquake.

12. Okay, So What Retrofitting Are You Really Going to Do?

You probably won't take all of these steps in making your home safer against earthquakes. Doing everything would be costly and might not increase the value of your home, unless it successfully rides out an earthquake. So you might decide to live with some risk.

Consider at least the following: (1) bolt your house to its foundation, (2) strengthen your cripple wall, (3) install flexible connections on all your gas appliances and make sure the main shut-off valve can be turned off quickly in an emergency, (4) secure your water heater, and (5) make sure that large pieces of furniture or large ceiling fixtures won't collapse on anyone in bed. This at least protects you against a catastrophic collapse of your house, and against fire or serious injury.

Suggestions for Further Reading

California Office of Emergency Services. An Ounce of Prevention: Strengthening Your Wood Frame House for Earthquake Safety.
Lafferty and Associates, Inc. 1989. Earthquake preparedness—for office, home, family and community. P.O. Box 1026, La Canada, CA 91012.
Seismic Safety Commission. 1992. The homeowner's guide to earthquake safety. 28p.

∽ 13 ∽
Earthquake Design
of Large Structures

"I don't know. This looks like an unreinforced masonry chimney to me."

Santa Claus, undated

1. Introduction

I t's impossible to earthquake-*proof* a building. A look at the intensity scale (Table 3-1) shows that for intensities of X and worse, even well-constructed buildings can fail. However, most earthquakes have maximum intensities of VIII or less, and well-designed buildings should survive these intensities.

Building codes should be designed so that a building will resist (1) minor ground motion without damage, (2) moderate earthquake ground-shaking without structural damage but possibly with some nonstructural damage, and (3) major ground motion with an intensity equivalent to the *maximum credible earthquake* for the region (Chapter 8) without structural collapse, although possibly some structural damage. In this last case, the building could be declared a total loss, but it would not collapse and people inside could escape safely.

Upgrading the building code does not have an immediate effect on the safety of large buildings. Building codes affect *new construction* or *major remodeling* of existing structures; if a building is not remodeled, it will retain the safety standards at the time it was built. The greatest losses in recent California earthquakes occurred in old, unreinforced masonry buildings. For example, forty-seven of the sixty-four people who died in the 1971 Sylmar Earthquake lost their lives due to the collapse of a single facility, the Veterans Administration Hospital (Figure 13-1). This was a reinforced concrete structure built in the 1920s, before the establishment of earthquake-related building standards after the 1933 Long Beach Earthquake. The collapsed buildings were designed to carry only vertical loads. Figure 13-1 is an aerial view of the hospital campus immediately following the earthquake. The building in the photograph that held up well had been reinforced after the 1933 earthquake. Clearly, retrofitting paid off in terms of lives saved.

Other examples are the collapse of masonry walls at the Pacific Garden Mall at Santa Cruz during the 1989 Loma Prieta Earthquake (Figure 13-2) and the destruction of the Cummings Valley School during the 1952 Kern County Earthquake (Figure 13-3). The Cummings Valley

Figure 13-1. Aerial view of the damage to the San Fernando Veterans Administration Hospital campus after the 1971 Sylmar Earthquake. Forty-seven of the sixty-four deaths attributed to the earthquake were a result of the collapse of this structure, built in 1926, before earthquake-resistance building codes were adopted. Adjacent building, reinforced after building codes were upgraded following the 1933 Long Beach Earthquake, did not collapse. Photo by E.V. Leyendecker, U.S. Geological Survey.

School was shaken down nineteen years after building codes for schools were upgraded by the Field Act, but the school had been built in 1910 and never remodeled. It was a time bomb for children.

It's much more expensive to retrofit a building for earthquake safety than it is to build in the same safety protection for a new building. Typically, a simple structure will cost nine to ten dollars per square foot to retrofit. A nonductile concrete-frame structure will be two to three times more expensive. The cost for a historic building could reach $100 per square foot. The owner of the building must consider the possibility that the money spent in upgrading might not be returned in an increased value of the building or increased income received from it. It is for these reasons that it takes so long to upgrade the building inventory of a city. Legislation can speed the process along.

2. Seismic Retrofitting

Traditionally, the goal of seismic retrofitting, like the goal of building codes, has always been to allow people inside the structure to survive the earthquake. Damage control and protection of property are secondary, except for certain historic buildings. Brittle structures behave poorly during earthquakes. Unreinforced masonry that bears the

Figure 13-2. Collapsed unreinforced masonry walls, Pacific Garden Mall, Santa Cruz, as a result of the 1989 Loma Prieta Earthquake. Photo by L. Carroll, U.S. Geological Survey.

Figure 13-3. Collapse of Cummings Valley School during 1952 Kern County Earthquake. School was built in 1910 with concrete walls and a wooden roof. Photo credit National Oceanic and Atmospheric Administration and National Geophysical Data Center.

structural load of a building with poorly tied floor and roof framing tends to fail by wall collapse. Nonductile concrete-frame buildings are subject to shear failure of weak, unconfined columns. Framed structures with large parts of their walls not tied together tend to behave structurally as soft-story structures (like the attached garage in the San Fernando Valley shown in Figure 12-5). In recent earthquakes these structures have failed catastrophically, with loss of life.

Strengthening of existing buildings must ensure that the added reinforcing is compatible with the material already there. For example, a diagonal steel brace might be added to a masonry wall. The brace is strong enough, but it would not carry the load during shaking until the masonry had first cracked and distorted. The brace can prevent total collapse, but the building might undergo enough structural damage to be considered a total loss.

Figure 13-4 shows several types of retrofit solutions for old buildings. The walls may be strengthened by infill walls, by bracing, by external buttresses (beautifully displayed by medieval Gothic cathedrals in western Europe), by adding an exterior or interior frame, or by base isolation. The building needs to behave as a unit during shaking, because the earthquake is likely to produce failure along weak joins.

The term *diaphragm* is used for a horizontal element of the building, such as a floor or a roof, that transfers horizontal forces between vertical elements such as walls (Figure 13-5a). The diaphragm can be considered as an I-beam, with the diaphragm itself the web of the beam and its edges the flanges of the beam (Figure 13-5b). In most buildings, holes are cut in the diaphragm for elevator shafts or skylights (Figure 13-5c). These holes interrupt the continuity and thereby reduce the strength of the diaphragm (Figure 13-5d).

Lateral forces from diaphragms are transmitted to and from the ground through *shear walls*. The forces are shear forces, those tending

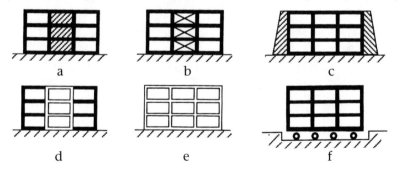

Figure 13-4. How to retrofit old buildings. (a) Infill walls. (b) Add braces. (c) Add buttresses. (d) Add frames, exterior or interior. (e) Completely rebuild. (f) Isolate building. From AIA/ACSA Council on Architectural Research, Washington, D.C.

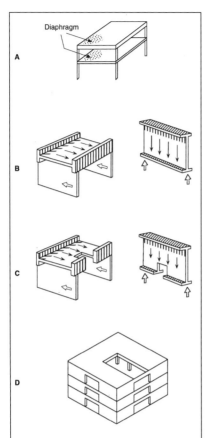

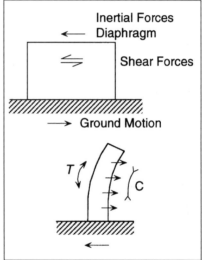

Figure 13-5. A. Horizontal diaphragm. Failure typically occurs at connections to vertical columns. B. Concept of diaphragm as a horizontal I-beam. C, D. Holes in beams or diaphragms for elevator shafts, large doors, etc., interrupt continuity and reduce strength. From AIA/ACSA Council on Architectural Research.

Figure 13-6 (above). Shear walls resist shear stresses transmitted from the ground and bending stresses in slender, tall buildings. C, compression; T, tension. From AIA/ACSA Council on Architectural Research.

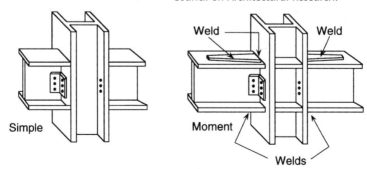

Figure 13-7. Joint used in a moment-resistant frame.

to distort the shape of the wall, or bending forces for slender structures like a skyscraper (Figure 13-6). Construction may include walls that have higher shear strength or diagonal steel bracing, or both.

Moment-resistant frames are steel-frame structures with rigid welded joints (Figure 13-7). These structures are more flexible than shear-wall structures; they are less likely to undergo major structural damage but more likely to result in damage to interior walls, partitions, and ceilings (Figure 13-8). Several steel-frame buildings failed in the 1994 Northridge Earthquake, but the failures were in large part due to poor welds at the joints—a failure in design, construction, and inspection.

3. Base Isolation

The normal approach to providing seismic resistance is to attach the structure firmly to the ground. All ground movements are transferred to the structure, which is designed to survive the inertial forces of the ground motion. This is the reason why your house is bolted to its foundation and your cripple wall is reinforced.

In large buildings, these inertial forces can exceed the strength of *any* structure that has been built within reasonable economic limits. The engineer designs the building to be highly ductile, so that it will deform extensively and absorb these inertial forces without collapsing. Moment-resistant steel-frame structures are good for this purpose, as are special concrete structures with a large amount of steel reinforcing.

These buildings don't collapse, but, as stated above, they have a major disadvantage. In deforming, they can cause extensive damage to ceilings, partitions, and building contents (Figure 13-8) such as filing cabinets and computers. Equipment, including utilities, will stop operating. High-rise buildings will sway and might cause occupants to become motion sick and panicky.

The problem with attaching the building firmly to the ground is that the earthquake waves are dissipated by the building and its contents, often destructively. Is there a way to dissipate the energy in the foundation *before* it reaches the main floors of the building?

In *base isolation*, the engineer takes the opposite approach: the objective is to keep the ground motion from being transferred into the building. This is the same objective as in automobile design—to keep the passengers from feeling all the bumps in the road. To accomplish this, the automobile is designed with air-inflated tires, springs, and shock absorbers to keep its passengers comfortable.

One way to do this is to put the building on roller bearings so that as the ground moves horizontally, the building remains stationary (Figure 13-9). A problem with this solution is that roller bearings would still transmit force into the building through friction. In addition, once the building began to roll, its inertia would tend to keep it moving. We

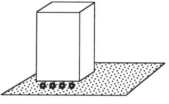

Figure 13-8. Failure of hanging light fixtures at library of Dawson Elementary School, fortunately unoccupied at time of earthquake. Note fallen ceiling tiles and plaster. Photo credit Earthquake Engineering Research Institute.

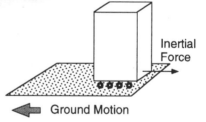

Figure 13-9. Mounting a building on roller bearings so that building remains stationary when the ground moves. The problem: how to stop it from moving. From AIA/ACSA Council on Architectural Research.

need a structure that allows horizontal movement with respect to the ground, but restrains, or dampens, this movement so that as the ground vibrates rapidly, the building vibrates much more slowly.

The solution is to separate the requirement for load bearing (vertical loads) from that for movement (horizontal loads). One way to do this involves a *lead-rubber bearing* (Figure 13-10). This bearing consists of alternating laminations of rubber and steel, which allow for up to six inches of horizontal movement without fracturing but are strong enough to support the building. A cylindrical lead plug is placed in the center of this bearing to dampen the oscillations in the ground produced by an earthquake, just like the shock absorbers in a car. The energy of the earthquake waves is absorbed by the lead plug rather than by the building itself. The lead plugs do not deform in small earthquakes or high winds; in that respect, they serve as "seismic fuses."

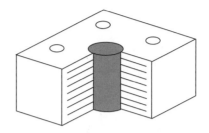

Figure 13-10. Base-isolation bearing. Alternating laminations of rubber and steel with a lead plug in the middle. From AIA/ACSA Council on Architectural Research.

Lead recovers nearly all of its mechanical properties after each deformation from an earthquake. This is analogous to the solid-state ductile deformation of lower crustal rocks without producing earthquakes. The lead-rubber bearings allow the ground under a building to move rapidly, but the building itself moves much more slowly, thereby reducing accelerations and maximum shear forces applied to the building. The building is allowed to move about six inches horizontally. A six-inch slot around the building is built for this purpose and covered by a replaceable metal grating. The damage to architectural and mechanical components of the building, and the ensuing costly repairs, are greatly reduced and, in some instances, almost eliminated.

Although base isolation adds to the cost of construction, some cost reduction is possible within the building itself because so much of the earthquake force is absorbed at the base of the building rather than transmitted into the structure.

Research is underway in Japan, New Zealand, and the United States to design other methods of base isolation. After the 1989 Loma Prieta Earthquake, the California State Legislature passed Senate Bill 920, requiring the state architect to select one new and two existing buildings to demonstrate new engineering technologies, including base isolation.

4. Special Problems

Each large building presents its own set of design problems in surviving earthquake forces, which means that architects must consider earthquake shaking in designing a large structure in a seismically hazardous region such as California. I consider two problems: *soft first stories* and the *tuning fork problem*.

In a building with a soft first story, the first floor is weaker than the higher floors. The first floor is taken up by a parking garage or contains large amounts of open space occupied by a department store or hotel ballroom. Instead of load-bearing walls, these spaces are supported by columns. Building codes commonly limit the height of soft stories to two normal stories, or thirty feet. But the result is that the ground floor is less stiff (has less strength) than the overlying floors. Since

Figure 13-11. Damage to the Los Angeles County Olive View Medical Center as a result of the 1971 Sylmar Earthquake. The first floor, with a lot of open space, behaved like a soft story, causing the upper floors to move relatively to the right, forcing out the stairwell. Photo by Robert Yeats.

earthquake forces enter the building at its base and are strongest there, the soft first story is a "stiffness discontinuity" that absorbs the force of the earthquake waves. Without a soft first story, the earthquake forces are distributed more equally throughout the entire building. With a soft first story, there is a tremendous concentration of forces on the ground floor and at the connection between the ground floor and the second floor. This can cause collapse or partial collapse of the higher floors, as happened at the Los Angeles County Olive View Medical Center during the 1971 Sylmar Earthquake (Figures 13-11 and 13-12). The upper floors were relatively undamaged, but the first floor and basement absorbed much of the force. The acceleration came from the right, and the building was forced toward the right, almost knocking down the stairwell. The problem can be alleviated by adding more columns, stiffening the existing structure.

The second problem might be called the tuning fork problem. A large pipe organ has pipes of different lengths so that the organ can play different notes. The deep bass notes are played on long pipes, and the high notes are played on short pipes. A xylophone works the same way: the high notes are played on short keys, and the low notes are played on long keys. These instruments are designed to take advantage of the *vibrational frequency* of the pipes or keys to make music. A tuning fork works in the same way. Strike the tuning fork and place it tines-up on a hard surface. You will hear a specific note, related to the length of

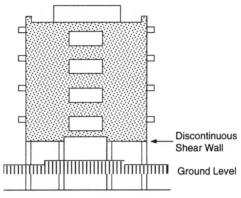

Figure 13-12. Diagrammatic representation of soft story at Olive View Medical Center. From AIA/ACSA Council on Architectural Research.

Discontinuous Shear Wall

Ground Level

the tuning fork, which generates sound waves of a specific frequency—the vibrational frequency of the tuning fork.

I recall a TV commercial in which a wine glass is shattered when a Wagnerian soprano sings a certain high note.

Buildings work in the same way. A tall building vibrates at a lower frequency than a short building, just like a tuning fork. The problem comes when the earthquake wave transmitted through the ground vibrates at the same frequency as the building. The building *resonates* with the earthquake waves, and the amplitude of the waves is intensified. All other things being the same, a building with the same vibrational frequency as the earthquake waves will suffer more damage than other buildings of different height.

In the Mexico City Earthquake of 1985, surface waves with a period of about two seconds were amplified by the soft clay underlying most of the city, which also extended the period of strong shaking. Buildings between ten and fourteen stories suffered the greatest damage, because they have a natural vibrational period of one to two seconds (Figure

Figure 13-13. Buildings have a vibrational frequency depending on their height. If the vibrational frequency resonates with that of the earthquake waves, shaking will be amplified and damage will be more severe, as was the case in the 1985 Mexico City Earthquake. From Bolt (1999).

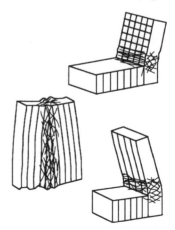

13-13). When waves of that characteristic frequency pushed the foundations of those buildings sideways, the natural resonance caused an accentuation of the sideways shaking and great structural damage. In contrast, a thirty-seven-story building built in the 1950s, with a vibrational period of 3.7 seconds, suffered no major structural damage.

5. Bridges and Overpasses

Freeways and bridges are lifelines, and their failure can disrupt the economy and kill people on or beneath them during an earthquake. The television images of people sandwiched in their cars in the collapse of the double-decker Interstate 880 Cypress Viaduct in Oakland (Figure 13-14), the collapsed span of the Oakland-San Francisco Bay Bridge, and the pancaked freeway interchanges in Los Angeles after the Northridge Earthquake (Figure 13-15) were dramatic reminders of the vulnerability to earthquakes of highways and railroads.

Freeway collapses during the Northridge Earthquake caused great disruption to commuters traveling from Santa Clarita and Santa Monica to downtown Los Angeles. Failure of the Golden Gate Bridge and Bay Bridge could isolate San Francisco from counties north of the Bay and from East Bay cities. In addition, bridge collapses on Highway 101 or State Highway 1 along the coast could isolate coastal communities for an indefinite period of time.

Figure 13-14. Collapsed section of the double-decker Nimitz Expressway, I-880, in which forty-one people lost their lives. Photo taken a day-and-a-half after the Loma Prieta Earthquake, by Michael Rymer, U.S. Geological Survey.

Figure 13-15. Damage to the Golden State Freeway (Interstate 5) and Foothills Freeway (Interstate 210) as a result of the 1971 Sylmar Earthquake. Photo by E.V. Leyendecker, U.S. Geological Survey.

Five bridges collapsed in the 1994 Northridge Earthquake—one on the Golden State Freeway, two on the Antelope Valley Freeway, one on the Simi Valley Freeway, and one on the Santa Monica Freeway. All of these structures were designed to pre-1974 standards, and none had been retrofitted. The Santa Monica Freeway had been targeted for seismic retrofit, but the earthquake got there first. In some cases, a collapsed bridge was adjacent to a recently retrofitted bridge that suffered little or no damage, even though it had been subjected to earthquake forces similar to those endured by the bridge that collapsed. Clearly, retrofit worked for bridges and overpasses.

The problem in the older bridges was in the columns supporting the freeway superstructure. There was inadequate column confinement, inadequate reinforcement connections between the columns and the footings on which they rested, and no top reinforcement in the footings themselves. When these problems were overcome in retrofitting, bridges rode through earthquakes fairly well.

California, through Caltrans, is the nation's leader in the seismic retrofit of bridges. Caltrans estimates that there are about seventeen hundred bridges in the state—about ten percent of California's bridges—that require retrofit to prevent collapse during a future strong-motion earthquake. Bridges such as the Oakland-San Francisco Bay Bridge, require special consideration, because a collapse could drop a large number of vehicles and passengers into the water. The cost of retrofitting all of these bridges is prohibitive if done in a very short period of time. Strengthening the two Carquinez Strait bridges and approach structures twenty-five miles northeast of San Francisco—one built in 1927 and one in 1958—would cost nearly $50 million. Decisions on which bridges to retrofit involve establishing priorities based on the potential magnitude of the loss, both directly in damages and lives lost and in economic losses, and then allocating the resources to do the job.

6. Engineering Against Ground Displacement

Up to this point, the main hazard discussed has been ground shaking. California law (Alquist-Priolo) seeks to avoid active fault traces. A large displacement of several feet, particularly vertical (dip-slip) displacement, will probably destroy a building constructed across the fault, but building foundations can be designed to survive displacements of a foot or less. It makes no difference whether the displacement is caused by faulting, ground subsidence, or incipient landsliding. Pipelines can be made flexible, and underground utility cables can have slack built in at fault crossings.

I recently served as a consultant on a housing development where there was potential for small-scale, distributed faulting on a large part of the property. The likelihood of a surface-rupturing earthquake was present but relatively low. The geologist determined the maximum amount of displacement expected based on backhoe excavations, and the structural engineer designed building foundations that would withstand that displacement without significant damage.

7. Decisions, Decisions, and Triage

The astronomical cost of retrofitting bridges brings up a major problem faced by society. As you look at the building inventory in your town or the bridge inventory in California, you soon recognize that in this era of budget cutbacks in government, the money is not available to retrofit even a sizeable percentage of the inventory. Decades will pass before dangerous buildings are retrofitted, with the retrofit decision commonly based on criteria other than earthquake shaking.

The decision on what to retrofit is a form of *triage*. In a major accident involving hundreds of severely injured people, limited medical aid requires decisions to help first those people who are more likely to survive. In earthquake retrofitting, the triage decision would be made to first retrofit those buildings that are most critical to the community, especially in an emergency, or structures whose destruction would be catastrophic to the population. These structures are called *critical facilities*. Let's consider the second category first.

In Chapter 6, mention was made of the proposed underground nuclear waste repository at Yucca Mountain, Nevada. Catastrophic failure of the underground repository and its surface facilities could

Figure 13-16. Van Norman Dam, San Fernando Valley, California, after the 1971 Sylmar Earthquake. About 800,000 yards of the embankment, including the parapet wall, dam crest, most of the upstream slope, and a portion of the downstream slope, slid into the reservoir, causing a loss of about thirty feet of dam height. Fortunately, the dam was only about half full at the time. Eighty thousand people living downstream from the dam were ordered to evacuate, and steps were taken to lower the water level in the reservoir. Photo by E.V. Leyendecker, U.S. Geological Survey.

result in the release of lethal amounts of radioactive gases and fluids, endangering the lives of hundreds of thousands of people. The Yucca Mountain repository is a critical facility; it must be designed to meet the highest seismic design criteria. The large dams in the foothills of the Sierra Nevada are also critical facilities, as are the nuclear power plants at Diablo Canyon and San Onofre. If a dam failed during an earthquake, it would release enormous volumes of water from the reservoir impounded behind it. These dams should be designed to withstand the highest conceivable amount of seismic shaking. The Van Norman Dam in the San Fernando Valley came very close to failure during the M 6.7 Sylmar Earthquake in 1971 (Figure 13-16). Had failure occurred, the waters impounded behind the dam would have overwhelmed many thousands of homes downstream, resulting in the loss of thousands of lives.

Continuing with our triage dilemma, what facilities in your town must continue to operate after an earthquake? Certainly the command structure of local government must function, because local government leaders will direct rescue efforts and make decisions that could avert spin-off disasters that can accompany an earthquake, such as major fires and tsunamis. So we should include the police and sheriff's departments, the fire department, city hall, and the county building, including the office of county emergency management services.

How about hospitals? Several hospitals were severely damaged in 1971 (Figures 13-1 and 13-11), and injured people had to be transported to distant hospitals that were not damaged. Schools? Most of the school children of Spitak and Leninakan, Armenia, were in their classrooms when the 1988 Spitak Earthquake struck. The classrooms were in poorly constructed, unreinforced-concrete buildings which collapsed, killing most of the pupils and teachers inside. There is a five- or six-year age gap in those communities in Armenia; most of the young people of that age were killed in the earthquake.

School buildings fared badly in the 1933 Long Beach Earthquake because so many of them were unreinforced brick buildings. It was providential that there were no children in those buildings at the time of the earthquake. Had the classrooms been full, hundreds of children might have died. This fact became obvious to parents after the Long Beach Earthquake, leading to passage of the Field Act requiring earthquake standards for school buildings. As a result, most school buildings have already been replaced or recycled.

Suggestions for Further Reading

Fratessa, P. 1994. *Buildings: Practical Lessons from the Loma Prieta Earthquake.* Washington, D.c.: National Academy Press.

Krinitsky, E., J. Gould, J., and F. Edinger. 1993. *Fundamentals of Earthquake Resistant Construction.* Wiley Series of Practical Construction Guides. New York: J. Wiley & Sons.

Lagorio, H.J. 1990. *Earthquakes: An Architect's Guide to Nonstructural Seismic Hazards.* New York: J. Wiley & Sons.

Necim, F., ed. 1989. *The Seismic Design Handbook.* London: Chapman & Hall.

⤺ 14 ⤻
The Federal Government and Earthquakes

" . . . the federal government shouldn't be expected to bail people out of natural disasters because they made poor choices in where to live."

Dennis Mileti, University of Colorado at Boulder

1. Introduction

The study of earthquakes is such a large-scale problem, with so many implications, that it seems impossible for the national government *not* to become involved. The government faces two difficulties: (1) defining the earthquake problem and dedicating the national resources to deal with it, and (2) informing the public about what has been done in such a way that the public can become a partner in reducing the earthquake hazards we face. A third difficulty is convincing the public a long time after the last earthquake that the government ought to be doing anything at all.

2. Historical Background

For most of recorded history, earthquakes were regarded as unpredictable calamities, acts of God—not subjects for government involvement except for dealing with the consequences. This began to change in 1891, when a killer earthquake devastated a large section of western Japan at the same time Japan was gearing up its economy to become an equal partner with Western countries. After the 1891 earthquake, the Japanese government authorized a long-term earthquake research program, including the mapping of active faults after a major earthquake, the deployment of seismographs (which had recently been invented), and the resurvey of benchmarks across active faults and along coastlines to look for crustal deformation. The Earthquake Research Institute was established at the University of Tokyo.

As a result, Japanese earthquake scientists became world leaders. Fusakichi Omori participated in the investigation of the 1906 San Francisco Earthquake (Part I). K. Wadati invented a magnitude scale before Charles Richter's invention of the one that bears his name. Wadati also was the first to recognize earthquakes hundreds of miles beneath the Earth's surface, outlining what would later be known as subduction zones. Two of the leading seismologists in the United States

312

are transplants from Japan: Hiroo Kanamori of Caltech, and Keiiti Aki, recently retired from the University of Southern California.

In the early twentieth century, seismograph observatories were established at the University of California at Berkeley and Caltech (Part I) and other places around the world. The Jesuits were important players, with a seismograph at Santa Clara College at San Jose. Seismology developed primarily as an academic pursuit, with earthquake research intertwined with using earthquake waves to image and explore the internal structure of the Earth.

The first federal funding for earthquake-related research was to the U.S. Weather Bureau, which was given the assignment of collecting earthquake observations at its weather stations. The Weather Bureau issued its own report on the 1906 San Francisco Earthquake. In several countries around the world, including Japan, the weather service still has a major responsibility in monitoring earthquakes.

Resurveying benchmarks in California by the U.S. Coast and Geodetic Survey (now the National Geodetic Survey) led to Professor Harry Reid's elastic rebound theory for the 1906 San Francisco Earthquake on the San Andreas Fault. A triangulation survey in the 1920s formed part of an earthquake prediction by Bailey Willis of Stanford University and a controversy that followed it (Part I). The Coast and Geodetic Survey confirmed Reid's observation that the area adjacent to the San Andreas Fault was continuing to build up strain, even as it had done before the earthquake.

For the most part, though, major government funding of earthquake research began only after the Soviets successfully tested nuclear weapons following World War II. This funding was not due to any concerns about earthquake hazards, but because of the Cold War. The United States and its NATO allies wanted to monitor Soviet (and later, Chinese) underground nuclear tests using seismographs. Seismologists showed that it was possible to distinguish between seismograms written by earthquakes and seismograms resulting from nuclear explosions, and also to determine the size of an underground nuclear test, just as seismologists are able to determine the magnitude of an earthquake.

By the early 1960s, the United States, in cooperation with other Western countries, had established a worldwide seismograph network, called WWSSN, to monitor the testing of nuclear weapons, particularly after the signing of the Nuclear Test Ban Treaty in 1963. The WWSSN had a spectacular, serendipitous scientific payoff. By allowing the world's earthquakes to be located much more accurately than before, the network provided evidence that these earthquakes follow narrow bands that were found to be the boundaries of great tectonic plates (Chapter 2). By 1966, the plate tectonics revolution had overturned the prevailing view of how the Earth works, and seismology, because of the WWSSN, had played a major part.

The U.S. Geological Survey (USGS) carried out detailed investigations of major earthquakes in Charleston, South Carolina in 1886 and in Alaska in 1899, and continued with USGS scientists participating in investigations of the 1906 San Francisco Earthquake and the 1959 Hebgen Lake Earthquake near Yellowstone Park. The USGS played a major role in the study of the great 1964 Alaska Earthquake. In carrying out these studies, the USGS was following in the tradition of the Geological Survey of India, which studied in detail great Himalayan earthquakes in 1897, 1905, and 1934. The USGS's involvement continued and accelerated following earthquakes in California in 1968 and 1971, leading to the establishment in 1977 of the USGS as the lead agency, together with the National Science Foundation (NSF), in a coordinated federal earthquake program (Part I).

3. The National Earthquake Hazard Reduction Program (NEHRP)

Two earthquakes in the mid-1970s strongly affected the decision to increase the involvement of the federal government in earthquake studies. The first was the Haicheng, China, Earthquake in February 1975, which had been predicted by the Chinese early enough to reduce greatly the loss of life (see Chapter 8). The second was an earthquake in August 1975, close to the Oroville Dam, in the foothills of the Sierra Nevada at the headwaters of the California Aqueduct (see Chapter 6). That earthquake, together with large earthquakes in China in 1962, Greece in 1966, and India in 1967—all of which had caused great loss of life—suggested that people can actually cause earthquakes by manipulating the water level of reservoirs and by the artificial pumping of fluids down boreholes for wastewater disposal or for improved recovery of oil. These two earthquakes finally laid to rest the view that earthquakes are acts of God in which humans play no role. The general public and, indeed, many people in the scientific community came to believe that earthquakes could be predicted and, by understanding the fluid pressures accompanying filling of reservoirs and pumping of fluids into or from wells, might even be controlled.

This led to passage of the *Earthquake Hazards Reduction Act of 1977* (Public Law 95-124), which directed the President to establish a *National Earthquake Hazards Reduction Program* (NEHRP, pronounced "Neehurp"). Among the objectives written into the law were (1) retrofitting existing buildings, especially critical facilities such as nuclear power plants, dams, hospitals, schools, public utilities, and high-occupancy buildings; (2) designing a system for predicting earthquakes and for identifying, evaluating, and characterizing seismic hazards; (3) upgrading building codes and developing land-use policies to consider seismic risk; (4)

disseminating warnings of an earthquake, and organizing emergency services after an earthquake; (5) educating the public, including state and local officials, about the earthquake threat, including the identification of locations and buildings that are particularly susceptible to earthquakes; (6) focusing existing scientific and engineering knowledge to mitigate earthquake hazards, and considering the social, economic, legal, and political implications of earthquake prediction; and (7) developing basic and applied research leading to a better understanding of control or modification of earthquakes.

Objective (6) contains a word, *mitigate,* which might be unfamiliar to many, but which appears so often in public statements as well as legislation that a definition should be presented here. To mitigate means to moderate, to make milder or less severe. The earthquake program thus does not take on the job of *eliminating* the earthquake threat, but rather of *moderating* the problem—an important distinction.

Although the 1977 law included several nonresearch objectives such as public education and upgrading of building codes, the legislation was primarily pointed toward research. The bill authorized new appropriations for two agencies, the USGS and the National Science Foundation, to conduct or to fund earthquake-related research through grants and contracts to universities and other nongovernmental organizations. The legislation did not indicate how the nonresearch objectives were to be implemented. Instead, the President was directed to develop a plan for implementation. Furthermore, the legislation left unclear which agency was in charge.

The President's implementation plan, sent to Congress in 1978, gave much of the responsibility for implementation of Public Law 95-124 to a lead agency, but, as in the law itself, the lead agency was not specified. A multi-agency task force was designated to develop design standards for federal projects. In the following year, Executive Order 12148, dated July 20, 1979, designated the newly created *Federal Emergency Management Agency (FEMA)* as the lead agency. This decision was included in 1980 in the first reauthorization legislation for the earthquake program. This legislation included a fourth agency, the National Bureau of Standards, later to be renamed the *National Institute of Standards and Technology (NIST),* as an integral—although small— part of NEHRP.

NEHRP was reauthorized five more times without significant change in the scope of the program. But by 1990 it was clear that Congress intended to make some changes. During the 1980s, it became apparent that the goal of earthquake prediction was not going to be achieved in the immediate future, as described in Chapter 8. The 1987 Whittier Narrows Earthquake struck Los Angeles and the 1989 Loma Prieta Earthquake struck the San Francisco Bay Area; neither had been predicted. Furthermore, as indicated in the Senate report accompanying the 1990 reauthorization bill, the application of NEHRP research findings to earthquake preparedness was considered slow and inadequate. The efforts of the four agencies were perceived as uncoordinated and unfocused. Finally, the goal of *earthquake control* was criticized as unrealistic and unattainable in the near future.

A mental exercise illustrates the problems facing the goal of earthquake control. An experiment in 1969 had shown that small earthquakes in an oil field at Rangely, Colorado could be turned on and off by increasing the amount of water injected into or withdrawn from the oil field. When water was withdrawn, earthquake activity decreased. The added water pressure along existing faults in the oil field weakened the fault zones and caused them to move, producing earthquakes. As in the case of filling the reservoir behind Oroville Dam, human activity was shown to have an effect on earthquakes.

The suggestion was then made: could this be done on a larger scale at a major fault, where the results could mitigate the earthquake hazard? Specifically, could it be done for the San Andreas Fault? The idea was simple: drill several very deep boreholes along the thinly populated 1857 rupture zone of the San Andreas Fault in central California and inject water, thereby weakening the fault. The idea was to weaken the fault enough to trigger a smaller earthquake of, say, M 6.5 to M 7 rather than wait for another earthquake as large as the 1857 rupture, which was M 7.9. The smaller earthquake, or series of smaller earthquakes, would cause much less damage than a repeat of the 1857 earthquake. It would be the earthquake equivalent of a controlled burn to alleviate hazard from forest fires.

There are two problems with this idea. First, the cost of drilling the holes for injection of water would be exorbitantly high—many millions of dollars to inject water deep enough to have an influence on the earthquake source ten miles or more beneath the surface. Second, what would be the legal implications of a triggered earthquake? What is the legal recourse for a person whose home or business is severely damaged in a triggered M 7 earthquake as opposed to the next M 7.9 earthquake, which might not have struck during his/her lifetime? What about the possibility of people being killed during the smaller event? Questions such as these led to the conclusion that earthquake control was not attainable in the near future, at least not by injecting fluids into a major, active fault zone. Returning to the forest-fire analogy: a controlled burn in the spring of 2000 went out of control and did severe damage to the town of Los Alamos, New Mexico. The legal fallout from that disaster has yet to be determined.

The 1990 reauthorization bill passed by Congress eliminated some references to earthquake prediction and control, and it expanded efforts in public education and in research on lifelines, earthquake insurance, and land-use policy. It marked the beginning of the shift from a predominantly research program toward a broader-based program including implementation and outreach. The role of FEMA as lead agency was clarified, including presentation of program budgets, reports to Congress, an education program, and block grants to states. New federal buildings were required to have seismic safety regulations, and seismic standards were established for existing federal buildings.

In the 1994 reauthorization, Congress again expressed concern about implementation and about coordination among the four agencies to achieve a unified, focused program. This led to an executive review by the White House Office of Science and Technology Policy (OSTP) and by the Office of Technology Assessment of the U.S. Congress. The OSTP review led to the establishment of the *National Earthquake Loss-Reduction Program (NEP)*, under the leadership of FEMA, with newly formulated goals to be developed in five-year plans by the principal agencies that are officially part of the federal earthquake program. The goals of NEP are to speed up the application of earthquake research to benefit society by reducing the vulnerability of communities to earthquakes. At the present time, both NEP and NEHRP are both in existence, although it was earlier believed that one would replace the other.

The amount allocated for NEHRP was less than $60 million in fiscal year (FY) 1978 and around $100 million in FY 1994. In terms of constant 1978 dollars, the program received less money in 1994 than it did at its start-up in 1978. In addition, there was commonly a disparity between the amount *authorized* and the amount actually *appropriated* by Congress. This disparity was greatest in FY 1979 and 1980, and again in FY 1992 and 1993. The effect of individual earthquakes was apparent. The only boost in constant dollars came in 1990 after the Loma Prieta "World Series" Earthquake in the San Francisco Bay Area, and the only time in the past ten years that appropriations were the same as authorization was after the Northridge Earthquake of 1994. On the other hand, the Landers Earthquake, which struck a thinly populated area in the Mojave Desert of California in 1992, had no impact on funding, even though it was larger than either the Loma Prieta Earthquake or the Northridge Earthquake.

The lesson here is that politicians respond to an immediate crisis, but they have short memories for solving the problem in the long haul—particularly after the last earthquake fades into memory. It is again a difference in the perception of time, as discussed in Chapter 1. To an Earth scientist, the 1989, 1992, 1994, and 1999 California earthquakes are part of a continuum, a response to the slow but inexorable movement of tectonic plates. To a public official, and indeed to the public at large, each earthquake is an instant calamity that must be dealt with in the short term, without serious consideration for when and where the next earthquake will strike.

We now consider the role of individual federal agencies, first those officially part of NEHRP, and then other agencies that play an important role in earthquake research but are not an official part of NEHRP.

4. Federal Emergency Management Agency (FEMA)

The Federal Emergency Management Agency (FEMA) has two roles within NEHRP: (1) leading and coordinating NEHRP, and (2) implementing mitigation measures. In the early years of its involvement in the program, it was mainly a coordinator rather than as a leader, resulting in congressional criticism in hearings before the 1990 and 1994 reauthorization bill. By 1994, FEMA's leadership responsibilities included (1) preparation of NEHRP plans and reports to Congress, (2) assessment of user needs, (3) support of earthquake professional organizations, (4) arranging interagency coordination meetings, (5) support of problem-focused studies, and (6) outreach programs, especially for small businesses.

In its implementation role, FEMA contributes to developing standards in new construction and retrofits, and to applying engineering design knowledge to upgrading building codes. Through its *State and Local Hazards Reduction Program*, FEMA provides grants to state governments and to multistate consortia to support earthquake hazard mitigation. In California, the state agency with objectives similar to those of FEMA is the Governor's Office of Emergency Services. Hazards include not only earthquakes but floods, wildfires, hurricanes, and other disasters. Activities include education, outreach, adoption of building codes, and training exercises. In California, this is coordinated by the FEMA Region 9 office in San Francisco.

At present, twenty-eight of the forty-three states and territories at some degree of seismic risk participate in this program. FEMA supports the program 100 percent in the first year, but requires 25 percent and 35 percent matches by the states in the second and third years, respectively, and 50 percent matches thereafter. The idea is for state and local governments to take over part of the financial responsibility after the first year: if it's worth doing, the federal government should not have to pay for it all. Participation by some states has declined when the fifty percent match year approached, and some states have not participated at all.

FEMA plays the lead role in preparing the federal government for national emergencies. Public Law 93-288 established a *Federal Response Plan* to coordinate federal assistance in any situation where a presidential disaster declaration is likely to be issued. The Federal Response Plan outlines the responsibilities, chain of command, and sequence of events for federal and local authorities to deal with the emergency. These activities include carrying out training exercises, getting local agencies to agree on emergency response plans, and supporting urban search and rescue teams.

When the President declares an area struck by an earthquake as a disaster area, FEMA swings into action. A coordinating officer is appointed, who sets up a disaster field office to manage the response, including rescue and small loans to businesses or individuals. The disaster field office coordinates response from other federal agencies, the Office of Emergency Services, and the Red Cross. The emergency response team deals with twelve support functions: transportation, communications, public works/engineering, firefighting, information and planning, mass care, resource support, health/medical services, urban search and rescue, hazardous materials, food, and energy.

In most cases, the governor of a state requests that the President declare a disaster area; however, the President may do so without the request of the governor. The disaster declaration varies from one disaster to the next. California is the largest recipient of federal disaster funds: forty-three percent of the total from 1989 to 1998—a time including both the Loma Prieta Earthquake and Northridge Earthquake, as well as other disasters such as floods and wildfires. So far, in the presidential declarations that have been issued in the past few years, this organization has worked reasonably well. However, the system has yet to be tested by an earthquake as large as the 1906 San Francisco Earthquake or a subduction-zone earthquake.

In 1997, FEMA started Project Impact, a plan to build disaster-resistant communities. Oakland, crossed by the Hayward Fault, was selected as one of the seven communities nationwide as a pilot project. The strategy is to build partnerships with local government, private companies, and individuals to prepare a community for a disaster before it happens, rather than simply picking up the pieces afterwards. With assistance from FEMA, communities do their own planning rather than accept a plan dictated by Washington or Sacramento. Communities may submit proposals to FEMA for support.

In 1997, FEMA started an initiative called HAZUS (Hazards United States), under a cooperative agreement with the National Institute of Building Sciences (NIBS). HAZUS uses a software program (newest version: HAZUS99) to map building inventories, soil conditions, known faults, and lifelines to estimate economic losses and casualties from a disaster. HAZUS was used for a study of the Portland, Oregon and Reno-Carson City, Nevada metropolitan areas. It has expanded nationwide, building up from local census tract data. In California, it's being used to estimate ground motion along the Hayward-Rodgers Creek Fault, the San Andreas Fault near Parkfield, and the San Jacinto Fault. FEMA

Region 9 and the Office of Emergency Services have established a HAZUS working group for the San Francisco Bay Area involving more than two hundred planners, managers, and other professionals.

Both programs represent a shift in focus from *hazard*—where the faults are, how big the earthquakes will be on these faults, and how the ground will respond—to *risk*—what the losses will be on a future earthquake. For example, the 1992 Landers Earthquake (M 7.3) in the Mojave Desert was a big hazard but did not represent a big risk because of the low population of the affected area. On the other hand, the 1987 Whittier Narrows Earthquake (M 5.9) was a much smaller hazard but a larger risk because it struck in the middle of Los Angeles.

FEMA has determined that average annual earthquake losses in California will be $3.9 billion to buildings alone, three-fourths of the nation's total. A third of these losses would be in Los Angeles County alone because of the large population at risk.

5. U.S. Geological Survey

The USGS receives the largest share of NEHRP funding, more than half in FY 1994. Funds are used to pursue four goals: (1) understanding what happens at the earthquake source, (2) determining the potential for future earthquakes, (3) predicting the effects of earthquakes, and (4) developing applications for earthquake research results. Research ranges from fundamental earthquake processes to expected ground motions to building codes.

More than two-thirds of NEHRP funding is spent internally to support USGS scientists in regional programs, laboratory and field studies, national hazard assessment programs, and the operation of seismic networks, including the Northern California network operated with the University of California at Berkeley, the Southern California network operated with Caltech, and the Great Basin network operated with the University of Nevada-Reno. The remainder is spent on grants to universities, consulting firms, and state agencies and partial support of the Southern California Earthquake Center. The external grants program is based on objectives established within the USGS with advice from outside. Grant proposals must address one or more of these objectives, which may change from year to year. The external grants program involves the best minds in the country, not just those of government scientists, to focus on earthquake hazard mitigation.

Much of the geographic focus has been on California, which received almost one-third of earthquake research funds in FY 1995. But starting in the mid-1980s, the USGS began a series of focused studies in urban areas at seismic risk, starting with the Salt Lake City urban corridor and continuing with the Puget Sound-Portland region in the Pacific

Northwest. However, the Bay Area and metropolitan Los Angeles continue to receive major research emphasis.

The California program has evolved from mapping active faults and their slip rates and paleoseismology to estimating ground motion, liquefaction, and earthquake-induced landslide hazards to probabilistic assessments of earthquake potential throughout the state, with a focus on urban areas.

Although this program has worked amazingly well over the past two decades, it nearly ran off track in 1995–96 as a result of the Contract with America from the new Republican majority in Congress. One of the objectives of the Contract was to eliminate several government agencies, and the USGS was on the hit list. As the USGS fought for its existence and tried to save the jobs of permanent staff members, the external-grants program of NEHRP suddenly found itself eliminated by a committee in the House of Representatives. The program was later restored. But before grants could be awarded, the government was temporarily shut down in early 1996, and the Department of the Interior, which includes the USGS, was forced to operate by continuing resolutions of the Congress for most of FY 1996 at significantly lower-than-normal appropriations. A year of earthquake research was lost.

The USGS provides financial support to the Southern California Earthquake Center and is coordinating a detailed paleoseismic investigation of Bay Area faults called BAPEX (Bay Area Paleoseismological Experiment). The USGS also operates the National Earthquake Information Center in Golden, Colorado to locate damaging earthquakes around the world as rapidly as possible and to collect and distribute seismic information for earthquake research.

Congress has given the USGS the job of developing a real-time alert system, and in addition, the USGS is proposing an Advanced National Seismic System with new, state-of-the-art instruments for better location and characterization of earthquakes.

6. National Science Foundation (NSF)

The National Science Foundation (NSF) receives about one-fourth of NEHRP funding, divided into two areas, administered by two directorates within NSF. The largest amount goes to earthquake engineering, including direct grants to individual investigators. Part of the budget goes to three earthquake-engineering research centers in New York (established in 1986), Illinois, and California (both established in 1997). The Pacific Earthquake Engineering Research Center in Richmond, California is operated by the University of California at Berkeley, one of the leading institutions in the world for earthquake engineering research.

Part of the budget of the engineering research centers comes from NSF, but an equal amount is expected to come from other sources. The Buffalo, New York center has received money from the Federal Highway Administration for research into the seismic vulnerability of the national highway system. Other research includes geotechnical engineering studies of liquefaction, tsunamis, and soil response to earthquakes, and the response of structures to ground motion. A category called *earthquake systems integration* includes research in the behavioral and social sciences and in planning, including code enforcement and how to decide whether to demolish or repair a building.

The directorate of NSF that includes the geosciences funds grants to individual scientists and to three university consortia—the Incorporated Research Institutions for Seismology (IRIS), the Southern California Earthquake Center (which also receives support from the USGS), and the University Navstar Consortium (UNAVCO), which provides technical assistance and equipment for geodetic studies of crustal deformation using GPS. IRIS is building a global network of state-of-the-art digital seismographs. IRIS provides NEHRP with assessments of the frequency of earthquakes worldwide and their expected ground motion. It is developing a program to deploy seismographs in the field immediately after a large earthquake or volcanic event. The Data Management Center of IRIS is housed in Seattle.

Direct grants from NSF to individual investigators include research into the study of earthquake sources, of active faults and paleoseismology, and of shallow crustal seismicity. In FY 1990, instrument-based studies in seismology and geodesy received the bulk of the funding.

Although the Ocean Sciences Directorate in NSF has no focused program in earthquake studies, projects attached to oceanographic cruises with other primary objectives have made important discoveries, including a set of seafloor faults that cut across the Cascadia Subduction Zone, discovered in an NSF-sponsored cruise in preparation for a research drilling program off Cascadia in 1992. A set of seismic-reflection profiles, also preparatory to the drilling project, imaged the plate-boundary fault directly. Tube worm and clam communities in the vicinity of the Cascadia Subduction Zone were discovered on a cruise to work out the migration of fluids in subduction zones; those fluids were found to travel along active faults. Cruises off southern California have mapped the San Clemente, San Diego Trough, and Coronado Bank faults in unprecedented detail. A new proposal for ocean drilling after 2003 includes major research on subduction zone earthquakes, including plans to acquire cores within the subduction-zone itself.

7. National Institute of Standards and Technology (NIST)

The National Institute of Standards and Technology (NIST), the old National Bureau of Standards, has received the least amount of funding of the four agencies comprising NEHRP. Its main role has been in applied engineering research and in code development. Its initial budget for earthquake research was less than $500,000 per year and now stands at $1.9 million. In FY 1994, it received a supplemental appropriation to respond to the Northridge Earthquake, resulting in a budget of $3.6 million. The 1990 reauthorization directed NIST to carry out "research and development to improve building codes and standards and practices for structures and lifelines."

8. National Oceanic and Atmospheric Administration (NOAA)

The agencies discussed in this section are not part of NEHRP. Yet two of them contribute significantly to earthquake research because of their technological focus on the sea (National Oceanic and Atmospheric Administration, NOAA) and in space (National Aeronautics and Space Administration, NASA). There are, of course, many informal working relationships between these agencies and NEHRP, but the lack of formal structure can lead to a lack of focus. Nonetheless, both NOAA and NASA have managed to make critical contributions to an understanding of earthquakes and earthquake hazard mitigation.

NOAA is part of the Department of Commerce, which until the early 1970s was the only government department, through the U.S. Coast and Geodetic Survey and the National Weather Bureau, with a federal mandate to study earthquakes. After a battle with the USGS for primacy in earthquake funding, the Department of Commerce withdrew from the field in the early 1970s, and the USGS took over (Part I). This might have been the reason NOAA was excluded from NEHRP in 1977.

NOAA is the principal federal agency responsible for tsunami hazards (see Chapter 10). Earthquake and tsunami data are distributed through its National Geophysical Data Center in Colorado. NOAA also provides real-time tsunami warnings for the United States and its territories through tsunami warning centers in Alaska and Hawaii (described in Chapter 10). After a tsunami generated by the 1992 Cape Mendocino Earthquake was detected on the northern California coast, Congress gave NOAA additional funds and responsibilities and established the National Tsunami Hazard Mitigation Program, designed to reduce risks from tsunamis. NOAA is the lead federal agency in this initiative, with participation by FEMA, USGS, and NSF (Chapter 10).

The U.S. Navy has declassified arrays of hydrophones (called SOSUS) on the sea floor that were used during the Cold War to monitor military ship traffic in the oceans and has allowed them to be used by NOAA. These hydrophones, in addition to recording ship engine noise and whale calls, monitor earthquake waves transmitted directly through water, called *T-phase waves*. These waves locatte earthquakes on the sea floor with much higher accuracy and to a much lower magnitude threshold than is possible from land-based seismographs. Furthermore, NOAA has located many times the number of earthquakes on the deep ocean floor than the land-based seismograph network.

Just as the USGS is responsible for topographic mapping, NOAA is responsible for mapping the topography (or *bathymetry*) of the sea floor using a ship-borne mapping device called *SeaBeam*. Earlier mapping techniques relied on individual soundings of water depth, followed later by profiles of the sea floor by depth recorders mounted in the hulls of passing ships. SeaBeam and similar techniques developed by the British, French, and Japanese map a swath of sea floor based on the echoes of sounds transmitted from several locations mounted in the ship's hull. NOAA swath bathymetry results in topographic maps of the sea bottom comparable in accuracy to topographic maps of dry land constructed by the USGS.

Once thought to be a barren, featureless landscape, the sea floor is now known to be marked by canyons, great faults, volcanoes, landslides, and active folds (Figures 2-4 and 9-9). Detailed understanding of sea floor topography has allowed scientists to map directly the Cascadia Subduction Zone off northern California, Monterey Submarine Canyon off central California, and the Santa Barbara Basin and California Borderland off southern California. Tectonic features of the deep ocean floor are not altered by erosion to the degree that land structures are.

The bathymetry is recorded digitally so that it can be displayed as a computer model in which the water has been stripped away, as shown in Figures 2-4 and 9-9. (Similarly, the USGS has digitized its land topographic maps permitting a new and revealing perspective on the tectonic forces that produce the topography above sea level, as illustrated in Figures 4-2, 4-7, 4-14, 5-1, 6-1, 6-7, 7-1, and the onshore portion of Figure 9-9.) SeaBeam bathymetry directs submersibles with observers and remote-controlled robotic vehicles to observe and map faults on the sea floor. An active research program involving submersibles, funded by NOAA's *National Undersea Research Program (NURP)*, has led to new detailed information on the Cascadia Subduction Zone and active faults and folds on the continental shelf and slope.

Because NOAA is not part of NEHRP, programs such as NURP earthquake hazards research and SeaBeam bathymetric mapping are at risk from budget cutters because except for tsunamis, earthquake hazard research is not a primary mission of NOAA.

9. National Aeronautics and Space Administration (NASA)

When LANDSAT cameras returned images of the Earth from space several decades ago, it changed our perspective forever. Faults such as the San Andreas were viewed in unprecedented clarity (see the space shuttle photo in Figure 4-3), and other, previously unknown earthquake-producing structures were also revealed. The *Geodynamics Program* at NASA was developed to take advantage of the new space platforms as a means to learn about the Earth, including plate tectonics, mineral resources, and an understanding of earthquakes. These activities are now coordinated in a program called *Earth Systems Enterprises*, managed by the Jet Propulsion Lab in Pasadena.

In December 1999, NASA launched a satellite named *Terra*, the Earth Observing System, to map the Earth in real time, tracking changes on the Earth's surface observed from space. In February 2000, the space shuttle *Endeavour* conducted an eleven-day radar mapping survey of the Earth, resulting in much more accurate topographic maps than had been available previously.

The greatest impact NASA has had on earthquake research has been in the measurement of crustal strain from space (described in Chapter 3). This includes the measurement of the relative motion of radio telescopes based on measuring signals from quasars in outer space (VLBI, or Very Long Baseline Interferometry), the measurement of strain through the Global Positioning System based on signals from NAVSTAR satellites, and the direct measurement of displacement during an earthquake based on radar interferometry. Much of this work is coordinated through NASA's Jet Propulsion Lab.

10. Other Federal Agencies

Earthquake research by other non-NEHRP agencies principally involves the earthquake safety of those critical facilities that are their responsibility. The *Nuclear Regulatory Commission* (NRC), the successor to the Atomic Energy Commission of the 1960s, has sponsored research into earthquake hazards related to the safety of nuclear power plants. With nuclear plants at Diablo Canyon and San Onofre (and formerly at Humboldt Bay) in California, all areas subject to earthquakes, the NRC took a strong interest in evaluating earthquake hazards in California as early as the 1970s. The *Department of Energy* (DOE) has also taken an interest in the earthquake safety of nuclear power plants as well as the Yucca Mountain site proposed for nuclear waste disposal.

Dams are critical facilities as well, and this has resulted in research by the *Army Corps of Engineers* and the *Bureau of Reclamation* of the Department of Interior. These agencies, together with the Veterans

Administration, have been responsible for installing instruments to measure strong ground motion. The *Department of Defense* has funded investigations through the Office of Naval Research and the Air Force Office of Scientific Research, which provides some support for IRIS and other seismic monitoring for nuclear test ban compliance.

12. Getting the Word Out to the Public

Scientists and engineers in the NEHRP program and in other federal agencies have made great advances in the understanding of earthquakes and of how to strengthen our society against future earthquakes. But how well has NEHRP succeeded in getting its research results out to society at large? Educating the public was one of the objectives of the original Earthquake Hazards Reduction Act of 1977, and this objective has been stated many times since, particularly at the prodding of Congress. Yet twenty years later, the public is still poorly informed about earthquakes. Why?

Many government scientists and their supervisors believe their job is done when their research results are published in a government document such as a USGS Professional Paper. But the publications branch of USGS is underfunded and inefficient. Because the papers represent the official position of a federal agency, they must be approved not only by other scientists but also by USGS management.

But most people don't have ready access to USGS publications, although instructions on how to obtain them are provided at the end of this book. Many USGS maps are available only online, which requires the user to have access to a large-format printer. To address the problem of ready access, the USGS has placed a list of all of its 110,000 publications from 1880 to the present on the World Wide Web, available at http://usgs-georef.cos.com. This list contains abstracts of some publications, and some of the more recent publications are available online.

Even if you are successful in finding the list and purchasing a publication, you discover that it is written for other scientists and engineers, not for the general public. The papers are full of technical jargon, and a background in earthquake science is necessary to understand fully the results. Many USGS scientists, frustrated by bureaucratic delays in their own publications branch, publish their results in scientific journals. Non-USGS scientists, including myself, do the same. This fulfills the scientist's professional obligation but still does not inform the public, because the scientific journal articles are also full of jargon.

The USGS and other agencies have responded by publishing circulars and fact sheets written in language easy for a nontechnical person to understand, and where available, these publications are listed in the

References. In addition, USGS officials have testified in public hearings on policy issues, and they have made themselves available to civic groups and classes for presentations on their specialty. All USGS offices have a public information officer ready to respond to questions and to arrange talks to civic groups. The Web pages of the USGS and other federal agencies have information that is useful and entertaining, geared to the general public. NOAA has slide sets of earthquake damage that are useful in instruction, and I have used them in my classes and in this book.

In general, though, the public is educated not by government documents, regardless of how well they are written, but by the broadcast and print media. A television reporter is interested in a breaking news story like an earthquake, not in public education. When a large earthquake strikes, my telephone rings off the hook for a day or a week, depending on how the story develops. Earthquake scientists, including myself, prefer to go about their lives unbothered by microphones or television cameras. During an earthquake, however, we get our fifteen minutes (or twenty-four hours) of fame, and any public education message has to be threaded into our response to the news story. That message often ends up on the cutting-room floor.

In some cases, the media have an agenda in pursuing a story, as was the case after the 1906 San Francisco Earthquake (Part I). The 1994 Northridge Earthquake ruptured a blind fault that was previously unknown to the scientific community, and CNN developed a story that had as its theme the withholding by the oil industry of subsurface oil well and seismic data that could have revealed the presence of the earthquake fault. Several of us use oil-company data in our earthquake studies, so I was one of those interviewed by CNN and asked about how difficult it was for me to get information from oil companies. I told the interviewer in Atlanta that oil companies had supplied me with all the information I had asked for, even hiring as summer interns my students working on earthquake projects. Nonetheless, the broadcast still carried the implication that oil companies had withheld data, and my comments stating the opposite were not used.

In the long run, the best way to get the word out is in the classroom, starting in elementary schools, where children are fascinated by earthquakes and volcanoes just as they are by dinosaurs. Earthquakes and volcanoes are generally included in courses in Earth science in high school, but these courses are not required and often are not even recommended in high school. Many high schools lack a teacher qualified or interested in teaching an Earth science course that would include a unit on earthquakes. I hope this book provides the resources to turn this problem around.

13. Summary and a Word about the Future

NEHRP, NASA's Earth Systems Enterprises, and NOAA's Tsunami Mitigation Program are mission-oriented, applied programs, not basic research programs. In the words of Sen. Barbara Mikulski (D., Maryland), this is *strategic* rather than *curiosity-driven* research. And yet NEHRP has been responsible for fundamental discoveries not only about earthquakes but about how the earth deforms and behaves through time. Not only this, but NEHRP has brought about world leadership in earthquake science for the United States since its beginning in the 1970s. Most of what has been presented in this book is the result of federally funded research. The U.S. earthquake program is the best in the world, even though it has not yet been able to weave an understanding of earthquake science and engineering into the fabric of society.

But U.S. leadership is now being challenged by the Japanese. The cost of the 1995 Kobe Earthquake was ten times the cost of the Northridge Earthquake the preceding year, and an additional cost was to the confidence of the Japanese in coping with the earthquake peril throughout most of their country. Accordingly, the Japanese government has ratcheted up its budget for earthquake hazards research to a much higher level than the American program, or that of any other country, possibly because so much of their country—including the capital city of Tokyo—is at great risk from earthquakes. The U.S. responded to the Northridge Earthquake with a one-year special appropriation with no long-range follow-up but instead an attempt by the Republican Congress in 1995 to dissolve the USGS, the principal agency responsible for earthquake research. Perhaps this is because earthquakes are still perceived as a California problem, despite the fact that earthquakes have caused great damage in Alaska, Hawaii, Massachusetts, Missouri, Montana, Nevada, Oregon, South Carolina, Tennessee, and Washington. Most people, if asked to list the things they would like the federal government to do, would not list earthquakes in the top ten, unless they live in an area that was recently struck by an earthquake, such as Northridge. Because of this prevailing public attitude, leadership in earthquake studies may return to where it was at the beginning of the twentieth century, to Japan.

Suggestions for Further Reading

Geschwind, C.-H. 2001. *California Earthquakes: Science, Risk, and the Politics of Hazard Mitigation, 1906–1977.* Baltimore: Johns Hopkins University Press.

↫ 15 ↫
The Role of State and Local Government

1. Introduction

Although the President can declare a disaster without consulting the governor or local officials, the role of the federal government is largely advisory. It is the State of California and its counties, cities, and multi-city governments that must establish and carry out policy regarding earthquakes. The USGS can advise the governor about earthquakes, and NOAA can advise about tsunamis, but the final call must be from the governor and from local elected officials.

FEMA operates through the Governor's Office of Emergency Services, which has disaster coordinators in every county, generally in the office of the sheriff. In some cities, emergency management is part of the Fire Department. The Department of Conservation, through the Division of Mines and Geology, identifies seismic hazards that are subject to special analysis before structures can be built on them. The Seismic Safety Commission makes recommendations to the governor, the legislature, and the general public about reducing earthquake losses and in recovering from earthquakes. The Department of Insurance regulates the insurance industry, including earthquake insurance, and it is responsible for the California Earthquake Authority, as described in Chapter 11. The state has a role in developing building codes and grading ordinances, but these are enacted at the county and city level. In addition, there are regional consortia of public and private agencies that deal with earthquakes.

2. Division of Mines and Geology

In 1853, five years after the start of the Gold Rush, a State Geological Survey was organized, with a prominent physician and geologist, John B. Trask, as the first State Geologist. Three years later, Trask, also a cofounder of the California Academy of Natural Sciences, began publishing compilations of earthquakes that had struck California. This was not to alert people to the hazard, but to show "that California quakes were no more severe or frequent than those felt on the East Coast."

Trask's Geological Survey expired about that time, but was followed in 1860 by a second State Geological Survey headed by Josiah D. Whitney. Whitney visited the area most heavily damaged in the 1872

Owens Valley Earthquake—the first time an earthquake had been studied by a scientist employed by the state. But Whitney's style was abrasive, and he was more interested in studying fossils whereas the legislature wanted him to work on gold deposits. No one saw any value in studying earthquakes. The last straw was when Whitney refused the personal request of Governor John Downey for help in his mining stock speculations. One thing led to another, and Whitney and his State Geological Survey were put out of business in 1874.

There was still interest in mining, though, and a State Mining Bureau was established in 1880, headed by a State Mineralogist. This arrangement stayed in place until 1929, when it was renamed the Division of Mines and placed under the new Department of Natural Resources, under the supervision of a Mining Board. In that same year, the Division hired its first geologist, Olaf P. Jenkins, whose assignment was to make a new geological map of the state. The Division of Mines continued under a State Mineralogist, one of whom was Jenkins, until 1961, when it was renamed Division of Mines and Geology and placed under the Department of Conservation. The head of the Division was named the State Geologist, the first with that title since Whitney.

But the mandate of the Division, like that of the USGS at the federal level, continued to be on mineral resources, although its geological staff had the expertise to work on environmental problems such as landslides and earthquakes. Things began to change in 1948, when Jenkins hired Gordon B. Oakeshott, a teacher at Compton Junior College. Oakeshott was born in Oakland sixteen months before it was shaken by the great San Francisco Earthquake, and he studied at Berkeley under "the King," Andrew Lawson, who had headed up the commission studying that earthquake. He and his family were badly shaken by the Long Beach Earthquake of 1933, while he was completing his Ph.D. studies on the San Fernando Valley and western San Gabriel Mountains. Oakeshott was captivated by earthquakes, and he carried this fascination to his new job with the state.

Oakeshott's chance came with the Kern County Earthquake of July 21, 1952. A party from the Division, including Oakeshott and Jenkins, visited the damaged area. At the time, earthquake studies were divided between Berkeley for northern California and Caltech for southern California; this earthquake clearly was in Caltech territory. At a meeting at Caltech, the Division of Mines agreed to publish a report to be edited by Oakeshott containing all the major scientific contributions from universities and government agencies alike. After the publication of this report in 1955, Oakeshott took the lead in earthquake studies within the Division, even though there was no clear authority from the legislature or the Mining Board for the Division to do so. He visited surface ruptures from earthquakes in Nevada in 1954, Montana in 1959, and Alaska in 1964.

In 1959, Ian Campbell, a professor of geology at Caltech, became the new Chief of the Division. By focusing on mining, the Division had mainly served the rural counties of the state, but Campbell believed that it should serve the cities as well. Urban sprawl was eliminating valuable deposits of sand and gravel, and Campbell justified an urban geology program to the Mining Board by calling it an assessment of sand and gravel resources around major cities. In 1960 he started a mapping program in the Palos Verdes Hills, an area affected by major landslides destroying expensive homes. Following the 1964 Alaska Earthquake, Campbell received approval from the Mining Board to start an urban hazards mapping program, including earthquake shaking, and to begin studies of the San Andreas Fault.

The Mining Board was reconstituted as the State Mining and Geology Board, and new appointees included earthquake geologist Clarence Allen, engineering geologist Richard Jahns, and earthquake engineer Karl Steinbrugge—all supporters of earthquake research. A broad-based earthquake program was started with a budget of $260,000 in 1969 (one-fifth of the Division total), increasing to more than $400,000 the following year. The popular Division publication, *Mineral Information Service* (renamed *California Geology* in 1971) began to publish articles on earthquakes that were easy for the general public to read. At the request of the California Disaster Office (later the Office of Emergency Services), the Division published a map showing where earthquake damage could be expected. In 1970, an agreement was reached with the Division of Real Estate to review all proposals for subdividing land, about fourteen hundred per year. The Division of Mines and Geology recommended that where appropriate, the Division of Real Estate should include a notice of possible earthquake hazard or other geologic hazard in its report to the public.

In 1969, following an earthquake-prediction scare in the Bay Area, State Senator Alfred Alquist of San Jose persuaded the legislature to appoint a Joint Committee on Seismic Safety, with himself as chairman. This legislative committee would be a driving force for earthquake legislation in the following decade.

On February 9, 1971, the Sylmar Earthquake struck the San Fernando Valley, which Oakeshott had mapped as a Ph.D. student; his report had been published by the Division in 1958. This earthquake produced unusually high accelerations, leading structural engineers to request more information on the strong motion of earthquakes. In addition, a previously unrecognized reverse fault cut across housing developments, roads, and freeways, causing great damage (for freeway damage, see Figure 13-15). It became clear that the Field and Riley Acts, which had been considered adequate to regulate building construction, did not offer enough protection. In addition, there was no requirement that active faults be taken into consideration in approving housing developments for construction.

Alquist's Joint Committee on Seismic Safety heard recommendations resulting from the 1971 earthquake, including one that the state establish a program to measure strong ground shaking during earthquakes. This program would be run by the Division of Mines and Geology and paid for by an assessment of 0.0007% of the value of new construction as part of the cost of the building permit—all except for Los Angeles and San Francisco, which already had such an assessment. The bill creating the Strong Motion Instrumentation Program was signed into law by Governor Ronald Reagan in October 1971. In the first three years of this program, the Division received nearly $1.25 million, an increase in its budget of about twenty-five percent.

Another law passed in 1971 was the requirement that cities and counties include a Seismic Safety Element as one of the components of their general plan, adding earthquakes to other natural and urban hazards. This was an outgrowth of a requirement put into place in 1937 and beefed up in 1955 that each city and county adopt a general plan to guide decisions regarding long-term development. The Division of Mines and Geology, along with other agencies, helped develop guidelines for preparing seismic safety elements and assisted several counties in preparing their plans, including emergency response plans; a plan for reducing hazards from old, unsafe buildings; and a map of local seismic hazards. However, most local agencies did not develop procedures for building permit review, which are necessary to implement the hazard-reduction policies of their general plans.

What about active faults, like the faults that had ruptured in the 1971 earthquake and damaged or destroyed buildings on top of them? Places like Daly City and the East Bay cities were building directly across faults that were known to be active. Geologist Clarence Allen of Caltech argued that the most likely place for a future fault rupture is where the fault has ruptured in the past. Evidence for past rupture could be determined by geological investigations.

Two months after the Sylmar Earthquake, Sen. Alquist, through the Joint Committee on Seismic Safety, introduced a bill to require the State Geologist to identify zones centered on the San Andreas Fault and other well-defined active faults, calling for special measures before construction on these zones could take place. Assemblyman Paul Priolo of Los Angeles introduced a similar bill, but both bills died in committee.

The next year, both Alquist and Priolo revised their bills with advice from the Joint Committee on Seismic Safety and the Division of Mines and Geology, including Wes Bruer, the State Geologist. Compromise was necessary to get the support of local government lobbying groups, including adding an urban planner and a representative of county government to the State Mining and Geology Board. The final bill, renamed the Alquist-Priolo Geologic Hazard Zone Act, was signed into law by Governor Reagan in late 1972.

In the following year, guidelines for cities and counties were drawn up by the Mining and Geology Board defining an active fault under the new law. An Alquist-Priolo fault must have evidence of movement in the Holocene, dated as starting eleven thousand years ago. A geologic report on the presence of active faults was required prior to development in an Alquist-Priolo zone. The law established a setback of fifty feet that would be off limits for construction. The setback could be widened or narrowed based on the recommendation of the geologist; a wider zone might be mandated based on a broader fault zone or on uncertainty in locating the fault. Another provision of the law was that a seller was required to inform a potential buyer that the property for sale lies in an Alquist-Priolo zone.

When the first fault maps appeared in late 1973, they were criticized because they "amount[ed] to libel of title to the lands inclosed" and "deprive[d] land owners of their property rights without due process of law." In response to this opposition, single-family homes not part of a subdivision (four or more lots) and buildings with up to three living units were excluded from the law, and the law was renamed the "Alquist-Priolo Special Studies Zone Act," a less threatening title than "Geologic Hazard Zone." An Alquist-Priolo fault was required to be *well defined* by the Division of Mines and Geology. This neutralized enough of the opposition that the fault zoning could continue.

The Alquist-Priolo Act has been amended thirteen times and is now known as the Alquist-Priolo Earthquake Fault Zoning Act. The Division has issued 549 maps at a scale of one inch equals 2,000 feet. On the basis of new evidence, 149 maps have been revised and 4 have been withdrawn. Zone boundaries are set at 500 feet away from most mapped faults but are as narrow as 200 feet for less significant faults. For each fault that has been reviewed under the Act, the Division prepares a Fault Evaluation Report documenting the reasons for zoning. Reports have been completed for 244 faults (Figure 15-1) and are available for public inspection. The geologic reports on proposed subdivisions required by the Act must be accepted by the local jurisdiction, after which they are filed with the Division of Mines and Geology where they, too, are available for public inspection. The fault-rupture hazard zones are described in detail by Hart and Bryant (1997).

What is the track record of Alquist-Priolo? The only major surface ruptures since the Act went into effect accompanied the 1992 Landers Earthquake (Figure 6-4) and 1999 Hector Mine Earthquake (Figure 6-6), both in thinly populated or unpopulated areas in the Mojave Desert.

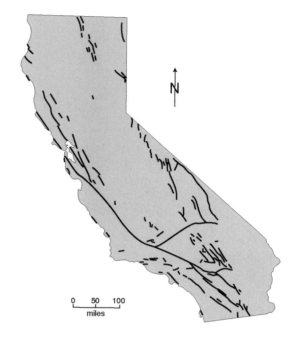

Figure 15-1. Map of California showing active faults zoned under the Alquist-Priolo Act. For a fault to be zoned, it must be shown to have been active in the Holocene (the past eleven thousand years). From Earl Hart, Division of Mines and Geology.

0   50   100
miles

Some of the faults that ruptured had been zoned under Alquist-Priolo, and others had not. The Act has not really been tested by a major earthquake with surface rupture in an urban area along an Alquist-Priolo Zone fault. For further analysis, see Hart and Bryant (1997).

Alquist-Priolo has been criticized as attacking the wrong problem: in the 1971 earthquake, the damage from surface rupture was considerably less than damage from other causes, such as strong shaking or liquefaction. The next three urban earthquakes, 1987 Whittier Narrows, 1989 Loma Prieta, and 1994 Northridge, were not accompanied by surface rupture at all, yet damage from the last two earthquakes ran into the billions of dollars. But the Chi-Chi, Taiwan Earthquake of September 21, 1999 on a reverse fault was accompanied by many miles of surface rupture in developed areas, and damage was nearly total along the fault rupture, with great loss of life, particularly in its hanging wall close to the fault (Figure 15-2). The surface rupture was on a mapped fault. If Alquist-Priolo had been in effect in Taiwan when these areas were developed, great losses would have been prevented and many lives saved.

The 1989 Loma Prieta Earthquake, with billions of dollars in damage, was not accompanied by surface rupture, so the Alquist-Priolo Act was of no help. It was clear that much of the damage was to buildings in areas that underwent liquefaction and landsliding. As noted in Chapter 9, geological and geotechnical studies are able to identify building sites

Figure 15-2. A test of the Alquist-Priolo Act in Fengyuan City, Taiwan, photographed five months after the September 21, 1999 Chi-Chi Earthquake of M 7.6. During the Chi-Chi Earthquake, the Chelungpu Reverse Fault ruptured across this developed area, producing the scarp visible to the left of the geologist. The cleared area on the hanging wall (left) side of the fault was formerly covered with buildings that were completely destroyed, with loss of life; the remains of these structures were subsequently removed. Damage to buildings on the footwall (far right) and on the hanging wall farther away from the fault was severe, but the buildings were not totally destroyed. If an Alquist-Priolo setback had been in effect prior to development of this area, losses of life and property would have been greatly reduced. Photo by Robert Yeats.

that are vulnerable to earthquake-related ground displacements. To address this hazard, the Seismic Hazard Mapping Act was signed into law in 1990, which requires that not only active faults but earthquake-induced liquefaction and landsliding must be taken into consideration in planning and development decisions.

Maps have been prepared for much of the Los Angeles metropolitan area and for the cities of San Francisco and Oakland, with additional maps being prepared (see the Division Web site at http://www.consrv.ca.gov/). Further guidance is provided in Division of Mines and Geology (1997) and Smith and McKamey (2000). The mapping program is supported by building permit fees supplemented by a grant from FEMA and the Office of Emergency Services. Cities and counties must use these maps to regulate development within areas identified as seismic hazards. Building permits must be withheld until the developer shows that the development plan will mitigate the hazard.

The law is not retroactive, but if a property within a seismic hazard zone is sold, the seller must disclose that fact to the buyer.

Does this cover all hazards? What about faults or folds that are clearly active but are not *well-defined* according to the Alquist-Priolo Act? For example, geotechnical investigations connected with the planned Los Angeles subway revealed a warp on the south side of the Repetto Hills and Elysian Hills in East Los Angeles called the Coyote Pass Escarpment. This is not a well-defined fault, but it would clearly result in damage if it deformed during an earthquake. This hazard is covered under the Seismic Hazard Mapping Act. Response to faults that are not well defined departs from the Alquist-Priolo strategy of *mitigation by avoidance* (don't build on an earthquake fault) to *mitigation by design* (recognize the zone of deformation, then design structures that will survive surface deformation on it, which is the intent of the Seismic Hazard Mapping Act.

The actions taken by the State of California starting in the early 1970s were ground-breaking, even revolutionary. In no state in the United States and in no country in the world, including Japan, has the government taken such steps to mitigate earthquake hazards. Earthquake programs in all other states lagged behind the establishment of a national earthquake program, and for the most part they have been financed by federal grants. California, on the other hand, *preceded* the establishment of a national program by more than four years!

3. Governor's Office of Emergency Services (OES)

The OES is the State's counterpart of FEMA, and federal disaster assistance is transmitted through OES. Like FEMA, the agency started out in civil defense in 1950, when the Soviets were ramping up their nuclear weapons program, and Chinese troops were battling Americans in Korea. By 1956, the agency became more involved in natural disaster operations, and the name was changed from the State Office of Civil Defense to the California Disaster Office. The Emergency Services Act was passed in 1970, and the agency's name was changed to the Governor's Office of Emergency Services.

The OES coordinates the response of state agencies to major disasters in support of local government. These disasters might be major brush fires, winter storms and floods, tsunamis, or earthquakes. They might be dam breaks, nuclear power plant emergencies, or major spills of hazardous materials. The state agencies most commonly called on are the National Guard, Highway Patrol, Department of Forestry and Fire Protection, Conservation Corps, Department of Social Services, Department of Health Services, and the Department of Transportation.

Communications vans and portable satellite units are available to be sent to disaster areas to ensure communications with remote areas as well as major cities where communications have been knocked out by an earthquake. One hundred twenty fire engines are available at fire stations in strategic locations. A warning center is staffed twenty-four hours a day, and daily contact is maintained with the National Warning Center and offices of emergency services located in every county. Regional OES resource centers are maintained in Los Alamitos, Oakland, and Santa Barbara.

OES is responsible for the State Emergency Plan, California's equivalent to the Federal Response Plan. This plan contains the organizational structure of state response to natural and man-made disasters. OES helps local governments and other state agencies in preparing their own emergency preparedness and response plans. A list of publications and videos is provided on the OES Web site at http://www.oes.ca.gov/

The Earthquake Program of OES provides assistance to local and regional governments, businesses, hospitals, schools, human service agencies, community organizations, and individuals in earthquake preparedness. This program began in 1993 by combining the Bay Area Regional Earthquake Preparedness Project (BAREPP) and the Southern California Earthquake Preparedness Project (SCEPP). This program has coordinated, through the Division of Mines and Geology, earthquake scenarios on the Cascadia Subduction Zone, the San Jacinto Fault in southeast California, and the Rodgers Creek Fault in the Bay Area. In April, the Earthquake Program sponsors the state's Earthquake Awareness Month.

4. Seismic Safety Commission

This commission was established by the legislature in 1975 as a state agency to advise the governor, the legislature, and the public on ways to reduce earthquake risk. The Commission manages the California Earthquake Hazard Reduction Program and reviews earthquake-related activities funded by the state. Fifteen of the seventeen commissioners are appointed by the governor, and the other two by the senate and assembly. In 1985, the California Earthquake Hazards Reduction Act charged the Commission with preparing an Earthquake Loss Reduction Plan to reduce earthquake hazards significantly by 2001. The Commission proposes earthquake bills to the legislature and will oppose legislation that would weaken the state's earthquake safety program.

The Commission issues reports on earthquake hazard reduction, including reports on building codes. Lists of publications are available at the Commission's web site at http://www.seismic.ca.gov One of these publications is The Homeowner's Guide to Earthquake Safety. If your house was built before 1960, and you want to sell it, state law requires you to deliver a copy of the Homeowner's Guide to the buyer.

5. Building Codes

One of the most important steps that can be taken by a community in defending itself against earthquakes is upgrading its building codes. Most codes are written such that a structure built under a seismic code should resist a minor earthquake without damage and to resist severe earthquakes without collapse of the building. They establish minimum standards based on average soil conditions. As discussed in Chapter 9, local conditions could generate seismic ground motions that exceed those in the code provisions.

Regulations to reduce property damage and loss of life have been in existence in America since the seventeenth century, when the main concerns were the spread of fire in densely populated New York City. Comprehensive building regulations were introduced in the mid-nineteenth century, and in 1905 the National Board of Fire Underwriters published a model building regulation aimed at fire damage. Because of the cover-up of the role of earthquake damage in the 1906 San Francisco Earthquake (discussed in Part I), nothing was done about extending building regulations to protect against earthquakes.

Building codes start at the local level, and as structural engineers began to recognize that buildings could be constructed to resist earthquakes, the situation began to change. Following the destructive Santa Barbara Earthquake of 1925, Santa Barbara and Palo Alto passed ordinances upgrading their building codes to take earthquakes into account. But it took the much more destructive Long Beach Earthquake of 1933 to produce statewide action, including an upgrade of building codes (discussed in Part I). The legislature passed the Field Act upgrading school construction standards and the Riley Act covering other buildings. Earthquake resistance was added to building codes in Los Angeles County and City, Long Beach, Santa Monica, Beverly Hills, and Pasadena, essentially putting an end to the use of unreinforced brick construction in California. Later, earthquake-resistance standards were applied to bridges, hospitals, and dams. Subsequent upgrades to the building codes, generally triggered by large earthquakes such as the 1971 Sylmar, 1989 Loma Prieta, and 1994 Northridge earthquakes, have produced the highest earthquake-resistant building standards in the United States.

The starting point for building codes in California is the *Uniform Building Code* (UBC), first published by the International Conference of Building Officials with its headquarters in Whittier. All cities and counties in the state are required to adopt the UBC or its equivalent. This model code, upgraded every three years, has as its objective "to provide minimum standards to safeguard life or limb, health, property, and public welfare while regulating and controlling design and construction." Priority is given to protecting the inhabitants of a building over the prevention of damage to the building itself. Building codes represent minimum standards; the owner may well choose to have higher standards than those required by the code. Other model building codes are published by the Building Officials and Code Administrators International, the Southern Building Code Congress International, and the Council of American Building Officials. These organizations have combined to work on an international building code, which is due to be completed in 2000 or 2001.

Two cautions should be made about building codes. The first tradeoff is cost. Upgrading seismic resistance can add up to five percent of the cost of a new building, and for retrofitting, the percentage increase is higher. For a new building, the revised codes set the standard, and the owner must decide whether or not to exceed these standards to get better building performance in an earthquake—a decision similar to obtaining earthquake insurance. For a retrofit, the decision is harder, because of the added cost to a business, or the added cost to taxpayers if a public building is retrofitted. Without better insight into earthquake forecasting than is now available, the owner's decision is a gamble.

The second caution is that upgrading the building code does not automatically make the area safe against earthquakes. New buildings will meet the standard, as will major remodels of buildings. But old buildings that are not remodeled will continue in the building inventory, and when these are unreinforced masonry (URM), they are potential time bombs. The greatest loss of life in the 1971 Sylmar Earthquake was in those buildings at the Veterans Administration Hospital that had not been retrofitted after the 1933 Long Beach Earthquake. Despite the existence of seismic building codes since 1933, there are still buildings constructed under earlier building codes that do not meet modern standards and are subject to collapse. It's important to know the year of construction (or last retrofit) of the building where you work or live.

A law has been passed in California that requires all hospitals to be strengthened against earthquakes by 2004 or be torn down. Cities and counties also are required to inventory their URM buildings and to develop a plan to retrofit them.

The insurance industry, through its Insurance Services Office, has established a system to grade the 454 building code enforcement departments in California on the effectiveness of their building codes, considering the quality of inspection and plan review as well as construction standards. The results of the grading will appear in an insurance publication called the Public Protection Classification Manual, which is read by more than a hundred thousand insurance agents and actuaries. A high grade should lead to discounts on insurance premiums for new construction, similar to discounts based on fire insurance grading systems.

The new 2000 International Building Code takes into consideration the largest-magnitude earthquake expected for a region, more precise shaking criteria, and contour maps developed by the USGS to quantify the seismic hazard, a refinement of the present system of seismic zones 1 through 4.

6. Grading Ordinances and Regulation of Building Sites

Building codes deal with the safety of buildings, but how about the site on which the building is constructed? A good example of a poor building site is the Leaning Tower of Pisa. The tower itself is in good shape, but the soils beneath the building are unable to hold it up, and it has settled differentially, causing it to lean.

A perfectly sound building is unsafe if it's built on a landslide, on a sea cliff subject to wave erosion, on soils subject to liquefaction, or on an active fault. As part of its public safety obligation, a city or county in California must take responsibility for evaluation of the safety of a building site, just as it takes responsibility for the structural integrity of a building. Ordinances passed for this purpose are called *grading ordinances*. Grading, which is one of the first steps in virtually any building project, can include excavation by a bulldozer or backhoe or it might involve placement of fill material to provide a flat surface for building. In either case the natural landscape is altered, and regulation is required to ensure that the alteration of the landscape will not harm residents of other sites—particularly those downhill, in addition to the potential residents or workers in buildings on the site in question.

Grading ordinances call into question the fundamental right of individuals to do with their land whatever they want. This differs from building codes, which might require a better-engineered and better-designed structure to be built for safety reasons but would not prevent some sort of structure from being built on a site. It's difficult for a landowner to accept the fact that the property might contain hidden geologic fatal flaws such as active faults or landslides that could prevent it from being developed at all. A site with a beautiful view over a steep hillslope should not be developed if the steep hillslope providing the view is the scarp of an active fault or a landslide. The site could become unstable because of the actions of the builder or owner, such as heavy use of irrigation sprinklers.

In 1952, the City of Los Angeles adopted the first grading ordinance in the United States and set up a grading section within the Department of Building and Safety. The city was growing out of the lowlands and up into the surrounding hills, and building sites there were found to be subject to major landslides, with extensive property losses.

The grading ordinance was upgraded in 1963 to require both engineering and geologic reports to be submitted, and to require that grading operations be supervised by both a *soils engineer* and an *engineering geologist*. Although responsibilities overlap, the soils engineer or geotechnical engineer deals directly with the strength and bearing capacity of earth materials on which a structure is to be built and on the tendency of a hillslope to slide, and an engineering geologist takes more account of the past geologic history of a building site, including old landslides, evidence of faulting, and the inclination of bedding and fracturing of rock formations on site. Engineers and geologists must be licensed to practice in the state.

In 1972 the State of California passed the Alquist-Priolo Act regulating construction on active faults, and in 1990 the Seismic Hazard Mapping Act regulated construction on zones subject to liquefaction and earthquake-induced landsliding, as discussed above in the section on the Division of Mines and Geology.

The standard reference for grading was Chapter 70 of the Uniform Building Code, written in the form of an ordinance that can be modified to fit the situation in the city or county where it's adopted. In the 1997 edition of the Code, the Grading Code appears in Chapter A-33. The local building official decides which sites pose a potential threat to life and public safety, requiring an evaluation of the site and supervision of grading. For commercial developments, Chapter A-33 provides for both a report by geotechnical and geological consultants employed by the developer and a review of the findings by soils engineers and geologists employed by the city or county for that purpose. The cost of a plan review, like the cost of a building inspection, is borne by the developer in the form of permit fees. A plan reviewer might ask questions such as: Is provision for drainage off the property adequate so that other property owners are not affected? Are cut slopes gentle enough that they would not be expected to fail by landsliding? Is the bearing strength of the soil sufficient to hold up the building? Do potentially active faults cross the property? This is covered by Chapter 16 of the Code, which also contains sample regulations that cover geotechnical tests for liquefaction and ground shaking.

California passed an addition to its Health and Safety Code requiring that all cities and counties adopt the UBC Grading Code or its equivalent. Unfortunately, many cities and counties lack the professional expertise to regulate grading effectively. In addition, implementation of the Grading Code in some communities has been opposed by developers and building contractors as well as a few politically well-connected landowners. However, where the Grading Code has been used, including review by consultants for the city or county, losses related to geologic conditions have dropped by ninety to ninety-five percent. The law works!

California requires property owners or their agents to disclose to prospective buyers the fact that a property is in a seismic hazard zone or an Alquist-Priolo fault zone. The disclosure requirement was added to the Alquist-Priolo law in 1975. Effective March 1, 1998, an amendment to these laws requires disclosure when one of two conditions are met: (1) the seller has actual knowledge that the property is within a seismic hazard zone; or (2) a map that includes the property has been provided to city and county officials by the State Geologist, and a notice has been posted at the offices of the county recorder, county assessor, and county planning agency.

Accompanying the increase in standards for grading is an increase in the number of lawsuits. A landslide or an earthquake can cause a house to be *red-tagged* (meaning that it must be demolished) or *yellow-tagged* (meaning that the occupants may not return until certain repairs have been made). If a landslide destroys or severely damages homes in an approved development, the landowner, the contractor, the engineering and geological firm, the city or county approving the plans, even the bank lending the money for the development can be sued. The plaintiff who loses his million-dollar home to a landslide argues that the city *should have known* that the site was unsafe. Were any of the parties negligent in approving the development? As the standards of practice are raised, so, too, are the conditions under which someone could be found negligent.

A problem is the difference between what can be done—"state of the art"—and what is the standard level of practice in the area. Clearly the standard level of practice is much higher in the Los Angeles and San Francisco metropolitan areas than it is for smaller cities and rural counties, although the "state of the art" is the same in all those areas. Jim Slosson, an engineering-geology consultant and former State Geologist, is the source of what has come to be called Slosson's Law, a corollary to Parkinson's Law: *"The quality of professional work will sink to the lowest level that government will accept."* This applies to building codes as well as grading ordinances.

7. Other State Agencies

The State Department of Insurance licenses and regulates insurance companies and manages a privately financed earthquake insurance plan, the California Earthquake Authority. This plan is discussed in detail in Chapter 11. Caltrans has the responsibility of maintaining the state's highways and bridges, and it funds research in earthquake engineering, particularly the earthquake resistance of bridges and overpasses. Other state agencies are responsible for interacting with the Office of Emergency Services in the event of a major earthquake.

8. Universities

Until the 1960s, most earthquake research in California was done at the universities. At the time of the 1952 Kern County Earthquake, northern California was taken care of by the University of California at Berkeley, and southern California was the responsibility of Caltech, each through its own seismological lab. The first seismograph in California (and one of the first in the world) was installed in the 1880s by an astronomer, Edward S. Holden, who was the first director of the Lick Astronomical Observatory on top of Mt. Hamilton, southeast of San Francisco, and was also the president of the University of California. A seismograph was also built on the University of California campus. The seismographs were set up to record earthquakes that were too small to be felt but might throw telescopes out of alignment. But Holden was also interested in earthquakes for their own sake; he believed that earthquakes might show a mathematical order and periodicity like the motion of planets. To test for periodicity, Holden began publishing a catalog of earthquakes in 1887. Holden, like his colleague Andrew Lawson prior to 1906, was not concerned about the danger posed by earthquakes. Seismographs, like telescopes, were a way to measure natural phenomena.

After the organization of the Seismological Society of America, the University of California added to its network, and at the present time, with support from NEHRP and in coordination with the USGS, it monitors earthquake activity in northern California.

Seismographs were not set up in the Los Angeles area until the 1920s, when Harry Wood of the Carnegie Institution, with the assistance of Charles Richter of Caltech, established a station in Pasadena and other stations in outlying regions. By 1932 the Caltech network consisted of 7 stations, which grew to 220 stations by 1990. A new collaborative project called Trinet—involving Caltech, USGS, and CDMG—is creating a newer network that will enable much quicker identification and characterization of southern California earthquakes, aiming for real-time notification. (As this book goes to press, funding for Trinet has expired and no new sources of money have been located.) The Caltech network included the region east of the Sierra Nevada, but later the northern part of this region became part of a network operated by the University of Nevada Reno. Although operated by the three universities, the networks are largely financed by the federal government.

Stanford University played an early role in conducting earthquake research and in advocating earthquake preparedness, starting with J.C. Branner and Bailey Willis. Following the establishment of a national earthquake program in the 1970s, earthquake research has been conducted at many California universities beside Berkeley, Caltech, and Stanford. Research on earthquake hazards on the northern

California coast is centered at Humboldt State University at Arcata, which has established the Humboldt Earthquake Education Center at the Department of Geology.

The work that is done at universities in seismology, earthquake geology, and earthquake engineering is nearly all funded by the federal government, as described in the previous chapter, and in small part by the State of California and other agencies. Faculty members have testified as private citizens to the state legislature and other commissions about earthquake hazards as part of their public service obligation, but not as official representatives of their universities. The Berkeley and Caltech seismological labs are generally the first to be called after a major earthquake, although in northern California this role is also filled by the Menlo Park office of the USGS.

9. Regional Organizations

The *Western States Seismic Policy Council* (WSSPC) is a partnership of emergency managers and state geoscience organizations to work on earthquake hazard mitigation, earthquake preparedness, emergency response, and recovery. It includes all the mountainous western states, Alaska, Hawaii, and Pacific island territories. Federal agencies that are part of WSSPC include the Department of Transportation, FEMA, NOAA, and USGS.

WSSPC is very much involved in training and technology transfer—in getting the message out to the public. It holds an annual conference, collects publications on earthquake matters produced by its member organizations, and helps find money to work on earthquake research. Its web site is www.wsspc.org

The *Southern California Earthquake Center* (SCEC) was established in 1991 with most of its funding from the National Science Foundation as a Science and Technology Center and from the USGS. The focus of SCEC is on earthquake hazards in southern California, particular its urban areas. SCEC operates from the University of Southern California and is governed by most of the major universities of southern California plus several outside the area with major research projects in the region. SCEC has brought together seismographers, geologists, and engineers to produce a detailed assessment of the earthquake sources of southern California, particularly Los Angeles, and the southern San Andreas Fault, which poses a hazard to southern California cities. One of its major goals is a *master model* of earthquake sources in southern California. A major part of SCEC's charge is outreach: bringing the earthquake hazard to the general public, to primary and secondary schools, and to general education students in colleges and universities. A widely disseminated free publication is *Putting Down Roots in Earthquake Country*, published in 1995 and available from the University of Southern California and several other sources. SCEC's charter ends in 2002, but plans are underway to continue the interdisciplinary working group, possibly at the state level. Its web site is www.scec.org

Another working group in the Pacific Northwest, including northern California, is the *Cascadia Region Earthquake Workgroup* (CREW), focused on mitigation against a Cascadia Subduction Zone earthquake. CREW includes representatives from FEMA; state emergency services agencies; the scientific community represented by USGS, universities, and state geological surveys; and private industry. The involvement of the private sector might be the most important hallmark of CREW. In addition to the expected concerns about loss of life and property, industries in the shadow of the Cascadia Subduction Zone are concerned about loss of market share in the event of a catastrophic earthquake. An example of the loss of market share is provided by the Port of Kobe, Japan, which became inoperable after the 1995 Kobe Earthquake. As a result, other ports in Japan took over the business that had previously gone to Kobe. It's unclear at present whether the Port of Kobe has regained its pre-earthquake level of business. A more focused group is the Redwood Coast Earthquake Study Group, concentrating on earthquake hazards on the northern California coast.

A nonprofit corporation called Consortium of Organizations for Strong-Motion Observation Systems (COSMOS) has been formed to encourage improvement in strong-motion measurements and applications, especially in urbanized areas, and to promote the wide dissemination of strong-motion instrument records after an earthquake. The organization is an outgrowth of discussions among the California Strong Motion Instrumentation Program of the Division of Mines and Geology, the USGS, the Bureau of Reclamation, and the Corps of Engineers. COSMOS has its headquarters at the Pacific Earthquake Engineering Research center at the University of California Berkeley, located at Richmond.

10. A Final Word

The people of California, spurred by disastrous earthquakes in 1933, 1971, 1989, and 1994, have enacted the strongest earthquake laws in the United States, and, indeed, in the world. If a fault is active, you can't build on it. If an area has a tendency to slide during earthquakes, you'll have to do a lot of remedial engineering to place a building on it. And if you're selling a property next to an active fault or within an area with the potential for liquefaction or earthquake-triggered landsliding, you'll have to tell the buyer about the problem.

This is revolutionary land-use legislation. It goes against the so-called inalienable right of a person to do whatever he or she can get away with on his or her own land, because to do otherwise diminishes the value of the land. It states that the value is based not only on a spectacular view but on hidden flaws that the nonspecialist might not be able to recognize, but are just as apparent to a geologist as a brain tumor is to a cancer specialist. Californians have accepted this infringement on their property rights—albeit grudgingly.

California is a pace-setter. If it's popular in California today, then it'll be popular everywhere else tomorrow. Is this true for California's earthquake laws as well?

Maybe not. Oregon, where I live, has upgraded its building codes close to California standards, but its land-use laws are essentially unchanged. On paper, the seller is required to tell a buyer about geological flaws on the property, but loopholes in the law make this requirement unenforceable. The state has made maps of Portland, Salem, and Eugene showing areas of potential liquefaction and landsliding, but no laws require a developer to abide by these maps. The earthquake problem in Oregon is a federal problem; except for tsunamis, the state has provided no money for earthquake hazard reduction, either from building permit fees or the General Fund.

California is the only state with strong earthquake legislation, but a lot of houses still rest on active faults or are perched atop beach cliffs that someday will slide into the sea, or sit on soft ground that will liquefy during an earthquake. But the life span of many California houses is mercifully short, and if we have patience, or luck, these houses will cycle out of the building inventory in a few generations and be replaced by houses that are bolted to their foundations with reinforced cripple walls. If state law is not degraded by future land capitalists, those houses built on the San Andreas Fault and Hayward Fault won't be followed by new houses in the same, precarious places. The San Andreas will emerge from the beach cliffs at Mussel Rock as a green belt, flanked by houses at safe setback distances, a green stripe visible from space merging with the undeveloped hillsides around San Andreas Lake and Crystal Springs Reservoir.

So in seventy or eighty years, if present state laws are allowed to remain in place, the old, unsafe buildings will be replaced, which should make for "earthquake-resistant communities," to borrow a phrase from James Lee Witt, Director of FEMA.

The problem is enforcement. The decisions that count are not made at the federal level nor even in Sacramento, which sets the standards but does not carry them out. These decisions are made by city councils asked to approve a land development, or planning commissions considering a zoning variance, or building inspectors checking out the welds on steel-frame buildings. Just as the "state of practice" drops precipitously at the state line, so also does it drop away from the cities around the Bay Area and metropolitan Los Angeles. Geologists from the Division of Mines and Geology have fanned out across the state to explain the new land-use laws to local governing bodies, only to find that many of them have never heard of the maps or don't know how to use them. The decisions that count are too often driven by a well-connected land developer rather than advice from faraway Sacramento.

Furthermore, pressure to weaken land-use laws will occur if there is a long period without headline-grabbing earthquakes. The landmark Field Act, upgrading school construction standards after the Long Beach Earthquake of 1933, came under immense pressure after World War II, when the remembrance of collapsed school buildings was overwhelmed by the surging postwar economy. The Seismic Safety Commission is a watchdog for such legislation at the state level, but what about zoning decisions in a faraway county or city that has yet to experience a disastrous earthquake?

My hope as I write this book is that the new laws are becoming so woven into the fabric of California life that attempts by developers to weaken them will be resisted—not only by scientists, engineers, and planners who are earthquake professionals, but by informed citizens who have the courage to hold their local elected officials to their responsibilities. Earthquakes are an environmental problem just as surely as logging old-growth forests, heap-leach mining in the back country, or spoiling a beautiful stretch of California coastline or a pristine mountain valley by housing developments. Let's hope we live up to the challenge.

Suggestions for Further Reading

California Division of Mines and Geology and State Mining and Geology Board. 1997. Guidelines for evaluating and mitigating seismic hazards in California. Calif. Div. Mines and Geology Spec. Pub. 117. 74p.

Mileti, D.S. 1999. *Disasters by Design: A Reassessment of Natural Hazards in the United States*. Washington D.C.: National Academy Press. 351p.

Smith, T.C., and B. McKamey. 2000. Summary of outreach activities for California's Seismic Hazards Mapping Program 1996–1998. California Division of Mines and Geology Special Publication 121. 38p. and appendices.

∽ 16 ∽
Preparing for the Next Earthquake

"Five minutes before the party is not the time to learn to dance."

Snoopy, 1982

1. Introduction

We are in denial about earthquakes. Starting with the 1933 Long Beach Earthquake, government officials began to accept the warnings from the scientific community that earthquakes are a major hazard to much of California and that more will arrive in the future. Government has responded by upgrading construction standards and establishing an infrastructure of emergency services down to the county level. Media reports take it as a given that there will be future damaging earthquakes.

Yet if the average Californian were to list the top ten concerns in his or her daily life, earthquakes probably would not make the list.

In terms of public perception, earthquakes might not be all that different from other disasters such as floods or forest fires. Television reports show expensive homes in Malibu burned out by brush fires, or homes flooded out in the Sacramento Delta, but since they own the land on which their former homes stood, people tend to rebuild in the same place, if local government will allow them to do so. In new suburbs of Los Angeles and San Francisco, some are opposed to laws restricting building next to an active fault. Nobody seems to learn anything.

There's the story about sheep grazing at the edge of a field. A wolf comes out of the forest, grabs a sheep, and carries it off. The other sheep scatter and bleat for a few minutes, then continue their grazing. The forest is still there, and the wolf will come back, but the sheep graze on.

So it is with earthquakes. A person living in Ventura, San Bernardino, or San Diego—cities not struck by a damaging earthquake during the time people have been keeping records—simply doesn't believe earthquakes are a problem. Local elected officials don't believe it either. The Northridge Earthquake was a major story in early 1994, but no great urban earthquake has struck since then. Earthquakes have dropped out of the news, and most people have forgotten about them.

It is in light of such public apathy that this chapter is written. You try to organize your household, your neighborhood, and your children's schools, but your efforts might result in your being called Chicken

Little, warning that the sky is falling. If you're serious, you must be determined and patient and have a thick skin. It won't be easy.

2. Getting Your Home Ready

Chapter 12 focused on steps you can take to make your home and its contents more resistant to earthquake damage. This chapter presents ways you can prepare yourself and members of your family to survive an earthquake and to help others survive as well. It's analogous to the fire drills in school or aboard an oceangoing ship. We're pretty sure our school or the ship will not catch fire, but we conduct the fire drills all the same. Fire drills are built into our culture. Earthquake drills are conducted in most schools, but they are often not taken seriously—even by the school officials who conduct them.

What can happen to your house in an earthquake? Shaking could cause a chimney to collapse, plate-glass windows to break, tall pieces of furniture to fall over, or a garage to cave in. Liquefaction or landsliding beneath your foundation could cause your house to move downslope, breaking up as it does so, and snapping underground utility lines. This happened in the Marina District of San Francisco in 1989 and in parts of Granada Hills in 1994. A severe winter storm might result in dozens of landslides, but a large earthquake could result in thousands of landslides, some more than a mile across. If you live on the coast, your house might be in danger of a tsunami, in which case you have only a few minutes to get to high ground, above the tsunami run-up line.

Some steps outlined here are not unique to earthquakes. They would apply if you were marooned by a flood or a landslide that cut off access to your house. But a large earthquake like Northridge or Loma Prieta differs in the large number of people impacted. The 9-1-1 emergency number would be overwhelmed and essentially useless. You could lose your phone service, electric power, water, sewer, and gas for days or weeks. Police and ambulance services would be diverted to the most serious problems such as collapsed apartment buildings or major fires. Access to your house or from your house to the nearest hospital could be cut off by a damaged bridge or a major landslide.

For these reasons, be prepared to survive without assistance or any public utilities (gas, water, sewer, electric power, or phone service) for up to three days. If you are at work, or your children are at school when the earthquake strikes, you should have a plan in place outlining what each member of the family should do. Designate a contact person *outside the potential disaster area* that everyone should contact if your family is separated.

Prepare an inventory of your household possessions and keep it away from your house, in a safe deposit box or with your contact person outside your area. This inventory will be necessary when you submit your insurance claim (Chapter 11).

3. Earthquake Preparedness Kit

Designate a kitchen cabinet or part of a hall closet in your house as the location of an earthquake preparedness kit. Everyone should know where it is and what's in it. Make it easy to reach in a damaged house. (The crawl space in your basement is *not* good, especially if you haven't reinforced your cripple wall.) The kitchen is okay, and so is an unused and cleaned-out garbage can in your garage—unless the garage is prone to collapse due to "soft-story" problems. Many items listed below are handy in *any* emergency—not just an earthquake. (Maybe you did this in the waning days of 1999 in preparation for Y2K!)

First-aid kit, fully equipped, including an instruction manual. Check expiration dates of medicines and replace when necessary. Liquids and glass bottles should be sealed in zip-lock storage bags. Keep your previous prescription glasses here; your prescription might have changed, but the glasses will do in an emergency.

Flashlights, one per person, preferably with alkaline batteries. Replace batteries every year. Keep extra batteries in the package they came in until ready for use. Several large *candles* for each room, together with matches. *Coleman lantern*, with an extra can of gas for it.

Portable radio with spare batteries. If the power is off, this will be your only source of information about what's going on. Your portable phone won't work if your phone service is cut off. Your *cell phone* might work, but heavy phone traffic could make it hard to get through.

Food, in large part what you would take on a camping trip. Granola bars, unsalted nuts, trail mix, and lots of canned goods (fish, fruit, juice, chili, beef stew, beans, spaghetti). Dried fruit, peanut butter, honey (in plastic containers, not glass), powdered or canned milk. We're talking about survival, not gourmet dining, but try to stock with food your family likes. Keep a manual can opener and other cooking and eating utensils separate from those you use every day. If you lose power, eat the food in your freezer first. It will keep for several days if the freezer door is kept shut as much as possible.

Fire extinguishers. Keep one in the bedroom, one in the kitchen, and one in the garage. Attach them firmly to wall studs so they don't shake off. Keep a bucket of sand near your fireplace during the winter, when the fireplace is in frequent use.

Drinking water. You'll need one gallon per person per day for at least three days; more is better. Large plastic containers can be filled with water and stored; change the water once a year. Two-and-one-half-gallon containers are available, but one-gallon containers are easier to carry. Your water heater and toilet tank are water sources, but if the water heater is not strapped and falls over, its glass lining may break, requiring the water to be filtered through a cloth. Empty the water heater by turning off the heater (remove its fuse or shut off its circuit breaker) and its hot-water source, then turn on a hot water faucet and fill containers. Water purification will be necessary. Do not use toilet tank water if the water has been chemically treated to keep the bowl clean (turns blue after flushing). Swimming pool or hot tub water is okay for washing but not for drinking.

Turn off your house water supply at the street to keep sewage from backing up into your water system. Plug bathtub and sink drains.

If you're a backpacker or you travel in underdeveloped countries, you already know about hand-operated water pumps, filters, and purifying tablets. A system called FirstNeed is available at outdoor stores. Iodine purifying tablets make the water taste terrible, but you can add other tablets to neutralize the taste. Store these with your preparedness kit, and use them if there is any doubt about the water, including water from the water heater or toilet tank. You can also use *liquid* bleach in a plastic container, but do *not* use *granular* bleach!

Tools. Keep a hammer, axe, screwdriver, pliers, crowbar, shovel, and Swiss Army knife in your kit, along with work gloves and duct tape. Buy a special wrench to turn off the gas at the source. Keep this at the gas valve, and make sure everyone knows where it is and how to use it. If you smell gas, turn your gas supply off *immediately* (Figure 12-6); the pilot light on your furnace would be enough to catch your house on fire. Don't turn it on again yourself—let a professional do it. Keep a wrench at the water meter to shut off your water at the source.

If your water is shut off, you won't be able to use the bathroom. Use your shovel to dig a hole in your yard for a temporary latrine. Line the hole with a large plastic garbage bag; alternatively, sprinkle with lime after each use (purchase the lime from a hardware store). If you are able to get to your bathroom, you could line the toilet with a small garbage bag, use the toilet, and dispose of the bag.

Camping gear. Keep in one place tents, sleeping bags, tarps, mattresses, ponchos, Coleman stoves and lanterns, and gas to supply them so they are as accessible as your preparedness kit. Picnic plates and cups, plastic spoons, paper napkins, and paper towels should be in your kit.

Other items. Large, zip-lock plastic bags; large and intermediate-size garbage bags with twist ties; toothbrushes and toothpaste; soap; shampoo; face cloths; towels; dish pan and pot; toilet paper; sanitary napkins; shaving items (your electric razor won't work); baby needs; and special medications (especially for elderly people).

Kits for elsewhere. Under your bed, keep a day pack with a flashlight, shoes, work gloves, glasses, car and house keys, and clothes for an emergency. Keep another day pack, along with a fire extinguisher, in the trunk of your car and—if you work in an isolated area—at your workplace.

4. Other Preparations

After a major earthquake, civil authorities will inspect your neighborhood to see whether damage has occurred, and they might determine that your house is dangerous to live in. This is due to fear that the structure might collapse with you inside. If your house is labeled with a *red tag*, you will not be permitted to live in it and the house will have to be torn down. If your house is labeled with a *yellow tag*, you will be ordered to leave and will not be allowed to return until the necessary repairs are made and your house is determined to be safe to live in. Accordingly, you should have ready those items you need if you are forced to leave your home for an extended period of time.

It's nice to have a first-aid kit, but make sure that you and your family know how to use it. Take a first-aid course and a CPR class (lots of reasons to do this, not just earthquake preparedness). You might be called on to help your neighbor, and access to a hospital may be blocked.

5. Neighborhood Plan

Many neighborhoods already have a "neighborhood watch" plan for security. Arrange a meeting once a year to discuss contingency plans in case of an earthquake. Are some of your neighbors handicapped or elderly? Are there small children? Do some of your neighbors have special skills? There are advantages to having a plumber, carpenter, nurse, or doctor for a neighbor. Do each of you know where your neighbors' gas shut-off valves are located? Be prepared to pool your resources. You can make lifelong friends during a major calamity. Your county emergency services coordinator, police department, and Red Cross office will be glad to help you get organized.

The Humboldt County Office of Emergency Services (707-268-2500) has information on forming a Neighborhood Emergency Service Team (NEST) in your neighborhood. These groups of neighbors, members of local organizations, and employees of local businesses, headed by an elected NEST captain, are organized against any disaster—not just an earthquake. For information about establishing a NEST in your neighborhood, contact your county Office of Emergency Services.

6. Your Child's School and Other Buildings You Use

Damaged school buildings were the impetus for the first state law upgrading building standards—the Field Act of 1933. Modern public elementary schools, high schools, and community colleges must meet the seismic safety specifications of the Field Act, and they have held up well in recent earthquakes. The Field Act does not apply to private schools, however. Seismic standards have been upgraded considerably after the Field Act was passed, and you are entitled to ask when the school was built or last remodeled. If the last time was prior to the 1971 Sylmar Earthquake, the Field Act seismic standards might not be enough. In addition, the school might be built on a site subject to liquefaction or landsliding—conditions the Field Act did not address. You also can look at the classroom for heavy bookcases that might topple on children at their desks or light fixtures that might come down on top of them (Figure 13-8).

Your school can take steps that cost little or no money, only time. Work through the PTA to ensure that the school has its own earthquake-preparedness supplies, an evacuation plan, and earthquake drills. School officials may not take earthquake drills seriously. Ask questions about the specifics of staff training and responsibilities. What is the school's plan to release children (or to house them in the school building) after an earthquake? Are hazardous materials stored properly?

Earthquakes seem to pick on universities. The 1989 Loma Prieta Earthquake caused more than $160 million in damage to Stanford University, including the building housing the Department of Geology. The university had previously been damaged severely by the 1906 San Francisco Earthquake; at that time it was a relatively new campus. The 1994 Northridge Earthquake trashed California State University at Northridge—again including the Department of Geology, which was still in temporary quarters two years later. The University of California at Berkeley is crossed by the Hayward Fault and is at risk from a M 7 earthquake in the near future. Seismic retrofit programs have been underway since 1978, with the expenditure of $250 million, but more than one-fourth of usable campus space is labeled "poor" or "very poor" in terms of earthquake resistance. Retrofitting these unsafe buildings over a period of twenty to thirty years will cost at least $1.2 billion.

Let's pray that the earthquake doesn't strike on a Sunday morning. Many cities have large church buildings constructed of unreinforced masonry. In most cases, the churches do not have earthquake insurance, nor do they have the money to bring their buildings up to code.

And how about those historic courthouses, built in the nineteenth century? Lovely to look at, but dangerous to work in. The Klamath County, Oregon, Courthouse was rendered useless after an earthquake of M 6 in 1993.

7. During the Earthquake

The strong shaking *will* stop. For a M 6 to M 7 earthquake, strong shaking will last less than a minute—in most cases less than thirty seconds—but it might seem the longest minute of your life. A subduction-zone earthquake can produce strong shaking of one to four minutes, but it too will stop.

The earthquake mantra is *duck, cover, and hold. Duck* under something such as a table or desk, and *cover* your face and neck with your arms. *Hold* on until the shaking stops. Teach this to your children, and make it part of your own family earthquake drill.

The greatest danger is something collapsing on you. So get under a big desk or table. Stay away from windows, chimneys, or tall pieces of furniture such as a refrigerator or china cabinet. Standing in a doorway is not a good option, unless you happen to live in an adobe house in a third-world country. The doorway might be in a wall that isn't braced against shear, and both wall and doorway could collapse, sandwiching you in between. Do not run outside, because you might be hit by debris or glass falling from the building.

If you can't get under something, sit or lie down with your feet and hands against a wall. Turn away from glass windows or mirrors. Don't hold or pick up your dog or cat; it will be so confused that it might bite you. Stay where you are until the strong shaking stops. If a vase is about to topple from a table, don't try to catch it.

Should you be at a stadium or theater, cover your head with your coat and stay where you are. Do not rush to the exits. The behavior of the California crowd when the Loma Prieta Earthquake struck at the beginning of the World Series game in October 1989 was exemplary. There was no panic, and people did not trample over others trying to get out of the ball park. There were no injuries. The important thing to remember is that there is no reason to leave. After the shaking stops, there will be plenty of time to head for the exits.

At work, get away from tall, heavy furniture or get under your desk. The fire sprinklers might come on. Stand against an inside wall. If you're in a tall building, do not try to use the elevator. If the lights go out, just stay where you are.

If you're in a wheelchair, lock your wheels and stay where you are. If you're out in the open, move only if you're close to a building where debris could fall on you.

Should you be outside in a business district with tall buildings, get as far away as you can from the buildings, where plate glass could shatter and masonry parapets could come crashing down on you. Stay away from tall trees. Watch for downed power lines.

If you're in your vehicle (with seat belt fastened), pull over to the side of the road. Do not stop under an overpass or on a bridge. Watch for places where sections of roadway might have dropped. Clarence Wayne Dean, a California Highway Patrol officer on his way to work on his motorcycle, drove off the end of a freeway overpass that had collapsed from the Northridge Earthquake, killing him. If wires fall on your car, stay in your car, roll up the windows, and wait for someone to help you. You might be waiting a long time, but the alternative—electrocution—makes the wait a safer if more boring choice.

8. After the Earthquake

Look for fires in your own home and the homes of your neighbors. Look out for downed power lines. Has anyone been injured? Is your house damaged enough to require it to be evacuated? Consider your chimney as a threat to your life until you have assured yourself that it's undamaged. Check for gas leaks, and if you smell gas, turn off the main gas valve to your house, which will extinguish all your pilot lights.

In case of a fire, try to put it out with your fire extinguisher or your bucket of sand. The most likely place for a fire is your wood stove if it has turned over. You have a few minutes to put the fire out. If the fire gets away from you, get everybody out of the house.

An earthquake might cause electric and telephone lines to snap. Even if you have no power, do not touch any downed power lines.

This is not the time to get in your car and try to drive around town looking at the damage. Roads will be clogged, making life tough for emergency vehicles. Stay where you are and turn on your portable radio. You'll be given status reports and told what to do and what not to do. If you're told to evacuate your neighborhood, do so. You will be told where to go. Do not decide on your own that you can tough it out where you are. Lock your house, unless it's too damaged to do so, to protect against looters.

9. Aftershocks or a Foreshock?

Crustal earthquakes and subduction-zone earthquakes have many aftershocks, and they will cause a lot of alarm. In a large earthquake, aftershocks will continue for months and even years after the main event. Many of these will be felt, and some can cause damage to already weakened buildings. This is one of the reasons you might be asked to leave your house. Though still standing after the main earthquake, it could be so weakened that it might not survive a large aftershock. Warn your family members that there will be aftershocks.

However, there is always the possibility that the earthquake you just experienced is a foreshock to an even larger one. The great 1857 Earthquake on the San Andreas Fault of M 7.9 was preceded by a foreshock of about M 6 at Parkfield. The Chinese have based their successful earthquake predictions on foreshocks—in some cases many foreshocks. Normal-fault earthquakes, occurring in crustal regions that are being extended or pulled apart, such as the Basin and Range of Nevada and eastern California, are more likely to have foreshocks.

10. Special Problems with Tsunamis

If you live on the coast, you will have the same problems everybody else has with shaking and unstable ground. But you'll have an additional problem: the threat of inundation from a large wave from the ocean.

In the case of a distant tsunami, such as the one that originated in Alaska and struck Crescent City in 1964, a warning will be issued by the Tsunami Warning Center in Alaska, including an expected arrival time of the tsunami. You will have time to evacuate to high ground. It's critical that you have a portable radio turned on to listen for tsunami warning updates. Most of the people who got into trouble in the Easter weekend tsunami of 1964 were just enjoying a normal spring holiday, without enough concern for events in the rest of the world to keep up with the news. With satellite communication and tsunami warning centers throughout much of the Pacific, the warning of a distant tsunami should be reliable, but you have to have your radio on to hear it. A coastal community is well advised to have a siren to warn those who aren't tuned in to their radio or television. This siren should be maintained by emergency-services or fire department personnel.

In the case of an earthquake on the Cascadia Subduction Zone, or on an offshore structure such as the Oak Ridge Fault in the Santa Barbara Channel, you'll have a much shorter time to react—twenty minutes or less. For this reason, if your area is subjected to very strong shaking lasting twenty seconds or more, don't wait for a tsunami warning. Leave immediately for high ground and stay there for an hour or so until you're sure there is no local tsunami. Here there could be false alarms, and some people recommend that you *not* leave. Coastal communities were strongly shaken by the 1906 San Francisco, 1989 Loma Prieta, and 1994 Northridge earthquakes, but there was no tsunami. The best solution is for local emergency management officials to develop a warning system in near-real time to determine whether an earthquake is likely to generate a tsunami or not.

There is no direct correlation between tsunami height and magnitude of the earthquake. A subduction-zone earthquake off the Pacific coast of Nicaragua on September 2, 1992 generated an unusually large tsunami for the size of the earthquake. It was found later that fault rupture was much closer to the surface, and fault motion took place much more slowly than for most subduction-zone earthquakes. In Papua New Guinea, coastal villagers were swept away by a tsunami generated by a landslide and by sea floor deformation. Earthquakes like this are sometimes called *tsunami earthquakes*; the tsunami is much more extreme than the seismic shaking would predict.

The other problem in coping with tsunamis from a distant source is the period of the waves. Frequently, the first wave is not the largest one. The people of Crescent City, California found this out the hard way. The first and second waves were small and caused little damage and people returned to the shoreline, only to be struck by much larger waves that crashed through the town.

Unlike ordinary storm waves, the period of a tsunami wave can be as long as an hour. So when the first wave rushes up and then recedes, for the next half hour or so you will notice only the ordinary surf. But don't think the tsunami is over. Wait at least two hours before you return. And just as a tsunami rises higher than ordinary waves, causing great damage, the tsunami also causes the water to recede much farther out to sea, exposing ocean floor not ordinarily seen even at the lowest tides. The temptation to rush to the beach at that time could be fatal.

11. Psychological Issues

Children are especially traumatized by earthquakes. Familiar surroundings—everything that is supposed to stay put in their lives—suddenly move, are damaged, or become a threat. Children might have to leave home for an extended period of time. They will fear that the shaking and destruction will get worse, or will happen again and again.

Assuring the physical safety of your child is only the first step. Include the child in all your activities, keep talking, and encourage the child to talk out fears. It might be necessary for your child to sleep with you for a few days until things return, more or less, to normal. Plenty of reassurance and just being present will help in overcoming your child's fears after an earthquake. Encourage the school to plan group activities that relate to psychological recovery from an earthquake.

Elderly or disabled persons also might feel a sense of helplessness and fear due to an earthquake. Some individuals of any age are prone to "disaster syndrome." This illness might not come on immediately after the disaster, but it builds up over days and weeks, with evidence of the disaster everywhere and with the telling and retelling of the stories of the event. In severe cases, these people will need counseling and might need to leave the area until they have recovered.

Suggestions for Further Reading

American Red Cross. 1985. The emergency survival handbook. Available from you local Red Cross office.

Lafferty and Associates, Inc. 1989. Earthquake preparedness—for office, home, family, and community. P.O. Box 1026, La Canada, CA 91012.

Morgan, L. 1993. Earthquake survival manual. Seattle: Epicenter Press. 160p.

National Science Teachers Association. 1988. Earthquakes: A teacher's guide for K–6 grades. NSTA Publications, 1742 Connecticut Ave. NW, Washington, DC 20009.

Seismic Safety Commission. 1992. The Homeowner's Guide to Earthquake Safety. SSC 92-01. 28p.

Yanev, P. 1974. *Peace of Mind in Earthquake Country: How to Save your Home and Life.* San Francisco: Chronicle Books.

∽ 17 ∽
An Uncertain Appointment with a Restless Earth

"In its relation to man, an earthquake is a cause. In its relation to the Earth, it is chiefly an incidental effect of an incidental effect."

G.K. Gilbert, 1912,
preface to U.S. Geological Survey Professional Paper 69

A very large earthquake will strike the San Andreas Fault! This is more acceptable in a geologic time frame of thousands of years, because the evidence is strong that the locked sections of the San Andreas Fault are visited by great earthquakes every few centuries. The last one was in 1906, nearly one hundred years ago. Because of much smaller earthquakes in 1933, 1971, 1989, and 1994, the structural engineering community has seen to it that building codes have been upgraded, resulting in much higher safety standards for new buildings than was the case a few decades ago. The governor of California would agree that there is an earthquake problem. Earthquake drills are conducted in schools, and partnerships are building between government and private industry in taking steps to deal with the earthquake hazard.

Yet there is a feeling of unreality about it all, a feeling extending even to those whose careers are in earthquake studies and preparedness. For example, I know that the place where I live and work has a potential for earthquakes, yet I have not taken all the steps called for in Chapters 12 and 16 to safeguard my home and family against earthquakes. I asked a friend of mine, a well-known seismologist, whether he had earthquake insurance. He hung his head sheepishly and replied, "No."

I had my own experience with an earthquake in 1978 in Mexico City, where my friend Chuck Denham and I were sitting in the bar of a small hotel, planning an ascent of Mount Popocatépetl. We were having a beer at nine o'clock in the morning because we didn't trust the water, and we didn't want to get sick halfway up the mountain.

Out of the corner of my eye I noticed a chandelier start to sway. At first I thought I was imagining things, but then I gained enough confidence in my senses to say something to Chuck. At that instant, the first strong waves struck. Glasses and bottles toppled from the bar, chairs scraped back, and people began to yell in Spanish. The entire building began to rumble, like the noise of a train. *Earthquake*, I thought.

The movement of the chandelier registered the P wave, and the strong shaking marked the S wave and the surface waves.

Despite all my wisdom about what to do in an earthquake, Chuck and I ran outside. I knew that it was the wrong thing to do, but rationality fled with the strong shaking. Fortunately, we were not bombarded by masonry or plate glass.

The scene in the street was surreal. The hotel was built very close to neighboring buildings, and each vibrated independently of the others so that their walls bounced together, like hands clapping. We waited for pieces of the building to fall off into the street, realizing at that instant how stupid it was for us to have run outside. Light poles waved back and forth. Parked cars rolled forward to hit the car in front, then backward to hit the car behind. The ground seemed like a thin sheet of plywood, bucking up and down, making it difficult to stand.

Then it was over. A siren wailed in the distance; otherwise it was deathly quiet. The buildings had not collapsed where we were, although we learned later that lives had been lost in other parts of the city.

Although aftershocks continued throughout the day, the whole experience seemed unreal, as though we had seen a UFO or heard a ghost in the attic. To this day, I find it hard to believe that the earthquake actually happened, even though every part of the experience is as vivid today as it was two decades ago. It was like a bad dream.

Perhaps this is our problem about earthquakes. An earthquake is an act of devastation, like the bombing of the World Trade Center, which happens, causes great damage and loss of life, and then is over. It's difficult for us to recognize this act of devastation as part of a continuum of Earth processes, of plate tectonics, of the raising of the San Gabriel Mountains and downwarp of the San Joaquin Valley.

The shaking of the Earth, a normal process to a geologist, is thought of as a bizarre aberration by everyone else—and perhaps even by geologists at the gut level, despite the knowledge gained by space satellites and seismographs. It is what scientists *feel* as opposed to what they *know*. Most people have only the feeling of unreality that an earthquake (or even the expectation of an earthquake) brings. An earthquake is so "unnatural" that it is almost impossible to believe, even when a person has experienced one.

One could describe this book as a morality play: the scientist points out the earthquake hazard to the public official, who refuses to take action, either through ignorance or greed. Taxpayers and their elected representatives refuse to pay for retrofit of buildings, living for today and gambling that they will be long gone and out of the game before the earthquake arrives to cash in its chips.

Our cholesterol level or our blood pressure is too high, or we smoke too much. But our personal feeling is that heart attacks, strokes, and cancer will always happen to the other guy. So it is with earthquakes. Even though an earthquake strikes a blow to Northridge or San Francisco, it's unbelievable that an even larger earthquake might strike San Bernardino or Los Angeles. It can't happen here.

Confronting the earthquake threat might be similar to visualizing the U.S. national debt. The debt is in the trillions of dollars, and our children will be the ones that have to deal with it. But this threat is so unreal that, like earthquakes, we put it out of our mind and allow our politicians to continue spending money rather than pay off the debt.

When Nikita Khrushchev banged his shoe on a table at the United Nations and said about the Soviet Union, "We will bury you," there was a great media outcry, and many people began to build bomb shelters. After a while, though, the bomb shelter craze passed, even though the threat of nuclear annihilation increased. It didn't seem real, and then, when the Soviet Union collapsed, it turned out that it hadn't mattered after all. We ignored the nuclear threat, and for the most part it went away.

Surely there is a middle path, and perhaps we are taking it. The upgrading of building codes and grading standards is an encouraging response of government to the earthquake problem. When the next earthquake strikes, I want to be in a building constructed under modern building codes rather than in an older building constructed under the weak codes of an earlier day. In a few generations, the older, unreinforced masonry buildings will be gone, and if an earthquake does not arrive beforehand, it might have proven sufficient.

The pressure needs to be kept on local, state, and national governments to protect their citizens against earthquakes, just as we now require protection against fires and windstorms. We must be sure that regional economies do not collapse and insurance companies are not forced out of business in the event of a great San Andreas Fault earthquake. Nuclear power plants, dams, hospitals, and government command centers must be able to operate after a major earthquake.

And finally, research must continue into the sources of earthquakes, just as we must continue to support research toward a cure for AIDS or for cancer. The Japanese took the Kobe Earthquake as a wake-up call, and they greatly boosted their efforts in preparedness and in research. Americans have not done the same, perhaps because the national command centers and population centers in the United States are on the East Coast, whereas the larger danger is on the West Coast.

To be ready for our uncertain appointment with the next earthquake, we as taxpayers and voters need to keep the earthquake issue high on the list of priorities of our elected officials and our neighbors. A politician who fails to act must pay a political price.

The effort starts with you and me.

∾ Appendix A ∾
Historical Earthquakes in California

Date	M	Name	Fault	Comments
Jan. 26, 1700	9	Cascadia	Subduction Zone	Tsunami in Japan; paleoseis evidence N. CA to Canada
Jul. 28, 1769	6	Santa Ana R.	?	Portolá expedition
Oct. 1800	?	San Juan Bautista	San Andreas Fault?	San Juan Bautista Mission destroyed
Nov. 22, 1800	6.5?	?	?	San Diego, San Juan Capistrano missions damaged
Dec. 8, 1812	7	San Juan Capistrano	San Andreas Fault	Surface faulting on San Andreas Fault at Wrightwood; 40 killed
Dec. 21, 1812	7	Santa Barbara	Offshore fault?	Epicenter offshore, tsunami at Santa Barbara, damage at Santa Maria
Jun. 10, 1836	6.8	Haywards	Hayward Fault?	Damage from San Pablo to Mission San Jose
Jun. 1838	7	San Francisco	San Andreas Fault	Damage from Santa Clara to San Francisco
Nov. 29, 1852	6.5	Fort Yuma	?	Epicenter 25–30 miles SE Yuma; mud volcano; steam eruption
Jul. 11, 1855	6?	Los Angeles	?	
Jan. 9, 1857	7.9	Fort Tejon	San Andreas Fault	200 mi. surface rupture; preceded by foreshock at ?Parkfield
Nov. 26, 1858	6.25	San Jose	?	
Dec. 16, 1858	6	San Bernardino	?	
Mar. 15, 1860	7	Pyramid Lake	?	Slides between Pyramid Lake and Carson City, NV
Jul. 4, 1861	5.8	San Ramon	Calaveras Fault	8 mi. surface rupture
May 27, 1862	6	San Diego	?	Probably offshore near San Diego
Feb. 26, 1864	6	South Bay Area	?	Southern Santa Cruz Mountains
Oct. 8, 1865	6.5	San Jose	?	Intensity IX at New Almaden; VIII at San Jose

Date	M	Name	Fault	Comments
Jul. 15, 1866	6		?	Western San Joaquin Valley
May 30, 1868	6	Virginia City	?	Western Nevada
Oct. 21, 1868	7.1	Haywards	Hayward Fault (S?)	30 mi. surface rupture; 30 killed; damage in San Leandro
Dec. 27, 1869	6.7	W. Nevada	Olinghouse Fault	Damage at Virginia City and Washoe City
Feb. 17, 1870	6	Los Gatos	?	
Mar. 2, 1871	6	C. Mendocino	?	Intensity VIII at Mattole
Mar. 26, 1872	7.7	Owens Valley	Owens Valley Fault	60 miles of surface rupture; 27 dead at Lone Pine
Nov. 23, 1873	6.7	Smith R.	Gorda slab earthquake?	Near California-Oregon border; damage to Crescent City
Jan. 24, 1875	6	Honey Lake	?	NE California
Nov. 15, 1875	6.25	Imperial Valley	?	
May 9, 1878	7	Punta Gorda	Mendocino F.Z.?	Chimneys collapsed in Petrolia; felt at Pt. Arena
Apr. 10, 1881	5.9	Parkfield?	San Andreas Fault	Minor damage from Stockton to Hollister
Sep. 5, 1883	6.0	Santa Barbara	?	Damage at Santa Barbara and Los Alamos
Mar. 26, 1884	6	Santa Cruz Mts	?	Santa Cruz Mountains
Apr. 12, 1885	6.2	Central CA	?	Felt in Sacramento, San Joaquin valleys, Coast Ra., Sierra foothills
Jun. 3, 1887	6.3	Genoa, NV	?	Intensity VIII at Genoa, damage at Carson City
Apr. 29, 1888	6	Mohawk Valley	?	
May 19, 1889	6.0	Antioch	?	Centered east of Bay Area; intensity VIII at Collinsville
Jun. 20, 1889	6	Susanville	?	Maximum intensity VII
Feb. 9, 1890	6.3	So. CA	San Jacinto, Elsinore F.?	Felt in Los Angeles, San Diego, Yuma, AZ
Apr. 24, 1890	6.0	SE Bay Area	San Andreas Fault?	5 mi. surface rupture? at Pajaro River at a railroad bridge
Jul. 25, 1890	6.0	Ferndale	?	Damage at Ferndale and Petrolia
Jul. 30, 1891	6	Colorado R.	?	Colorado River delta region

Date	M	Name	Fault	Comments
Feb. 24, 1892	7.0	Laguna Salada	Laguna Salada Fault	In Baja Calif. near border; more than 13 mi. surface rupture
Apr. 19, 1892	6.5	Vacaville	blind thrust?	Highest intensity between Vacaville and Winters
Apr. 21, 1892	6.2	Vacaville	blind thrust?	Same intensity distribution as Apr. 19 shock
May 28, 1892	6.3	SE CA	San Jacinto or Elsinore Fault?	Strongly felt from Los Angeles to Yuma
Jul. 30, 1894	6	Inland Emp.		Lytle Creek region
Sep. 30, 1894	6.5	Cape Mendocino	Mendocino Fracture Zone?	Intensity VII in S. Humboldt County
Aug. 17, 1896	6	?		Southeast Sierra Nevada region
Jun. 20, 1897	6.2	Gilroy	Calaveras Fault?	Intensity VIII, Gilroy, San Felipe; surface rupture Calaveras F.?
Mar. 31, 1898	6.2	Mare Island	?	Intensity VIII
Apr. 15, 1898	6.8	Mendocino	?	Mendocino coast from Ft. Bragg to Greenwood; intensity to IX
Apr. 16, 1899	6.4	Arcata	Gorda Plate?	Offshore Arcata; damage to Eureka
Jul. 22, 1899	6.4	Inland Empire	?	Damaging from Orange County to Barstow
Dec. 25, 1899	6.4	Hemet	San Jacinto Fault?	Intensity of VIII, San Jacinto and Hemet; 6 deaths
Mar. 2, 1901	6	Parkfield	San Andreas Fault	
Sep. 3, 1903	6	Wonder, NV	?	In Wonder Mining District
Apr. 18, 1906	7.9	San Francisco	San Andreas Fault	More than 360 miles of surface rupture; several thousand killed
Apr. 19, 1906	6.2	Imperial Valley	?	
Oct. 29, 1909	6.4	W. of Scotia	?	Damage in Rio Dell, Rohnerville, and Upper Mattole
Mar. 19, 1910	6	Petrolia	?	Offshore Petrolia
May 15, 1910	6	Temescal Valley	Elsinore Fault	9 mi. surface rupture
Oct. 3, 1915	7.6	Pleasant Valley	4 normal faults	In western Nevada S. of Winnemucca; 37 mi. surface rupture

Date	M	Name	Fault	Comments
Nov. 21, 1915	7.1	Volcano L.	Cerro Prieto Fault?	Mud volcano steam eruption near Cerro Prieto Fault, Baja Calif.
Dec. 31, 1915	6.2–6.5	Cape Mendocino	?	Offshore Cape Mendocino
Apr. 21, 1918	6.9	Hemet	San Jacinto Fault	Damage to Hemet and San Jacinto
Jul. 15, 1918	6–6.5	Arcata	?	Offshore Arcata
Jan. 26, 1922	6	Cape Mendocino	Mendocino Fracture Zone?	Offshore Cape Mendocino
Jan. 31, 1922	7.3–7.6	W. of Arcata	Gorda Plate	37 mi. W of Arcata
Mar. 10, 1922	6.5	Cholame	San Andreas Fault	
Jan. 22, 1923	6.5–7.3	Cape Mendocino	Mendocino Fracture Zone	Damage at Petrolia
Jun. 4, 1925	6	Orick	?	Offshore W. of Orick
Jun. 29, 1925	6.4	Santa Barbara	?	Damage in Santa Barbara, 12 killed
Dec. 10, 1926	6	W. of Eureka	Gorda Plate	80 mi. W of Eureka
Nov. 4, 1927	7	Lompoc	Hosgri Fault or thrust?	Offshore; tsunami runup 5–6 ft.
Jun. 6, 1932	6.4	Arcata	?	One death at Arcata; damage at Eureka
Dec. 21, 1932	7.2	Cedar Mtn.	largely strike slip	Back country E of Gabbs and Mina, Nevada
Mar. 11, 1933	6.4	Long Beach	Newport-Inglewood Fault	Epicenter off Newport Beach; 115 killed; damage to schools
Jan. 30, 1934	6.3	Excelsior Mt.	?	Mineral County, NV
Jun. 7, 1934	6	Parkfield	San Andreas Fault	Surface rupture reported
Jul. 6, 1934	6.5	W. of Trinidad	Gorda Plate	56 mi. W of Trinidad
Dec. 30, 1934	6.5	Cerro Prieto	Cerro Prieto Fault	Northern Gulf of California, Mexico
Dec. 31, 1934	7.1	Cerro Prieto	Cerro Prieto Fault	60 mi. of surface rupture on Cerro Prieto Fault; horiz. disp. >12 feet

Date	M	Name	Fault	Comments
May 19, 1940	7.1	Imperial V.	Imperial Fault	40 mi. surface rupture; up to 18 feet horizontal displacement
Feb. 9, 1941	6.6	NW. C. Mend.	?	60 mi. W of Eureka
May 13, 1941	6	Offshore Cape Mendocino	?	Offshore Cape Mendocino
Oct. 2, 1941	6.4	NW. Cape Mendocino	?	30 mi. W of Cape Mendocino
May 19, 1945	6.2	Off C. Mend.	?	Offshore Cape Mendocino
Apr. 10, 1947	6.2	Manix	Manix Fault	First earthquake in 20th century Eastern California Shear Zone sequence
Dec. 14, 1950	5.6	Honey Lake Valley	Fort Sage Fault	NE California Basin and Range; surface rupture
Oct. 8, 1951	5.8–6	Offshore Cape Mendocino	Mendocino Fracture Zone	Offshore 10 mi. W of Petrolia, 6 mi. W of Punta Gorda
Jul. 21, 1952	7.5	Kern County	White Wolf Fault	12 dead, 2 more in an aftershock; $50 million damage; 20 mi. rupture
Jul. 6, 1954	6.3	Rainbow Mt.	Rainbow Mt. Fault	SE edge of Carson Sink, Nevada; 11 mi. surface rupture
Aug. 24, 1954	7.1	Stillwater	Rainbow Mt. Fault	Stillwater Marsh, Nevada; 23 mi. surface rupture
Nov. 25, 1954	6.5	Offshore Cape Mendocino	Mendocino Fracture Zone	65 mi. W of Punta Gorda
Dec. 16, 1954	7.2	Fairview Pk.	Fairview Pk. Fault	Fairview Peak, Nevada; 42 miles of surface rupture
Dec. 16, 1954	7.1	Dixie Valley	Dixie Valley Fault	E. range front of Stillwater Range, Nevada; 28 mi. surface rupture
Dec. 21, 1954	6.6	Crustal	Mad River Fault?	12 mi. NE Arcata; $12 million damage; one death
Feb. 9, 1956	6.8	N. Baja Calif.	San Miguel Fault	12 miles surface rupture
Oct. 11, 1956	6	Offshore Cape Mendocino	?	Offshore NW of Cape Mendocino; slight damage in Ferndale
Aug. 9, 1960	6.0 –6.2	Offshore Cape Mendocino	?	Felt in southern Oregon to San Francisco

Date	M	Name	Fault	Comments
Jun. 28, 1966	6.4	Parkfield	San Andreas Fault	23 mi. surface rupture; looked like 1934 earthquake
Apr. 9, 1968	6.5	Borrego Mtn.	Coyote Creek	Part of San Jacinto Fault Zone; first paleoseismology trench
Feb. 9, 1971	6.7	Sylmar	San Fernando Fault	10 mi. surface rupture led to Alquist-Priolo Act; 64 killed
May 31, 1975	5.2	Galway Lake	Galway Lake Fault	4 mi. surface rupture; Eastern California Shear Zone
Aug. 1, 1975	5.7	Oroville	Cleveland Hill Fault	Probably induced by filling of Lake Oroville
Nov. 26, 1976	6.3	NW of Eureka	Gorda Plate	93 mi. NW of Eureka
Aug. 13, 1978	4.6	Stephens Pass	Stephens Pass Fault	More than a mile of surface rupture; within Cascade Range
Mar. 15, 1979	5.6	Homestead Valley	Homestead Valley Fault	2 mi. surface rupture; Eastern California Shear Zone
Aug. 6, 1979	5.9	Coyote Lake	Calaveras Fault	9 mi. surface rupture
Oct. 15, 1979	6.4	Imperial Val.	Imperial Fault	19 mi. surface rupture on part of fault that broke in 1940
Jan. 24, 1980	5.6	Livermore V.	Greenville Fault	4 mi. surface rupture
May 25,1980	6.1	Mammoth L.	Hilton Creek Fault	12 mi. surface rupture, probably secondary; largest of 3 earthquakes
Nov. 8, 1980	7.4	W. of Trinidad	Gorda Plate	30 mi. W of Trinidad; $1.75 million damage; collapsed bridge
Apr. 26, 1981	5.6	Westmorland	Imperial Fault	11 mi. surface rupture; same amount on Superstition Hills Fault
Oct. 1, 1982	5.2	Little Lake	Little Lake Fault	4 mi. surface rupture
May 2, 1983	6.7	Coalinga	Blind thrust	Growth of Coalinga Anticline in Coast Ranges
Sep. 10, 1984	6.6	Gorda Plate	Gorda Plate	166 mi. W of Eureka
Aug. 4, 1985	5.9	Avenal	Blind thrust	Growth of North Kettleman Hills Anticline in Coast Ranges

Date	M	Name	Fault	Comments
Jul. 8, 1986	6	North Palm Springs	Banning Fault	Part of San Andreas Fault; 5 mi. surface rupture
Jul. 21, 1986	6.2	Chalfant Valley	White Mtns. Fault	6 mi. surface rupture on range-front fault of White Mtns.
Oct. 1, 1987	5.9	Whittier Narrows	blind thrust	Uplift of anticlines in East Los Angeles
Nov. 24, 1987	6.2	Elmore Ranch	Elmore Ranch Fault	Left-lateral surface faulting; foreshock to Superstition Hills Eq.
Nov. 24, 1987	6.6	Superstition Hills	Superstition Hills Fault	Right-lateral surface faulting; part of San Jacinto Fault System
Oct. 17, 1989	6.9	Loma Prieta	near San Andreas Fault	Oblique-reverse fault next to San Andreas F.; no primary surface rupture
Jul. 13, 1991	6.7–6.9	Gorda Plate	Gorda Plate	Offshore 50 mi. WNW of Crescent City
Aug. 16, 1991	5.9–6.3	Gorda Plate	Gorda Plate	Offshore 62 mi. W of Crescent City
Aug. 17, 1991	6–6.2	Honeydew	Crustal	Chimney, foundation damage; landslides
Aug. 17, 1991	6.9–7.1	Gorda Plate	Gorda Plate	Offshore 62 mi. W of Crescent City
Apr. 22, 1992	6.1	Joshua Tree	E. California Shear Zone	N. of San Andreas Fault; no surface rupture
Apr. 25, 1992	7.1	Cape Mendocino	Cascadia Subduction Zone Gorda Plate	5 mi. N of Petrolia, tsunami, coastal uplift, $48 million damage
Apr. 26, 1992	6	Scotia	Gorda Plate	30 mi. WNW of Petrolia; Scotia Shopping Center destroyed
Jun. 28, 1992	7.3	Landers	E. California Shear Zone	Johnson Valley, Homestead Valley, Emerson, Camp Rock Faults
Jun. 28, 1992	6.2	Big Bear	?	Left lateral fault beneath San Bernardino Mountains
Jun. 28, 1992	5.6	Little Skull Mountain	?	Largest earthquake in Nevada Test Site in more than a century

Date	M	Name	Fault	Comments
Apr. 26, 1993	6.5	W. of Petrolia	Gorda Plate	15 mi. W of Petrolia
May 17, 1993	6.2	Eureka Valley	?	In southeastern Sierra Nevada
Sep. 20, 1993	6	Klamath Falls	unnamed	W. boundary fault of Klamath Lakes, Oregon, graben; no surface break
Jan. 17, 1994	6.7	Northridge	Northridge Fault	Blind E. projection of Oak Ridge Fault
Sep. 1, 1994	7	Cape Mendocino	Mendocino F.Z.	85 mi. W. of Cape Mendocino
Sep. 20, 1995	5.8	Ridgecrest	Airport Lake Fault	Largest of 2 earthquakes to strike China Lake area; 1.5 mi. surface break
Oct. 16, 1999	7.1	Hector Mine	Lavic L., Bullion F.	In Mojave Desert NE of Eastern California Shear Zone; surface rupture
Sep. 3, 2000	5.2	Yountville	unnamed fault	25 injured, 1 critically; $50 million damage

⇜ Appendix B ⇝
Glossary

acceleration—Rate of increase in speed of an object.

accelerometer—A seismograph for measuring change in ground speed (motion) with time.

active fault—A fault along which there is recurrent movement, which is usually indicated by small, periodic displacements or seismic activity.

active tectonics—Tectonic movements that are expected to occur within a future time span of concern to society.

aftershock—Smaller earthquakes following the largest earthquake and in the same general area.

amplitude—Maximum height of a wave crest or depth of a wave trough.

anticline—A fold, convex upward, whose core contains the older rocks.

asperity—Roughness on the fault surface subject to slip. Region of high shear strength on the fault surface.

asthenosphere—The layer or shell of the Earth below the lithosphere, which is weak and in which isostatic adjustment take place, magmas might be generated, and seismic waves are strongly attenuated.

attenuation—The reduction in amplitude of a wave with time or distance.

basalt—A general term for dark-colored igneous rocks, commonly extrusive but locally intrusive (e.g., as dikes), composed chiefly of feldspar and pyroxene. The principal constituent of oceanic crust, which includes gabbro, the coarse-grained equivalent of basalt.

base isolation—A process of foundation construction whereby forces from the ground are not transmitted upward into the building.

bathymetry—Topography of the sea floor; measuring depths in the sea.

blind fault—A fault that does not break the surface, but can be expressed at the surface as a fold or broad warp.

body wave—A seismic wave that travels through the interior of the Earth.

brittle—1. Said of a rock that fractures at less than three to five percent deformation or strain. 2. In structural engineering, describes a building that is unable to deform extensively without collapsing.

capable fault—A fault along which it is mechanically feasible for sudden slip to occur.

characteristic earthquake—An earthquake with a size and generating mechanism typical for a particular fault source.

colluvial wedge—In cross section, a wedge of coarser grained material fallen off or washed down from a fault scarp, commonly taken as evidence in a backhoe trench of an earthquake with surface rupture.

colluvium—A general term applied to any loose, heterogeneous, and incoherent mass of soil material and/or rock fragments deposited by rain or slow, continuous downslope creep, usually collecting at the base of gentle slopes or hillsides.

continent—One of the Earth's major land masses, including both dry land and continental shelves.

continental crust—That type of the Earth's crust which underlies the continents and the continental shelves, ranging in thickness from about twenty miles to as much as forty miles under mountain ranges.

core (of Earth)—The central part of the Earth below a depth of 1,800 miles. It is thought to be composed mainly of iron and silicates and to be molten on the outside with a solid central part.

cripple wall—Short studs between the mudsill and foundation and the floor joists of the house.

critical facility—A structure that is essential to survive a catastrophe because of its need to direct rescue operations or treat injured people, or because if it were destroyed (such as a dam or nuclear power plant), the effects of that destruction could be catastrophic to society.

crust—The outermost layer or shell of the Earth, defined according to various criteria, including the speed of seismic waves, density and composition; that part of the Earth above the Mohorovičić discontinuity.

crystalline rock—An inexact but convenient term designating an intrusive igneous or metamorphic rock as opposed to a sedimentary rock.

density—Mass per unit volume.

deterministic forecast—An estimation of the largest earthquake or most severe ground shaking to be found on a fault, or in a region, the **maximum credible earthquake**, or MCE.

diaphragm—Horizontal element of a building, such as a floor or a roof, that transmits horizontal forces between vertical elements such as walls.

dip—The angle between a layer or fault and a horizontal plane.

dip-slip fault—A fault in which the relative displacement is in the direction of fault dip.

ductile—1. Said of a rock that can sustain, under a given set of conditions, five to ten percent deformation before fracture or faulting. 2. In structural engineering, the ability of a building to bend and sway without collapsing.

earthquake segment—That part of a fault zone or fault zones that has ruptured during individual earthquakes.

elastic limit—The greatest stress that can be developed in a material without permanent deformation remaining when the stress is removed.

epicenter—The point on the Earth's surface that is directly above the focus (hypocenter) of an earthquake.

epoch—A geologic time unit shorter than a period.

era—A geologic time unit next in order of length above a period; e.g., the Paleozoic, Mesozoic, and Cenozoic eras.

eustatic—Pertaining to worldwide changes of sea level that affect all the oceans, largely caused in the Quaternary by additions of water to, or removal of water from, the continental icecaps.

fault—A fracture or a zone of fractures along which there has been displacement of the sides relative to one another parallel to the fracture.

fault creep—Movement along a fault unaccompanied by earthquakes.

feldspar—An abundant rock-forming mineral constituting sixty percent of the Earth's crust.

first motion—On a seismogram, the direction of motion at the beginning of the arrival of a P wave. By convention, upward motion indicates a compression of the ground; downward motion, a dilation.

focal depth—The depth of the focus below the surface of the Earth.

focus—The place at which rupture commences.

footwall—The underlying side of a fault.

forecast (of an earthquake)—A specific area or fault is identified as having a higher statistical probability of an earthquake of specified magnitude range in a time window of months or years.

foreshocks—Smaller earthquakes preceding the largest earthquake of a series concentrated in a restricted crustal volume.

frequency—Number of waves per unit time; unit is Hertz, or one cycle (one complete wave) per second.

free face—Exposed surface of a scarp resulting from faulting; may be modified by erosion.

friction—The resistance to motion of a body sliding past another body along a surface of contact; may generate heat.

g—Acceleration due to the gravitational attraction of the Earth, a rate of thirty-two feet (9.8 meters) per second, per second.

geodesy—The science concerned with the determination of the size and shape of the Earth and the precise location of points on its surface.

geomorphology—The science that treats the general configuration of the Earth's surface; specifically the study of the classification, description, nature, origin, and development of present landforms and their relationships to underlying structures, and of the history of geologic changes as recorded by these surface features.

geothermal gradient—Increase of temperature in the Earth with depth.

GPS—Global Positioning System, in which surveying is accomplished by determining the position with respect to the orbital positions of several NAVSTAR satellites. Repeated surveying of ground stations can reveal tectonic deformation of the Earth's crust.

graben—A crustal block of rock, generally long and narrow, that has dropped down along boundary faults relative to adjacent rocks.

granite—A deep-seated rock in which quartz constitutes ten to fifty percent of the light-colored mineral components and in which feldspar is the other light-colored component. Broadly applied, any completely crystalline, quartz-bearing rock found at depth in the Earth's crust.

Gutenberg-Richter recurrence relationship—The observed relationship that, for large areas and long time periods, numbers of earthquakes of different magnitudes occur systematically with the relationship $M = a - bN$, where M is magnitude, N is the number of events per unit area per unit time, and a and b are constants representing, respectively, the overall level of seismicity and the ratio of small to large events.

hanging wall—The overlying side of a fault.

hazard—Danger; a feature such as an earthquake or volcano that is dangerous. Equivalent to "peril" in insurance. In insurance, something that increases the danger.

Holocene—The past 10,000 years; an epoch of the Quaternary. For the Alquist-Priolo Act, the Holocene started 11,000 years ago.

indemnity—Insurance against, or repayment for, loss or damage.

inertia—The tendency of matter to remain at rest or continue in a fixed direction unless acted upon by an outside force.

intensity (of earthquakes)—A measure of ground shaking, obtained from the damage done to structures built by humans, changes in the Earth's surface, and reports about what people felt or observed.

isoseismal—Contour lines drawn to separate one level of seismic intensity from another.

isostasy—That condition of equilibrium, analogous to floating, of the units of the lithosphere above the asthenosphere.

Law of Large Numbers—The larger the number of insurance contracts a company writes, the more likely the actual results will follow the predicted results based on an infinite number of contracts.

left-lateral fault—A strike-slip fault on which the displacement of the far block is to the left when viewed from either side.

liquefaction—The act or process transforming any substance into a liquid.

lithosphere—A layer of strength relative to the underlying asthenosphere for deformation at geologic rates. It includes the crust and part of the upper mantle and is up to sixty miles (100 km) in thickness.

load—The forces acting on a building. The weight of the building is its **dead load**. Weight of contents, or snow on the roof, etc., are **live loads**.

magma—Naturally occurring molten rock material, generated within the Earth and capable of intrusion and extrusion as lava, from which igneous rocks such as volcanoes are thought to have been derived through solidification and related processes.

magnitude (of earthquakes)—A measure of earthquake size, determined by taking the common logarithm (base 10) of the largest ground motion recorded during the arrival of a seismic wave type and applying a standard correction for distance to the epicenter

mantle—The zone of the Earth below the crust and above the core, which is divided into the upper mantle and the lower mantle.

meizoseismal region—The area of strong shaking and significant damage in an earthquake.

mitigate—To moderate or to make milder or less severe.

modulus of elasticity—The ratio of stress to its corresponding strain under given conditions of load, for materials that deform elastically.

Mohorovičić discontinuity—The boundary surface or sharp seismic-velocity discontinuity that separates the Earth's crust from the underlying mantle, marked by an abrupt change in speed of seismic waves.

moment (of earthquakes)— A measure of earthquake size based on the rigidity of the rock times the area of faulting times the amount of slip. Dimensions are dyne-cm or Newton-meters.

moment magnitude (Mw)—Magnitude of an earthquake estimated by using the seismic moment.

moment-resistant frame—Steel frame structures with rigid welded joints, more flexible than shear-wall structures.

mudsill—The lowest board between a house and its foundation.

neotectonics—1. The study of the post-Miocene structures and structural history of the Earth's crust. 2. The study of recent deformation of the crust, generally Miocene and younger. 3. Tectonic processes now active, taken over the geologic time span during which they have been acting in the presently observed sense, and the resulting structures.

normal fault—A fault in which the hanging wall appears to have moved downward relative to the footwall.

ocean basin—The area of the sea floor between the base of the continental slope, and the mid-ocean ridge.

olivine—An olive-green, grayish-green, or brown mineral, common in basalt and peridotite.

P wave—The primary or fastest wave traveling away from a seismic event through the rock and consisting of a train of compressions and dilations of the material.

paleoseismology—That part of earthquake studies that deals with geological evidence for earthquakes and fault rupture.

peridotite—Rock composed predominantly of the minerals pyroxene and olivine; the major component of the Earth's mantle.

peril—The risk, contingency, event, or cause of loss insured against, as in an insurance policy.

period—1. The time interval between successive crests in a wave train; the period is one divided by the frequency of a cyclic event. 2. The fundamental unit of the geological time scale, subdivided into epochs, and subdivisions of an era.

plate—A large, relatively rigid segment of the Earth's lithosphere that moves in relation to other plates over the deeper interior.

plate tectonics—A theory of global tectonics in which the lithosphere is divided into a number of plates whose pattern of horizontal movement is that of rigid bodies that interact with one another at their boundaries, causing seismic and tectonic activity along these boundaries.

Pleistocene—An epoch of the Quaternary Period, after the Pliocene and before the Holocene.

precursor—A change in the geological conditions that is a forerunner to earthquake generation on a fault.

prediction (of earthquakes)—The estimation of the time, place, and magnitude of a future earthquake.

premium—An amount payable for an insurance policy.

probability—The number of cases that actually occur divided by the total number of cases possible; the likelihood that an event will take place.

probability of exceedance of a given earthquake size—The odds that the size of a future earthquake will exceed some specified value.

pyroxene—A group of dark, rock-forming silicate minerals.

quartz—Crystalline silica, an important rock-forming mineral.

Quaternary—The second period of the Cenozoic era, following the Tertiary, consisting of the Pleistocene and Holocene epochs.

radiometric—Pertaining to the measurement of geologic time by the study of the disintegration rates of one element or isotope to another.

recurrence interval—The average time interval between earthquakes in a seismic region or along a fault.

reinsurance—A contract in which the insurer becomes protected by obtaining insurance from someone else upon a risk that the first insurer has assumed.

retrofit—Reinforcement or modification of an existing building.

reverse fault—A fault that dips toward the block that has been relatively raised.

Richter scale—Logarithm to the base 10 of the maximum seismic-wave amplitude, in thousandths of a millimeter, recorded on a Wood-Anderson seismograph at a distance of sixty miles (100 km) from the earthquake epicenter.

rheology—The study of the deformation and flow of matter.

right-lateral fault—A strike-slip fault on which the displacement of the far block is to the right when viewed from either side.

rigidity—The resistance of an elastic body to shear.

risk—The amount of loss, and the chance of loss occurring.

S wave—The secondary seismic wave, traveling more slowly than the P wave and consisting of elastic vibrations at right angles to the direction of wave travel.

seafloor spreading—A hypothesis that oceanic crust is being created by convective upwelling of magma along the mid-oceanic ridges or world rift system and by a moving-away of the new material at a rate of a fraction of an inch to five inches per year.

seismic gap—An area in an earthquake-prone region where there is a below-average release of seismic energy

seismic moment—See moment (of earthquakes).

seismic wave—An elastic wave in the Earth usually generated by an earthquake or explosion.

seismicity—The occurrence of earthquakes in space and time.

seismogenic—Characterized by earthquakes.

seismogram—Record of an earthquake written on a seismograph.

seismograph—An instrument for recording as a function of time the motions of the Earth's surface that are caused by seismic waves.

seismology—1. The study of earthquakes, including geodesy, geology, and geophysics. 2. The study of earthquakes, and of the structure of the Earth, by both naturally and artificially generated seismic waves.

serpentine—Green, streaky rock formed by the addition of water to peridotite. The California state rock.

shear wall—A wall of a building that has been strengthened to resist horizontal forces.

shoreline angle—The boundary between a freshly-cut sea cliff and the marine wave-abraded platform.

slip—The relative displacement of formerly adjacent rock materials on opposite sides of a fault, measured in the fault surface.

soft story—A section or horizontal division of a building extending from the floor to the ceiling or roof above it characterized by large amounts of open space that reduces its resistance to horizontal forces, such as a two-car garage or a ballroom in a hotel.

soil—1. A natural body consisting of layers or horizons of mineral and/or organic constituents of variable thicknesses, which differ from the parent material in their morphological, physical, chemical, and mineralogical properties and their biological characteristics. 2. All unconsolidated materials above bedrock (engineering).

stick slip A jerky, sliding motion associated with fault movement.

strain—Change in the shape or volume of a body as a result of stress.

stress—Force per unit area.

stress drop—The sudden reduction of stress across a fault during rupture.

strike—The direction of trend taken by a structural surface as it intersects the horizontal.

strike slip—In a fault, the component of movement that is parallel to the strike of the fault.

strike-slip fault—A fault on which the movement is parallel to the strike of the fault.

subduction—The process of one lithospheric plate descending beneath another.

subduction zone—A long, narrow belt in which subduction takes place.

surface-wave magnitude (Ms)—Magnitude of an earthquake estimated from measurements of the amplitude of earthquake waves that follow the Earth's surface.

surface waves—Seismic waves that follow the Earth's surface only, with a speed less than that of S waves. There are two types of surface waves—Rayleigh waves and Love waves.

swarm (of earthquakes)—A series of earthquakes in the same locality, no one earthquake being of outstanding size.

syncline—A fold of which the core contains the stratigraphically younger rocks; it is concave upward.

tectonic geomorphology—The study of landforms that result from tectonic processes.

tectonics—A branch of geology dealing with the broad architecture of the outer part of the Earth; that is, the regional assembling of structural or deformational features, a study of their mutual relations, origin, and historical evolution.

tephrochronology—The dating of tephra (pyroclastic material, such as ash, from a volcano).

teleseism—Record of an earthquake that occurs far from the recording seismograph, generally thousands of miles away.

thrust fault—A fault with a dip of forty-five degrees or less over much of its extent, on which the hanging wall appears to have moved upward relative to the footwall.

topography—The general configuration of a land surface or any part of the Earth's surface, including its relief and the position of its natural and man-made features.

trace—The intersection of a geological surface with another surface, e.g., the trace of bedding on a fault surface, or the trace of a fault or outcrop on the ground surface.

transform fault—A plate boundary that ideally shows pure strike-slip displacement.

trend—A general term for the direction or bearing of the outcrop of a geological feature of any dimension.

trench—1. Long, narrow, arcuate depression on the sea floor which results from the bending of the lithospheric plate as it descends into the mantle at a subduction zone. 2. Shallow excavation, dug by bulldozer, backhoe, or by hand, revealing detailed information about near-surface geological materials.

triple junction—Point where three plates meet.

tsunami—An ocean wave caused by seafloor movements in an earthquake, submarine volcanic eruption, or submarine landslide.

turbidite—A sediment or rock deposited from a turbidity current, a flow of sediment-charged water.

ultimate strength—The maximum differential stress that a material can sustain under the conditions of deformation.

underwriting—The writing of one's signature at the end of an insurance policy, thereby assuming liability in the event of specific loss or damage.

URM—Unreinforced masonry, a type of construction that is not strengthened against horizontal forces from an earthquake.

volcanology—The branch of geology that deals with volcanoes.

wavelength—The distance between two successive crests or troughs of a wave.

∽ Appendix C ∽
Credits

I. Boosters and Shakers: Three Centuries of Living with Earthquakes in California: The major source for the period between the San Francisco Earthquake of 1906 and the Long Beach Earthquake of 1933 was Carl-Henry Geschwind's fully-referenced Ph.D. dissertation at Johns Hopkins University, augmented by the history from 1933 to the establishment of the National Earthquake Hazards Reduction Program (NEHRP) in 1977 in his book, *California Earthquakes: Science, Risk, and the Politics of Hazard Mitigation, 1906–1977*, published by Johns Hopkins University Press in 2001. For pre-1900 earthquakes, I relied on CDMG Open-File Report 81-11 (1981) by Tousson Toppozada and colleagues, updated for the Bay Area by Martitia Tuttle and Lynn Sykes in CDMG Special Publication 113 (1993). Philip Fradkin's book, *Magnitude 8*, contained many new insights into the 1865 and 1868 earthquakes in the Bay Area. The San Francisco Earthquake cover-up was brought to light by careful research by Gladys Hansen, the "Death Lady of San Francisco," and Emmet Condon, a former chief of the San Francisco Fire Department, in their book, *Denial of Disaster*. Stephen J. Pyne's book, *Grove Karl Gilbert: A Great Engine of Research*, published by University of Texas Press in 1980; and Francis Vaughan's book, *Andrew C. Lawson: Scientist, Teacher, Philosopher*, published in 1970 by Arthur Clark Co., were useful in the roles of those scientists in the San Francisco Earthquake investigation. J.R. Goodstein's book, *Millikan's School*, described the founding of Caltech and the establishment of the Seismological Lab as a center of excellence in applied physics. Excerpts from a forthcoming biography of Charles Richter by Michael Forrest appeared in the Southern California Earthquake Center newsletter. For the period leading up to the establishment of NEHRP, the comments of Robert Wallace of the USGS (as well as his EERI Oral History) and Robert Hamilton of the National Academy of Sciences were most useful because they were closely involved in the negotiations leading up to NEHRP. The Mammoth Lakes controversy was discussed in detail by John Nance in *On Shaky Ground*, and by Kerry Sieh and Simon LeVay in *The Earth in Turmoil*; and a perspective from a USGS participant was provided by David Hill. The chapter was reviewed by Carl-Henry Geschwind, Robert Hamilton, and Robert Wallace.

1. A Concept of Time: Standard textbooks on historical geology were used in this chapter. In the time scale, dating of Los Angeles earthquakes was based on paleoseismic trenching by James Dolan of the University of Southern California. Timing of San Andreas earthquakes was based on work by Kerry Sieh and his students, especially Lisa Grant; Ray Weldon of the University of Oregon and his students; and Tom Fumal, David Schwartz, and others of the USGS.

2. Plate Tectonics: The basic information is provided in textbooks, some of which are cited. The plate tectonics of California for the past 30 million years has been worked out by Tanya Atwater of the University of California Santa Barbara, William R. Dickinson of the University of Arizona, and many others. Atwater has produced a video of Figure 2-6.

3. Earthquake Basics: Most of this is based on textbooks in structural geology and seismology. For structural geology, see Yeats et al. (1997), and for seismology, see Bolt (1999) and Brumbaugh (1999); these textbooks discuss the subjects at a very basic level, suitable for the nonscientist. GPS is too new to be featured in a textbook except for Yeats et al. (1997). I received a lot of help from Ken Hudnut of SCIGN and his colleagues at the Jet Propulsion Lab. Jim Savage of the USGS was featured, but major contributions were also made by Will Prescott, Mike Lisowski, and others of the USGS; and Andrea Donnellan, Michael Heflin, Frank Webb, and others at the Jet Propulsion Lab; and Yehuda Bock of the University of California San Diego.

4. The San Andreas Fault System: The Big One: Thurston Clarke's book gave me the idea of describing the San Andreas Fault in terms of the cities and countryside it passes through. I repeated his tour to bring it up to date and give a geologist's perspective. I have highlighted the regional mapping of the fault by Thomas Dibblee, Jr., but many others have contributed to San Andreas mapping. These include John Crowell and his students at UCLA and the University of California Santa Barbara; Ray Ingersoll of UCLA; Levi Noble, Jack Vedder, Bob Wallace, Bob Powell, Doug Morton, Warren Addicott, and John Sims of the USGS; Clarence Allen of Caltech; Mason Hill of ARCO; Red Smith of Shell; and Allen Barrows, James Kahle, Gordon Oakeshott, and Harold Weber of CDMG. The paleoseismic mapping started with Kerry Sieh (described by him in Sieh and LeVay, 1998) and has continued with his students Ray Weldon, Lisa Grant, Sally McGill, Carol Prentice, and Doug Yule, Weldon's students Gordon Seitz and Glenn Biasi, Charles Rubin of Central Washington University, and consultants Thom Davis and Scott Lindvall. Other major contributors have been Tom Fumal, Michael Rymer, and David Schwartz of the USGS, Tina Niemi of Stanford, Bill Cotton of Cotton and Associates, and Tim Hall of Geomatrix. For Bay Area strike-slip faults, William Lettis, Keith Kelson, and Gary Simpson of Lettis and Associates have played major roles. Tom Rockwell and his students at San Diego State University have done much of the paleoseismology of the San Jacinto, Elsinore, and Imperial faults in southeastern California; he, Eldon Gath, and Tania Gonzales of Earth Consultants International have done the paleoseismology of the Whittier Fault. The segmentation of the San Andreas Fault into strong segments (the 1857 and 1906 ruptures and the unruptured southeastern segment) and weak segments in the middle was done by Clarence Allen of Caltech. For the section on fault pioneers, the biographies of Andrew Lawson by F.E. Vaughn and of G.K. Gilbert by N.J. Pyne were useful, as was the obituary of H.F. Reid by Lawson. The chapter was reviewed by Kerry Sieh and Carol Prentice.

5. The Transverse Ranges: LA in the Squeeze: T. Toppozada et al. (1981) did the research on the 1812 earthquake at Santa Barbara. Geologic mapping of most of the Transverse Ranges was done by Thomas Dibblee, Jr., as in other parts of California, but others have contributed much as well: Jerry Treiman, Richard Saul, Allan Barrows, Gordon Oakeshott, and Harold Weber of CDMG; Robert Yerkes and Russell Campbell of the USGS for the Santa Monica Mountains; Tom Bailey, formerly of Shell; Jerry Winterer of Scripps Institute of Oceanography for the east Ventura basin; my own students and myself for the hills between the Santa Clara Valley and the Santa Monica Mountains; Perry Ehlig of California State University Los Angeles for the San Gabriel Mountains; Gene Fritsche of California State University Northridge; John Crowell of the University of California Santa Barbara for the mountainous country east and west of Interstate 5 south of Tejon Pass and their offset counterparts across the San Andreas Fault in southeastern California; A.O. Woodford of Pomona College and Robert Yerkes, Jack Vedder, D.L. Durham, and Jack Schoellhamer of the USGS for the Puente Hills south of the San Gabriel Valley; and Bob Powell and Doug Morton of the USGS for the eastern Transverse Ranges. My own students and I have mapped the subsurface geology of the Ventura and northern Los Angeles basins based on petroleum industry data, as have Thom Davis and Jay Namson, consultants; John Suppe of Princeton; and John Shaw of Harvard. Detailed summaries of subsurface data were prepared by Tom Wright of Chevron for the Los Angeles Basin and Tom Hopps of Rancho Energy for the Ventura Basin. The Quaternary geology and landscape evolution, begun by W.C. Putnam of UCLA, has been worked out by Ed Keller of the University of California Santa Barbara and his students, especially Tom Rockwell. Paleoseismology based on trench excavations in the Ventura and Los Angeles basins has been done by James Dolan and Tom Rockwell, with other contributions from Scott Lindvall of Lettis and Associates, Charles Rubin of Central Washington University, and Jerry Treiman of CDMG. A three-dimensional perspective has been presented by Egill Hauksson of Caltech based on seismicity and the behavior of seismic waves as they pass through the Earth's crust; Hauksson and Lucy Jones of USGS and Peter Shearer of the University of California at San Diego have mapped the earthquake distribution in the region. The chapter was reviewed by Ed Keller.

6. Shakes in the Back Country: Decades of Violence, Millennia of Silence: The 1872 Owens Valley Earthquake and Fault were studied by Sarah Beanland of the Institute of Geological and Nuclear Sciences of New Zealand and Malcolm Clark of the USGS. The geology and hazard at Mammoth Lakes have been studied by Roy Bailey and others at the USGS, in addition to Dave Hill. The geology of the Eastern California Shear Zone has been described by Roy Dokka of Louisiana State University and many others. Charles Richter described the faulting accompanying the 1947 Manix Lake Earthquake, and Ross Stein worked on the 1979 Homestead Valley Earthquake. The 1992 Landers Earthquake led to a study by geologists from the Southern California Earthquake Center, USGS, and CDMG; a paper describing this work was published by Sieh et al. (1993). Paleoseismic work has been done by Tom Rockwell, Charles Rubin of Central Washington University, and others. Work on the Central Nevada Seismic Zone was pioneered by Vincent Gianella and Burt Slemmons of the University of Nevada Reno, followed by Bob Wallace of USGS (for the 1915 earthquake), Craig dePolo (for the 1932 earthquake), and John Bell and John Caskey (for the 1954 earthquakes). Slemmons used aerial photography taken in early morning or late evening to highlight subtle fault scarps on the desert floor. dePolo and John Anderson of the University of Nevada Seismological Lab and their colleagues developed an earthquake scenario for the Reno-Carson City area and organized a workshop to consider earthquake hazards in Las Vegas; both studies contributed much to this chapter. The USGS circular by Hanks et al. and the paper by Ewing (1999) provided useful insights into the proposed Yucca Mountain nuclear waste repository. The "desert rats" of the Death Valley Fault Zone include Benny Troxel of CDMG and Lauren Wright of Pennsylvania State University. The Garlock Fault has been studied by G.I. Smith of the USGS, and paleoseismology has been done by Sally McGill of California State University at San Bernardino. Recent work on the Kern County Earthquake was done by Ross Stein and Wayne Thatcher, following earlier work by Charles Richter and J.P. Buwalda. Thatcher headed a team that used GPS to show that strain is concentrated in the Eastern California Shear Zone and the country between the Sierra Nevada and the Central Nevada Seismic Zone; their results were confirmed by Tim Dixon and Brian Wernicker. The chapter was reviewed by Craig dePolo, Tom Hanks, Dave Hill, and Wayne Thatcher.

7. Cascadia: The major contributors to the recognition of the Cascadia Subduction Zone as a major earthquake source have been acknowledged elsewhere (Yeats, 1998) and in the text of this chapter. The active faults and folds of the California north coast have been described in detail by faculty and students at Humboldt State University, especially Gary Carver. Kenneth Lajoie of the USGS first described the tectonic deformation of marine terraces near Cape Mendocino, followed by Dorothy Merritts of Franklin and Marshall College. Each of the crustal faults has been characterized as a seismic source by Pat McCrory of the USGS. Earthquakes from a seismic network in support of a nuclear power plant at Humboldt Bay were described by Bob McPherson, together with

Lori Dengler of Humboldt State University and David Oppenheimer of the USGS. Historical earthquakes were summarized by Dengler and by Bill Bakun of the USGS. Dengler has been the driving force behind the Humboldt Earthquake Education Center, an outreach program for north coast residents. The chapter was reviewed by Lori Dengler and Pat McCrory.

8. Memories of the Future: The Uncertain Art of Earthquake Forecasting: An analysis of the Iben Browning prediction of an earthquake at New Madrid, Missouri was done by William Spence of the USGS. Several of California's "earthquake sensitives" were interviewed by Clarke (1996). The Brady prediction for Lima, Peru was the subject of a book by Olson (1989). Ma et al. (1990) discussed earthquake prediction in China; an evaluation of these predictions is provided by Bolt (1999), among others. The pros and cons of the VAN method of earthquake prediction were reviewed by Seiya Uyeda (pro) and Dave Jackson and Yan Kagan (con) (1998) in the Transactions of the American Geophysical Union, with references to earlier work. The controversy over our ever being able to predict earthquakes has been presented by Robert Geller, Chris Scholz, and Lowell Whiteside, among others. Probabilistic and deterministic forecasting was based on Clarence Allen's chapter in Yeats et al. (1997). C. Allin Cornell, Art Frankel, Tom Hanks, Ellis Krinitzky, David Boore, W.B. Joyner, and Robin McGuire have contributed much to this field. A good general reference is Reiter (1990). An unpublished report that helped me was "Probabilistic Seismic Hazard Analysis: A Beginner's Guide," by Tom Hanks and Allin Cornell. The emerging field of stress triggering of earthquakes and the stress shadow caused by the 12906 San Francisco Earthquake has benefited from the work of Ruth Harris, Bob Simpson, and Bill Ellsworth of the USGS and Steve Jaumé and Lynn Sykes of Columbia University, in addition to those cited in the chapter. The possibility of earthquake forecasting using both long- and short-term precursors was explained to me by Mike Kozuch of the New Zealand Institute of Geological and Nuclear Sciences, who shared a house with me in Wellington in 1999. The chapter was reviewed by Clarence Allen, Bill Ellsworth, and Tom Hanks.

9. Solid Rocks and Bowls of Jello: My understanding of liquefaction and lateral spreading is largely based on the work of Obermeier (1996) of the USGS. Earthquake-induced landslides have been described by Keefer (1984) and Jibson (1996). The chapter was reviewed by Eldon Gath and Steve Obermeier.

10. Tsunami! I learned much from Lori Dengler and the publications of Satake (1992) and Bernard et al. (1991). The submarine landslides generating tsunamis accompanying the 1964 Alaska Earthquake were described by Hampton et al. (1993). The effect of the tsunami in Seward and Valdez, Alaska, is based on the account by Nance (1988). I used the archives of the Seattle *Times* to follow the 1964 tsunami down the coast of Vancouver Island, Washington, and Oregon. The book by Griffin (1984) presents the story of the tsunami at Crescent City in the words of those who survived it. The 1960 tsunami is discussed in Atwater et al. (1999). George Priest of DOGAMI provided information about the Oregon tsunami hazard mitigation program. Information about tsunami hazard mitigation was obtained from the NOAA web site and from Lori Dengler, who has been active in tsunami mitigation in California. The chapter was reviewed by Frank Gonzalez of NOAA and Lori Dengler of Humboldt State University, and an early draft was reviewed by Kenji Satake of the Geological Survey of Japan.

11. Earthquake Insurance: Betting Against Earthquakes: The Western States Seismic Policy Council publication on the Earthquake Insurance Summit was very useful, as was a conference in 1996 sponsored by the Southern California Earthquake Center. I used information from a California Dept. of Conservation publication (1990), and an insurance-industry perspective of political issues involving earthquake insurance was provided by a publication by the Insurance Services Office (1996). The story of the CEA was ably told from the Department of Insurance perspective by Richard J. Roth, Jr., and from the consumer's perspective by the United Policyholders' publication, *What's UP*. The CEA's viewpoint was given by Mark Leonard. The relationship between damage to homes by the Northridge Earthquake and the age of construction was worked out by Richard Roth. I learned about the New Zealand earthquake insurance story from David Middleton of the New Zealand Earthquake Commission. The chapter was reviewed by Jack Watts of State Farm Insurance Co., Richard Roth of the State Dept. of Insurance, Amy Bach of United Policyholders, and David Middleton of the New Zealand Earthquake Commission.

12. Is Your Home Ready for an Earthquake? I began with *Sunset Magazine*'s two-part series on earthquake protection, published in 1990 after the Loma Prieta Earthquake. Other useful references are Lafferty and Associates (1989), a booklet by the Seismic Safety Commission (1992), and publications by the Office of Emergency Services. For wood stoves and propane tanks, I used information from "Living on Shaky Ground," by the Humboldt Earthquake Information Center.

13. Earthquake Design of Large Structures: I received much information from Tom Miller, a structural engineer at Oregon State University, who provided me with the information from AIA/ACSA Council on Architectural Research. Bolt (1999) was also useful.

14. The Federal Government and Earthquakes: Geschwind (2001) and Bob Wallace's oral history (Scott, 1999) presented the background to the establishment of NEHRP, and the early days of NEHRP legislation and presidential declarations are detailed in the report by the Office of Technology Assessment (1995), for which I was an advisor. Reports by Hanks (1985) and Page et al. (1992) provide insights into the USGS management of NEHRP. Examples of how the USGS responded to a major earthquake are provided by Plafker and Galloway (1989) and USGS (1996). The chapter was reviewed by Robert Hamilton, who was there for much of the beginning of NEHRP. An earlier version of this chapter was reviewed by Ian MacGregor of NSF and Craig Weaver of USGS.

15. The Role of State and Local Government: For the Division of Mines and Geology, the memoirs of Olaf Jenkins (1976) and Gordon Oakeshott (1989) were useful as well as the account by Geschwind (2001). Bill Bryant and Bob Sydnor also provided me information. Geschwind was also the best source for the legislative history of state involvement in earthquake preparedness, starting with the 1933 earthquake and continuing through the establishment of Alquist-Priolo and other legislative acts. Web sites for OES and the Seismic Safety Commission were very useful. I received a lot of help in understanding building ordinances from Walter Friday of Linhart Petersen Powers Associates. Diane Murbach of the City of San Diego was a great help in getting me information about California grading ordinances. The chapter was reviewed by Eldon Gath of Earth Consultants International, who has worked under California regulations for his entire career; and Earl Hart of the Division of Mines and Geology, who was involved in carrying out the provisions of the Alquist-Priolo Act almost from the beginning.

16. Preparing for the Next Earthquake: See references for Chapter 12.

Appendix A. Table of Significant Earthquakes in California.
Compilations by Bill Bakun, Lori Dengler, Bill Ellsworth, and Tousson Toppozada, and the table of earthquakes with surface rupture from Yeats et al. (1997), were used to prepare this table. Nevada earthquakes were compiled by Craig dePolo and his colleagues at the Nevada Bureau of Mines.

Bibliography

Sources of Information and Websites

Advanced National Seismic System website: http://pasadena.wr.usgs.gov/
eqhaz/ANSS.html

Alaska Tsunami Warning Center, 910 S. Felton Street, Palmer, AK99645. 907-
745-4212. Website: http://www.alaska.net/~atwc/index.html

A.M. Best, the standard insurance company rating system. Website:
www.ambest.com

American Red Cross, 2700 Wilshire Boulevard, Los Angeles, CA 90057, 213-
739-5200; 550 Sutter St., San Francisco, CA 94109, 415-202-0780.

Association of Bay Area Governments website: www.abag.ca.gov

Association of Engineering Geologists website: www.aegweb.org

Bay Area Regional Earthquake Preparedness Project, 101 Eighth Street, Suite
152, Oakland, CA94607. 415-540-2713.

California Department of Insurance website: www.insurance.ca.gov

California Division of Mines and Geology, P.O. Box 2980, Sacramento, CA
95812-2980; 107 S. Broadway, Los Angeles, CA 90012, 213-620-3560; 185
Ferry St., San Francisco, CA 94107-1725, 415-904-7707. 916-445-5716.
Website: www.consrv.ca.gov/dmg

California Governor's Office of Emergency Services, 11200 Lexington Drive,
Bldg. 283, Los Alamitos, CA 90720-5002. 310-795-2900. Website for
earthquake program: www.oes.ca.gov:8001/html/eqprog/eqprog.html

Cascadia Regional Earthquake Workgroup, Website:
www.geophys.washington.edu/CREW

Consortium of Universities for Research in Earthquake Engineering, 1301
S.46th St., Richmond, CA 94804. 510-231-9557. Website: www.curee.org

Earthquake Engineering Research Institute, 499 14th Street, Suite 320,
Oakland, CA 94612-1934. 610-451-0905. Website: http://www.eeri.org e-
mail eeri@eeri.org

Federal Emergency Management Agency, P.O. Box 70274, Washington, DC
20024; The Presidio, Bldg. 105, San Francisco, CA 94129, 415-923-7100;
245 South Los Robles, Pasadena, CA 91101, 818-451-3000. Website:
fema.gov/homepage.html HAZUS website: www.hazus.org

Humboldt Earthquake Education Center, Department of Geology, Humboldt
State University, Arcata, CA 95521-8299. 707-826-3931. Website: http://
sorrel.humboldt.edu/~geodept/earthquakes/eqk_info.html

Incorporated Research Institutions in Seismology. Website:
www.iris.washington.edu http://www.iris.washington.edu/seismic/
60%5F2040%5F1%5F8.html Monitor earthquakes around the world in
near-real time, visit worldwide seismic stations. Earthquakes of M 6 or
larger are linked to special information pages that explain the where,
how, and why of each earthquake.

Institute for Business and Home Safety. Website: www.ibhs.org

Insurance Institute for Property Loss Reduction: e-mail iiplr@aol.com

International Conference of Building Officials website: www.icbo.org (latest
information on building codes)

International Tsunami Information Center, Box 50027, Honolulu, HI 96850-
4993. 808-541-1658.

Multidisciplinary Center for Earthquake Engineering Research, State University of New York at Buffalo, Red Jacket Quadrangle, Buffalo, NY 14261. 716-645-3391 Website: http://mceer.buffalo.edu/outreach/

National Earthquake Information Center website: gldss7.cr.usgs.gov e-mail neic@usgs.gov

National Geophysical Data Center (NOAA), 325 Broadway, Boulder, CO 80303. 303-497-6215. Website: www.ngdc.noaa.gov/ngdc.html

National Information Service for Earthquake Engineering: Website: nisee.ca.berkeley.edu

National Institute of Building Sciences, 1201 L Street NW, Suite 400, Washington, DC 20005-4024. 202-289-7800.

National Landslide Information Center: e-mail nlic@usgs.gov

National Oceanic and Atmospheric Administration website: National Tsunami Hazard Mitigation Program http://www.pmel.noaa.gov/tsunami-hazard/

NOAA Pacific Marine Environmental Laboratory (PMEL) website: http://www.pmel.noaa.gov/tsunami

National Science Foundation: Website: www.nsf.gov

Nature of the Northwest Information Center, 800 NE Oregon Street #5, Suite 177, Portland, OR 97232. 503-872-2750.

Nevada Bureau of Mines and Geology, University of Nevada Mail Stop 178, Reno, NV 89557-0088. 775-784-6691. Website: www.nbmg.unr.edu e-mail nbmgsales@unr.edu

Northern California Earthquake Data Center: Website: quake.geo.berkeley.edu

Oregon Department of Geology and Mineral Industries, 800 NE Oregon St. #28, Suite 965, Portland, OR 97232. 503-872-2750.

Pacific Disaster Center (tsunami warnings): Website: www.pdc.org

Pacific Earthquake Engineering Research Center, University of California, 1301 S. 46th Street, Richmond, CA 94804-4698. 510-231-9554. Website: http://peer.berkeley.edu e-mail eerclib@nisee.ca.berkeley.edu

Pacific Tsunami Warning Center, 91-270 Fort Weaver Road, Ewa Beach, HI 96706-2928. 808-689-8207.

Paleoseismology Information: inqua.nlh.no/commpl/paleoseism.html

Redwood Coast Tsunami Work Group, Humboldt Earthquake Education Center, Humboldt State University, Arcata, CA 95521. 707-826-3115. Website: http://glinda.cnrs.humboldt.edu/earthquakes/rctwg/toc

Seismic Safety Commission, 1755 Creekside Oaks Drive, Suite 100, Sacramento, CA 95833. 916-263-5506. Website: www.seismic.ca.gov

Seismological Society of America, Suite 201, Plaza Professional Building, El Cerrito, CA 94530-4003. www.seismosoc.org

Seismosurfing website: www.geophys.washington.edu/seismosurfing.html

Southern California Earthquake Center, University of Southern California, University Park, Los Angeles, CA 90089-0742. Website: www.scec.org Information on recent earthquakes in California, with maps: www.scecdc.scec.org/recenteqs and www.scecdc.scec.org/earthquakes/current.txt (text). Weekly coverage of earthquake news at http://www.scec.org/instanet

Southern California Earthquake Preparedness Project, 1110 E. Green Street, Suite 300, Pasadena, CA 91106. 818-795-9055, and 1350 Front Street, Suite 4015, San Diego, CA 92101. 619-238-3321.

Southern California Integrated GPS Network (SCIGN) website designed as a learning module: http://scign.jpl.nasa.gov/learn/

United Policyholders, 110 Pacific Ave. #262, San Francisco, CA 94111. Website: www.unitedpolicyholders.org. e-mail info@unitedpolicyholders.org.

U.S. Geological Survey, Earth Science Information Center, 345 Middlefield Road, Menlo Park, CA 94025. 415-329-4390. Website: www.usgs.gov Earthquake information website (Menlo Park, CA): earthquakes.usgs.gov Includes an earthquake education website entitled "Earthquakes for Kids & Grownups."

U.S. Geological Survey Long Valley Caldera website: http://quake.wr.usgs.gov/VOLCANOES/LongValley/

University of Nevada Seismological Laboratory/174, Mackay School of Mines, Reno, NV 89557-0141. 702-784-1766, 784-1833. Website: www.seismo.unr.reno

Western States Seismic Policy Council, 121 Second Street, 4th Floor, San Francisco, CA 94105.   Website: www.wsspc.org For online discussion group e-mail wsspc@wsspc.org

References

Ad Hoc Working Group on the Probabilities of Future Large Earthquakes in Southern California, 1992, Future seismic hazards in southern California: Phase I: Implications of the 1992 Landers earthquake sequence: National Earthquake Prediction Evaluation Council, California Earthquake Prediction Evaluation Council, and Southern California Earthquake Center, 42 p.

American Red Cross, 1985, *The emergency survival handbook*: (local Red Cross office).

Atwater, B.F., Cisternas V. M., Bourgeois, J., Dudley, W.C., Hadley, J.W., and Stauffer, P.H., compilers, 1999, Surviving a Tsunami—Lessons Learned from Chile, Hawaii, and Japan: U.S. Geol. Survey Circular 1187, 18 p.

Ball, H., 1986, *Justice Downwind: America's Atomic Testing Program in the 1950s*: New York, Oxford University Press, 280 p.

Bakun, W.H., 2000, Seismicity of California's north coast: Bulletin of the Seismological Society of America, v. 90, p. 797-812.

Barker, M.E., 1998, *Three Fearful Days*: San Francisco, Londonborn (Box 11246, San Francisco 94107), 335 p. A gripping account of the San Francisco Earthquake of 1906.

Bean, W., and J.J. Rawls, 1988, *California - an interpretive history*, 5th ed.: New York, McGraw-Hill Book Co., 522 p.

Beanland, S., and Clark, M.M., 1994, The Owens Valley Fault Zone, Eastern California, and Surface Faulting Associated with the 1872 Earthquake: U.S. Geol. Survey Bull. 1982, 29 p., 4 pl.

Bell, B., 1999, The liquid earth: Atlantic Monthly, January 1999, p. 58-72.

Benz, H., Filson, J., Arabasz, W., Gee, L., and Wald, L., 2000, Advanced National Seismic System Info Sheet; see also http://geohazard.cr.usgs.gov/pubs/circ

Bernard, E.N., et al., 1991, *Tsunami Hazard: A Practical Guide for Tsunami Hazard Reduction*: Dordrecht, The Netherlands, Kluwer Academic Publishers.

Bolt, B.A., 1999, *Earthquakes*: New York, W.H. Freeman & Co., 366 p.

Bronson, W., 1959, *The earth shook, the sky burned: a photographic record of the 1906 San Francisco earthquake and fire*: San Francisco, Chronicle Books, 192 p.

Brumbaugh, D.S., 1999, *Earthquakes: Science and Society*: Upper Saddle River, NJ, Prentice-Hall.

California Department of Conservation, 1990, Seismic Hazard Information Needs of the Insurance Industry, Local Government, and Property Owners of California: California Department of Conservation Special Publication 108.

California Division of Mines and Geology and State Mining and Geology Board, 1997, Guidelines for evaluating and mitigating seismic hazards in California: Calif. Div. Mines and Geology Spec. Pub. 117, 74 p.

California Office of Emergency Services, An Ounce of Prevention: Strengthening Your Wood Frame House for Earthquake Safety: video and booklet.

Carter, W.E., and Robertson, D.S., 1986, Studying the earth by very-long-baseline interferometry: *Scientific American*, v. 255, no. 5, p. 46-54. Written for the lay person.

Clarke, S.H., and Carver, G.A., 1992, Late Holocene tectonics and paleoseismicity, southern Cascadia subduction zone: *Science*, v. 255, p. 188-192.

Clarke, T., 1996, *California fault: Searching for the spirit of state along the San Andreas*: New York, Ballantine Books, 417 p.

Crampin, S., 1999, Stress-forecasting earthquakes: *Seismological Research Letters*, v. 70, p. 291-293.

Dengler, L., Carver, G., and McPherson, R., 1992, Sources of North Coast seismicity: *California Geology*, v. 45, p. 40-53.

Dengler, L., Moley, K., McPherson, R., Pasyanos, M., Dewey, J.W., and Murray, M., 1995, The September 1, 1994 Mendocino Fault earthquake: *California Geology*, v. 48, p. 43-53.

Dengler, L., and Moley, K., 1999, Living on shaky ground: how to survive earthquakes & tsunamis on the North Coast: Humboldt Earthquake Education Center, Humboldt State University, 3rd edition, 24 p.

dePolo, C.M., ed., 1998, Proceedings of a conference on seismic hazards in the Las Vegas region: *Nevada Bureau of Mines and Geology Open-File Report 98-6*, 107 p.

dePolo, C.M., et al., 1996, Planning scenario for a major earthquake in western Nevada: *Nevada Bureau of Mines and Geology Special Publication 20*, 128 p.

dePolo, D.M., and dePolo, C.M., 1999, Earthquakes in Nevada 1852-1998: *Nevada Bureau of Mines and Geology Map 119*.

Dixon, T.H., 1991, An introduction to the Global Positioning System and some geological applications: *Reviews of Geophysics*, v. 29, p. 249-276.

Dokka, R.K., and Travers, C.J., 1990, Late Cenozoic strike-slip faulting in the Mojave Desert, California: *Tectonics*, v. 9, p. 311-340.

Dudley, W.C., and Lee, M., 1988, *Tsunami!*: Honolulu, University of Hawaii Press.

Earthquake Commission and Centre for Advanced Engineering (New Zealand), 1995, *Wellington after the Quake: The Challenge of Rebuilding Cities*: Published by the Earthquake Commission, Wellington, 284 p.

Earthquake Engineering Research Institute, 1996, Construction quality, education, and seismic safety: EERI Endowment Fund White Paper: Earthquake Engineering Research Institute, 499 14th St., Suite 320, Oakland, CA 95612-1934, 68 p.

Earthquake Engineering Research Institute, 1996, Public policy and building safety: EERI Endowment Fund White Paper: Earthquake Engineering Research Institute, 499 14th St., Suite 320, Oakland, CA 95612-1934, 57 p.

Earthquake Engineering Research Institute, 2000, *Resisting the Forces of Earthquakes:* video

Ellsworth, W.L., Earthquake history, 1769-1989, in Wallace, R.E., ed., The San Andreas fault system, California: *U.S. Geol. Survey Professional Paper 1515*, p. 153-187.

Elnashai, A.S., and Antoniou, S., 2000, *Implications of Recent Earthquakes on Seismic Risk*: Imperial College Press. Order from www.worldscientific.com

Ewing, R.C., 1999, Less geology in the geological disposal of nuclear wastes: Science, v. 286, p. 415-417.

Forrest, M.R., 1998, Charles Richter: *Southern California Earthquake Center Quarterly Newsletter*, v. 3, no. 4, p. 6-9; v. 4, no. 1, p. 26-29.

Fradkin, P.L., 1989, *Fallout, an American Nuclear Tragedy*: Tucson, University of Arizona Press, 300 p.

Fradkin, P.L., 1998, *Magnitude 8: Earthquakes and life along the San Andreas Fault*: Berkeley, University of California Press, 226 p.

Frankel, A., et al., 1996, National seismic hazard maps, documentation June 1996: U.S. Geol. Survey Open-File Report 96-532, 110 p.

Fratessa, P., 1994, *Buildings: Practical Lessons from the Loma Prieta Earthquake*: Washington, D.C., National Academy Press.

Freeman, J.R., 1932, *Earthquake Damage and Earthquake Insurance*: New York, McGraw-Hill, 904 p.

Geller, R.J., 1997, Predictable publicity: *Seismological Research Letters*, v. 68, p. 477-480.

Gere, J.M., and Shah, H.C., 1984, *Terra Non Firma: Understanding and Preparing for Earthquakes*: New York, W.H. Freeman and Co., 203 p.

Geschwind, C.-H., 1996, Earthquakes and their interpretation: The campaign for seismic safety in California, 1906-1933: Baltimore, Johns Hopkins University PhD dissertation, 256 p.:

Geschwind, C.-H., 2001, *California Earthquakes: Science, Risk, and the Politics of Hazard Mitigation, 1906-1977*: Baltimore, Johns Hopkins University Press, in press.

Glen, W., 1982, *The Road to Jaramillo*: Stanford, Calif., Stanford University Press. An account of the plate tectonics revolution.

Goodstein, J.R., 1991, *Millikan's School*: New York, W.H. Norton & Co., 317 p.

Gore, R., 1995, Living with California's faults: National Geographic, v. 190, no. 4.

Gore, R., and Richardson, J., 1998, Cascadia: Living on Fire: *National Geographic*, v. 193, no. 5, p. 6-37

Governor's Office of Emergency Services, 1996, Tsunami! How to survive the hazard on California's coast. (Free pamphlet available from OES)

Griffin, W., 1984, *Crescent City's Dark Disaster*: Crescent City, CA., Crescent City Printing Co., 381 H Street, Crescent City, CA 95531, 188 p.

Hampton, M.A., Lemke, R.W., and Coulter, H.W., 1993, Submarine landslides that had a significant impact on man and his activities: Seward and Valdez, Alaska: *U.S. Geol. Survey Bull. 2002*, p. 122-134.

Hanks, T.C., 1985, The National Earthquake Hazards Reduction Program—Scientific Status: *U.S. Geol.Survey Bull. 1659*, 40 p.

Hanks, T.C., Winograd, I.J., Anderson, R.E., Reilly, T.E., and Weeks, E.P., 1999, Yucca Mountain as a radioactive waste repository: *U.S. Geol. Survey Circular 1184*, 19 p.

Hansen, G., and E. Condon, 1989, *Denial of disaster*: San Francisco, Cameron and Co.

Harris, R.A., 1998, The Loma Prieta, California, earthquake of October 17, 1989—forecasts: *U.S. Geol. Survey Professional Paper 1550-B*.

Hart, E.W., and Bryant, W.A., 1997 (revised), Fault-rupture hazard zones in California: *Calif. Div. Mines and Geology Spec. Pub. 42*, 38 p. (Revised periodically)

Hauksson, E., and others, 1988, The 1987 Whittier Narrows earthquake in the Los Angeles metropolitan area, California: *Science*, v. 239, p. 1409-1412.

Health Plus, 1986, Getting ready for the big one: 694 Tennessee Street, San Francisco, CA 94107.

Hill, D.P., 1998, Science, geologic hazards, and the public in a large, restless caldera: *Seismological Research Letters*, v. 69, p. 400-404.

Hill, M.L., 1981. San Andreas fault: History of concepts: *Geological Society of America Bulletin*, v. 92, p. 112-131.

Iacopi, R.L., 1996. *Earthquake Country*, 4th. ed.: Tucson, AZ, Fisher Books, 146 p.

Kearey, P., and Vine, F.J., 1990, *Global Tectonics*: London, Blackwell Scientific Publications, 302 p.

Hill, M.R., Oakeshott, G.B., Greensfelder, R.W., and Kahle, J.E., 1972, The great Owens Valley Earthquake of 1872: *California Geology*, v. 25, p. 51-61.

Hyndman, R.D., 1995, Great earthquakes of the Pacific Northwest: *Scientific American*, v. 273, no. 6, p. 50-57.

Insurance Service Office, Inc., 1996, *Homeowners insurance: Threats from without, weakness within*: ISO Insurance Issues Series, 62 p.

International Conference of Building Officials, 1997, *1997 Uniform Building Code* in 3 volumes, available in hard copy or CD-ROM: ICBO, 5360 Workman Mill Road, Whittier, CA 90601-2298, web page www.icbo.org.

Jackson, D.D., Kagan, Y., and Uyeda, S., 1998. The VAN method of earthquake prediction: *EOS, Trans. American Geophysical Union*, v. 79, p. 573, 579-580. (Jackson and Kagan argue against; Uyeda argues for)

Jenkins, O.P., 1976, *Building a State Geological Survey, California, 1928-1958*: Monterey, CA, Angel Press, 124 p.

Jibson, R.W., 1996, Using landslides for paleoseismic analysis, in McCalpin, J.P., ed., *Paleoseismology*: San Diego, Academic Press, p. 397-438.

Jochim, C.L., Rogers, W.P., Truby, J.O., Wold, R.L., Jr., Weber, G., and Brown, S.P., 1988, Colorado landslide hazard mitigation plan: *Colorado Geological Survey Bull. 48*, 149 p.

Kanamori, H., Hauksson, E., and Heaton, T., 1997, Real-time seismology and earthquake hazard mitigation: *Nature*, v. 390, p. 481-484.

Keefer, D.K., 1984, Landslides caused by earthquakes: *Geological Society of America Bulletin*, v. 95, p. 406-471.

Keller, E.A., 1988, *Environmental Geology*, 5th ed.: Columbus, Ohio, Merrill Publishing Co., 540 p.

Kimball, V., 1988, *Earthquake ready*: Roundtable Publishing, Santa Monica, CA, 225 p.

Kramer, S.L., 1996, *Geotechnical Earthquake Engineering*: Englewood Cliffs, N.J., Prentice-Hall.

Krinitsky, E., Gould, J., and Edinger, F., 1993, *Fundamentals of Earthquake Resistant Construction*: Wiley Series of Practical Construction Guides: New York, J. Wiley & Sons.

Kunreuther, H., and Roth, R.J., Sr., 1998, *Paying the Price: The Status and Role of Insurance against Natural Disasters in the United States*. Washington , D.C., Joseph Henry Press.

Lafferty and Associates, Inc., 1989, *Earthquake preparedness—for office, home, family and community*: P.O. Box 1026, La Canada, CA 91012.

Lagorio, H.J., 1990, *Earthquakes: An Architect's Guide to Nonstructural Seismic Hazards*: New York, J. Wiley & Sons.

Lawson, A.C., and others, 1908, *The California earthquake of April 18, 1906: Report of the State Earthquake Investigation Commission*: Carnegie Institution of Washington Publ. 87.

Lee, W.H.K., 1992, Seismology, observational: Academic Press, *Encyclopedia of Physical Science and Technology*, v. 15, p. 17-45.

Leonard, M., 2000, A history of the California Earthquake Authority: Earthquake Quarterly, Spring 2000, Western States Seismic Policy Council, p. 15-17.

LeVay, S., 1999, Stress test: *Scientific American*, v. 281, no, 12, p. 28-29.

Lillie, R.J., 1999, *Whole-Earth Geophysics*: Englewood Cliffs, N.J., Prentice-Hall, 361 p.

Lindeburg, M., *Seismic Design of Building Structures*, 7th ed.: Belmont, CA, Professional Publications.

Lomnitz, C., 1994, *Fundamentals of earthquake prediction*: New York, John Wiley & Sons, 326 p.

Ma Z., Fu Z., Zhang Y., Wang C., Zhang G., and Liu D., 1990, *Earthquake prediction: Nine major earthquakes in China (1966-1976)*: Beijing, Seismological Press, and Berlin, Springer-Verlag, 332 p.

Mader, G. G., et al., 1988, *Geology and planning: The Portola Valley experience*: Spangle, W., and Associates, Inc., 3240 Alpine Road, Portola Valley, CA 94025, 75 p.

Manolis, G.D., Beskos, D.E., and Brabbia, C.A., 1996, *Earthquake Resistant Engineering Structures*: Computational Mechanics, 728 p.

McCrory, P.A., 1996, Evaluation of fault hazards, northern coastal California: *U.S. Geol. Survey Open-File Report 96-656*, 87 p.

McPhee, J., 1993, *Assembling California*: New York, The Noonday Press, 304 p.

McPherson, R.C., and Dengler, L.A., 1992, The Honeydew Earthquake: *California Geology*, v. 45, p. 31-39.

Michael, A.J., Ross, S.L., Schwartz, D.P., Hendley, J.W., II, and Stauffer, P.H., 1999, Major quake likely to strike between 2000 and 2030—understanding earthquake hazards in the San Francisco Bay Region: *U.S. Geological Survey Fact Sheet 152-99*, 4 p.

Mileti, D.S., 1999, *Disasters by Design: A Reassessment of Natural Hazards in the United States:* Washington, National Academy of Sciences, 351 p.

Morgan, L., 1993, *Earthquake survival manual*: Seattle, Epicenter Press, 160 p.

Naeim, F., ed., 1989, *The Seismic Design Handbook*: London, Chapman and Hall.

Muir, J., 1912, *The Yosemite*: The Century Company, republished by Doubleday and Co., Inc., New York.

Nance, J.J., 1988, *On Shaky Ground*: New York, William Morrow and Co.

National Science Teachers Association, 1988, *Earthquakes: A teacher's guide for K-6 grades*: NSTA Publications, 1742 Connecticut Ave. NW, Washington, DC20009.

Nevada Bureau of Mines and Geology, 2000, *Living with Earthquakes in Nevada*: Special Pub. 27, 36 p.

Oakeshott, G.B., 1989, My California: Autobiography of a Geologist: Published by Gordon B. Oakeshott, 194 p.

Obermeier, S.F., 1996, Using liquefaction-induced features for paleoseismic analysis, in McCalpin, J.P., ed., *Paleoseismology*: San Diego, Academic Press, p. 331-396.

Office of Technology Assessment, Congress of the United States, 1995, *Reducing earthquake losses*: Washington, Government Printing Office, OTA-ETI-623, 162 p.

Olson, R.S., 1989, *The politics of earthquake prediction*: Princeton, N.J., Princeton University Press, 187 p.

Oppenheimer, D., and others, 1993, The Cape Mendocino, California, earthquakes of April 1992: subduction at the triple junction: *Science*, v. 261, p. 433-438.

Oregon Department of Geology and Mineral Industries, 1997, Tsunami hazard map of the Yaquina Bay area, Lincoln County, Oregon: *Department of Geology and Mineral Industries Publication IMS-2*

Page, R. A., Boore, D.M., Bucknam, R.C., and Thatcher, W.R., 1992, Goals, opportunities, and priorities for the USGS Earthquake Hazard Reduction Program: USGS Circular 1079, 60 p.

Palm, R., Hodgson, M., Blanchard, R.D., and Lyons, D., 1990, *Earthquake Insurance in California: Environmental Policy and Individual Decision Making*: Boulder, Colorado, Westview Press.

Palm, R., and Carroll, J., 1998, *Illusions of Safety: Cultural and Earthquake Hazard Response in California and Japan*: Boulder, CO, Westview Press.

Pellegrino, C.R., 1985, *Time Gate: Hurtling Backward through History*. Blue Ridge Summit, PA, TAB Books, Inc., 275 p.

Peterson, M.D., and Wesnousky, S.G., 1994, Fault slip rates and earthquake histories for active faults in southern California: *Bulletin of the Seismological Society of America*, v. 84, p. 1608-1649.

Plafker, G., and Galloway, J.P., eds., 1989, Lessons learned from the Loma Prieta, California, earthquake of October 17, 1989: *U.S. Geological Survey Circular 1045*, 48 p.

Prescott, W.H., Davis, J.L., and Svarc, J.L., 1989, Global positioning system measurements for crustal deformation: Precision and accuracy: *Science*, v. 244, p. 1337-1340.

Rogers, J.J.W., 1993, *A History of the Earth*. Cambridge University Press, 312 p.

Priest, G.R., 1995, Explanation of mapping methods and use of the tsunami hazard maps of the Oregon coast: *Oregon Department of Geology and Mineral Industries Open-File Report O-95-67*.

Priest, G.R., 1995, Explanation of mapping methods and use of the tsunami hazard map of the Siletz Bay area, Lincoln County, Oregon: *Oregon Department of Geology and Mineral Industries Geologic Map Series Report*.

Pyne, N.J., 1980, *Grove Karl Gilbert—A Great Engine of Research*: Austin, University of Texas Press, 306 p.

Reiter, L., 1990, *Earthquake Hazard Analysis: Issues and Insights*: New York, Columbia University Press.

Richter, C.F., 1958, *Elementary Seismology*: San Francisco, W.H. Freeman and Co., 468 p.

Roth, R.J., Jr., 1997, Earthquake basics: insurance: What are the principles of insuring natural disasters? Earthquake Engineering Research Institute, Suite 320, 499-14th Street, Oakland, CA 94612-1934.

Rubin, C.M., Lindvall, S.C., and Rockwell, T.K., 1998, Evidence for large earthquakes in metropolitan Los Angeles: *Science*, v. 281, p. 398-402.

Satake, K., 1992, *Tsunamis*: Academic Press: Encyclopedia of Earth System Science, v. 4, p. 389-397.

Scholz, C., 1990, *Mechanics of Earthquakes and Faulting*: Cambridge University Press, 439 p.

Scholz, C.H., 1997, Whatever happened to earthquake prediction? *Geotimes*, v. 42, no. 3, p. 16-19.

Scott, S., interviewer, 1999, Robert E. Wallace: *Connections, the EERI Oral History Series*: Earthquake Engineering Research Institute: Earthquake Engineering Research Institute OSH-6

Schwab, W.C., Lee, H.J., and Twichell, D.C., eds., 1993, Submarine landslides. Selected studies in the U.S. Exclusive Economic Zone: *U.S. Geol. Survey Bull. 2002*, 204 p.

Scullin, C.M., Excavation and grading code administration, inspection, and enforcement (available through ICBO).

Seismic Safety Commission, 1992, *The Homeowner-s Guide to Earthquake Safety*: SSC 92-01, 28 p.

Shaw, J.H., and Shearer, P.M., 1999, An elusive blind-thrust fault beneath metropolitan Los Angeles: *Science*, v. 283, p. 516-518.

Sieh, K., 1978, Prehistoric large earthquakes produced by slip on the San Andreas fault at Pallett Creek, California: *Journal of Geophysical Research*, v. 83, p. 3907-3939.

Sieh, K., et al., 1993, Near-field investigations of the Landers earthquake sequence: Science, v. 260, p. 171-176.

Sieh, K., and LeVay, S., 1998, *The Earth in Turmoil*: New York, W.H. Freeman, 324 p.

Silver, P.G., and Valette-Silver, N.J., 1992, Detection of hydrothermal precursors to large northern California earthquakes: *Science*, v. 257, p. 1363-1368.

Silver, P.G., and Wakita, H., 1996, Search for earthquake precursors: *Science*, v. 273, p. 77-78.

Smith, T.C., and McKamey, B., 2000, Summary of outreach activities for California's Seismic Hazards Mapping Program 1996-1998: *California Division of Mines and Geology Special Publication 121*, 38 p. and appendices.

Southern California Earthquake Center, 1995, *Putting Down Roots in Earthquake Country*. Available free from Southern California Earthquake Center, University of Southern California.

Stanley, S.M., 1989, *The Earth and Life through Time*. New York, J.W. Freeman & Co., 689 p.

Stein, R.S., 1999, The role of stress transfer in earthquake occurrence: *Nature*, v. 402, p. 605-609.

Stein, R.S., and Hanks, T.C., 1998, M $\geq$ 6 earthquakes in southern California during the twentieth century: no evidence for a seismicity or moment deficit: *Bulletin of the Seismological Society of America*, v. 88, p. 635-652.

Stein, R.S., and Yeats, R.S., 1989, Hidden earthquakes: *Scientific American*, v. 260, p. 48-57.

Stein, R.S., King, G.C.P., and Lin, J., 1994, Stress triggering of the 1994 M = 6.7 Northridge, California, Earthquake by its predecessors: *Science*, v. 265, p. 1432-1435.

Stein, R.S., King, G.C.P., and Lin, J., 1997, Change in failure stress on the southern San Andreas fault system caused by the 1992 magnitude = 7.4 Landers earthquake: *Science*, v. 258, p. 1328-1332.

Sunset Magazine, 1990, Quake—2 part series in October and November, 1990, issues, available as reprints (Sunset Quake '90 Reprints) from Sunset Publishing Company, 80 Willow Road, Menlo Park, CA 94025.

Sykes, L.R., and Nishenko, S.P., 1984, Probabilities of occurrence of large plate rupturing earthquakes for the San Andreas, San Jacinto, and Imperial faults, California: *Journal of Geophysical Research*, v. 89, p. 5905-5927.

Thatcher, W., et al., 1999, Present-day deformation across the Basin and Range Province, western United States: *Science*, v. 283, p. 1714-1718.

Thomas, G., and M.M. Witts, 1971, *The San Francisco Earthquake*: New York, Dell Publishing Co., 301 p.

Toppozada, T., Borchardt. G., Haydon, W., Peterson, M., Olson, R., Lagorio, H., and Anvik, T., 1995, Planning scenario in Humboldt and Del Norte Counties, California, for a great earthquake on the Cascadia Subduction Zone: *California Division of Mines and Geology, Special Publ. 115*, 157 p.

Toppozada, T., Real, C., and Parke, D., 1981, Preparation of isoseismal maps and summaries of reported effects for pre-1900 California earthquakes: California Division of Mines and Geology Open-File Report 81-11, 182 p.

U.S. Geological Survey, 1996, USGS Response to an Urban Earthquake: Northridge '94. *U.S. Geological Survey Open-File Report 96-263*, 78 p.

U.S. Geological Suirvey, 1999, An assessment of seismic monitoring in the United States: Requirements for an advanced national seismic system: *U.S. Geological Survey Circ. 1188.*

United Policyholders: Tips on Earthquake Claims: What's UP (newsletter);

Vaughan, F.E., 1970, *Andrew C. Lawson: Scientist, Teacher, Philosopher*: Glendale, CA, A.H. Clark Co., 474 p.

Vere-Jones, D., Harte, D., and Kozuch, M.J., 1988, Operational requirements for an earthquake forecasting programme for New Zealand: *Bulletin of the New Zealand Society for Earthquake Engineering*, v. 31, no. 3, p. 194-205.

Wallace, R.E., editor, 1990,*The San Andreas Fault System, California*: U.S. Geol. Survey Prof. Paper 1515, 293 p.

Western States Seismic Policy Council and the Council of States Governments-WEST, 1998. Earthquake Insurance: Public Policy Perspectives from the Western United States: Earthquake Insurance Summit: 354 p. Available from Western States Seismic Policy Council.

Whiteside, L.S., 1998, Earthquake prediction is possible: Seismological Research Letters, v. 69, p. 287-288.

Wicander, R., and Monroe, J.S. 1980, *Historical Geology*. St. Paul, MN: West Publishing Co., 578 p.

Working Group on California Earthquake Probabilities, 1995, Seismic hazards in southern California: Probable earthquakes 1994-2024: *Bulletin of the Seismological Society of America*, v. 85, 379-439. (SCEC Phase II Report)

Working Group on Northern California Earthquake Potential, 1996, Database of potential sources for earthquakes larger than magnitude 6 in northern California: *U.S. Geological Survey Open-File Report 06-705*, 40 p.

Working Group on California Earthquake Probabilities, 1999, Earthquake probabilities in the San Francisco Bay Region: 2000 to 2030 - a summary of findings: *USGS Circular 1189* (in press) and http://quake.usgs.gov/study/wg99/of99-517/index.html

Yanev, P., 1974, *Peace of mind in earthquake country: How to save your home and life:* San Francisco, Chronicle Books.

Yeats, R.S., 1998, :*Living with Earthquakes in the Pacific Northwest*: Corvallis, Oregon State University Press, 309 p.

Yeats, R.S., and Huftile, G.J., 1995, The Oak Ridge fault system and the 1994 Northridge earthquake: *Nature*, v. 373, p. 418-420.

Yeats, R.S., Sieh, K.E., and Allen, C.R. 1997, *The Geology of Earthquakes*. New York: Oxford University Press, 568 p.

Ziony, J.J., ed., 1985, *Evaluating Earthquake Hazards in the Los Angeles Region —An Earth Science Perspective*: U.S. Geol. Survey Professional Paper 1760, 516 p.

Index